# ALCOHOL AND CULTURE:
# COMPARATIVE PERSPECTIVES FROM
# EUROPE AND AMERICA

ANNALS OF THE NEW YORK ACADEMY OF SCIENCES

Volume 472

# ALCOHOL AND CULTURE: COMPARATIVE PERSPECTIVES FROM EUROPE AND AMERICA

*Edited by Thomas F. Babor*

*The New York Academy of Sciences*
*New York, New York*
*1986*

**Library of Congress Cataloging-in-Publication Data**

Alcohol and culture.

(Annals of the New York Academy of Sciences ; v. 472)
Papers from a conference sponsored by the National Institute on Alcohol Abuse and Alcoholism, and others, held May 5–7, 1983, in Farmington, Conn.
Bibliography: p.
Includes index.
1. Alcoholism—Cross-cultural studies—Congresses. 2. Alcoholism—Prevention—Cross-cultural studies—Congresses. 3. Drinking of alcoholic beverages—Cross-cultural studies—Congresses. I. Babor, Thomas. II. National Institute on Alcohol Abuse and Alcoholism (U.S.) III. Series.
Q11.N5 vol. 472    500 s        86-16258
[HV5009]        [362.2'921]
ISBN 0-89766-339-X
ISBN 0-89766-340-3 (pbk.)

CCP
Printed in the United States of America
ISBN 0-89766-339-X (cloth)
ISBN 0-89766-340-3 (paper)
ISSN 0077-8923

ANNALS OF THE NEW YORK ACADEMY OF SCIENCES

Volume 472
July 11, 1986

## ALCOHOL AND CULTURE:
## COMPARATIVE PERSPECTIVES FROM EUROPE AND AMERICA[a]

*Editor*
THOMAS F. BABOR

## CONTENTS

[a] This volume is the result of a conference entitled Alcohol and Culture: Comparative Perspectives from Europe and America, held on May 5-7, 1983 in Farmington, Connecticut, and
sponsored by the National Institute on Alcohol Abuse and Alcoholism, the World Health Organization, the International Council on Alcohol and Addictions, and the Connecticut Alcohol
and Drug Abuse Commission.

### Part III. Socialization and Acculturation in the Etiology of Alcoholism

### Part IV. Alcoholism Treatment in Cross-Cultural Perspective

### Part V. Implications for Research and Prevention Policy

**Financial assistance was received from:**
- HEUBLEIN CORPORATION
- NATIONAL INSTITUTE ON ALCOHOL ABUSE AND ALCOHOLISM

# Preface

THOMAS F. BABOR

*Alcohol Research Center*
*University of Connecticut School of Medicine*
*Farmington, Connecticut 06032*

The research conference for which the papers in this volume were commissioned was organized by the University of Connecticut Alcohol Research Center and was jointly sponsored by the National Institute on Alcohol Abuse and Alcoholism, the World Health Organization, the International Council on Alcohol and Addiction, and the Connecticut Alcohol and Drug Abuse Commission. Financial support was provided by the National Institute on Alcohol Abuse and Alcoholism (Grant No. P50-AA03510) and the Heublein Corporation. We are particularly grateful that these organizations have seen fit to lend their good names and good offices to the sponsorship of this conference.

Beyond the institutional support, a number of individuals have played a crucial role in shepherding this project from concept to reality. Robin Room is to be thanked for his helpful suggestions on the program, and for the copious notes he provided when our tape recorder failed to capture Dr. William Meyer's speech. Roger Meyer, Jerome Jaffe, Bernard Glueck, Ron Kadden, and Ovide Pomerleau, as well as Michie and Victor Hesselbrock, provided the kinds of local support and encouragement necessary to launch and manage an endeavor of this magnitude. Albert Powlowski of the NIAAA is owed a large debt of gratitude for his efforts in obtaining funding for the conference through the Alcohol Research Center's program. Margie Meadows supervised the organizational details with exquisite care and attention, while Kathy McDermott, Debbie Sandberg, Janet Keener, Meredith Weidenman, Sandy Margoles, Lynn Virgilio, Linda Rheaume, Kim Palmisano, and Nancy Carter-Menendez — practically the entire staff of the University of Connecticut Alcohol Research Center — all pitched in with the technical support needed to run a successful conference. And Barbara Bacewicz helped quite a few people write their papers on her WANG word-processor.

Finally, a word should be said in recognition of the speakers, discussants and the more than 100 members of the audience who spent two and one-half days sequestered in a high-technology industrial park on a beautiful spring weekend. Despite a tremendous diversity in language, nationality, and professional affiliations, those attending the conference managed to maintain a remarkable degree of involvement in both the formal and informal aspects of the proceedings.

# Taking Stock: Method and Theory in Cross-National Research on Alcohol[a]

THOMAS F. BABOR

*Alcohol Research Center*
*University of Connecticut School of Medicine*
*Farmington, Connecticut 06032*

When cocktail party conversation turns to the subject of alcohol, it is not uncommon to hear boastful comparisons about the drinking prowess of different ethnic, religious, or national groups. The Irish are thought to drink more than the Scandinavians, American Indians more than Japanese-Americans, Catholics more than Methodists. The incidence of alcohol-related problems among such groups is also thought to vary, presumably because of the biological or cultural characteristics shared by their members.

The comparison of the drinking habits of different cultural groups has also been a favorite pastime of armchair alcohologists. Greek writers often contrasted the abstemious Spartans with the intemperate Athenians. Fra Salimbene of Parma, an incisive thirteenth-century ethnographer of European drinking customs, noted that the "French and English make it their business to drink full goblets; wherefore the French have bloodshot eyes. . . . We must forgive the English if they are glad to drink good wine when they can, for they have but little wine in their own country" (quoted in Coulton, 1908).

With the emergence of the world temperance movement in the nineteenth century, international comparisons of drinking patterns and alcohol problems took on new meaning. The American temperance crusade of the 1830s spread quickly to England and the Continent through the medium of the transatlantic community of evangelical Christians. Their cause was given impetus and justification by the publication of international statistics on production, consumption and problems—issues that became common themes in the temperance literature. One use to which these comparative statistics were put was epidemiology, the understanding of how alcohol problems are distributed among different population groups. Another purpose was to monitor trends in alcohol consumption and to evaluate the impact of alcohol-control policies in different countries. For example, at the Fourth International Congress against the Abuse of Alcoholic Beverages, the Rev. L. L. Rochat presented liquor-consumption data from six European countries between 1870 and 1892. He argued that countries with active total abstinence societies (Sweden, Switzerland, England, Norway) had effectively suppressed liquor consumption, while those without temperance organizations (Belgium, France) had witnessed a dramatic increase in the drinking of spirits.

Yet another common theme in the early comparative studies of alcohol is suggested in the title of Dr. N. S. Davis' address to the Seventh International Congress against the Abuse of Alcoholic Beverages (1900): "Is there any Causative or Etiological relation between the extensive use of alcoholic drinks and the continued increase of epilepsy, imbecility and insanity, both mental and moral in all the countries of Europe and

[a] This work was supported in part by Grant No. P50-AA03510 from the National Institute on Alcohol Abuse and Alcoholism.

1

America?" Davis, like many physicians of his time, was intrigued by cross-national similarities in the etiology and manifestation of alcoholism. The rapid dissemination of the term *alcoholismus chronicus* within the international medical lexicon is in itself testimony to the common belief that there were invariant and universal elements to alcoholism.

These two facets of the comparative method—the explanation of culturally patterned differences and the identification of transcultural universals—have become increasingly recognized as fundamentally important to the understanding of the consequences of alcohol use and its control (Paulson, 1973; Mäkelä *et al.*, 1981). As illustrated by the papers in this volume, the comparative method has benefited greatly in recent years from advances in alcohol theory and research technology. The authors of these papers were chosen because they are all seasoned social scientists who have used the comparative method as a means to investigate drinking behavior. Their contributions are designed to cover the major areas where comparative research has been applied and to summarize the major trends and initiatives currently taking shape within the U.S. National Institute on Alcohol Abuse and Alcoholism (NIAAA) and the World Health Organization (WHO).

# SYNOPSIS

In Part I of this book, which concerns social epidemiology, Esa Österberg, Klaus Mäkelä, and Bruce Ritson provide much more than an introduction to current research on the distribution and determinants of alcohol problems in various parts of the world. Their papers also represent three of the most ambitious and significant comparative studies ever conducted in the field. Future generations will view the International Study on Alcohol Control Experiences (ISACE) as a landmark in comparative research methods and cross-cultural analysis. To the extent that history creates culture, including the social institutions within which individuals carry on their behavior, comparative history becomes one of the most important sources of hypotheses about the forces that operate on individual drinking at any given time. The static, cross-sectional approach that has characterized much comparative research needs to be broadened to include a longitudinal view of the social forces that determine not only the complementarity between drinking patterns and alcohol problems, but also the reciprocal effects of alcohol problems and societal responses. Despite tremendous differences in the nature and prevalence of alcohol problems in the ISACE countries, the study identified remarkably similar responses taken by modern industrialized societies. For the most part, these took the form of a rapid shift in the societal management of alcohol problems from the agencies of social control to the newly developed social and medical services.

Klaus Mäkelä's study of attitudes toward alcohol in four Scandinavian countries, while more focused than the ISACE study, demonstrates again how comparative analysis gives new meaning to the notion of cultural relativity. Using semantic differential rating scales to bridge linguistic barriers, and the comparison of age cohorts to identify intergenerational trends, this is one of the few studies to evaluate one of the time-honored clichés in alcohol and culture theory. Like Jellinek's typology of alcoholism, David Pittman's typology of drinking cultures owes its longevity less to its intrinsic merits than to the logistics of testing alcohol theory on an international plane. In other words, theories are easier made than tested. What Mäkelä shows is that the cultural dynamics of alcohol control may be more complex than a simple continuum of attitudes ranging from abstinence to overpermissiveness. Societies, like individuals, do not distinguish their drinking according to nutritional versus intoxicant uses of alcohol.

Bruce Ritson's paper on lessons from the Community Response Study is guaranteed to entice but then disappoint anyone familiar with the World Health Organization project. No brief report such as this could do justice to that study, but it does serve admirably as an illustration of the potential of international collaborative research to serve as an instrument for the development of rational social policy. As the paper suggests, the traditional reluctance of social scientists to involve themselves in applied research may be ending, particularly as advances are made in ethnography, epidemiology and the coordination of research on an international scale. Mexico, Zambia and Scotland are as far apart culturally as they are geographically, yet each country benefited equally from the impact of a methodology employing community plans to respond to alcohol problems. More than any previous international study, this project was an adventure in relevance, guided less by theory than by a conviction that social research has a place and a purpose in both developing and developed countries. In its attempt to demonstrate a research process, the influence of this project promises to go far beyond the findings it has generated.

The next section, which deals with the manifestation and meaning of alcoholism, introduces a new approach to the exploration of cultural relativity and pancultural generality. Missing from many cross-cultural portrayals of the disparate nature of alcohol problems is the notion of alcoholism as an organizing principle. The concept of cultural relativity emphasizes the *differences* among cultures in social organization and practice that are presumably related to the differential prevalence and patterning of alcohol-related problems. The pancultural or generalist view emphasizes the similarities in alcohol-related consequences across cultures, particularly at the levels of biological function and personality disorganization.

These concepts are nicely illustrated in the papers in this section dealing with cross-national and interethnic differences among clinical samples of diagnosed alcoholics. Løberg and Miller's cross-national comparison of American and Norwegian samples, placed within the context of an exhaustive review of the international literature, suggests that certain universal aspects of alcoholism do indeed exist, especially with respect to neuropsychological impairments and personality subtypes. Nevertheless, they speculate that population differences in drinking patterns, such as the spacing of drinking, the alcohol and congener content of different beverages, and associated dietary customs, may all color the nature and degree of neuropsychological deficits and personality disorder. Løberg and Miller also point out the inferential problems involved in interpreting cross-national differences in drinking behavior and symptoms. All too often researchers have failed to control for such personal and demographic factors as age, socioeconomic status, and educational level before attributing observed differences to hypothetical cultural constructs. In the studies reported by Babor and colleagues, multivariate statistical procedures are employed to adjust and control for sociological differences between ethnic and/or national groups of alcoholics. Without such precautions, researchers fail to do justice to their data, and take the risk of confounding structural variables with the real object of their analysis.

Two studies in this section deal with social attitudes toward alcohol and concepts of alcoholism. Among alcoholics it is interesting to note that the meaning of alcoholism seems to differ in ways suggested long ago by E. M. Jellinek (1962). American alcoholics endorse the disease concept to a much greater degree than do patients treated in France and Québec. Miller's survey of treatment ideology in Europe and America seems to show a similar disparity in medical/psychiatric as opposed to behavioral/environmental views of the management of alcohol problems.

The papers in Part III address the issues of etiology and socialization of drinking patterns. George Vaillant's paper adds depth as well as credibility to Babor and Mendelson's findings that ethnicity accounts for more variance than family history in determining the degree of alcoholic symptoms. Boris Segal's broad psychohistorical interpretation of Irish, American, and Russian drinking reminds us again that culture is inextricably linked to historical circumstances, and that etiology may take its rise as well as its pattern according to the social context.

Social attitudes surrounding the initiation of alcohol use in adolescents have long intrigued cross-cultural theorists, but it was not until recently that sophisticated multivariate statistical techniques became available to explore the relative contributions of sociodemographic, interpersonal, and intrapersonal variables. The paper by Thomas Harford illustrates the extent to which social researchers are now capable of testing complex causal models by means of parallel analyses of cross-cultural data sets. While Harford also finds similarities in the environmental factors affecting alcohol use by black and nonblack American students, his data suggest that differences in attitudes and exposure to peer drinking models may explain the later onset of drinking among blacks.

Part IV is devoted to studies of alcoholism treatment, the one area in this collection where the comparative method has been least rigorous. The relative dearth of comparative research on treatment is surprising in view of the importance that specialized alcoholism treatment systems have recently assumed within the health care industry in Western countries. Both the ISACE and WHO Community Response studies take on added importance in light of the valuable data they assemble on treatment systems in various countries. The four papers contained in this section provide a much more subtle view of the impact of culture on treatment, since they focus on process, rather than structure.

Serkka-Liisa Säilä's paper on detoxification centers highlights one of the more important aspects of the treatment-versus-social-control dialectic identified in the ISACE study as a major feature of the postwar period. The detoxification centers of Finland, Poland, the United States and many other countries are, in a sense, a humanitarian Band-Aid that harks back to the time when alcohol was seen as the cause of poverty, crime, and insanity. Like the poor, chronic inebriates will always be with us, at least as long as industrialized societies fail to meet the basic needs for food, shelter, and gainful employment, preferring instead to shift the blame to the person and the bottle.

The next three papers focus on the relationship between American ethnic minorities and the specialized, residential treatment programs that have become the cornerstone of alcoholism treatment. The papers by Frank Iber and Roberta Hall at first reading seem to contradict one another. Iber suggests that all alcoholism treatments are effective, regardless of the staff's ideology or the patient's cultural affiliation. In contrast, Hall's paper implies that culturally appropriate treatments work best, especially those, like the Indian sweat lodge, that are in tune with the *Weltanschauung* of a people. Iber's point is that motivating patients to seek treatment and getting them to comply with it are the keys to success. Both agree that the key to motivation and compliance is cultural appropriateness.

Westermeyer's paper adds another dimension to the relationship between culture and treatment, the post-treatment environment. While culturally attuned programs may be effective, we may expect far too much of what for many alcoholics amounts to a 4-week respite from a chaotic environment. To the extent that the culture of that environment supports and encourages heavy drinking, then the recovering patient, as exemplified by Westermeyer's successful Indian alcoholics, might do well to try a different way of living, at least for a time.

Part V closes this collection with two appropriate notes: (1) the pessimistic note of the technocrats, who are sorry to say that alcohol problems are not easily prevented, and (2) the optimistic note of the bureaucrats, who tell us that research can play a crucial role in the definition of social reality, if not in its manipulation. William Mayer's candor sets the stage for subsequent papers. From his vantage point, at the time of this writing, as Administrator of the Alcohol, Drug Abuse and Mental Health Administration, Mayer says with authority that alcoholism is both treatable and preventable. But as chief health officer for the new social diseases, he also cautions us that medicine and science are not likely to produce a repetition of past public health victories. Norms, values, and attitudes conducive to the prevention of alcohol problems cannot be inculcated through mental sanitation or social vaccination — nor through alcohol education, if we are to believe Marcus Grant's masterful review of the Western European and American literature. According to Reginald Smart, the illusory targets and elusive goals of prevention efforts in developed countries are not even an important consideration in many Latin American countries, where the widespread consequences of excessive drinking are not clearly recognized, much less considered a proper domain for the investment of scarce health resources. His recommendation is to study how culture controls alcohol availability, and then to act on that knowledge. It is the policymakers, not the schoolchildren, who need alcohol education, especially concerning the functions, complexities, and public health implications of alcohol-control policies.

The final papers, by Leland Towle and Marcus Grant, provide complementary opinions regarding the optimistic outlook for social research in the coming years. For better or for worse, social research on alcohol is now a highly specialized and multidisciplinary enterprise dependent on the fortunes of national and international health bureaucracies. For this reason, it is important for us to understand how the makers of research and health policy see the future of cross-national research on alcohol.

Leland Towle uses these proceedings as a forum for explaining NIAAA's expanding international role in technical cooperation, cross-national research, exchange of scientists, and the collation of statistical data. Considered in the light of NIAAA's recent designation as a WHO collaborating center, these international programs reflect a growing recognition by the premier American alcohol research agency that alcohol problems have no national boundaries, nor do their solutions.

Equally important to the future of social research on alcohol is the role of WHO's ambitious alcohol program, as outlined in Marcus Grant's contribution. The objectives of the WHO include the collection and exchange of statistical data, development of coordinating mechanisms for transferring knowledge and experience, coordination of international research using common research methods, development of treatment and secondary prevention strategies within the framework of each nation's primary health care system, and the encouragement of collaborating relationships among centers of excellence in order to build an international network of researchers and practitioners.

What is encouraging about this impressive demonstration of institutional support from WHO and NIAAA is the implicit recognition it confers on the increasingly important role social research has played in the study of alcohol, and on the future role social researchers may be asked to play in the treatment and prevention of alcohol-related problems. That role will depend not only on the methods and theories social scientists contribute to alcohol research, but also on the professional manpower that can be marshalled to conduct alcohol research on a national and international level. In a sense, these proceedings are testimony to the emergence of an international research infrastructure comprising investigators speaking a common language, and to the existence of generally accepted research methods and theories, national research centers having stable funding, and resources (such as books, journals, and meetings) for formal and informal communication among scholars.

## SYNTHESIS

All too often, edited volumes such as this are simply an expedient assemblage of previously published papers available from authors known personally to the editor. This was not the rationale for the present volume. Through a choice of what are perhaps the most representative set of recent comparative studies, an attempt has been made to take stock of the kinds of research questions being asked, the methods being applied to answer those questions, and the findings which have begun to emerge. Like a piece of a jigsaw puzzle, no single study provides more than a clue to the nature of the larger picture. But when all the pieces have been fitted in their proper places, we have something more than the sum of its parts. What emerges from a careful reading of these papers are several themes which, when considered together, say a great deal about the present and future status of cross-cultural research on alcohol.

The word *culture* may have as many definitions as the word *alcoholism*. As Dwight Heath points out in his closing comments, rarely are the nature and underlying dynamics of culture defined operationally. As with other complex concepts, research proceeds vigorously despite the lack of widespread agreement on an exact definition. But when culture is defined so broadly that it is all-encompassing, it is indicative of nothing very much in particular. In many instances, the word is used vaguely to refer to some combination of language, customs, socialization practices, skin color, and country of origin.

The concept of culture implicit in many of the empirical studies in this book is closely tied to the assumed differences between modern nation states. Although nations like the U.S. and the U.S.S.R. are complex and subculturally heterogeneous, there is some evidence (Hofstede, 1980) to suggest that modern nations do have dominant national character traits which are related to attitudes, values, and structural characteristics. To the extent that drinking customs, alcohol availability, alcohol-control policy, and religious attitudes are determined by the legal, economic, and social structures of national governments, one would expect to find national variations in drinking patterns.

This is not to deny the importance of subcultural variations in drinking behavior, the second aspect of culture underlying many of these comparative studies. If we define culture as a common set of learned beliefs and sorts of behavior shared by a group of individuals over time, then drinkers typically belong to many cultural groups defined by age, sex, socioeconomic status, ethnicity, and religion. If one is interested in only one type of subculture (for example, ethnic group), then other subcultural differences should be matched or controlled before it can be inferred that culture is the deciding influence.

The ultimate aim of alcohol research is to formulate and test theories that explore the nature and consequences of drinking. Tools of this exploration process often include speculation, description, classification, and sometimes experimentation. Unfortunately, research can be parochial and misleading. Examination of single samples, rarely accepted as a basis for scientific inference, at best provides only limited generalizations over the broad spectrum of human drinking. Replication using other samples in various contexts increases the credibility of generalizations. The research process exemplified by all of the empirical studies in this book can be called quasiexperimental. Exposure to different national cultures or ethnic subcultures is hypothesized to account for similarities or differences in drinking behavior. The comparative method is used to approximate the experimental method in which various groups are similar in all respects except culture.

As indicated by the brief historical review of cross-cultural comparisons of drinking, there has been a tendency to use the comparative method to stress unique aspects and, to a lesser extent, comparable aspects of different cultures. The distinction between the unique and the general, the specific and the comparable, has been defined in sociology as the idiographic versus nomothetic styles of scientific inquiry (Hofstede, 1980). The idiographic style favored by historical and anthropological disciplines looks for unique configurations of events, conditions, or developments; the nomothetic style, more characteristic of the natural sciences, looks for general laws. A similar distinction has been made by cross-cultural psychologists and anthropologists using the terms "emic" and "etic" to distinguish the study of unique and specific wholes from the application of general, polycultural classification schemes. The study of alcohol often provides the meeting ground of the natural and social sciences and it is not surprising to find both approaches within the domain of cross-cultural comparisons.

Another way of describing these fundamental differences in research styles is in terms of the distinction between pancultural generality versus cultural relativity. The concept of cultural relativity implies that the differences among countries in social organization and practice are related to differences in drinking behavior. This leads to the expectation of wide variations in attitudes toward alcohol, drinking patterns, and alcohol-related problems. The pancultural-generalist view emphasizes similarities in the context and functions of drinking across societies. Biologically, all humans are members of the same species, susceptible in the same way to intoxication, dependence, and liver damage. Socially, almost all humans find alcohol reinforcing. Ecologically, drinking is a means of adapting to environmental conditions. This would lead one to expect certain common features in drinking behavior, especially at the biological and psychological levels of analysis. The beauty of the comparative method is that it allows researchers to explore both similarities and differences related to culture.

TABLE 1 provides examples of the studies that illustrate these research strategies, confirming what Frijda and Jahoda (1966) meant when they said that "Cross-cultural research is like virtue—everybody is in favor of it, but there are widely differing views of what it is and ought to be" (p. 122). In the table, the distinction between the search for similarities (nomothetic/etic) and the search for differences (idiographic/emic) is further subdivided according to two levels of analysis: (1) micro-level variables and their relationships measured within societies or ethnic groups; (2) macro-level or ecological variables and their relationships measured at the level of societies. For example, a study by Kandel *et al.* (1981) attempted to prove the universality of micro-level laws governing the initiation of "substance use" by adolescents. In contrast, micro-level studies by Harford, and Babor and Mendelson have a more idiographic/emic orientation. By showing differences among ethnic groups, these investigators illustrate the uniqueness of each and suggest the important role of context in drinking behavior and its consequences. Both types of study compare groups at the micro-level, without necessarily specifying what "culture" stands for. In a sense, culture is treated as a "black box" whose reality is assumed as a given, but whose contents are unknown. If basic similarities are found, then it does not matter what is in the black box. But when differences are found between groups or societies, the black box becomes Pandora's box, since

**TABLE 1.** Classification of Illustrative Comparative Studies According to Different Research Strategies

| Level of Analysis | Research Strategy | |
|---|---|---|
| | Nomothetic/Etic Pancultural Generalist Approach | Idiographic/Emic Cultural Relativist Approach |
| Micro-level studies | Sequencing of alcohol/ drug initiation (Kandel *et al.*, 1981) | Alcoholic symptomatology (Babor and Mendelson) |
| Macro-level studies | Per capita consumption trends (Österberg) | Alcohol-related problems (Segal) |

the concept of culture is often invoked to explain differences that are not clearly attributable to it.

At the macro-level level of analysis, comparative studies focus on either similarities or differences on the basis of ecologic variables. For example, Österberg reviews the ISACE study results showing that consumption trends that are similar in industrialized societies are not necessarily related to drinking problems in the same way. Nevertheless, trends in the societal responses to these problems are quite similar. Segal's study of the U.S.S.R., the U.S., and Ireland, on the other hand, finds that differences in economic systems, national character, and historical circumstances all have contributed to national differences in drinking patterns. Here the concept of culture is specified to a much greater degree than in micro-level studies.

The studies in this volume also provide evidence that the methodological problems inherent in any social science research, as well as basic research strategies used in comparative research, are amplified by the number of societies studied. The limitations and difficulties of conducting cross-cultural research on drinking have been discussed by Everett et al. (1976), Rootman and Moser (1984), Westermeyer (1979), and Mäkelä et al. (1981). Broader discussions of cross-cultural research methods can be found in Manaster and Havighurst (1972), Triandis and Brislin (1984), Williams and Best (1982), and Hofstede (1980). The major methodologic pitfalls can be summarized under the concepts of representativeness, equivalence, and measurement bias. If samples are not representative of the populations to which they belong, then generalizations to those broader populations will not be valid. Of equal importance is the problem of equivalence. Before attempting to compare samples in terms of behavior, symptoms, or attitudes, it should first be determined that they are equivalent with respect to background and demographic characteristics such as age, social position, and education. These variables are known to vary with drinking patterns and seem to influence social behavior independently of other aspects of culture. Failure to control for gross differences in these variables might confuse any analysis of cross-national or interethnic differences.

One strategy to improve equivalence is to make the samples very heterogeneous in order to randomize subcultural differences. This procedure attempts to make the sample representative of the population as a whole. Another strategy is to make the samples very narrow, drawing from similar subcultures in different countries. A third strategy is to control statistically for subcultural differences. All three are illustrated among the studies in this volume.

Measurement bias can result from a variety of sources in cross-cultural research. In micro-level studies where self-report measures are used, linguistic equivalence can only be approximated, even after the tedious process of translation and back translation. When rating scales are employed it is important to consider the intrusion of differential and culture-specific response bias, such as the tendency to agree, disagree, or favor socially desirable answers. In macro-level comparative studies, the researcher must contend with the limitations of alcohol problems statistics, whose meanings are determined not only by their relation to alcohol use, but also by the relations to alcohol use perceived by those who generate statistics. Attributional practices and record-keeping methods both change over time, and these may affect the quality of data available for comparative research.

## CONCLUSION

Cross-cultural comparative research is at a crossroads. On the one hand, there is an ever-increasing demand for empirically based data to guide policy decisions in areas such as alcoholism treatment and alcohol abuse prevention. On the other hand, comparative research has yet to develop an identity, a common methodology, or a sense of purpose in any way comparable to those of biological or psychological areas of alcohol research. Despite more than a century of interest in comparative analysis, alcohol researchers are just beginning to realize the potential applications of their trade for theory development and policy planning at both the national and international levels. What seems to be guiding this realization is the general conviction that sociocultural factors are crucial to an explanation of the prevalence and patterning of alcohol problems in society. Genetic determinants, biological risk factors, and psychological vulnerability all may play a role, but the variability observed among human social groups (where these factors are presumably distributed randomly) suggests that sociocultural analysis may be the most fruitful line of inquiry for the purposes of treatment and prevention policy.

If the readers of this volume begin their survey with the impression that more questions have been raised than solutions provided, they should at least be consoled by the truism that no answer has meaning without being defined by an appropriate question.

## REFERENCES

COULTON, C. C. 1908. From St. Francis to Dante . . . the Chronicle of the Franciscan Salimbene. London.

DAVIS, N. S. 1900. Is there any causative or etiological relation between the extensive use of alcoholic drinks and the continued increase of epilepsy, imbecility and insanity, both mental and moral in all the countries of Europe and America? Annexe No. 4, VII Congrès International contre l'Abus des Boissons Alcooliques, Session de Paris 1899, Vol. 2. :53–59. Union Francaise Antialcoolique. Paris, France. pp. 53–59.

EVERETT, M. W., J. O. WADDELL & D. B. HEATH, Eds. 1976. Cross-Cultural Approaches to the Study of Alcohol: An Interdisciplinary Perspective. Mouton. The Hague, the Netherlands.

FRIJDA, N. & G. JAHODA. 1966. On the scope and method of cross-cultural research. Int. J. Psychol. 1: 109–127.

HOFSTEDE, G. 1980. Culture's Consequences: International Differences in Work-Related Values. Sage Publications. Beverly Hills, CA.

JELLINEK, E. M. 1962. Cultural differences in the meaning of alcoholism. In Society, Culture and Drinking Patterns. D. J. Pittman & C. Snyder, Eds. :382–388. Southern Illinois University Press. Carbondale, IL.

KANDEL, D. B., I. ADLER & M. SUDIT. 1981. The epidemiology of adolescent drug use in France and Israel. Am. J. Publ. Health 71: 256–265.

MÄKELÄ, K., R. ROOM, E. SINGLE, P. SULKUNEN & B. WALSH. 1981. Alcohol, Society and the State: A Comparative Study of Alcohol Control, Vol. 1. Addiction Research Foundation. Toronto, Canada.

MANASTER, G. J. & R. J. HAVIGHURST 1972. Cross-National Research: Social-Psychological Methods and Problems. Houghton Mifflin. Boston, MA.

PAULSON, R. W. 1973. Women's Suffrage and Prohibition: A Comparative Study of Equality and Social Control. Scott, Foresman. Glenview, IL.

ROCHAT, L. L. 1893. Receptions. Compte-rendu du 4ieme Congrès International contre l'Abus des Boissons Alcooliques. :80–82. The Hague, the Netherlands.

ROOTMAN, I. & J. MOSER. 1984. Guidelines for Investigating Alcohol Problems and Developing Appropriate Responses. WHO Offset Publication No. 81. World Health Organization. Geneva, Switzerland.

TRIANDIS, H. C. & R. W. BRISLIN. 1984. Cross-cultural psychology. Am. Psychol. 39: 1006–1016.

WESTERMEYER, J. 1974. Alcoholism from the cross-cultural perspective: A review and critique of clinical studies. Am. J. Drug Alcohol Abuse 1: 89–105.

WILLIAMS, J. E. & D. L. BEST. 1982. Measuring Sex Stereotypes: A Thirty-Nation Study. Sage Publications. Beverly Hills, CA.

# Alcohol-Related Problems in Cross-National Perspective: Results of the ISACE Study

ESA ÖSTERBERG

*Social Research Institute of Alcohol Studies*
*00100 Helsinki 10, Finland*

## INTRODUCTION

This paper presents an international overview of alcohol-related problems in cross-national perspective as derived from the results of the International Study of Alcohol Control Experiences (ISACE), a comparative study which began in 1976 and ended in 1981.

The idea of ISACE was to analyze the social history of the postwar alcohol experience in seven societies — those of California, Finland, Ireland, the Netherlands, Ontario, Poland, and Switzerland. The first goal of the project was to trace the historical development of alcohol-control policy and its determinants. Secondly, it aimed at assessing the potential influence of control policy on the consumption of alcohol and its adverse consequences (Mäkelä *et al.*, 1981).

The national and cross-national aspects of the project were closely intertwined and, as a result of this, the final report of ISACE was published in two complementary volumes. Volume 2, the national case studies, contains the alcohol-control experiences in the seven societies (Single *et al.*, 1981). Volume 1, the international report, presents the theoretical and policy implications of these case studies (Mäkelä *et al.*, 1981). A third volume, concentrating on the developments in alcohol-related problems in the seven societies, has also been published (Giesbrecht *et al.*, 1983).

ISACE was mainly concerned with alcoholic beverage controls and with the state's role in managing the production and distribution of alcoholic beverages. For ISACE, the term "alcohol control" refers to any government measure that relates to the purchase, production or trade of alcoholic beverages, whatever the measure's aim may be. ISACE was not, therefore, specifically concerned with cross-cultural comparisons of alcohol-related problems. Describing alcohol-related problems was, however, an important part of the project. There were two reasons for this. First, the project dealt with alcohol-related problems, both as one of the determinants of alcohol-control policy and as phenomena to which alcohol-control policies are directed or which are affected by alcohol-control policies. Secondly, being able to give overall descriptions of social history of national alcohol experiences also presupposed charting the course of the development of alcohol-related problems.

When describing social history, ISACE treated alcohol-related problems as no different from other aspects of the alcohol question. The guidelines for data collection first outlined a few crucial indicators which each country was supposed to take special pains to collect. But the project also included the collection of other indicators; each country was entitled to resort to indicators that they felt important. What was obtained was a batch of national papers dealing with the development of alcohol-related problems (cf. Mäkelä et al., 1981, pp. 131–135). These later served as parts of the national case studies, on the one hand, and as basic material for the international report, on the other. What follows in the next eight sections is an almost direct summary of the alcohol problems section of the ISACE international report.

## ALCOHOL PROBLEMS STATISTICS AND THEIR MEANING

Alternative prevalence estimates of alcoholism yield different rankings among societies. This, among other things, is an indication of the real variability of alcohol-related problems between societies and highlights the need to focus separately on specific alcohol-related problems and specific problem indicators. After all, there is no single indicator that can reliably estimate the magnitude of alcohol problems in all countries at a specific time or in a single country over time.

Different societies define social problems in different ways and they also disagree about the extent to which these problems are related to alcohol. Furthermore, societies change over time in terms of their readiness to attribute different social problems to drinking. Important national differences also exist in the division of resources among the authorities concerned with the management of alcohol-related problems. The manner in which resources are shared among the police, penal institutions, and social and medical authorities, for instance, affects when and how alcohol problems are tackled. The division of resources has an effect on statistics as well; most records that are used as problem indicators are kept by officials as part of their work. This in turn means that problem indicators also reflect changes in the autonomous activity of different authorities or in statistical practice.

The way in which ISACE regarded the disparities in alcohol-related problems among different societies was by no means unique. Neither was ISACE particularly naive with respect to the use of problem indicators as portrayors of changes in alcohol-related problems. What was unique was that ISACE did not capitulate, as many other studies have done, before the problems inherent in using problem indicators as means of describing changes in the alcohol scene. ISACE countered the problems of comparing the nature and extent of alcohol-related problems by striving to measure two different dimensions: alcohol's role in problematic events or situations and the cultural dimension of the definition of problems and their attribution to alcohol (Mäkelä et al., 1981, p. 41).

In practice, ISACE did not have access to anything like the standard of data it would have liked. The available time series came from four health and social statistical systems: statistics on mortality, hospitalization (particularly for mental hospitals), arrests and convictions for public drunkenness, and road accidents. These statistical series reflected differing mixtures of "objective" reality and social definition and attribution. The available measures were thus severely limited as a vehicle for describing and comparing actual alcohol problems in the seven societies studied.

Administrative statistics on control undertakings are, however, also of interest in their own right, whether or not they accurately reflect the objective consequences of drinking. In some instances, control measures constitute the most important consequences of drinking both from the point of view of the individual in question and of society as a whole. Changes in problems statistics may therefore reflect fluctuations in the social and health systems' response to alcohol-related problems and changes in the social awareness of these problems. In addition, alcohol problem statistics may provide an indication of trends in drinking patterns. Consequently, ISACE examined the available statistics on alcohol problems from three perspectives: as indicators of actual changes in the alcohol problems of a society; as indicators of changes in the social health systems' response to these problems; and as indicators of trends in the drinking practices.

## CULTURAL VARIATION IN ALCOHOL PROBLEMS

At the beginning of the 1950s, the aggregate consumption in all seven societies studied in ISACE was on a low or moderate level (FIG. 1). Correspondingly, somatic health ailments related to prolonged drinking were not very conspicuous, with the possible exception of the subjects in Switzerland and California. There were, however, substantial differences in the ratio of mortality from cirrhosis to the total consumption of alcohol, and even more striking cultural differences in the rates and nature of social conflicts related to drinking.

In both Poland and Finland, the level of overall consumption was very low; distilled spirits accounted for the lion's share of consumption (TABLE 1). Social conflicts related to drinking were common. Both countries had high rates of arrests for drunkenness and of fatal alcohol poisoning. Conflict-prone drunken behavior was not confined to isolated subgroups of inebriates.

In the Netherlands, the level and beverage structure of consumption were very similar to those of Finland and Poland, but there were few signs of disruptive drinking or significant numbers of people drunk in public. Of the societies with a somewhat higher aggregate consumption, Ireland was perhaps the most closely comparable to Finland and Poland. Disruptive drunken behavior was more an outgrowth of culturally accepted patterns of drinking than confined to deviant subgroups. The rate of prosecutions for drunkenness was, however, quite low.

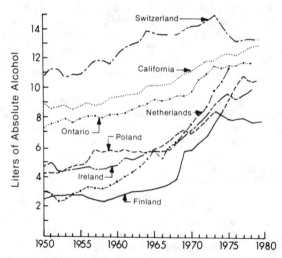

**FIGURE 1.** Total consumption of alcoholic beverages (in liters of absolute alcohol per head) of population aged 15 years and over in countries studied in ISACE, from 1950–1980. (SOURCE: Mäkelä et al., 1981 [Table 2.1]. Reprinted by permission of the Addiction Research Foundation.)

**TABLE 1.** The Share of Distilled Spirits in Total Consumption in 1950 and in 1980 in Countries Studied in ISACE

| Country | 1950 | 1980 |
|---|---|---|
| Finland | 80% | 47% |
| Poland | 78% | 71% |
| Netherlands | 70% | 32% |
| California | 43% | 43% |
| Ontario | 28% | 39% |
| Ireland | 26% | 32% |
| Switzerland | 15% | 19% |

SOURCE: Mäkelä et al., 1981 (Table 2.1).

Public drunkenness was quite conspicuous in California and in Ontario, although to a lesser degree than in Poland and Finland. Arrests for drunkenness were disproportionately confined to a socially visible subgroup of chronic public inebriates. Switzerland had the highest level of aggregate consumption. Despite variations in patterns of drinking among cantons, there were few signs of social conflicts related to disruptive drunken behavior.

A number of cultural idiosyncrasies in problem perception also deserve mention. Californians tend to emphasize drunken driving as the single most important alcohol issue. Alcohol as a factor endangering productivity seems to receive more public attention in Poland than in other societies. In Poland, opinion polls also indicate great concern about family disturbances related to drinking.

At the beginning of the study period, the division of labor among various public agencies in the management of disruptive drinking varied widely over the seven societies. In Finland, Poland, California, Ontario and, to a lesser degree, in Ireland, arrests for drunkenness were important means of control. In Finland and in the English-speaking societies, jail sentences (frequently in lieu of unpaid fines) resulted in a longer-term isolation of deviant drinkers.

Psychiatric institutions played a considerable role in the management of disruptive drinking in Ireland, and to a lesser degree in California and Ontario. In the Netherlands and in Switzerland, where the incidence of disruptive drinking was low, the role of the police was correspondingly small. In Switzerland, cantonal legislation often delegated wide powers to social and health authorities to use repressive measures to control disruptive drinking. Similar stipulations also existed in the Netherlands, but mandatory confinements were relatively rare.

Although there were national idiosyncrasies in the detailed organizational arrangements, general patterns related to the frequency and nature of social conflicts caused by drunken behavior can still be detected in each of the societies. Where the rate of social conflict was high, the primary agencies of problem-handling tended to be the police and the judicial system. Where there was a low incidence of such conflict, the primary agencies tended to be social welfare authorities and psychiatric institutions. Differences in problem mixture were undoubtedly influenced by variations in problem-handling, but each society's control system was also responsive to its peculiar problems.

## ALCOHOL-RELATED HEALTH AILMENTS

The overall picture of trends in alcohol-related health ailments known to be etiologically related to drinking in the 1950–1975 period shows a substantial increase for most

**TABLE 2.** Cirrhosis Mortality Rates per 100,000 Population Aged 25 Years and Over in Countries Studied in ISACE: 1950–1975

| Country | 1950 | 1955 | 1960 | 1965 | 1970 | 1975 |
|---|---|---|---|---|---|---|
| California | 26.2 | 29.0 | 33.3 | 39.4 | 40.3 | 36.3 |
| Finland | 3.7 | 6.1 | 5.8 | 6.0 | 7.4 | 10.1 |
| Ireland | 3.6 | 4.2 | 3.4 | 5.7 | 6.2 | 5.7 |
| Netherlands | 4.5 | 5.8 | 6.4 | 6.3 | 7.1 | 8.0 |
| Ontario | 7.7 | 9.7 | 12.9 | 13.9 | 18.0 | 22.2 |
| Poland | – | – | 6.1 | 10.9 | 15.2 | 18.0 |
| Switzerland | – | 21.1 | 19.2 | 25.0 | 25.2 | 20.4 |

SOURCE: Mäkelä et al., 1981 (Table 3.1).

indicators in the majority of the societies studied in ISACE, though the rate of increase varies from one disease and society to another (Mäkelä et al., 1981, pp. 47–50). The most complete data are those available for cirrhosis mortality, and here the increase has been substantial for all the societies studied with the exception of Switzerland (TABLE 2). The rate of increase, however, does not necessarily vary from one society to another as a function of the rate of growth of the aggregate consumption of alcohol.

The study societies differed in their mixture of health problems related to drinking, and there was little sign of convergence in the study period. The societies with a historic pattern of extreme drinking and associated consequences—notably Finland and Poland, where substantial alcohol poisoning fatalities occur—experienced, in a period of increasing consumption, increases in these consequences and in the consequences of prolonged drinking as well. On the other hand, Switzerland, which had a relatively high consumption level at the beginning of the study period and a drinking culture not given to drunkenness, experienced modest increases in health consequences despite a large increase in consumption.

Data on alcohol-specific diseases only gives a partial picture of the impact of drinking on public health. Mortality in persons treated for alcoholism is commonly in excess of that of the general population, because of both drinking-related diseases and other causes as well. In most of these other health ailments, drinking is only implicated in a minority of cases; trend data on the number of alcohol-related cases were generally not available. Nevertheless, numerous special studies indicate that health consequences related to single drinking occasions, such as alcohol-related traffic deaths, still play a significant role from the perspective of overall public health (Giesbrecht et al., 1983).

## SOCIAL CONFLICTS RELATED TO DRUNKEN BEHAVIOR

There are many social conflicts in which alcohol use is implicated, such as public drunkenness, fights and quarrels, violent crimes, and family troubles. The statistical series more generally available, however, only relate to public drunkenness. Because the persons involved in such offenses often come from the lower social stratum, differences in the presence and size of the skid row population have a bearing on the volume of public drunkenness. Any interpretation of arrest rates for public drunkenness also has to take into account changes in legislation and rule-enforcement practices. These changes are also of interest in their own right, as reflections of changing attitudes towards drunkenness as a social problem.

There was considerable variation among the societies studied in the rate of official

**TABLE 3.** Rates of Public Drunkenness per 100,000 Inhabitants Aged 15 Years and Over in 1960 and 1975 in Countries Studied in ISACE

| Country | 1960 | 1975 |
|---|---|---|
| California | 2.390 | 1.325 |
| Finland | 4.247 | 7.485 |
| Ireland | 160 | 220 |
| Netherlands | 90 | 21 |
| Ontario | 1.095 | 615 |
| Poland | 1.856 | 1.646 |

SOURCE: Mäkelä et al., 1981, (Table 3.2).

response to public drunkenness around 1960 (TABLE 3). Public drunkenness is not included at all as an offence in the Swiss penal code. The Netherlands also had very few recorded cases of public drunkenness. The arrest rate was quite high in California and Poland and reached even higher levels in Finland. The rate of official response to public drunkenness was quite high in Ontario, while the Irish rate fell below that of Poland, California, and Ontario.

During the last years of the period, the growth in alcohol consumption was accompanied by increasing rates of public drunkenness in the three countries — Finland, Ireland, and Poland — where intoxication and conflict-prone drunken behavior are an outgrowth of culturally accepted traditional patterns of drinking. Because of a declining trend in the first half of the 1960s, the overall level in Poland in 1975 was below the figures for 1960. In the Netherlands, on the other hand, the rise in alcohol consumption since the 1960s was substantial, but the conviction rate was small and declining. Ontario and California fall in between: public drunkenness rates, once high, declined despite the rise in consumption. In Finland, Poland, and Ireland, rates of public drunkenness also tended to lag behind consumption.

Actual changes in drinking styles, occasions, and places, as well as shifts in perceptions of public drinking or drunkenness seem to have contributed to the decline in the perception of public drunkenness as a social problem. In some of the societies studied, decriminalization of public drunkenness led to the establishment of medical substitutes for police "drunk tanks." By 1966 in Poland, more drunks were already being attended to at sobering-up stations than in police stations. In California and Ontario, at least a proportion of public inebriates are now sent to detoxification centers. No new medical facilities were established in Finland, but decriminalization saved a substantial group of drunks from serving their sentences in prison.

## DRINKING AND ROAD TRAFFIC

Over the last two decades, alcohol-related traffic problems have been identified as a primary indicator of social problems linked to drinking. In all the societies studied in ISACE, it is an offence to drive a motor vehicle when the blood alcohol content exceeds a certain level. Nevertheless, the definition of drunken driving and enforcement practices varies greatly from society to society. Arrests for drunken driving, therefore, should not be used as an indicator of the relative seriousness of drunken driving in different countries. Alcohol-related traffic accident rates are also affected by changes in recording or investigation practices. In most situations, however, accident rates can

**TABLE 4.** Percentage Changes between Selected Years in the Number of Drinking and Driving Offences and Fatal or Injury Accidents in Countries Studied in ISACE

| | Year | Drinking and Driving Offences | Fatal or Injury Accidents/Drivers Involved in Fatal or Injury Accidents/Persons Killed or Injured in Road Accidents | |
| --- | --- | --- | --- | --- |
| | | | All Cases | Alcohol-Related Cases |
| California | 1960–75 | + 549 | + 53 (drivers) | + 73 (drivers) |
| Finland | 1960–75 | + 320 | + 28 (accidents) | + 128 (accidents) |
| Ireland | 1961–75 | + 532 | – | – |
| Netherlands | 1961–75 | + 155 | – | – |
| Ontario | 1960–75 | + 325 | + 185 (drivers) | + 243 (drivers) |
| Poland | 1964–74 | + 66 | + 94 (persons) | + 86 (persons) |
| Switzerland | 1963–75 | + 79 | – 4 (persons) | + 21 (persons) |

SOURCE: Mäkelä et al., 1981 (Table 3.4).

be used as a partially independent check on the picture obtained from legal statistics on drunken driving.

In general, drinking and driving offences and alcohol-related road accidents increased greatly between the early 1960s and the mid-1970s (TABLE 4). Absolute changes are not very informative, however, because of traffic growth, changes in enforcement practices, and better safety precautions. The growth rate of alcohol-related accidents may therefore best be compared with the growth rate of all accidents. In four of the five societies for which data are available, there was a faster increase in alcohol-related accidents than in all other types. Despite the continuous traffic growth, the overall number of fatal or injury accidents leveled off or showed a slight decrease during the last years of the study period, but alcohol-related accidents continued to increase. Trends in alcohol-related accidents thus generally run counter to the declining rates for all accidents. It is thus likely that the upward trend in alcohol consumption, and particularly the related diversification of drinking patterns and styles, contributed to an actual increase in the prevalence of drinking and driving.

Drinking and driving intervention is in unique contrast to the moves toward decriminalization of public drunkenness and the expansion of nonpunitive responses to other alcohol problems. This is evident in general developments in legislation and law enforcement, such as the introduction and expanded use of Breathalyzer equipment. In a wider sense, concern about alcohol and traffic accidents has widened the definition of "problem drinkers" to more than just public inebriates or those under care for alcohol problems. The approach taken towards drunken driving also differs from that for other alcohol-related social problems. For drunken driving, the overriding trend has been to emphasize general deterrence through criminal penalties and the taking away of a driver's licence. Of the societies studied in ISACE, only in California has the tendency to regard drinking problems as medical ones been extended to drunken driving. Nevertheless, like the other study societies, California has adopted blood alcohol limits, mandatory blood-alcohol testing, and increased drunken driving penalties.

## CHANGES IN ALCOHOL-RELATED PROBLEMS IN
## RELATION TO CONSUMPTION

Alcohol consumption levels rose in every society studied in ISACE. Alcohol-related problems, on the other hand, showed a more complicated pattern. The rise in alcohol consumption was accompanied by increases in the incidence of many physical ailments known to be etiologically related to prolonged drinking, although the rate of increase varied from one disease and society to another. The evidence in regard to consequences of single-drinking occasions is less conclusive, but even in the societies where conflicts related to drinking have increased in absolute figures, their rate of increase has fallen below the increase in aggregate consumption. This can be seen as an indication of less conflict-prone patterns of drinking behavior. Drunken driving is perhaps the only type of behavior related to single-drinking occasions which steadily gained in importance. The absolute number of alcohol-related road accidents increased in each of the societies studied, and with the reduced overall rate of accidents, the proportion of alcohol-related cases of all accidents tended to rise (TABLE 5).

The rate of increase of physical ailments related to prolonged drinking tended to be higher than the rate of increase of conflicts related to single-drinking occasions. Because of the different rate of growth of various types of drinking problems, variations across societies tended to diminish. Nevertheless, persistent cultural differences exist. In Finland and Poland especially, social conflicts related to drunken behavior are still extremely important. The health consequences of single-drinking occasions are similarly quite important in comparison with the health consequences of prolonged drinking.

In broad terms, the results may be interpreted in the following fashion: Each so-

**TABLE 5.** Alcohol-Related Cases in Percent of all Road Accidents by Type of Accident in Selected Years in Countries Studied in ISACE

| | | Alcohol-Related Cases (%) of: | |
| | | Nonfatal Injury Accidents/Drivers Involved in Injury Accidents/Persons Injured in Accidents | Fatal Accidents/Drivers Involved in Fatal Accidents/Persons Killed in Accidents |
|---|---|---|---|
| California | 1960 | 11.5 | 20.9 |
| | 1975 | 12.9 | 33.7 |
| | | (drivers) | (drivers) |
| Finland | 1960 | 8.3 | 13.0 |
| | 1975 | 14.8 | 23.0 |
| | | (accidents) | (accidents) |
| Ontario | 1960 | 10.0 | 15.4 |
| | 1975 | 11.8 | 26.4 |
| | | (drivers) | (drivers) |
| Poland | 1964 | 15.5 | 20.7 |
| | 1974 | 15.0 | 18.3 |
| | 1975 | 19.4 | 30.0 |
| | | (persons) | (persons) |
| Switzerland | 1963 | 6.4 | 14.5 |
| | 1975 | 8.0 | 19.2 |
| | | (persons) | (persons) |

SOURCE: Mäkelä et al., 1981 (Table 3.5).

ciety has certain specific social circumstances and drinking habits, and the mixture of alcohol-related problems thus varies accordingly. In cross-sectional comparisons these differences and differences in the management of alcohol-related problems lead to a situation where there are few if any positive relationships between the consumption level and the incidence of given alcohol-related problems at a specific time. Nevertheless, looking at the historical experience of each cultural setting, problems are not unrelated to temporal variations in aggregate consumption.

Even in a given cultural setting, however, the relationship between consumption level and problems is by no means a simple one. First of all, the cultural patterns of drinking and drunken behavior do change. Second, many other factors besides actual drinking behavior determine the rate and seriousness of alcohol problems. Urban ecology influences the probability that public drunkenness will result in social conflicts, medical technology has an impact on the incidence of fatal delirum, and so on.

At the end of the study period, drinking problems were less strictly confined to social outcasts and visibly deviant subgroups. There was a shift in the locus of problems from the lower class and deviant subgroups to the middle class. Skid row inebriates were supplanted or joined by middle class cirrhotics and drunken drivers. The diffusion of drinking into practically all segments of the population and a growing number of social situations has made it more difficult to localize the alcohol problem in a particular population group or to associate it with particular lifestyle. More than ever, problems stem not only from pathologic or deviant drinking, but also from an outgrowth of socially integrated patterns of consumption.

During the postwar period in particular, cultural perceptions of alcohol problems changed radically. Alcohol problems tended to be redefined as medical problems. Behavior that had earlier been looked upon as reprehensible conduct and dealt with by social and legal authorities was redefined as a symptom of an underlying disease which had to be treated. There was also a growing awareness of alcohol as an etiologic factor in a number of somatic ailments in addition to the classic alcoholic diseases of cirrhosis and pancreatitis. The role of drinking as a causal factor in social disturbance began to be seen as less prominent as well. Whereas drinking was considered a sufficient explanation for a wide array of disturbances ranging from wife-beating to sports hooliganism early on, by the 1970s the mass media and public discussion had played down the role of drinking in these situations. Poland and the U.S. are perhaps exceptions to this trend: the public and the media in those countries continue to associate alcohol with a wide range of social evils. The 1970s also saw the resurrection of alcohol as an explanation for the problems found in many of the societies studied.

## CHANGES IN THE SOCIETAL HANDLING
## OF ALCOHOL PROBLEMS

Among the trends in societal response, the most pervasive was the expansion of service facilities for heavy drinkers organized and financed under a medical rubric. In many of the societies studied in ISACE, this expansion took the form of setting up specialized institutions or services for alcohol problems rather than integrating alcohol problem management into the general health-care system. Detoxification facilities, halfway houses, behavior modification clinics, drunken driver reeducation programs, pickup services for drunks, hotlines and referral services, and industrial alcoholism programs are services that were new or reformulated in the postwar period.

In general, services for alcohol problems shifted away from large inpatient facilities to outpatient services and smaller community-based facilities. This reflected, particularly in the 1960s, a strong trend against the propensity of large public mental hospitals and similar institutions to depersonalize, label, and segregate their patients. Also, as wages for service occupations rose, inpatient treatment became extraordinarily costly. In most of the societies studied in ISACE, there were fewer involuntary commitments to treatment. Nevertheless, coercion into treatment may have changed less *de facto* than *de jure*. The decline in involuntary commitments was associated with a trend toward deinstitutionalization, and also reflected developing notions of civil liberties and patients' rights.

The timing of the expansion of services for alcohol problems was remarkably similar in the societies studied, seemingly irrespective of the baseline mixture of alcohol problems in each society. Common solutions were adopted for very different problems. The first modern wards of clinics specializing in alcoholism treatment were founded in the 1940s or 1950s, but the quantitative expansion occurred in the late 1960s and early 1970s. The expansion of special health services for alcohol problems coincided with a general wave of investment in public health and social security in most industrial countries.

## THE POSTWAR ERA AND THE FUTURE

The increase in alcohol consumption slowed down or leveled off in many industrialized countries in the 1970s, and some decreases were recorded. It is possible that the standstill is not only an interlude related to economic recession, but also signifies the end of the long wave of increasing alcohol consumption.

The overall level of drinking problems is likely to remain at a permanently higher level than that before the growth in alcohol consumption. The mixture of problems is unlikely to change to any significant extent. Event-type consequences will continue to be important, both from a public health perspective and from the perspective of the quality of social life. Given the surprising endurance of traditional patterns of drinking, cultural variation in the mixture of alcohol problems may be expected to remain significant.

There are many signs of coming changes in the social response to drinking problems. The optimism about the treatment of "alcoholism" as a disease seems to be wearing off. Over the study period, the increasing drinking problems were absorbed by the expanding treatment system. In view of the financial strain on the public sector providing health and welfare benefits, it is doubtful that the integrative and service-oriented approach will continue in the future. The trend towards a redefinition of public health in terms of individual responsibility is likely to be first extended to self-induced conditions such as alcohol problems.

A possible revival of drinking as a moral issue may reinforce tendencies towards punitive and disciplinary control of individual deviant drinkers. At the same time, it is possible that preventive control policies may regain popular support. In popular moral sentiments, these two options are not necessarily alternatives to each other. Nevertheless, from a policy perspective, the distinction between individualized repressive control and preventive alcohol-control policies may become increasingly important.

## DISCUSSION

There exists, despite numerous confounding factors, a relationship between the amount of intake and the various social consequences of drinking at an individual level. Cross-regional comparisons of alcohol problems, too, tend to exhibit a positive correlation between mean consumption and a number of ailments related to alcohol; this is especially true of cirrhosis of the liver. There were, however, few cross-cultural comparisons of the social consequences of drinking prior to the ISACE project. Furthermore, the scant research which had been conducted was usually unable to find any positive or significant correlation between alcohol consumption and varying sets of social consequences.

In the early stages of ISACE, a great deal of effort was spent in trying to ensure that the guidelines for data collection would really guarantee the collection of comparable data. ISACE, however, never gave birth to an international data bank. But, despite having to make do with data that were inadequate in many ways, ISACE was able to complete a comparison of alcohol problems in different countries. This entitles us to conclude that the principles of cross-cultural comparison which the project adhered to brought about practical benefits, and that the methodology used in ISACE represents an improvement on the correlation hypothesis which previously dominated the field. In other words, in order to compare alcohol-related problems in different countries — or even in one country over time — one must have access to information on the role alcohol plays in problematic events or situations and measures of how the culture defines problems and their attribution to alcohol. One also has to examine the available statistics from three perspectives: as indicators of the actual changes in alcohol-related problems; as indicators of changes in the social health systems' response to these problems, and as indicators of trends in drinking practices. In addition, the fact that alcohol-related problems form a process that can be studied at different stages and by different authorities means that statistical series should be used in combination rather than separately.

## REFERENCES

GIESBRECHT, N., M. CAHANNES, J. MOSKALEWICZ, E. ÖSTERBERG & R. ROOM, Eds. 1983. Consequences of Drinking: Trends in Alcohol Problem Statistics in Seven Countries. Addiction Research Foundation. Toronto, Ontario, Canada.

MÄKELÄ, K., R. ROOM, E. SINGLE, P. SULKUNEN, B. WALSH, R. BUNCE, M. CAHANNES, T. CAMERON, N. GIESBRECHT, J. DE LINT, H. MÄKINEN, P. MORGAN, J. MOSHER, J. MOSKALEWICZ, R. MÜLLER, E. ÖSTERBERG, I. WALD, & D. WALSH. 1981. Alcohol, Society, and the State. 1. A Comparative Study of Alcohol Control. Addiction Research Foundation. Toronto, Ontario, Canada.

SINGLE, E., P. MORGAN & J. DE LINT, Eds. 1981. Alcohol, Society and the State. 2. The Social History of Control Policy in Seven Countries. Addiction Research Foundation. Toronto, Ontario, Canada.

# Attitudes towards Drinking and Drunkenness in Four Scandinavian Countries

### KLAUS MÄKELÄ

*Finnish Foundation for Alcohol Studies*
*00100 Helsinki 10, Finland*

This report, which attempts to discuss drinking cultures over time, is part of a comparative survey of drinking in Scandinavia.[a] One of the aims of the project is to compare the interactions of drinking behaviors and the consequences of drinking in various structural and cultural settings. Attitudes towards drinking and drunkenness were examined in an attempt to describe the cultural climate prevailing in each of four Scandinavian countries as one crucial factor affecting personal experiences related to drinking.

## CONCEPTUAL BACKGROUND

In order to be able to discuss change we first have to classify. On the surface, it seems to be a straightforward task to compare cultures in terms of prevailing attitudes towards drinking, on the one hand, and drunkenness on the other. Indeed, one major attempt to classify the alcohol-using cultures of the world (Pittman, 1967) makes use of precisely these two features. On closer inspection, however, the content of both drinking and drunkenness proves to be more complex than expected (Mäkelä, 1983). The point of departure for the following analyses is that the cultural dynamics of the control of excessive drinking vary according to the historically dominant uses of alcohol.

The importance of the historically dominant use of alcohol is easily seen by comparing some of the cultures occupying the same category in David Pittman's well-known classification of drinking cultures. Pittman classifies both the Jewish and the Italian as permissive cultures which tolerate moderate drinking but condemn drunkenness. Among orthodox Jews, however, alcohol is used as a ritual beverage on sacral occasions, but it plays no role whatsoever in the daily caloric intake. In Italy, wine is mainly used as a foodstuff. In the same fashion, one may seriously doubt whether both the French and the Bolivian Camba should be classified as belonging to the same group, as they do in Pittman's classification. In France, the nutritional use of wine is widespread, and heavy intoxication is culturally condemned, even if daily consumption is much higher than in Italy and drinking outside meals is fully accepted. In contrast, in the Camba society extreme drunkenness is sought as an end in itself, but the consumption is limited to specific occasions.

---

[a] The project group consists of Ragnar Hauge, Björn Hibell, Olav Irgens-Jensen, Klaus Mäkelä, Tom Nilsson, Hildigunnur Olafsdottir, and Jussi Simpura.

With respect to the dominant uses of alcohol, Italy and France, on the one hand, and the Jews, Scandinavians and Camba, on the other hand, are variations of two basic types. In Italy and France, nutritional use of alcohol is historically dominant, but the French have developed more tolerant attitudes towards the intoxicant side effects of wine. Among the Jews, the Scandinavians and the Camba alike, alcohol is an intoxicant, but these three cultures have developed alternative normative solutions to the regulation of the use of this intoxicant. The orthodox Jews have succeeded in isolating alcohol into a sacral corner, the Camba use it up to extreme drunkenness but only on clearly demarcated occasions, and the Scandinavians vacillate between Dionysiac acceptance and ascetic condemnation of drunkenness.

In Scandinavia, the role of alcoholic beverages in the intake of calories has been minimal, and drinking has not been part of daily meals. Moreover, drinking has not been part of everyday sociability but has been isolated from the normal flow of daily life. The dominant use of alcohol as an intoxicant has deeply influenced the *structure* of Scandinavian attitudes toward alcohol. On the level of general opinion, attitudes towards drinking have been nearly synonymous with attitudes towards (occasional) drunkenness. The main culturally given choice has been one between acceptance of drinking *and* the core features of factually prevailing patterns of drinking or condemnation of drinking in general. If rules of moderation have been advocated, their purpose has been to domesticate the intoxicant, not to keep within boundaries the happy side effects of the nutrient.

The dominant use of alcohol also affects the structure of situational norms about drinking. In principle, we could expect that cultures classify situations in three categories with more or less distinct boundaries: situations where no drinking is permitted, situations where moderate drinking is permitted but drunkenness proscribed, and situations where intoxication is normatively accepted. In countries where alcohol is an intoxicant, the number of situations where drunkenness is permitted may vary, but the main feature is that the zone of prescribed moderation will be narrow.

Alcohol can be set apart from the daily flow of social life in two senses: First, it can be used in culturally regulated special occasions and ritual festivities. Drinking then marks a collective break in routine chores and signifies a culturally regulated transition from toil to celebration. This pattern is typical of many peasant societies. But drinking can also signify an individual breaking out from the normal flow of social life and from responsibilities towards work and family. An extreme example would be a drinking bout of a dipsomaniac, but a similar individual withdrawal from everyday normal social responsibilities is clearly present in many instances of proletarian male drinking. In analyzing situational norms about drinking we thus should distinguish between annual festivities that punctuate ritual passages in the collective rhythm of social life and "the new leisure" which is defined solely as a negation of work or other social obligations (Määttänen, 1982; Falk, 1983).

No cultural codes can, of course, be regarded as permanently given or totally resistant to change. It is always possible for an individual or a group to rise above the set of choices given by a cultural code. An American Indian may leave the reservation and adopt the American middle-class system of choices with respect to drinking. On the reservation, however, it is difficult for him to drink in a middle-class fashion, not only because the content of the norms are in conflict with the surrounding culture, but also particularly because the structure of the normative system diverges from the Indian system of normative classification.

It is important to note that the codes underlying normative choices are not eternal and do themselves change. Our argument here is simply that cultural change cannot be adequately understood unless the structure and not only the content of individually held attitudes and norms is taken into consideration.

In the postwar era, there has been a world-wide normalization of drinking as a social activity. Age and sex segregation has been breaking down, and drinking has become integrated with other social activities and is accepted in a much wider repertoire of situations than before. Particularly in countries where drinking was traditionally an occasion for intoxication, occurring in well-defined and relatively rare situations, the modal pattern has changed towards one in which more moderate quantities are drunk more frequently but with less ceremony. In many countries, however, the spread of alcohol into new situations has not displaced the tradition of occasional heavy drinking (Mäkelä et al., 1982, pp. 19–30).

Corresponding to this change in time, we may postulate two extreme types of norm systems regulating drinking in Scandinavia. The "traditionally Scandinavian" type accepts drinking in specific and well-defined situations only, where not only drinking but drunkenness as well would be culturally accepted. The "modern" norm system is more permissive of drinking in general, but makes a clearer distinction between moderate drinking and intoxication. Our survey data can correspondingly be used to compare countries on the dimension of traditionality and modernity with respect to integration of drinking with other social activities. Moreover, by comparing various age groups, we can learn about the transformation of the structure of culturally held alcohol norms over time.

## THE MATERIAL

In February 1979, identical questionnaires were mailed to representative samples of the population between 20 and 69 years of age in Finland, Iceland, Norway and Sweden (for sampling operations and data collection, see Hauge and Irgens-Jensen, 1981a). The sample sizes and response rates are given in TABLE 1. Despite considerable variation in the response rate from one country to another, the analysis of the representativeness of the samples indicated that they are well suited for cross-cultural comparisons (Hauge and Irgens-Jensen, 1981b).

Our aim was to describe attitudes towards drinking and drunkenness in such a way as to obtain a measure of the relative distance between the two. This was done on two levels. First, two sets of semantic scales were presented to the respondents in order to measure the generalized emotive meaning of the two concepts of *alcohol* and *being drunk*. Second, the measures of generalized emotive meanings were complemented by presenting to the respondents two sets of identical situations in order to assess situational attitudes towards drinking and slight intoxication.

The analysis of attitudes and norms aims at internal comparisons of the countries studied and at locating Scandinavia among the alcohol-using cultures of the world. The goal is to describe cultures. We are therefore interested in demographic variation only insofar as it reflects variations between cultures. For example, for our present

**TABLE 1.** Sample Sizes and Response Rates in the Scandinavian Drinking Survey

|  | Finland | Iceland | Norway | Sweden |
|---|---|---|---|---|
| Number of respondents |  |  |  |  |
| Men | 1018 | 1047 | 838 | 877 |
| Women | 1119 | 1111 | 789 | 910 |
| Total | 2137 | 2158 | 1627 | 1787 |
| Response rate (%) | 71.3 | 63.1 | 54.5 | 58.3 |

purposes sex differences would be important only insofar as the direction or magnitude of the difference would vary from one country to another. Because such differences between countries were not found, both sexes will be combined in the following analysis. Correspondingly, differences in attitudes held by various age groups are not of primary concern, but will be analyzed as indirect indications of cultural change.

## EVALUATION OF ALCOHOL AND DRUNKENNESS

The questionnaire included seven semantic differential scales in order to measure the connotative meaning of the two concepts of alcohol and drunkenness. Four of the scales belong to Osgood's dimension of evaluation. Two of the scales measure activeness and one measures potency. It is well known, however, that the content of the concepts to be rated affects the intercorrelations of semantic scales (Osgood *et al.*, 1957, p. 177; Husu, 1980). It was thus no surprise that the scales designed to measure Osgood's basic semantic dimensions did not turn out to be independent. Furthermore, the structure of the factor loadings of some of the scales varied considerably from one country to another. It was therefore decided to construct only one composite index to measure the dimension of evaluation and to include only those scales that behaved identically in all countries in the item analysis. The indices reported here represent the sum score of the following scales: unpleasant–pleasant; bad–good; dull–exciting; and worthless–valuable. The respondents marked their response on a seven-step graphic scale defined by each pair of adjectives. The most positive alternative was scored as 7 and the most negative was given the value of 1. A score of 4 on any subscale (or, correspondingly, the score of 16 on the summary index) thus indicates a neutral attitude. The composite index was coded as nonresponse as soon as information was lacking for one of its items. The reliabilities of the semantic scores vary between 0.8 and 0.9. The semantic scales proved difficult, especially for older women, and the rate of nonresponse turned out to be quite high (Mäkelä, 1981).

The Icelanders evaluate both *alcohol* and *being drunk* most positively, followed by the Norwegians and the Finns (FIG. 1). The Swedes are the most negative in their

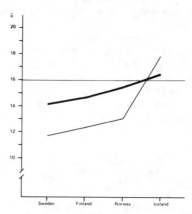

**FIGURE 1.** Evaluation of attitudes toward alcohol and being drunk in Sweden, Finland, Norway and Iceland. *Thick line*, alcohol; *thin line*, being drunk. High values indicate positive evaluation of alcohol and being drunk.

evaluations. In Sweden, Finland and Norway, both averages fall below the neutral line, i.e., both *alcohol* and *being drunk* are negatively evaluated. Only in Iceland is the overall evaluation of these two concepts positive. In Sweden, Finland and Norway, *being drunk* is more negatively evaluated than *alcohol*, and the distance between the two concepts is about the same in the three countries, but in Iceland *being drunk* is more positively evaluated than *alcohol*.

It would have been interesting to compare the distance between *alcohol* and *being drunk* among various age groups as representing different strata of a culture undergoing change, but the high and probably selective nonresponse in the older groups renders this unfeasible.

## ACCEPTANCE OF DRINKING AND INTOXICATION BY SITUATION

Ideally, our set of situations should include work situations and other daily routines as well as a selection of both ritual festivities and modern leisure situations. What we have in the questionnaire falls far short of this. The respondents were asked to indicate how fitting they think it is for a man in his thirties with no special drinking problem (1) to drink a bottle of beer or two, and (2) to drink so much as to become slightly intoxicated in the following five situations: an ordinary weekday dinner at home, having food at work, being together with friends on a Saturday evening, an evening on holiday abroad, and New Years's Eve. The response alternatives for this question were given the following scores: 1 = unfitting, 2 = not very fitting, 3 = reasonably all right, 4 = quite all right.

For a detailed cultural description it is useful to study each situation separately. For the sake of economy, summary measures have to be constructed if the normative distance between drinking and intoxication is to be compared among multiple demographic groups. For this purpose, an item analysis was carried out separately for the questions dealing with drinking at all and those dealing with slight intoxication. In both series, the correlations between the three leisure situations were quite high, and the inclusion of the two everyday situations would have decreased the reliability of the composite index in all countries. The item analysis further indicated that leisure situations and everyday situations represent two distinct dimensions, even if the separateness of the dimensions was not as clear in all countries. The correlations of the work situation were consistently low, as the response distributions were very skewed with few respondents accepting even drinking a beer or two in this case. It was decided to construct two indices for both series. The indices were constructed as simple sums of the precoded raw scores of the items. Each composite index was coded as nonresponse as soon as information was lacking for one of its items. Because of the very skewed distributions of the work questions, the reliabilities of the everyday indices are dangerously low (between 0.5 and 0.6 except for the reliability of acceptance of drinking in Norway, which is only 0.3). The reliabilities of the leisure indices are all above 0.9 (Mäkelä, 1981).

TABLE 2 can be read situation by situation as well as country by country. Despite the limited number of items, the contours of a classification of situations into those where no drinking is permitted, those where moderate drinking is permitted but drunkenness proscribed, and those where intoxication is culturally accepted can be read out of TABLE 2. During working hours, no alcohol consumption at all is allowed. A substantial minority (and in Sweden, a majority of respondents) regard it as all right to have a beer or two at a weekday dinner at home, but even slight intoxication is not permitted. A strong majority of respondents permit slight intoxication on an evening

**TABLE 2.** Percentage of Approval of Moderate Drinking and Slight Intoxication in Selected Situations

| | With Food at Work | Weekday Dinner at Home | Evening on Holidays Abroad | With Friends on a Saturday Evening | New Year's Eve | n |
|---|---|---|---|---|---|---|
| Approval of drinking[a] | | | | | | |
| Finland | 4 | 41 | 73 | 80 | 79 | 2096–2104 |
| Iceland | 3 | 21 | 84 | 83 | 83 | 2074–2099 |
| Norway | 1 | 36 | 81 | 84 | 84 | 1592–1603 |
| Sweden | 12 | 59 | 86 | 87 | 84 | 1761–1768 |
| Approval of intoxication[a] | | | | | | |
| Finland | 0 | 7 | 59 | 64 | 72 | 2091–2100 |
| Iceland | 1 | 3 | 75 | 73 | 78 | 2052–2091 |
| Norway | 0 | 4 | 57 | 59 | 67 | 1601–1606 |
| Sweden | 1 | 7 | 60 | 57 | 66 | 1763–1768 |

[a] Drinking/slight intoxication "reasonably all right" or "quite all right."

on holidays abroad, with friends on a Saturday evening, and on New Year's Eve. In leisure situations, very few permit drinking without taking the next step of permitting intoxication. It is also worth noting that the response patterns are very similar for all three leisure situations: there seems to be relatively little normative differentiation between leisure as nonwork and a particular ritual occasion such as New Year's Eve, although intoxication is somewhat more commonly permitted on New Year's Eve. It may also be that in order to differentiate seasonal festivities from simple nonwork, questions about more extreme drunkenness would have been required.

The questionnaire turned out not to include any situation where a very large majority would have approved of moderate drinking but condemned even slight intoxication. Such situations might have been found by adding new items to the list, but it can also be that this zone of prescribed moderate drinking really does not exist or is quite ephemeral in Scandinavia.

From a comparative perspective, the unanimity of the Scandinavians in separating drinking from work is worth noting. Prior to the Industrial Revolution and all through the nineteenth century, work and drinking appear to have been inseparable in many countries (Fillmore, 1981), and even today drinking and work coexist in many cultures (Lolli *et al* 1958; Sadoun *et al.*, 1965).

All in all, TABLE 2 reveals three characteristic features of the Scandinavian drinking culture: drinking and working are kept strictly separate; drinking is still not integrated with everyday meals; and the main normative division tends to be one between non-drinking situations and situations where not only drinking but intoxication as well are culturally accepted.

In TABLE 2, the variation across situations is, of course, much more striking than the variation across countries. Nevertheless, there are some interesting differences in the normative climate in the four countries (FIG. 2).

Approval of drinking in leisure situations is at the same level in all four countries with the only exception that Finns are somewhat less permissive with respect to drinking on an evening on holidays abroad.

There is more cultural variation with respect to everyday drinking. Drinking with food at work is slightly more commonly approved of in Sweden than in the three other

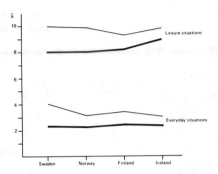

**FIGURE 2.** Approval of moderate drinking and slight intoxication in everyday (*bottom*) and leisure (*top*) situations. *Thick line*, approval of slight intoxication; *thin line*, approval of a beer or two. High values indicate approval of drinking and intoxication.

countries, and in normative expectations concerning weekday dinners there is considerable variation across countries. Only a relatively small minority of the Icelanders, but a substantial majority of the Swedes, permit any drinking at a weekday dinner at home, with the Finns and the Norwegians falling in between.

With respect to slight intoxication, the differences between countries in everyday situations are small. In leisure situations, approval of slight intoxication is at the same level in Finland, Norway and Sweden, but the Icelanders are consistently more permissive of intoxication.

The normative distance betweeen drinking and intoxication can be analyzed by comparing the means of the composite indices in each country (FIG. 2). Both for everyday situations and for leisure situations, the normative distance between drinking and feeling the effects of alcohol is shortest in Iceland and longest in Sweden, with Finland and Norway falling in between.

Inter-Scandinavian differences in the normative culture may be summarized as follows. In two respects, an emergent zone of prescribed moderate drinking is most clearly visible in Sweden and least developed in Iceland. First, moderate drinking at weekday meals is more commonly permitted in Sweden than in other Scandinavian countries, with Iceland at the other extreme. Second, the step from accepting drinking to accepting feeling the effects of alcohol in leisure situations is shortest in Iceland and longest in Sweden.

A broader international perspective is provided by TABLE 3, where data from the Nordic study can be compared with figures from the WHO Community Response Study. In the Nordic study, the questions referred to the drinking of "a man in his thirties with no special drinking problems." In the Community Response Study, respondents were asked "How much should a man/woman of about your age feel free to drink?" in each situation. In order to minimize the impact of differences in question wording, only male respondents are included in TABLE 3. The situations asked about in both studies are not identical, and the response alternatives presented to the respondents differed. Because of the rarity of cross-cultural comparative data, however, it was felt that compiling TABLE 3 was worth the effort.

The overall picture presented by TABLE 3 is one of cross-cultural uniformity, and the exceptions to this uniformity are not easily interpreted in a conceptually coherent fashion. In none of the eight countries is drinking enough to feel the effect accepted during working hours, and only in Scotland and Sweden do more than very few respon-

**TABLE 3.** Approval of Drinking and of Drinking Enough to Feel the Effects of Alcohol in Selected Situations in Males in Four Scandinavian Countries and in Scotland, Mexico, Zambia and Ontario[a]

| | During Working Hours | With Food at Work | In a Party at Someone Else's House | When out at a Bar with Friends | With Friends on a Saturday Night |
|---|---|---|---|---|---|
| Approval of drinking (%) | | | | | |
| Finland | | 6 | | | 84 |
| Iceland | | 3 | | | 86 |
| Norway | | 2 | | | 86 |
| Sweden | | 15 | | | 89 |
| Ontario | 7 | | 96 | 96 | |
| Scotland | 18 | | 98 | 99 | |
| Mexico | 5 | | 91 | 92 | |
| Zambia | 7 | | 75 | 81 | |
| Approval of drinking enough to feel the effects of alcohol (%) | | | | | |
| Finland | | 1 | | | 71 |
| Iceland | | 1 | | | 79 |
| Norway | | 1 | | | 66 |
| Sweden | | 1 | | | 67 |
| Ontario | 1 | | 69 | 51 | |
| Scotland | 0 | | 65 | 78 | |
| Mexico | 0 | | 50 | 52 | |
| Zambia | 2 | | 57 | 62 | |

[a] The figures for Scotland, Mexico and Zambia are from the WHO Community Response Study. In Mexico, representative samples of the population were interviewed in two arbitrarily selected communities, one urban and one rural. In Zambia, three communities were selected, one rural and two urban. The Scottish sample was representative of the Lothian region, including both urban and rural communities. The general population surveys were carried out in 1978–79. The WHO interview schedule asked respondents to answer the question "How much should a man/woman of about your age feel free to drink?" in a series of nine different situations. The answer categories were "no drinking," "one or two drinks," "enough to get high but not drunk," "getting drunk sometimes all right." The last three categories are included in "approval of drinking" and the last two in "approval of drinking to feel the effects." The figures refer to the adult population 18 years and older (Roizen, 1981).

The figures for Ontario are from a survey of a representative sample of the adult population 18 years and older residing in the Regional Municipality of Durham. The data were collected in 1978. The questions were the same as in the WHO Community Response Study (Smart and Liban, 1981). Reginald G. Smart kindly provided unpublished data by sex of the respondent.

dents approve of any drinking at all at work. With respect to drinking in leisure situations, Scotland and Ontario are the most permissive and Zambia perhaps the least permissive, with Mexico and the Scandinavian countries falling in between. With respect to drinking enough to feel the effect the order of the countries is changed. Mexico is now the least permissive country, whereas the Scandinavian countries are quite tolerant of intoxication. Two leisure items from the Community Response Study were included in TABLE 3 in order to show the dangers inherent in too-straight forward comparisons of single questions and in order to point out the possibility of national ideosyncracies. The rank order of Ontario and Scotland is reversed depending on the situation choosen.

In FIGURES 3 and 4, the mean summary scores of the situational expectations are

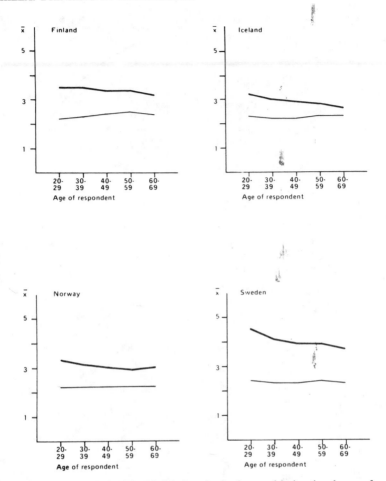

**FIGURE 3.** Approval of drinking and slight intoxication in everyday situations by age of respondent. *Thick line*, drinking; *thin line*, intoxication. The number of respondents in each age group is above 200.

presented by age of respondent. Differences among age groups revealed by cross-sectional analysis can either be related to age roles and aging or reflect persistent differences among birth cohorts. In our particular case, there are strong indications that in all older birth cohorts attitudes towards alcohol have changed over time in a more liberal and "modern" direction (cf. Mäkelä, 1982). The remaining differences among age groups are probably not effects of aging but reflect historical changes from one generation to the next. We can thus discuss various age groups as representing different layers of a culture undergoing change.

With respect to *intoxication* in everyday situations, the differences between age groups are very small. With respect to *drinking* in the same situations, there is a slight tendency for younger respondents in each country to be somewhat more permissive.

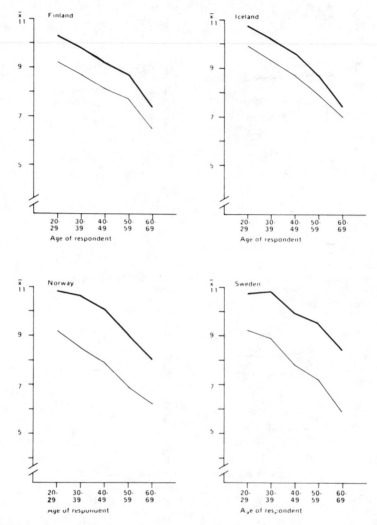

**FIGURE 4.** Approval of drinking and slight intoxication in leisure situations, by age of respondent. *Thick line*, drinking; *thin line*, intoxication. The number of respondents in each group is above 200.

As a consequence, the normative distance between drinking and intoxication tends to be a little longer among the young than among the old.

In leisure situations, young respondents are considerably more permissive of both drinking and intoxication than are older respondents. The normative distance between drinking and intoxication remains practically the same when we move from older to younger age groups. Although attitudes seem to have changed in a more permissive direction over time, there is little to indicate that this change would have been accompanied by a strengthening of any zone of prescribed moderate drinking.

FIGURES 3 and 4 also illustrate differences between countries with respect to the normative distance between drinking and intoxication. In both figures, the distance is shortest in Iceland and longest in Sweden.

## SUMMARY AND DISCUSSION

In Sweden, Finland and Norway, being drunk is more negatively evaluated than alcohol, and the distance between the two concepts is about the same in the three countries, whereas in Iceland being drunk is more positively evaluated than alcohol.

Situational norms reveal three characteristic features of the Scandinavian drinking culture: drinking and working are kept strictly separate; drinking is still not integrated with everyday meals; and the main normative division tends to be one between nondrinking situations and situations where not only drinking, but intoxication as well, are culturally accepted. The response patterns are very similar for all three leisure situations: there is little normative differentiation between leisure as nonwork and a particular ritual occasion such as New Year's Eve, although intoxication is slightly more commonly permitted on New Year's Eve.

In two respects, an emergent zone of prescribed moderate drinking is most clearly visible in Sweden and least developed in Iceland. First, moderate drinking at weekday meals is more commonly permitted in Sweden than in other Scandinavian countries, with Iceland at the other extreme. Second, the step from accepting drinking to accepting feeling the effects of alcohol in leisure situations is shortest in Iceland and longest in Sweden.

When age groups are compared as representing different strata of a culture undergoing change, attitudes seem to have changed in a more permissive direction over time, but there is little to indicate that this change would have been accompanied by a strengthening of any zone of prescribed moderate drinking in leisure situations. In everyday situations, the normative distance between drinking and intoxication tends to be a little longer among the young than among the old.

The questions on moderate drinking state the exact amount to be consumed, whereas the questions on intoxication are formulated in terms of feeling the effects of alcohol. It should also be pointed out that a more detailed classification of situations might require a third series about more extreme drunkenness. In Scandinavia, such a third category may be necessary in order to distinguish leisure as nonwork from special festivities.

The phrasing of the questions refers to either the amounts consumed or with *feeling* intoxicated, not *acting out* one's drunkenness. As a result, important nuances about situational drinking norms may remain hidden. "The domestication of the intoxicant" may have occurred not so much by regulating the amounts consumed as by ever tighter control of the kinds of behavior that are permitted in drinking situations (Virtanen, 1982). Nevertheless, the changes in a more permissive direction of the context of attitudes towards drinking have not been accompanied by changes in the *structure* of situational drinking norms.

Drinking cultures should not be discussed primarily in terms of whether they require moderation or accept intoxication, but rather in terms of the historically dominant use of alcohol. The French and Italian culture represent different responses to the nutritional use of alcohol. Correspondingly, the orthodox Jews and the Scandinavians have adopted alternative normative solutions to the regulation of the use of alcohol as an intoxicant. If ideals of moderation are to be disseminated in Scandinavia, due attention has to be paid to the fact that alcoholic beverages in these countries have for centuries been intoxicants and not nutrients.

32     ANNALS NEW YORK ACADEMY OF SCIENCES

## REFERENCES

FALK, P. 1983. Humalan historia [A history of intoxication]. Unpublished licenciate's thesis, University of Helsinki, 1983.
FILMORE, K. M. 1981. Research as a handmaiden of policy: An appraisal of estimates of alcoholism and its cost in the workplace. Paper presented at the 1981 National Alcoholism Forum of the National Council on Alcoholism, New Orleans, April 15, 1981.
HAUGE, R. & O. IRGENS-JENSEN. 1981a. Scandinavian Drinking Survey: Sampling Operations and Data Collection. Reports from the National Institute for Alcohol Research No. 44. Oslo, Norway.
HAUGE, R. & O. IRGENS-JENSEN. 1981b. Scandinavian Drinking Survey: Demographic Variables and Representativeness of Samples. Reports from the National Institute for Alcohol Research No. 45: Oslo, Norway.
HUSU, L. 1980. Kulttuurierojen tutkiminen ja semanttinen differentiaali [The study of cultural variation and the semantic differential]. Sosiologia XVII(2): 110–117.
LOLLI, G., E. SERIANNI, G. M. GOLDER & P. LUZZATTO-FEGIZ. 1958. Alcohol in Italian Culture. The Free Press. New Haven, Conn.
MÄÄTTÄNEN, K. 1982. The contexts of social drinking and the quality of social interaction in work, family, and leisure. Paper presented at the Meeting of the Alcohol Epidemiology Section of the ICAA in Helsinki, June 28–July 2, 1982.
MÄKELÄ, K. 1981. Scandinavian Drinking Survey: Construction of Composite Indices of Drinking Attitudes and Personal Experiences Related to Drinking. Reports from the National Institute for Alcohol Research No. 47. Oslo, Norway.
MÄKELÄ, K. 1983. The uses of alcohol and their cultural regulation. Acta Sociol. XXVI(1): 21–31.
MÄKELÄ, K. 1982. Permissible starting age for drinking in four Scandinavian countries. Reports from the National Institute for Alcohol Research No. 60. Oslo, Norway.
MÄKELÄ, K., R. ROOM, E. SINGLE, P. SULKUNEN, B. WALSH, R. BUNCE, M. CAHANNES, T. CAMERON, N. GIESBRECHT, J. DE LINT, H. MÄKINEN, P. MORGAN, J. MOSHER, J. MOSKALEWICZ, R. MÜLLER, E. ÖSTERBERG, I. WALD & D. WALSH. 1981. Alcohol, Society and the State. 1: A Comparative Study of Alcohol Control. Addiction Research Foundation. Toronto, Canada.
OSGOOD, C., G. SUCI & P. TANNENBAUM. 1957. The Measurement of Meaning. University of Illinois Press. Urbana-Champaign, IL.
PITTMAN, D. J. 1967. International overview: Social and cultural factors in drinking patterns, pathological and nonpathological. In Alcoholism. David J. Pittman, Ed.: 3–20. Harper & Row. New York, NY.
ROIZEN, R. 1981. The World Health Organization Study of Community Responses to Alcohol-Related Problems: A Review of Cross-Cultural Findings. Annex 41: Final Report of Phase I of the WHO Study of Community Response to Alcohol-Related Problems. World Health Organization.
SADOUN, R., G. LOLLI & M. SILVERMAN. 1965. Drinking in French Culture. Rutgers Center of Alcohol Studies. New Brunswick, NJ.
SMART, R. G. & C. B. LIBAN. 1981. The need for attitude changes concerning drinking and drinking problems. J. Alcohol Drug Ed. XXVII(1): 47–61.
SULKUNEN, P. 1976. Drinking patterns and the level of alcohol consumption. In Research Advances in Alcohol and Drug Problems, Vol. 3. R.J. Gibbins et al., Eds.: 223–281. John Wiley. New York, NY.
VIRTANEN, M. 1982. Änkyrä, tuiske, huppeli [Varieties of intoxication]. WSOY. Juva, Finland.

# Research and Action: Lessons from the World Health Organization Project on Community Response to Alcohol-Related Problems[a]

E. BRUCE RITSON

*Alcohol Problems Clinic*
*Royal Edinburgh Hospital*
*Edinburgh EH10 5HD, Scotland*

## INTRODUCTION

The 28th World Health Assembly in 1975 asked the Director General of the World Health Organization (WHO) to direct special attention to the "extent and seriousness of the individual, psychological, and social problems associated with the current use of alcohol in many countries of the world and the trend towards higher levels of consumption and to study what measures could be taken to control the increase in alcohol consumption involving danger to public health."

The Community Response to Alcohol-Related Problems Project was one of a number of initiatives aimed at responding to this request (WHO, 1983). The project was a collaborative venture drawing on the technical and financial commitment of the countries involved and the support of the National Institute of Alcohol Abuse and Alcoholism and WHO.

The range of interests involved in this project reflects the political importance of alcohol. In some countries it plays a crucial part in the economy. In many countries it has a symbolic significance — as a taboo substance or as a focal point in religious ritual, for example. In still other countries the growing availability of alcohol symbolizes a significant transition in the country's history, especially where alcohol was forbidden to native inhabitants by colonial powers (Pau, 1975). Permission to drink or to get drunk may be a faithful reflection of the status systems within a culture. Thus, each country attributes to alcohol, drinking, and drunkenness a meaning that is specific to that culture. A country also develops its own way of defining alcohol-related problems and of responding to them.

Some might conclude that the multiplicity of factors involved and the sheer diversity of their nature is so great as to frustrate any attempt to study, and particularly to compare, alcohol problems in different countries. It is true, however, that alcohol

[a] This work was supported by Contract No. ADM 281-76-0028 from the National Institute of Alcohol Abuse and Alcoholism and grants from the Alcohol, Drug Abuse, and Mental Health Administration and the Department of Health and Human Services of the government of the United States; by the governments of Zambia, Mexico, and the United Kingdom; and by the World Health Organization.

itself, although varying in strength from beverage to beverage, remains basically the same drug, ethyl alcohol, and it is thus perhaps the only constant whose impish ways can be traced throughout the course of this study.

The WHO project was first conceived as a pilot effort to be carried out in one country. This initial plan was discarded when it was recognized that the development of a single research strategy, however elegantly packaged by a single country, might have a very limited value in other settings. It was therefore decided that several countries at different stages of socioeconomic development should be involved in the project from the start. Several countries initially showed interest in the project, but finally Zambia, Mexico, and Scotland were chosen. They were selected with the agreement and active support of their governments—each had shown an interest in the project and had personnel who were willing to see it through.

A priority in the Community Response Study was to evolve models that were relevant to a disparate range of countries at different levels of socioeconomic development. Between-country comparisons were therefore not a priority concern of the project, although such comparisons are of interest and of particular relevance to the present agenda.

From the point of view of WHO, the project afforded a chance to enlarge the WHO program on alcohol problems and to tilt the program significantly toward the developing world, as is intended now for all WHO programs. It was also envisioned that the project would provide a model for action-oriented research, a technique for actualizing community change. In the subsequent phases of the project, it was hoped that the methods derived in this research would serve as a basis for the diffusion of techniques and expertise back and forth between the collaborating countries and eventually to neighboring and other countries. From the perspective of the countries who participated, the project gave them the chance of developing or extending their knowledge and expertise in dealing with alcohol problems. It was therefore evident that the countries selected would have to give some sign of having a commitment to action about alcohol and its effect on the patient's health.

## AIMS OF THE COMMUNITY RESPONSE STUDY

The purposes of the project, as presented in the statement of work, were:

(1) to assist in the initiation and development of a long-term multinational collaborative program on community response to alcohol-related problems;

(2) to develop basic epidemiologic and psychosocial data in a sample of widely differing cultural and socioeconomic settings, including at least one of rapid social change; and

(3) to develop information on community resources that are available and community capability to deal with alcohol-related problems in these settings.

## CONCEPTUAL BACKGROUND TO THE ENQUIRY

In many industrialized countries surveys are an established means of obtaining information about drinking practices and problems (Cahalan et al., 1969; Edwards et al., 1972). Such surveys had hitherto been uncommon in developing countries, where an understanding of drinking habits usually came from anthropologists' ethnographic studies, which often focused on traditional village cultures (Heath, 1976). With notable exceptions, we have to rely on anecdotes to furnish an understanding of the drinking patterns which exist in the rapidly growing urban populations of the developing countries.

Both these approaches have their strengths and weaknesses. The ethnographic approach often gives the clearest sense of meaning, while the social survey provides a demographic snapshot frozen at one point in time.

The aim of the general population study was to obtain a quantitative description of drinking patterns and problems in the study sites which would provide a factual basis for planning at the local level (perhaps for the first time). As previously stated, cross-national comparability was a bonus rather than a primary aim of this data collection.

From the outset the project teams adopted an agreed-upon list of alcohol-related disabilities and made no assumptions about the existence of alcoholism as an entity. There was, however, an acknowledged interest in identifying features of an "alcohol-dependence syndrome" which might present differently in different cultures and the agenda for this research included investigation of the transcultural universality of such a syndrome.

In developed countries there are evidently "two worlds" of alcohol problems—the population known to agencies and the much larger number of problem drinkers in the general population who have never been in touch with any treatment agency (Room, 1980). This "two worlds" formulation raised a number of research questions, since it was clear that the drinker is not born into the clinical population but enters it or is "elected" to it by others. To what extent and in what manner was the second population drawn from the very much larger first one? If one can speak of those in treatment for alcohol problems having been extruded from or picked out of the general population, how does the process of extrusion work? Under what circumstances do the informal social controls of drinking break down and how and by whom are the more formal responses of the alcoholism treatment system or the other social agencies brought into play? Such questions are posed in a way that is appropriate for an industrialized society which has devised services for identified problem drinkers. In other areas similar processes doubtless exist, but the labels and assumptions under which the agencies' or communities' responses operate are not well known.

The project sought to elucidate this "extrusion process" in each community by identifying individuals with alcohol-related problems in three different contexts and simultaneously studying the responses that such problems evoked. These contexts were those in which (1) individuals reported alcohol problems in the population survey, but were not in touch with any agency; (2) alcohol problems appeared unrecognized by agencies; and (3) identified problem drinkers either attended specialist agencies or were in contact with and labeled as problem drinkers by other agencies.

## DESIGN OF THE PROJECT

A principal investigator was appointed in each community. Initially all three appointees were psychiatrists who had experience in research and in developing services for problem drinkers in their own area. Workers from other disciplines subsequently joined each team. From the start these "alcohol problem teams" had to engage the interest of local and national bodies and try to work closely with them throughout the project.

The following criteria were adopted to choose the communities to be studied:

(1) The area would not be grossly unrepresentative of the country;

(2) it should be accessible;

(3) it should preferably be a recognizable administrative unit;

(4) a disturbing level of alcohol problems should have been noted;

(5) political will for research and potential for response should be present; and

(6) both rural and urban areas should be included

The following locales were selected:

(1) one urban and one rural community in Mexico within the delegation of Tlalpan, which is 23 kilometers from the center of Mexico City;

(2) the Lothian Region of Scotland incorporating the city of Edinburgh and surrounding semirural areas;

(3) urban, peri-urban, and suburban areas of Lusaka in Zambia and a rural health demonstration zone.

A project manager was appointed by WHO to coordinate the study and a group of experienced advisers joined in all meetings of the project. Other consultants were invited to advise on specific issues from time to time.

The project manager was crucial in keeping the alcohol problem teams focused on the task and in linking them with their colleagues in other countries. Collaboration was maintained by regular six-monthly meetings of the principal workers throughout the period 1978–1980. This meeting of investigators was held at each study site on at least one occasion so that all the teams could gain some first-hand understanding of the communities concerned.

The principal aims referred to earlier were broken down into a series of interlinked objectives:

(1) To describe and measure the extent and nature of drinking patterns and alcohol-related problems in the community;

(2) to describe and measure responses to such problems;

(3) to explore factors contributing to alcohol-related problems and responses;

(4) to assay the strength and efficacy of existing responses and to make tentative proposals for desirable changes and methods for achieving these; and

(5) to promote interest in the development of policies focused on the prevention and alleviation of alcohol-related problems.

Five different approaches were considered in an attempt to answer these questions. Each will be considered in turn along with the methodological problems that they highlighted.

## COLLATION OF BACKGROUND INFORMATION

Guidelines were drafted for the collection of general and alcohol-related background information at a national and local community level (Rootman and Moser, 1984).

The range of information being sought was extensive and included the geographic, demographic, economic, sociocultural, health, and historic aspects of the country as well as those items that were more specifically concerned with alcohol.

This information provided a backdrop against which to view the selected study site to see how far it was typical of the country and it placed that community's problems in a national perspective. A number of subsidiary objectives were served by this study. It revealed gaps in the available data and deficiencies in the method of collating information, established a basis for national planning, and either opened up or strengthened links between the project team and individual bodies concerned with alcohol-related problems, thereby giving public visibility to the project.

It was surprising how often topics that seemed quite arcane suddenly revealed their importance to the project itself. For example, the climate of a country is obviously important in determining the nature of the crops from which alcohol is derived, but the seasons of the year in rural Zambia had a very significant effect on home-brewing and hence on availability, which was not the case in more industrialized communities, which were independent of the vagaries of the climate. Climate, again, influenced the survey methodology. In certain seasons, floods made it impossible to conduct a survey in certain parts of a country. And the climate in Scotland may be a factor in determining both the place and the style of drinking, in which long, dark winter evenings are spent in the snug warmth of a local pub.

National demography was obviously of considerable influence, notably the age structure of the population. This was particularly evident in countries such as Zambia in which there was a very large number of young people, many of whom rarely drink. As the age structure of the population changes, so may the per capita consumption patterns.

Sociocultural factors are fundamental to an understanding of the context of drinking. Literacy and education influenced the way in which the questionnaire could be phrased. Religion was a prominent issue in some areas, but seemed to be of minimal significance in others.

The distribution and character of the social welfare services was a factor which varied almost beyond useful comparison from one country to another. The plethora of social agencies in Lothian can be contrasted with the one social work department in Lusaka, while the church occupies a prominent role as a social agency in Mexico. The nature of the health service, staffing, patterns of population coverage, and the use of traditional systems (such as native healers) would dictate the response to alcohol problems and the degree to which the community could afford to view such "problems" as special or health issues. No overview of a country or community would be complete without a sense of its history, which may be very important in determining existing attitudes towards alcohol. The history of the Temperance Movement and its influence is a well-known example. There is no doubt that collecting data for this study did help to engage the interest of local and national bodies. It also high-lighted problems in data collection. For instance, in Scotland it was evident that detailed information about the production and, to a lesser extent, the consumption of alcohol was available for the entire United Kingdom; it was extremely difficult to obtain data related to Scotland alone and impossible to obtain useful data pertaining to the local community itself.

## General Population Survey

A population survey was used as the principal means of obtaining an overview of the existing drinking practices in the community and an understanding of the prevailing attitudes towards alcohol and alcohol-related problems. The questionnaires used were developed out of a conference between the collaborators and their advisers and were tried out in each community prior to reaching consensus about the final content. Inevitably they drew heavily on the experience of earlier drinking surveys, most of which had been based on North American or Northern European experience.

No hard and fast rules about sampling were set down. It was simply agreed that investigators should "seek representative samples" from their study areas. Confidentiality of data collected in this way was assured throughout.

The general population survey constituted the major investment of time, personnel, and finance in each of the countries. It also provided the principal data set from which any comparative analyses could be made. The survey approach and the questionnaire did, however, raise a number of questions. For example, sampling was very hard in some areas because no census or even mapping of population existed. One of the first discoveries for a European researcher was that sampling methods in developing countries are different from the traditonal European ones. Households become "those who share a common cooking pot," maps have to be drawn of an area before samples can be made, techniques such as aerial photography prove impossibly expensive and yet may be the only sensible means of making a random sample of a thinly populated rural area.

Translation was another problem. In Zambia there are a large number of local languages, some of which did not exist in written form. In that respect the authors of the Zambian report felt it might have been preferable not to attempt a translation from English but rather to train the interviewers to translate at the time of the interview into local language.

The training of interviewers also presented difficulties. There was a striking contrast between the group of young uniformed men who conducted the interviews in Zambia and the collection of largely middle-aged and middle-class housewives who formed the dominant group in the survey team in Lothian.

These and many other problems will have to be addressed by anyone striving for comparability of survey methods in very differing settings.

### Agency Study

In each community a sample of agency workers was interviewed in depth to provide information about the way in which they perceived and reacted to alcohol problems. Inevitably the numbers and varieties of these agencies varied greatly among communities. In some areas it was difficult to choose between agencies within a plethora of alternatives, as in Lothian. In other places there were no alcohol-specific agencies. Indeed, the concept of an "agency" seemed foreign in rural Mexico and even more so in Zambia. Ultimately the following categories of agencies were included: (1) medical, (2) social, (3) specialized alcohol, (4) penal, (5) nonstatutory (religious, political, traditional).

Workers at different levels within each agency were selected for an approximately one-hour interview, which was a free-ranging discussion around a number of preidentified issues. These were:

(1) the nature of the agent's perception of alcohol problems;

(2) the agency's sensitivity to alcohol problems;

(3) access and use made of other resources;

(4) the level of competence and confidence the agent possessed in responding to alcohol problems;

(5) the extent to which the agent personally dealt with alcohol problems.

This method provided a valuable means of learning how the agent perceived alcohol problems within the community. It did not provide data that readily lent themselves to statistical analysis and was particularly unsuitable for cross-cultural comparisons. In Lothian, however, it proved a valuable means of tuning in to themes that were of major concern to the caregivers and agents of control in that community. As a reasonably cheap and effective means of raising community interest and gleaning some valuable information, this method had much to commend it; as a research tool, it had serious limitations.

### Study of Clients of Agencies

It was our hope to sample clients attending agencies. Unfortunately, lack of funds made it virtually impossible to study every agency. A number of pilot studies in each area were completed. The aim had been to interview 100 clients of each agency or one month's intake, if fewer than 100 had attended in that time. Only new cases aged 15 or over were studied, a new case being defined as someone who had not contacted the agency within the previous 6 months. All the clients were given a "brief case report form." This form described the presence and nature of alcohol involvement in the caseload of various health and social work agencies. If this screening questionnaire suggested alcohol problems, the client was reinterviewed in greater detail with questions similar to those in the general population survey. The client interview form described the drinking habits and characteristics of the clients found to have alcohol problems. By means of this information these clients could then be compared to members of the general population who were drinking in a similar way and experiencing similar problems, but who had not come into contact with any agencies.

### Observational Study

Investigators were asked to identify situations where they felt observational studies could be carried out in their own country, focusing particularly on those agencies providing the client studies described above. However, the envisioned participant observation studies and descriptive accounts of agencies and other alcohol-related dramas never materialized.

This paper is concerned with describing the project rather than discussing the findings, which are detailed elsewhere (WHO, 1983). Some themes, however, were particularly striking: The prevalence of abstinence, which is common in Zambia and Mexico but rare in Scotland (FIG. 1), certainly reveals how misleading per capita consumption data can be unless it is taken within the context of the known distribution of alcohol consumption. "All-or-none" drinking in Zambia and Mexico gives rise to very high levels of drunkenness and problems both personal and social among those who do drink (TABLES 1 and 2). In Scotland, drinking is a near-universal pursuit, but most is apparently problem-free. Drinking locales differed greatly among communities, and

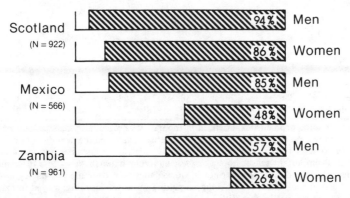

**FIGURE 1.** Proportions of male and female respondents aged 18 and over classified as drinkers in Scotland, Mexico, and Zambia.

**TABLE 1.** Self-Reported Frequency of Getting Drunk in Past Year (Base: Current Drinkers Only)

| | n | Drunk at Least Once a Week | Less Than or About Once a Month | Not during Last Year | Total[a] |
|---|---|---|---|---|---|
| *Scotland* | | | | | |
| Males | 562 | 9 | 37 | 54 | 100% |
| Females | 338 | 1 | 17 | 82 | 100% |
| *Mexico* | | | | | |
| Males | 296 | 15 | 59 | 25 | 99% |
| Females | 90 | 1 | 27 | 72 | 100% |
| *Zambia* | | | | | |
| Males | 209 | 58 | 28 | 13 | 99% |
| Females | 117 | 45 | 32 | 24 | 101% |

[a] Totals may vary due to rounding.

these differences influence the pattern of problems. In each community it was in the family that most alcohol-related problems were expressed, but the character of the conflict presumably differs when men drink together away from home than when the family drinks together at home. (This merits further exploration. We may discover valuable approaches by paying attention to the way families cope with alcohol.)

Such dramatic differences intrigue the researcher concerned with cross-cultural studies, but it is essential to keep in mind that the principal focus of the Community Response Study was to assess the impact of a method on community plans. Thus the concern here is to show the way in which this abundance of information available for the first time in some areas, such as Zambia, could be turned to best account by the local community. This was in essence the task of Phase 2 of the project. The experience

**TABLE 2.** Personal Problems Score (Base: Current Drinkers)

| | Number of Subjects | Number of Problems | | | | | | | Total |
|---|---|---|---|---|---|---|---|---|---|
| | | 0 | 1 | 2 | 3 | 4 | 5 | 6+ | |
| *Scotland* | | | | | | | | | |
| Males | 565 | 63% | 20 | 9 | 5 | 2 | 1 | [a] | 100% |
| Females | 338 | 88% | 8 | 3 | 1 | 0 | 0 | [a] | 100% |
| *Mexico* | | | | | | | | | |
| Males | 302 | 26% | 18 | 17 | 16 | 11 | 7 | 7 | 102% |
| Females | 93 | 58% | 23 | 7 | 5 | 3 | 2 | 2 | 100% |
| *Zambia* | | | | | | | | | |
| Males | 241 | 23% | 30 | 21 | 17 | 6 | 2 | 1 | 100% |
| Females | 137 | 40% | 30 | 18 | 4 | 2 | 4 | 2 | 100% |

NOTE: Personal problems experienced in the past year were described as follows: Felt you should cut down on your drinking or stop altogether; awakened the next day not being able to remember some of the things you had done while drinking; sometimes got drunk even when there was an important reason to stay sober; had your hand shake or loss of memory after drinking; told by a doctor or other health worker that your drinking was having a bad effect on your health; took a drink first thing on getting up in the morning; stayed intoxicated for several days at a time. Each positive answer scores one on the scale.

[a] Less than half a percent.

of the methods adopted in Phase 1 was reviewed and the lessons learned were distilled into "model guidelines" which would provide useful information for other investigators developing studies of this kind in their own community (Rootman and Moser, 1984).

## PHASE 2 OF THE PROJECT

This part of the study sought to use the data already collected in Phase 1 to assist change and planning at the local and national level. The objectives of this phase of the project as stated in the contract were:

(1) to develop general guidelines and procedures for the application of the method for community analysis and planning developed in the current collaborative project to other interested countries;

(2) to study how community and national planning was carried out in the original three countries;

(3) to develop a report on the detailed procedures for monitoring the implementation of plans in these three countries over an extended period of time.

It was also hoped that neighboring countries would show an interest in all or part of the approach adopted and pursue similar projects in their own area. Three principal steps were involved in the process:

1. Data were presented to each local community and various action plans followed.

2. A national meeting was called to examine the implications of the project for national alcohol strategies.

3. An international conference was planned with neighboring countries who might share similar problems with alcohol and had expressed an interest in the Community Response Study from their own point of view.

Throughout this time changes were monitored and fed back to the relevant community, the aim being to evaluate change on a continuous basis.

One of the objectives of this phase was to "study the process of implementation of community and country planning." Monitoring protocols were developed for this purpose. Phase 2 inevitably unfolded differently in each country and the overall process is perhaps best illustrated by a brief summary of the progress in each site.

### Mexico

The Mexican team adopted an objective of "developing specific actions oriented towards the improvement of the responses to alcohol-related problems." The Mexican team employed a number of techniques to track developments throughout Phase 2. They kept logbooks, interviewed participants in the new program, and recorded observations of the meetings that occurred.

### Local Level

At the local level Phase 2 concentrated on Miguel Hidalgo, the urban community where the survey was first conducted. An educational program was introduced aimed at increasing not only knowledge, but also skills in decision-making and self-help. They used the already existing infrastructure in the area to create an organized group which would promote health. They created feedback programs based on the results of Phase 1. The Mexican team strove hard to establish a trusting and cooperative relationship between the researcher and the community. A number of key local individuals (such as teachers, social workers, doctors, and priests) were invited to participate in the feedback program. The "Center for the Integral Development of the Family" showed the greatest enthusiasm for the project. Women's groups at this center became very active in participating in and furthering the program.

Phase 1 of the project revealed that the role of women in relation to drinking in Mexico is very clearly defined. In comparison with women in the other countries, Mexican women were very abstemious and complained about the consequences of male drinking for the family. it is therefore most interesting that they showed particular concern for responding to drinking problems. This sense of concern has been paralleled in Scotland, where women in local communities have been in the forefront in articulating community problems. A more general question can be raised, namely that of the traditional role commonly played by women in "coping" with problems. Such speculation is beyond the scope of this paper, but is worth doing nonetheless.

*National Level*

The Mexican team organized a national meeting. The meeting was held in June 1981 and was attended by representatives of the newly formed "National Council on Alcoholism" and relevant government departments and treatment agencies. This meeting resulted in a list of recommendations for action.

*International Meeting*

Representatives of Argentina, Brazil, Costa Rica, Honduras, and Panama were observers at the national meeting and directly after it conferred about the possibility of involvement in similar projects in their own area.

## Scotland

The Scottish team monitored the impact of Phase 1 by keeping records and diaries of subsequent events and collecting minutes and reports of all relevant meetings and happenings. They also used the data of the population survey of 1978 as a baseline for a subsequent survey in 1981. During this period the price of alcoholic beverages in Scotland rose by 61 percent and for the first time in 30 years the price of alcohol had risen faster than the retail price index so that it proved possible to study the effect of a price rise on the drinking habits of a known population.

*Local Level*

The Scottish project team held a series of meetings with the agencies who had participated in the study followed by a larger conference attended principally by workers in social work, health education, and voluntary agencies. The meetings were therefore focused at the level of primary care workers. Some examples may serve to illustrate the way in which the project influenced planning.

The agency study had shown that many frontline workers recognized alcohol problems, but were extremely pessimistic about their capacity to do anything about them.

In response to this identified need, the alcohol problems clinic and the Council on Alcoholism both gave priority to educating workers in these primary care positions, including those in industry, and to providing them with easier access to specialist support and consultation. The Council on Alcoholism has also responded to critical comments about accessibility of services by outposting voluntary counsellors in health centers and in two communities noted for their high levels of unemployment.

## National Level

The project team has participated in the Scottish Health Education Coordinating Committee in developing an area plan for alcohol education and primary prevention throughout Scotland. In February 1983 a national meeting was held which debated the implications of the Community Response Project. Politicians from local and national government attended along with representatives of the civil service, health, social work, the Churches, law, education and voluntary agencies. This was followed by an international meeting with participants from West Germany, Holland, France, Sweden, Norway, Spain, Greece and the USSR. Rather than examining exclusively the Community Response project, delegates were asked to explore a number of themes drawing on their own experience and other documents. The themes were: public awareness and understanding, preventive strategies, collection, dissemination and use of data on alcohol consumption and alcohol-related problems, and coordination of activities. At the close of this meeting, a number of European countries expressed an interest in pursuing the Community Response method in their own country.

### Zambia

The project team here embarked on a policy of establishing local networks which could examine the implications of alcohol problems in their community and devise means of describing and recording these problems and monitoring the effectiveness of local responses to such problems. The four main "strands" of their strategy were: (1) working with communities of local residents, (2) working with the health services, (3) working with the police, who had been shown in Phase 1 to be a salient group in dealing with alcohol problems, and (4) designing and distributing information.

## Local Activity

Developments were monitored by careful recording of meetings, monthly progress reports, and the maintenance of a log book. Community Action Groups were created which focused on issues of local significance, such as illegal brewing, and excessive drinking by women, leading in one community to the exclusion from bars of women with children. In one urban area it was suggested that small-scale industries be introduced to assist home brewers in finding an alternative source of income. In the rural community, efforts to establish community action groups were unsuccessful, but there was general concern with "excessive drinking" by villagers who identified cattle-rustling, the harmful influence of urban visitors, prostitution by urban girls, and uncontrolled bar-opening times as specifically contributing to alcohol-related problems.

Another village brought the following suggestion to the head man: "that home-brewers should be encouraged to sell their beer after working hours only, that brewing be done alternately among villages and that concerted efforts at promoting sports activities be encouraged as an alternative to drinking."

The International Theatre Institute initiated a "popular theatre" which performed plays illustrating the nature of alcohol problems. This appeared to be a useful means of spreading information in villages and had previously been adopted in Mexico.

In addition to the work done directly with local communities, the project team also worked with health workers and police to clarify their experience and perceptions of alcohol problems. They also helped the police to consider playing a more preventive rather than punitive role. Their strategy throughout was to combine research and demonstration.

### National Meeting

A national conference was held in November 1981. The recommendations from the conference were sent to the Mental Health Coordinating Group of the Ministry of Health and to other ministries within the government. The National Conference was used as an opportunity to interest neighboring countries in the project. Delegations from Botswana, Kenya, Lesotho, Swaziland and Tanzania joined in a discussion on the implications for their own areas. The Institute for African Studies has since worked with WHO in developing further phases of the Community Response Project in other African countries.

## CONCLUSIONS

It proved possible for the teams in each country to monitor developments at national and local levels using the techniques suggested in the monitoring protocols: this was accomplished with limited resources. The project stimulated many activities, involved large numbers of people, built networks for future collaboration, and produced research strategies and materials that will, it is hoped, prove of value in other settings.

Survey methodology, so familiar in industrialized nations, needs to be rethought when applied to developing countries. The efforts to do so were worthwhile because they help less-developed countries learn optimum ways of establishing databases for alcohol problems, from which communities can develop appropriate responses. In this respect the agency interviews were extremely informative and proved a cost-effective way of obtaining the opinion of primary workers. This approach, like others that rely on key informants, runs the risk of simply confirming stereotypes unless it is supported by a systematic enquiry from a random sample of the population. Without such sampling it is easy to overlook the diversity within a community and to make plans that meet the needs of only its most vociferous representatives.

Generalizations about an entire country are hazardous and although the data support them to a degree, they can only ultimately refer to the specific communities studied. This caveat needs to be taken seriously and it must therefore seem excessively presumptuous to then make between-country comparisons from the same local database. The reasons for doing this rest on the care which was taken to achieve comparability, the methods adopted, and the questions asked, particularly in the survey data reported elsewhere. This paper has attempted to show some of the problems and limitations encountered by this audacious but not uncritical attempt to achieve comparability, and it is against this background that the findings should be considered.

## ACKNOWLEDGMENTS

This paper is drawn from the detailed reports listed in the reference section. I am particularly indebted to Dr. Irving Rootman, who prepared much of the final report for Phase 1 and 2. For those who wish to understand the extent and detail of the project, there is no substitute for reading these longer reports.

## REFERENCES

CAHALAN, D., I. CISIN & H. CROSSLEY. 1969. American Drinking Practices: A National Study of Drinking and Attitudes. Monograph 6, Rutgers Center of Alcohol Studies. New Brunswick, NJ.

EDWARDS, G., A. HAWKER & C. HENSMAN. 1972. Drinking in a London suburb. Q. J. Stud. Alcohol Suppl. 6: 69–93.

HEATH, D. 1976. Anthropological perspectives on alcohol: An historical review. In Cross Cultural Approaches to the Study of Alcohol. M. W. Everett et al., Eds. Mouton. The Hague, the Netherlands.

PAU, L. 1975. Alcohol in Colonial Africa. Finnish Foundation for Alcohol Studies. Helsinki, Finland.

ROOM, R. 1980. Treatment-seeking populations and larger realities. In Alcoholism Treatment and Transition. Edwards and Grant, Eds. Croom Helm. London.

ROOTMAN, I. & J. MOSER. 1984. Guidelines for Investigating Alcohol Problems and Developing Appropriate Responses. WHO Offset Publication No. 81. World Health Organization. Geneva.

WORLD HEALTH ORGANIZATION. 1983. Final Report: Community Response to Alcohol Related Problems, Phase 1. World Health Organization. Geneva.

# Ethnic/Religious Differences in the Manifestation and Treatment of Alcoholism[a]

THOMAS F. BABOR AND JACK H. MENDELSON

*Alcohol Research Center*
*University of Connecticut School of Medicine*
*Farmington, Connecticut 06032*

## INTRODUCTION

A rather extensive literature now exists documenting the extent to which patterns of drinking and rates of alcoholism differ across cultural, religious, and racial boundaries (Everett *et al.*, 1976). An important assumption underlying much of this literature is that socially learned norms, values and attitudes exert a powerful influence on drinking behavior, and that some "drinking subcultures" are more conducive than others to the development of alcoholism (Greeley *et al.*, 1980). With a few exceptions (Westermeyer, 1974; Kane, 1981; Wanberg *et al.*, 1978) comparative studies have focused their attention on noninstitutionalized drinkers identified through population surveys or ethnographic studies of a community. Perhaps because the word *alcoholism* implies the existence of a unitary disease syndrome, considerably less attention has been devoted to the study of differences in the symptoms of institutionalized alcoholics belonging to different drinking subcultures. Such an approach would seem to be important for practical as well as theoretical reasons.

First, cultural factors may affect how alcohol problems are defined, what criteria are used to diagnose alcoholism, and how persons with alcohol problems gain access to treatment. Second, cultural factors may influence the etiology of different types of alcoholism. For example, culturally patterned differences in drinking styles, beverage preferences, and dietary habits have been advanced as possible explanations for differences observed in cross-national comparisons of alcoholics (Lolli *et al.*, 1958; Babor *et al.*, 1974). Third, to the extent that cultural factors are deemed to be important in the mainifestation of only certain kinds of alcoholic symptoms, this in itself may help to identify a common core of "biosocial universals" characterizing all alcoholics.

Finally, cultural identification may influence the patient's response to treatment. Modes of treatment may differ in their appropriateness for various population groups. Treatment personnel may respond differentially to patients by using ethnic stereotypes

[a] This work was supported in part by Grants 1K01AA00-25, AA05624, AA06252, and 1P50AA03510 from the National Institute on Alcohol Abuse and Alcoholism, and Research Scientist Award DA00064 to J. H. M. from the National Institute on Drug Abuse.

to assign treatments. Patients may respond differently to treatment personnel who do not belong to the same cultural group. And after treatment is concluded, the patient's long-term prognosis may be influenced by the attitudes toward alcoholics existing in different cultures, and by the norms applied to sanction their drinking behavior.

Evidence for the cultural patterning of alcohol-related disabilities within hospitalized groups of diagnosed alcoholics would serve to extend the previous work of social researchers who have focused almost exclusively on general population and community samples. This research has shown that members of specific ethnic and religious groups have different drinking patterns and different types of drinking problems. Drinkers of Irish descent drink more, in greater amounts, and experience more alcohol-related problems, while Italians and Jews have lower problem rates in spite of the small numbers of total abstainers in these groups (Cahalan et al., 1969; Cahalan and Room, 1974). Swedish and English drinkers occupy intermediate positions between the Irish, on the one extreme, and the Italians and Jews, on the other (Greeley et al., 1980). Black American drinkers have been found to be particularly affected by liver cirrhosis (Herd, 1983). High rates of excessive drinking, alcohol-related accidents, and cirrhosis of the liver have also been found in studies of American Indian groups, although rates vary considerably among and within tribes (Noble, 1978).

Various cultural, socioeconomic and historical hypotheses have been advanced to explain the observed differences among American ethnic groups. Irish drinking patterns have been attributed to the bachelor lifestyle and the solidarity of the male drinking group (Stivers, 1976; Bales, 1946). The relative absence of drinking problems among American Italians and Jews has been explained by the traditional use of wine by these groups, integration of drinking into family life, the predominant dietary functions of alcohol, and in the case of Jewish drinkers, the religious significance attached to alcohol and sobriety (Snyder, 1958; Lolli et al., 1958). The drinking patterns and problems of American Indians and blacks have been discussed in terms of their historical role in discrimination and alienation (Harper, 1976). Hispanic drinking is most often characterized in terms of *machismo* or male dominance (Panitz et al., 1983).

Although there is some evidence that ethnicity is declining as an important factor in some groups (Blane, 1977), Greeley et al. (1980) argue that ethnic heritage tends to endure migration and that despite pressures toward assimilation, certain ethnically linked traits, including alcohol consumption, have remarkable durability. Given the multidimensional nature of alcohol problems and the social, psychological, and biological heterogeneity found in diagnosed alcoholics (Horn and Wanberg, 1969), it might be expected that cultural factors would influence the patterning of alcoholism. In support of this notion, Wanberg et al. (1978) found that in contrast to the Caucasian and black alcoholics, American Indian and Hispanic alcoholics tended to drink more gregariously, in greater amounts, and with greater disruption in social role functioning. Kane (1981) and others have compared patients having minority ethnic status with alcoholics identified with the dominant Caucasian culture. Their findings also support the notion that ethnicity plays an important role in the symptoms and problems alcoholics experience. Nevertheless, as Boscarino (1980) points out, a major shortcoming of ethnic drinking research has been the lack of proper statistical controls to separate cultural influences from the demographic differences among ethnic groups (e.g., age, socioeconomic status).

The present study was undertaken to determine whether persons identified with different American ethnic/religious groups do in fact differ in the symptoms they present at the time they reach treatment when demographic factors are held constant. A second goal was to examine how ethnicity affects the referral of patients to treatment, and the type of aftercare prescribed following treatment.

## METHOD

### Subjects

Social, demographic and clinical data were obtained from 10,885 consecutive admissions to 13 private hospitals operated by the Raleigh Hills Hospitals in the western part of the continental United States. A preliminary descriptive analysis of the first 3411 cases recruited has been published previously (Mendelson et al., 1982). Only male patients from the total sample having a primary diagnosis of alcoholism are included in the present analysis. A primary diagnosis of alcoholism was made when alcoholism was entered as the first and primary reason for hospital admission. An additional criterion for inclusion was the patient's self-identification with any one of nine ethnic/religious groups. These groups were listed in a series of three interview questions pertaining to national origin (Irish, Italian, Scandinavian, French, German, other), "racial" background (black, American Indian, Oriental, Caucasian, Spanish-speaking American, other), and religion (Catholic, Jewish, Protestant, Mormon [Latter Day Saints], other, none). The questions were phrased in general terms and were designed only to obtain a measure of the patient's perception of group identification or religious affiliation. No attempt was made to determine the length of time the patient, his parents, or his grandparents had been living in the United States. Also included in the analysis were patients who chose not to identify themselves by national origin. This group is Caucasian and is referred to as the "no ethnicity group." Excluded from the analysis were patients classified as "other," and for statistical reasons patients identified with groups having a total sample size of less than 100. The sample of 8155 male patients was distributed among the following relatively homogeneous ethnic/religious groups: Irish (25.4%), German (12.0%), Scandinavian (6.3%), Hispanic (6.3%), Mormon (5.5%), French-Canadian (3.9%), black (3.8%), Italian (1.9%), and American Indian (1.7%). Patients classified into the category of "no ethnicity" constituted 33.2% of the sample.

TABLE 1 summarizes data for each group pertaining to marital status, occupational category, and employment. The majority of patients in all groups were married, although German and Mormon alcoholics indicated higher proportions of intact marriages. Italian, French-Canadian and black patients had higher proportions of bachelors, while blacks showed the highest rate of divorce. More than one-third of the sample was currently unemployed, with the highest rates occurring among the Irish, black and Indian patients. Even though the majority of patients in most groups had skilled occupations, other occupational status levels were represented in significant proportions. Scandinavian, German, Irish, and those having no ethnicity had the largest representation of professional and managerial workers. Given the large number of patients in the various categories of marital status, employment status and occupational type, it is not unexpected that the differences among groups on each of these variables were highly significant according to the $\chi^2$ statistic ($p < 0.01$).

These demographic data indicate that Raleigh Hills patients identified with various ethnic/religious groups differ markedly in their sociological makeup. To the extent that sociological variables affect access to treatment, manifestional symptoms, drinking patterns, alcohol-related problems, and aftercare referrals, then these variables should be controlled before speculating about the influence of cultural variables.

Data pertaining to the patient's present condition, past history, and hospital treatment were obtained from three sources: (1) a series of routine medical and laboratory examinations conducted soon after admission; (2) personal interviews conducted by the admitting physician and nursing staff at the time of admission; (3) standardized

**TABLE 1.** Personal and Demographic Characteristics of Alcoholic Patients Classified by Ethnic Identification

| | Mean Age (yr) | Marital Status (%) | | | Employment Status: Unemployed (%) | Occupational Category (%) | | | |
| --- | --- | --- | --- | --- | --- | --- | --- | --- | --- |
| | | Single | Married | Divorced | | Professional/ Managerial | White Collar/ Small Business | Skilled Labor | Unskilled Labor |
| No ethnicity (n = 2657) | 46.3 | 9.7 | 59.9 | 30.3 | 37.1 | 29.3 | 14.5 | 44.6 | 8.5 |
| Mormon (n = 443) | 45.0 | 6.5 | 63.9 | 29.6 | 33.0 | 18.4 | 12.3 | 55.8 | 10.6 |
| Irish (n = 2029) | 46.5 | 8.8 | 58.9 | 32.2 | 41.7 | 28.3 | 13.0 | 47.8 | 7.4 |
| Italian (n = 151) | 42.3 | 17.9 | 50.3 | 31.8 | 31.3 | 19.9 | 16.3 | 47.5 | 8.5 |
| Scandinavian (n = 505) | 46.5 | 9.3 | 60.4 | 30.3 | 34.0 | 33.0 | 11.1 | 45.3 | 7.0 |
| French-Canadian (n = 314) | 46.8 | 11.8 | 56.7 | 31.5 | 36.7 | 27.7 | 14.2 | 49.3 | 6.1 |
| German (n = 957) | 45.7 | 7.7 | 64.6 | 27.7 | 32.6 | 30.2 | 13.4 | 44.7 | 7.4 |
| Indian (n = 135) | 40.4 | 9.6 | 60.7 | 29.6 | 40.6 | 10.3 | 12.9 | 61.2 | 11.2 |
| Hispanic (n = 506) | 44.1 | 8.9 | 60.7 | 30.4 | 39.1 | 10.9 | 6.8 | 56.0 | 20.7 |
| Black (n = 300) | 42.7 | 12.3 | 52.0 | 35.7 | 40.5 | 12.2 | 7.4 | 50.0 | 25.7 |

ratings and other treatment-related information provided by staff members during the course of treatment.

Data derived from these sources were used individually or in combination in a series of multivariate analyses which describe the relationship between a set of predictor variables (representing personal, social, and demographic factors) and a set of dependent variables (representing prognostic indicators, drinking behavior, severity of dependence, alcohol-related disabilities). The statistical procedure employed is multiple classification analysis (MCA), a multivariate technique related to analysis of variance which assesses how several predictive factors simultaneously determine a dependent variable. In the series of MCAs described here, four categorical independent variables were used in each analysis. These were: (1) ethnic/religious designation (10 categories); (2) marital status (single, married, divorced/widowed); (3) familial alcoholism (positive if at least one parent indicated drinking problems or heavy drinking, negative if neither did); (4) pattern of drinking (daily or intermittent). In addition, two covariates (age and an index of socioeconomic status) were entered to control for differences in these variables.

The reason for including variables other than ethnicity in the analysis was both statistical and heuristic. Given the fact that MCA examines the relationship between each predictor and the dependent variable while adjusting for covariates and the remaining independent variables, it was considered desirable to include marital status and drinking pattern so that these variables could be controlled. Another reason for combining these variables in a single analysis is to compare the relative influence of each in explaining the variance of various dependent variables. It was of interest, for example, to consider the extent to which ethnicity and familial alcoholism were independently associated with drinking problems, since both variables may be highly intercorrelated.

Eight dependent variables were employed in the MCA series to be described. Three measures were derived from evaluations provided by treatment personnel. The first was an estimate of the amount of care needed by the patient, given on a three-point scale (1 = less than average, 2 = average, 3 = more than average). The second staff evaluation was based on independent ratings of prognosis provided by the treatment nurse and the patient's counselor on a three-point scale (1 = poor, 2 = fair, 3 = good). The third staff evaluation was derived from the counselor's judgment of the patient's sincerity and attitude toward treatment. Each was rated on a four-point scale (1 = poor, 2 = fair, 3 = good, 4 = very good). Because the two ratings were highly intercorrelated, they were combined into a single estimate of patient attitude in order to improve the reliability of the measure.

The remaining dependent measures were derived from information provided directly by the patient. An estimate of the daily amount of absolute alcohol consumed was constructed from three questions about the usual daily consumption (in total ounces) of distilled spirits, wine and beer during the three months prior to hospital admission. Before combining the amounts given in the three questions, the total ounces reported for each beverage type were converted to absolute alcohol by the following formula: liquor (45%), wine (12%), beer (5%). In view of the central role alcohol dependence is likely to play in the development of other alcohol-related disabilities, a composite measure of this construct was derived from a series of questions dealing with symptoms of addiction. These included mental confusion, personality change, tolerance, blackouts, shakes, dry heaves, heavy sweating, and epigastric pain relieved by alcohol. Each symptom was scored by the interviewer as either present or absent, and the total dependence score was derived from the sum of positive responses. An estimate of the extent of alcohol-related psychosocial disability was developed by summing the number of positive responses to four questions dealing with personal problems associated with drinking: loss of job, friends' comments on drinking, marital problems, and decreased ability to perform usual duties. In addition to this global measure of psychosocial problems, two additional indicators were considered. The first was a count of the number of times the individual had been cited for driving under the influence of alcohol, the second a weighted estimate of abnormal liver function modeled after a procedure developed by Orrego *et al.* (1979). The latter was based on the results of five common liver function tests: gamma glutamyl transpeptidase (GGT), lactate dehydrogenase (LDH), aspartate aminotransferase (SGOT), alkaline phosphatase, and bilirubin. Weights ranging from 1 to 3 were assigned to reflect the severity of disorder associated with elevated test values on these tests (GGT = 1, LDH, SGOT, and alkaline phosphatase = 2; bilirubin = 3), and the weights were summed to provide an index of abnormal liver function.

## RESULTS

At the time of hospital admission patients were asked to describe how they were referred to treatment. TABLE 2 summarizes the proportions in each ethnic/religious group attributing their referral to each of four major categories of recruitment. Media referrals accounted for the largest proportion of patients admitted to treatment. Although radio and print advertising were included in this category, television solicitations accounted for the majority of the media referrals. Among the different ethnic groups, blacks (with 66.2%) and Hispanics (with 56.8%) responded to media advertising in greater proportions than the other groups.

The second major category of referral was the patient's social network. This included any references by friends or family, both alcoholic and nonalcoholic. Thirty-one percent of the sample said they were referred to treatment by persons in their social network. Groups contributing disproportionately to network referrals were Indians (42.0%), Mormons (38.0%), Irish (36.5%), and Italians (34.1%).

The two remaining sources of recruitment were referrals from physicians or social service agencies and self-referrals. These accounted, respectively, for 8.1% and 6.0% of the total referrals. Patients identifying their ethnicity as German (14.4%) and Scandinavian (11.5%) were recruited in higher proportions than were the other groups from professional or agency referrals. In contrast, Italians (8.9%), blacks (7.2%), and persons

**TABLE 2.** Percentage Distributions within Each Ethnic Group for Sources of Referral for Treatment

| Ethnic Group | Physician or Agency (%) | Social Network (%) | Media (%) | Self-Referral (%) |
|---|---|---|---|---|
| No ethnicity | 11.1 | 33.1 | 48.7 | 7.1 |
| Mormon | 5.6 | 38.0 | 49.7 | 6.7 |
| Irish | 9.4 | 36.5 | 48.2 | 5.9 |
| Italian | 9.8 | 34.1 | 47.2 | 8.9 |
| Scandinavian | 11.5 | 31.5 | 51.0 | 6.0 |
| French-Canadian | 8.9 | 31.5 | 53.3 | 6.2 |
| German | 11.5 | 30.5 | 51.3 | 6.8 |
| Indian | 5.4 | 42.0 | 48.2 | 4.5 |
| Hispanic | 5.5 | 32.8 | 56.8 | 4.9 |
| Black | 6.3 | 20.3 | 66.2 | 7.2 |

**TABLE 3.** Method of Bill Payment According to Ethnic Identification

|  | Third-Party Insurance (%) | Personal Resources (%) | Both (%) |
|---|---|---|---|
| No ethnicity | 62.8 | 10.8 | 26.4 |
| Mormon | 66.7 | 7.9 | 25.4 |
| Irish | 66.7 | 7.6 | 25.7 |
| Italian | 63.4 | 12.4 | 24.1 |
| Scandinavian | 59.2 | 7.5 | 33.3 |
| French-Canadian | 65.5 | 6.8 | 27.7 |
| German | 61.3 | 8.3 | 30.4 |
| Indian | 71.0 | 9.9 | 5.4 |
| Hispanic | 78.7 | 4.9 | 16.4 |
| Black | 81.4 | 3.4 | 15.2 |

having no ethnic identification (7.1%) accounted for the highest proportions of self-referrals.

TABLE 3 summarizes information about the patient's method of hospital-bill payment. Third-party insurance, provided by insurance companies, employees, Medicare, Medicaid, or CHAMPUS, accounted for the majority of each group's bill payment. Personal resources accounted for the least, while in approximately 25% of the cases patients paid with a combination of insurance and personal resources. Scandinavians, Germans, Italians, and persons with no ethnic identification relied the least on exclusive third-party covervage, while Hispanics and blacks had the highest proportion of insurance coverage. In contrast, Italians, Indians and patients with no ethnic identification relied most on personal resources.

TABLE 4 summarizes the results of the multiple classification analyses. Because the results of this procedure can be affected by large numerical disparities among the classification groups, it was desirable to equalize the numbers of the various ethnic/religious classifications. Accordingly, a random exclusion procedure was employed to reduce the numbers of cases in the larger groups (i.e., "no ethnicity," Irish, German).

**TABLE 4.** Summary of Eight Separate Multiple Classification Analyses

| Dependent Variables | Independent Variables | | | | | | | |
|---|---|---|---|---|---|---|---|---|
|  | Ethnicity | | Marital Status | | Familial Alcoholism | | Drinking Pattern | |
|  | F | Beta | F | Beta | F | Beta | F | Beta |
| Patient's attitude | $5.64^a$ | 0.13 | $7.08^a$ | 0.07 | 35.6 | 0.04 | 2.22 | 0.03 |
| Prognosis | $4.60^a$ | 0.12 | $28.45^a$ | 0.14 | 0.15 | 0.01 | 2.60 | 0.03 |
| Care needed | $3.27^a$ | 0.11 | $4.09^b$ | 0.06 | 0.00 | 0.00 | 3.22 | 0.04 |
| Daily absolute alcohol | $3.58^a$ | 0.11 | 1.13 | 0.03 | $4.83^b$ | 0.04 | $6.42^b$ | 0.05 |
| Dependence | 0.77 | 0.05 | $4.50^b$ | 0.06 | $6.28^b$ | 0.05 | $45.82^a$ | 0.13 |
| Drinking problems | 1.05 | 0.06 | $107.27^a$ | 0.28 | $4.43^b$ | 0.04 | 3.57 | 0.04 |
| DUI citations | $2.08^a$ | 0.11 | $9.17^a$ | 0.09 | 0.43 | 0.01 | $24.09^a$ | 0.11 |
| Liver function index | 1.40 | 0.07 | 0.20 | 0.01 | 0.31 | 0.01 | $52.79^a$ | 0.15 |

$^a p < 0.01.$
$^b p < 0.05.$

The resulting groups vary in size from a low of 91 (American Indians) to a high of 378 (Hispanic), with an average group size of 253.

The table shows that ethnicity produced significant main effects on all dependent variables except dependence and drinking problems. Marital status produced significant differences in alcohol consumption, dependence symptoms, and drinking problems, while drinking pattern (daily versus intermittent) produced differences only on dependence, drinking problems, and DUI citations. To the extent that the beta coefficients (standardized partial correlation coefficients) represent the relative degree of association between dependent and independent variables, TABLE 4 shows that ethnicity is among the strongest predictors on most variables.

FIGURES 1 through 6 summarize the results of the multiple classification analyses. Each figure shows deviations from the grand mean for each independent variable found to have a statistically significant main effect ($p < 0.05$). The deviation scores have been adjusted for age and occupational status through covariance analysis, as well as for the effects of the other independent variables included in the analysis. What these figures portray, then, are the relative differences among ethnic groups after adjustments have been made for age, social position, marital status, familial alcoholism, and drinking pattern. Also shown are the adjusted deviation scores for any other independent variable (in addition to ethnicity) demonstrating a significant main effect.

FIGURE 1 shows that while all groups were rated slightly above average in their attitude toward treatment, the Mormons (Latter Day Saints), Italians, and Scandinavian patients scored noticeably above the other groups. In contrast, Hispanic and black patients were thought by treatment personnel to have a poorer treatment attitude than the other groups. Marital status was also found to have a significant main effect on ratings of treatment attitude, although this variable accounted for less variance (beta = 0.07) than ethnicity (beta = 0.13). According to the treatment personnel, single and divorced patients had a poorer treatment attitude than did married patients.

Another evaluative dimension rated by the treatment personnel was prognosis. As shown in FIGURE 2, the results were similar to the ratings of treatment attitude. Hispanic, German and black patients were throught to have the poorest prognosis, while Scandinavians were given the best prognosis. Interestingly, the Indian alcoholics were rated

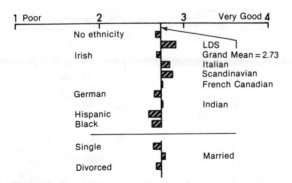

**FIGURE 1.** Counselor's rating of patient's sincerity and attitude toward treatment. Adjusted deviation scores from grand mean according to ethnic/religious group.

Prognosis

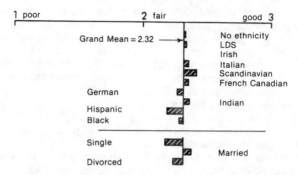

**FIGURE 2.** Prognosis rating provided by treatment nurse and patient's counselor. Adjusted deviation scores from grand mean according to ethnic/religious group.

second to the Scandinavians. Married patients were given a better prognosis than single and divorced alcoholics.

As shown in FIGURE 3, the groups also differed in the extent to which treatment personnel rated them in amount of "care needed." Hispanic, Indian, German, and French-Canadian patients were thought to require "more than average" care, as were single and divorced patients. Irish and Mormon patients were rated closer to "average" on this scale. Estimated daily absolute alcohol consumption, in ounces, is shown in FIGURE 4. Indian, Scandinavian and patients of no ethnicity reported the highest amounts of daily consumption, Hispanics the least.

A frequently used diagnostic indicator of alcohol-related social impairment is arrests or convictions for driving under the influence (DUI) of alcohol. As portrayed graphically in FIGURE 5, main effects were obtained by ethnicity, marital status, and

Care Needed

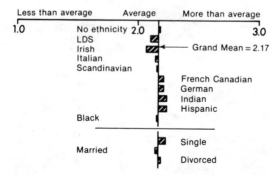

**FIGURE 3.** Treatment staff evaluations of amount of care needed by patient at admission to alcoholism treatment. Adjusted deviation scores from grand mean according to ethnic/religious group.

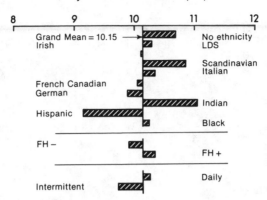

**FIGURE 4.** Estimated absolute alcohol consumed per day (in ounces). Adjusted deviation scores from grand mean according to ethnic/religious group.

drinking pattern. Mormon (LDS), Irish, Indian and Hispanic patients admitted to the greatest number of DUI citations, as did divorced and intermittent drinkers.

TABLE 5 presents information describing the discharge plans recommended to patients at the termination of their treatment. The groups differed significantly with respect to the proportions recommended to psychiatric referrals, Alcoholics Anonymous, and outpatient medical care. Psychiatric care was recommended most to patients with no ethnic identification (10.7%) and least to the Mormon alcoholics (5.2%). Black, Hispanic and Indian patients received disproportionate numbers of AA referrals. Black and Hispanic patients were referred more often to outpatient medical care than were other groups.

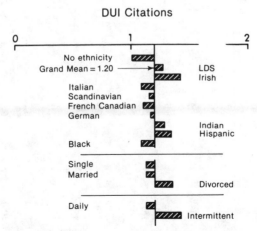

**FIGURE 5.** Number of citations for driving under the influence (DUI) of alcohol. Adjusted deviation scores from grand mean according to ethnic/religious group.

**TABLE 5.** Recommended Discharge Plans According to Ethnic Group: Percentage of Patients Receiving Referrals to Six Different Kinds of Aftercare Treatment

| | Psychiatric Referral (%) | Psychological Referral (%) | Group Therapy (%) | Social Service Agency (%) | AA (%) | Outpatient Medical Care (%) |
|---|---|---|---|---|---|---|
| No ethnicity (n = 2657) | 10.7 | 16.0 | 22.3 | 13.9 | 41.5 | 25.2 |
| Mormon (n = 443) | 5.2 | 15.6 | 23.3 | 19.3 | 48.7 | 19.2 |
| Irish (n = 2029) | 8.1 | 15.2 | 23.5 | 14.9 | 43.7 | 25.6 |
| Italian (n = 151) | 8.3 | 19.9 | 29.4 | 16.1 | 47.4 | 30.8 |
| Scandinavian (n = 505) | 6.7 | 14.9 | 30.2 | 18.2 | 42.7 | 32.9 |
| French-Canadian (n = 314) | 6.9 | 18.3 | 22.9 | 17.9 | 40.5 | 21.6 |
| German (n = 957) | 8.0 | 15.3 | 22.7 | 15.6 | 39.6 | 24.2 |
| Indian (n = 135) | 7.1 | 13.1 | 25.6 | 20.5 | 50.6 | 22.0 |
| Hispanic (n = 506) | 8.0 | 13.9 | 19.1 | 10.5 | 54.6 | 35.0 |
| Black (n = 300) | 6.9 | 17.2 | 26.6 | 14.0 | 56.7 | 48.9 |
| Chi square | 17.1 | 4.4 | 16.0 | 16.5 | 47.5 | 91.9 |
| Significance level | .05 | NS | .10 | .10 | .001 | .001 |

## DISCUSSION

In recent years the planning and implementation of alcoholism treatment policy has been influenced by a concern for the assumed needs of "special population" groups such as women, youth, and ethnic minorities (Noble, 1978). The special needs of these groups are formulated most often in terms of improved access to treatment and of programs, personnel, and therapeutic approaches appropriate for the kinds of alcohol-related problems they experience. Although evidence suggests that ethnic minorities are underserved by the treatment system, there are little empirical data indicating that the kinds of alcohol-related problems they experience are different from those of the Caucasian majority. What is often lost in these discussions is the fact that many alcoholics counted in the dominant culture's majority are in fact members of older ethnic minorities, whose drinking and alcohol problems may be subject to the same cultural patterning as the more recent ethnic groups. As the findings of the present study suggest, ethnicity, regardless of racial origins, social position, degree of integration within the dominant culture or linguistic isolation, seems to be a powerful determinant of access to treatment, manifestational symptoms, certain alcohol-related problems, and the type of aftercare recommended after discharge.

The findings indicate that even within the relatively broad ethnic/religious groups defined in the present study, certain patterns of treatment referral, presenting symptoms, drinking behavior, and social consequences can be reliably linked to different drinking subcultures in American society. They further indicate that many ethnic/religious group differences are not primarily attributable to sociological characteristics, since they cannot be readily explained by such influences as age, occupational level, and marital status after these variables have been controlled.

A major issue in the planning and equitable distribution of treatment resources is the extent to which psychological, social, and economic barriers prevent certain population groups from obtaining access to treatment. For example, Fitzgerald and Mulford (1981) found that the overrepresentation of lower socioeconomic patients in publically funded treatment facilities may be explained by the greater severity of alcoholism in these clients. The study also suggested, however, that affluent patients may be more capable of avoiding the stigma associated with entering public treatment facilities. The present study provided a unique opportunity to study ethnic differences among predominently middle-income alcoholics, and how recruitment into treatment is affected by different referral mechanisms. The results showed that the more affluent German, Scandinavian and "no ethnicity" alcoholics responded more to professional advice than the other groups, while the more economically disadvantaged black, Hispanic, and French-Canadian patients were influenced more by media advertising. The large proportions of all groups responding to media referrals suggest the need for further research to determine whether these patients would never have sought specialized treatment in the absence of advertising. Social-network referrals were lowest among the blacks, and highest among the Indians, Hispanics, and Mormons (TABLE 2). These differences might be explained by the relative differences in network density within these groups. Strug and Hyman (1981) found that dense networks composed of close friends and confidants were associated with greater pressures to enter into treatment.

Another apparent inducement to enter treatment, particularly among lower socioeconomic status groups, is insurance coverage. Third-party coverage was indicated most frequently by black, Indian, and Hispanic patients, the three groups having the highest proportions of both unskilled laborers and unemployment. These data suggest that insurance coverage, media advertising, and social-network contacts may have a powerful influence on whether or not alcoholics from disadvantaged minorities seek specialized treatment, and in what kinds of setting they choose to receive it.

# 58 ANNALS NEW YORK ACADEMY OF SCIENCES

The results of the multiple classification analysis showed that ethnicity was among the strongest predictors of a variety of dependent variables when considered in relation to marital status, familial alcoholism, and drinking pattern. Treatment attitude and prognosis are the two dependent measures most susceptible to influence by the subjective attitudes and biases of treatment personnel. It is, therefore, interesting to note the pattern of ethnic differences since this may suggest the extent to which a patient's minority status affects both his acceptance of treatment, as organized and structured by the dominant culture's representatives, and the expectations held by treatment personnel for his eventual recovery. While FIGURE 1 shows that Hispanic and black patients are throught to have the worst attitude toward treatment of all the groups, it is also important to note that Germans and patients with no ethnic identification are also below the average. Hispanic, black and German patients were rated lowest on prognosis, as were single and divorced patients. It is impossible to determine whether these judgments are influenced by clinical experience of the treatment personnel or by their ethnic stereotypes.

Indians, Scandinavians, and alcoholics with no ethnic identification reported the greatest daily amounts of alcohol consumption, as did persons having a positive family history. Indians were also found to be the heaviest drinking alcoholics by Wanberg *et al.* (1978). The latter study reported greater social disruption among the Indian and Hispanic alcoholics, findings consistent with the present study if DUI citations and ratings of "care needed" are considered. Although the groups did not differ significantly on the global index of alcohol-related problems, further analysis showed that Indian patients had the highest prevalence of alcohol-related job loss (35.1%) and suicide attempts (19.1%). The results suggest that the three most socially disadvantaged groups (Indians, blacks and Hispanics) have the greatest rehabilitation needs. Nevertheless, it should also be noted that while the "no ethnicity" group indicated fewer problems than the other groups, at least one of the other Caucasian groups scored as poorly as the minority groups on each of the problem indicators. It is also interesting that the groups did not differ on the measure of dependence severity, suggesting that these symptoms constitute a "biosocial universal" common to alcoholics regardless of cultural influences.

Finally, it appears the ethnic differences played a role in the decisions by treatment personnel to recommend specific kinds of aftercare following inpatient treatment. Alcoholics Anonymous was recommended most to black, Hispanic, and Indian alcoholics, despite the strong association of the fellowship with the value system of the dominant American culture. Two explanations might be advanced to account for this apparent anomaly. Treatment personnel might recommend AA disproportionately to socially disadvantaged patients because it costs nothing. Alternatively, ethnic minorities might have difficulty becoming involved in traditional group and individual therapies, preferring instead the less intensive gregarious experience of the AA fellowship, which is often structured along ethnic lines in geographically segregated communities.

Although ethnic differences in the patterning of alcohol-related problems have been documented in this study, the treatment implications of this research for "special population" groups is not evident. The findings do suggest, however, that ethnotherapy, a new treatment technique employing ethnic and religious identity as a basic medium of intervention, may have application beyond patients belonging to socially disadvantaged ethnic groups.

## ACKNOWLEDGMENTS

Statistical analyses for this study were supported by a grant from the Raleigh Hills Foundation, Irvine, California. Access to the research data was provided by Mr. Herbert Pratt, former president of Raleigh Hills Hospitals and Dr. Robert Schmitz, former Medical Director. Their assistance and cooperation is gratefully acknowledged.

## REFERENCES

BABOR, T. F., P. MASANES & J. P. FERRANT. 1974. Patterns of alcoholism in France and America: A comparative study. *In* M. E. Chafetz, Ed. Alcoholism, A Multilevel Problem. U.S. Government Printing Office. Washington, DC.

BALES, R. F. 1946. Cultural differences in rates of alcoholism. Q. J. Stud. Alcohol **4**: 480–499.

BLANE, H. T. 1977. Acculturation and drinking in an Italian American community. J. Stud. Alcohol **38**: 1324–1346.

BOSCARINO, J. 1980. Isolating the effects of ethnicity on drinking behavior: A multiple classification analysis of barroom attendance. Addictive Behav. **5**: 307–312.

CALAHAN, D., I. H. CISIN & H. M. CROSSLEY. 1969. American Drinking Practices: A National Study of Drinking Behavior and Attitudes. Rutgers Center for Alcohol Studies. New Brunswick, NJ.

CALAHAN, D & R. ROOM. 1974. Problem Drinking among American Men. Rutgers Center for Alcohol Studies. New Brunswick, NJ.

EVERETT, M. W., J. O. WADDELL & D. B. HEATH. 1976. Cross-Cultural Approaches to the Study of Alcohol: An Interdisciplinary Perspective. Mouton. The Hague, the Netherlands.

FITZGERALD, J. L. & H. A. MULFORD. 1981. Social attributes, problem drinking and alcoholism treatment contacts. J. Stud. Alcohol **42**: 403–413.

GREELY, A. M., W. C. MCCREADY & G. THEISEN. 1980. Ethnic Drinking Subcultures. Praeger. New York, NY.

HARPER, F. D., Ed. 1976. Alcohol Abuse and Black America. Douglass Publishers. Alexandria, VA.

HERD, D. Migration, cultural transformation and the rise of black cirrhosis. Paper presented at the Alcohol Epidemiology Section, International Council on Alcohol and Addiction, Padova, Italy, June 1983.

HORN, J. L. & R. W. WANBERG. 1969. Symptom patterns related to excessive use of alcohol. Q. J. Stud. Alcohol **30**: 35–68.

KANE, G. P. 1981. Inner City Alcoholism: An Ecological Analysis and Cross-Cultural Study. Human Sciences Press. New York, NY.

LOLLI, G., E. SERIANNI, G. M. GOLDER & P. LUZZATO-FEGIZ. 1958. Alcohol in Italian Culture: Food and Wine in Relation to Sobriety among Italian and Italian Americans. Rutgers Center for Alcohol Studies. New Brunswick, NJ.

MENDELSON, J., K. D. MILLER, N. K. MELLO, H. PRATT & R. SCHMIDTZ. 1982. Hospital treatment of alcoholism: A profile of middle income Americans. *In* Alcoholism: Clinical and Experimental Research **6**: 377–383.

NOBLE, E. P., Ed. 1978. Third Special Report to the U.S. Congress on Alcohol and Health. Department of Health, Education and Welfare. Washington, DC.

ORREGO, M., H. KALANT, Y. ISREAL, J. BLAKE, A. MEDLINE, J. G. RANKIN, A. ARMSTRONG & B. KAPOR. 1979. Effect of short-term therapy with Propyithiouracil in patients with alcoholic liver disease. Gastroenterology **76**: 105–115.

PANITZ, D. R., S. MCCONCHIE, S. R. SAUBER & J. A. FONSECA. 1983. The role of machismo and the Hispanic family in the etiology and treatment of alcoholism in Hispanic American males. Am. J. Family Ther. **11**: 31–44.

STRUG, D. L. & M. M. HYMAN. 1981. Social networks of alcoholics J. Stud. Alcohol **42**: 855–884.

SNYDER, C. R. 1958. Alcohol and the Jews: A Cultural Study of Drinking and Sobriety. Rutgers Center of Alcohol Studies. New Brunswick, NJ.

STIVERS, R. 1976. A Hair of the Dog: Irish Drinking and American Stereotype. Pennsylvania State University Press. University Park, PA.

WANBERG, K., R. LEWIS & F. M. FOSTER. 1978. Alcoholism and ethnicity: A comparative study of alcohol use patterns across ethnic groups. Int. J. Addictions **13**: 1245–1262.

WESTERMEYER, J. 1974. Alcoholism from the cross-cultural perspective: A review and critique of clinical studies. Am. J. Drug Alcohol Abuse **1**: 89–105.

# Patterns of Alcohol and Drug Abuse in Drug Treatment Clients from Different Ethnic Backgrounds

R. L. HUBBARD, W. E. SCHLENGER, J. V. RACHAL,
R. M. BRAY, S. G. CRADDOCK, E. R. CAVANAUGH,
AND H. M. GINZBURG[a]

*Research Triangle Institute*
*Research Triangle Park, North Carolina 27709*

*[a]National Institute on Drug Abuse*
*Rockville Maryland 20857*

## INTRODUCTION

Alcohol abuse has been widely reported among persons using drugs (Johnston *et al.*, 1981; Lowman *et al.*, 1982; Gelb *et al.*, 1978; Green and Jaffe, 1977; Green *et al.*, 1978; Stimmel, 1979; and Schlenger *et al.*, 1984), and cultural differences have been examined in the patterns and problems of alcohol use in blacks (King, 1982) and Hispanic-Americans (Alcocer, 1982). The drug treatment client population offers a unique blend of cultures and extensive combined use of alcohol and other drugs. This paper attempts to look at the patterns and problems of alcohol use among individuals from different ethnic backgrounds who use other drugs heavily. Examination of individuals at this end of the continuum of substance abuse may suggest explanations for cultural differences in alcohol abuse.

The data in this paper are drawn from the Treatment Outcome Prospective Study (TOPS). Funded by the National Institute on Drug Abuse (NIDA), in cooperation with the National Institute of Justice (NIJ), the Treament Outcome Prospective Study is aimed at providing current and timely data on treatment given to individuals with drug problems. TOPS is a long-term large-scale longitudinal investigation of the natural history of drug abusers who sought services in federally funded drug-abuse treatment programs. This longitudinal research tracks a multiyear census (1979–1981) of persons identified as eligible for treatment at selected drug treatment programs and at the Treatment Alternatives to Street Crime (TASC) programs.

The TOPS research is designed to access the behavior of clients entering a variety of stable, functioning drug treatment programs. A series of reports (Bray, *et al.*, 1981 and Craddock, *et al.*, 1982) described the characteristics, behaviors, and outcomes during treatment for the complete sample. Although none of the programs participating in TOPS specifically focused on alcohol-use problems, alcohol was commonly a drug of abuse among clients. A more complete discussion of alcohol use among all clients in TOPS appears in Schlenger *et al.* (1984).

None of the programs participating in the TOPS research was specifically designed to meet the needs of different cultural groups, but treatment modalities and some programs differed greatly in their ethnic mix. This paper focuses on alcohol use and problems for white, black, and Hispanic male clients, ages 21–30, entering three different kinds of drug treatment program (outpatient methadone, residential, and outpatient drug-free) from 1979–1981. In the following sections we will examine the characteristics, problems, and behaviors of these clients.

# METHOD

The complexities of studying the behavior of clients in natural settings pose many design, analysis, and interpretation problems. The TOPS research program was principally a descriptive and correlational assessment of client behavior which employed a survey design for the data collection. More formally, TOPS used a longitudinal prospective cohort research design.

## Sample

The intreatment study population consisted of all clients who applied for treatment in selected programs in ten geographically disparate communities. Clients contacted by the TASC programs in five of the communities constituted a separate but overlapping population. Major emphasis was placed on a reasonable, manageable number of selected programs in order to tightly control the study, to minimize nonresponse, and to maximize quality control. Over the three years of the study, 12 outpatient methadone, 14 residential, and 11 outpatient drug-free programs participated in TOPS.

The first year of the full-scale intreatment study began in January 1979 and involved the voluntary participation of more than 3400 clients from intake to treatment and during treatment in six cities (Chicago, Des Moines, New Orleans, New York, Phoenix, and Portland). The Intreatment Study activities were expanded for calendar years 1980 and 1981. Four treatment programs in Miami and three in San Francisco were added in 1980, and an additional four programs in Detroit and four in Philadelphia were added in January 1981. The programs in Phoenix, New York, and Miami had the majority of Hispanic clients, although some Hispanic clients were interviewed in all the cities. Intreatment data collection was terminated in December 1981. Although some TOPS programs were discontinued, almost 8000 clients were included in the study in 1980 and 1981 for a three-year total of more than 11,000 persons.

For the analyses in this paper, the sample was restricted to male clients aged 21–30 years to minimize the effects of age differences in the behaviors measured. Thus, covariation of age and ethnicity should not confound the results. In the later sections of this paper, clients are categorized further by their pattern of drug abuse. We have found a great deal of similarity among clients with the same type of drug-abuse patterns. Thus, the analysis of patterns of drug abuse offers a good opportunity to assess the nature of ethnic differences in alcohol use among these groups.

## Data Collection

Detailed background information for each client was collected at intake for the year before entry into treatment. Intreatment interviewing took place at 1 month, 3 months, and quarterly thereafter for as long as 2 years if the client remained in treatment. Follow-up interviews were conducted with a sample of 1979 clients 12 and 24 months after treatment and with a sample of 1980 clients 3 and 12 months after treatment.

Clients were first interviewed when they applied for admision to a TOPS program. In this interview they were first asked to provide information about their background including their education, training, current living arrangements, and their contact with the treatment program. They were then asked to report on their use of alcohol and drugs during the previous 3 months and the previous 12 months, to indicate their perceived alcohol-related problems, and to describe their treatment histories. In addition, they were questioned about a variety of other activities, including criminality and employment.

Since a major goal of the intreatment interviews was to trace changes over time for TOPS clients, the intreatment interviews generally followed the format described above for the intake interview, but the focus was on behavior occurring during a specific time period based on the admission date. In addition, information was gathered about the status of the client in the treatment program during this time. The follow-up questionnaires used questions and time periods consistent with those of the intake questionnaire to obtain information about the behavior of clients during several periods after leaving the TOPS treatment program. Some questions were asked about treatment and behavior immediately prior to discharge and in the 10th through 12th months after termination of treatment. In addition, an extensive section on knowledge and utilization of community services was included. The follow-up interviews also obtained more extensive information on lifestyle, support networks, and family stability than the intake interview did. The follow-up data collection was completed in December 1982.

## RESULTS AND DISCUSSION

This paper focuses primarily on the characteristics and patterns of alcohol use prior to treatment and secondly on the assessment of the nature and extent of alcohol-related problems. In the first section we look primarily at ethnic differences per se. In the next section we control for the different drug-use patterns and generate information on possible interactions. In a final section we identify some peer group and family composition variables that may have an impact on alcohol use.

### Overall Ethnic Differences

In this section we examine overall ethnic differences in current alcohol consumption, initiation of alcohol use, and alcohol-related problems.

#### Alcohol Consumption

Alcohol consumption was assessed in TOPS in several ways. During the intake interview, clients were asked to describe how frequently they drank alcohol (of any kind) during the prior 12 months. Responses to this item were intended to provide an indication of the clients' "typical" drinking behavior.

More detailed information was collected concerning alcohol consumption during the 3 months before treatment. Clients were asked to estimate how frequently they

**TABLE 1.** Level of Alcohol Use and Ounces of Absolute Alcohol per Day for White, Black, and Hispanic Males Aged 21-30 Years and Admitted to TOPS Treatment Programs in 1979-1981

| | White ($n$ = 1994) | Black ($n$ = 1013) | Hispanic ($n$ = 572) |
|---|---|---|---|
| Level of Use | | | |
| Abstainer | 20.5 | 35.4 | 24.1 |
| Infrequent/light | 11.5 | 7.4 | 12.6 |
| Moderate | 30.6 | 25.2 | 29.0 |
| Heavier | 37.4 | 32.0 | 34.3 |
| | 100.0 | 100.0 | 100.0 |
| Ounces of absolute alcohol per day | | | |
| 0 | 20.6 | 35.8 | 24.3 |
| 0.01-0.21 | 18.2 | 13.5 | 19.8 |
| 0.22-0.99 | 20.8 | 14.7 | 17.4 |
| 1.00-2.49 | 14.6 | 11.9 | 15.1 |
| 2.50+ | 25.8 | 24.1 | 23.4 |
| | 100.0 | 100.0 | 100.0 |

consumed beer, wine, and liquor and to describe the typical quantity consumed when they drank each beverage during the 3 months before treatment. From this information, a quantity-frequency index was constructed for each beverage type. Fifteen categories of consumption (and nonconsumption) were defined by cross-classifying the quantity and frequency categories and then mapping them into five drinking types (nondrinkers and infrequent, light, moderate, and heavier drinkers).

The composite measure for each of these ethnic groups is shown in TABLE 1. Consistent with previous literature, we find that blacks have a greater proportion of abstainers (35.4%) than do the other two ethnic groups. Only 20.5 percent of whites and 24.1 percent of Hispanics did not report drinking in the 3 months prior to treatment. The highest proportion of heavier and moderate drinkers was found among the white clients (37.4 and 30.6 percent respectively). Blacks (32.0 percent heavier and 25.2 percent moderate) and Hispanics (34.3 percent heavier and 29.0 percent moderate) had somewhat lower proportions in these categories. The black clients tended to distribute more at the extremes than did either the white or the Hispanic clients.

The general finding of more abstainers and fewer heavier drinkers among the blacks has been previously demonstrated in a variety of other studies comparing ethnic groups (Alcocer, 1982; King, 1982). The result also appears to be confirmed in the drug treatment population. However, unlike other studies, we found very few persons who report never drinking. Only about 1 percent of whites, 8 percent of blacks, and 3 percent of Hispanics report never drinking any alcohol. These rates compare with about 15 percent for males 21-30 in the most recent general population survey (Clark and Midanik, 1981).

An alternative way of looking at a client's drinking behavior is through examination of the average amount of "alcohol" consumed in a given time period (e.g., average amount of alcohol consumed per day). The average daily intake for each of the three beverages was computed by multiplying the number of drinking days times the typical amount per drinking occasion (converted to absolute alcohol equivalents) for each beverage and dividing by the total number of days in the time period. The averages for the three beverages were then summed to create an index of total average daily alcohol consumption. The strength of this averaging approach is that it is standardized and provides a quantitative measure of alcohol intake. However, because alcohol intake is averaged over time, such a measure is unable to capture the episodic nature of drinking. For example, a client who drinks a moderate amount of alcohol every day and another who drinks rarely but drinks heavily on every drinking occasion may have the same average daily alcohol intake, yet their drinking behaviors are clearly different. The longer the period of time over which intake is averaged, the greater the potential for such disparities.

Again in TABLE 1, we see patterns similar to those for level of use. About 25 percent of the clients in each ethnic group drink 2.5 ounces of absolute alcohol each day. On the other hand, a larger proportion of blacks are abstainers. Although there are some differences in ethnic groups among the intermediate categories, the major differences are in abstention rather than quantity consumed.

## Age at Involvement

In TABLE 2 we present some data on ethnic differences in the age at first use and when first drunk. These data may give some clues to the development of later drinking patterns and problems. White and Hispanic youth appear to use alcohol on a weekly basis at a somewhat earlier age than blacks. Two of five white and Hispanic young men who eventually enter drug treatment programs report using alcohol weekly or more often prior to their 16th birthday.

The difference between white and Hispanic men and black men is even greater when age when first drunk is reported. Again, higher proportions of white and Hispanic youth report being drunk prior to the age of 16. Sixty-three percent of whites and 55 percent of Hispanic men compared with 40 percent of black men report being drunk before turning 16.

**TABLE 2.** Age at First Weekly Alcohol Use and Age at First Episode of Drunkenness for White, Black, and Hispanic Males Aged 21–30 Admitted to TOPS Treatment Programs in 1979–1981

|  | White (n = 1994) | Black (n = 1013) | Hispanic (n = 572) |
|---|---|---|---|
| Age at first weekly use |  |  |  |
| ≤13 | 18.4 | 13.3 | 14.4 |
| 14–15 | 21.3 | 18.4 | 24.7 |
| 16–19 | 40.0 | 35.0 | 33.8 |
| 20+ | 8.7 | 12.9 | 10.9 |
| Never | 11.5 | 20.4 | 16.3 |
|  | 99.9 | 100.0 | 100.1 |
| Age at first episode of drunkenness |  |  |  |
| ≤13 | 33.3 | 18.0 | 27.8 |
| 14–15 | 29.8 | 21.7 | 27.1 |
| 16–19 | 30.2 | 33.0 | 28.1 |
| 20+ | 3.5 | 7.0 | 5.9 |
| Never | 3.2 | 20.3 | 11.2 |
|  | 100.0 | 100.0 | 100.1 |

It should also be noted that one-fifth of the blacks do not report ever being drunk, a much higher proportion than for either the white (3.2%) or the Hispanic (11.2%) clients. When these individuals who report never being drunk are excluded from the analysis, we still find strong support for ethnic differences. Of the men who report ever being drunk, two-thirds of the Hispanics and whites report being drunk prior to age 16. About half the blacks who report ever being drunk said that their first episode of drunkenness occurred prior to age 16.

It appears that alcohol use may begin at a later age for blacks compared with persons from other ethnic groups who eventually enter drug treatment programs. This result is at some variance with the studies reviewed by King (1982). He reported that incidence of drinking was increasing for young blacks. Although the incidence may be increasing among black males who come to drug treatment, the age of initiation of weekly alcohol use and the first episode of drunkenness are reportedly much later for blacks than for whites and Hispanics. As indicated in the previous section, however, the level of heavier drinking for all three ethnic groups is similar. Despite apparent differences in the developmental pattern of drinking, similar proportions of persons in the ethnic groups entering drug treatment programs reach the same level of heavier drinking by age 21–30.

## Alcohol-Related Problems

Ethnic differences with respect to the nature and extent of alcohol abuse and alcohol-related problems have also been reported. Problem drinking, indicated by alcohol-related arrests and deaths, is greater for Hispanics (Alcocer, 1982). The recognition of biomedical problems appears to be more common among blacks than the recognition of alcohol abuse and alcoholism (King, 1982).

**TABLE 3.** Number of Alcohol-Related Problems, Need for Alcohol Treatment, and Prior Alcohol Treatment for White, Black, and Hispanic Males Aged 21–30 Admitted to TOPS Treatment Programs in 1979–1981

|  | White (n = 1994) | Black (n = 1013) | Hispanic (n = 572) |
|---|---|---|---|
| Number of alcohol-related problems |  |  |  |
| None | 63.9 | 78.3 | 79.6 |
| 1–2 | 15.9 | 11.0 | 11.4 |
| 3 or more | 20.2 | 10.7 | 9.0 |
|  | 100.0 | 100.0 | 100.0 |
| Need for alcohol treatment |  |  |  |
| No problem | 76.7 | 79.9 | 87.1 |
| Secondary problem | 14.0 | 14.8 | 10.4 |
| Primary problem | 9.4 | 5.3 | 2.5 |
|  | 100.1 | 100.0 | 100.0 |
| Prior alcohol treatment |  |  |  |
| Never | 84.4 | 91.4 | 92.3 |
| In the past year | 11.3 | 6.0 | 4.6 |
| More than a year ago | 4.3 | 2.7 | 3.2 |
|  | 100.0 | 100.1 | 100.1 |

The data presented in TABLE 3 indicate that these general findings may not be applicable to the drug treatment client population. White clients report greater numbers of alcohol-related problems, express a more pressing need for alcohol treatment, and indicate more prior alcohol treatment. One-fifth of the white clients report three or more alcohol-related problems compared with about 10 percent of the black and Hispanic clients. Twenty-three percent of white clients and 20 percent of black clients say they need alcohol treatment. Only about one in eight Hispanic clients says he needs alcohol treatment. Fifteen percent of the white clients reported prior treatment for alcohol compared with less than 10 percent for blacks and Hispanics.

Thus, it appears that white drug treatment clients perceive themselves as having more alcohol-related problems and are more likely to perceive a need for help than are minority clients. However, we must be cautious in concluding that black and Hispanic clients have fewer problems with alcohol and are less in need of alcohol treatment. As we saw in TABLE 1, the rate of heavier drinking is similar for the three ethnic groups. As King and Alcocer report, there is a problem of recognition of alcohol abuse and alcohol-related problems in the black and Hispanic communities. This may result in a depressed report of problems and need for treatment among black and Hispanic drug treatment clients.

### Ethnic Differences within Drug-Use Patterns

In this section we attempt to examine ethnic differences within various categories of drug use. As shown in the next section, the ethnic groups of clients entering treatment differ greatly with respect to the prevalence of the type and number of drugs used. Furthermore, prevalence of use patterns differs from city to city, depending on the availability of drugs and the subculture of drug abusers. In order to partially account for these differences, we divided the sample into seven different use patterns on the basis of the work of Bray et al. (1982), and we looked at ethnic differences in alcohol use within these patterns.

The classification measure selected for use with TOPS data consists of a set of seven patterns (see Bray et al. [1982] for a complete discussion of this measure and others that were examined). Weekly or greater use of eight drug types (heroin or illegal methadone, other narcotics, barbiturates or sedatives, cocaine, amphetamines, minor tranquilizers, marijuana, and alcohol) was the principal criterion used to create the patterns.

The seven patterns of drug use were defined using the following hierarchical rules. First, a weekly heroin/other narcotics pattern classification was created that included all clients who reported weekly or more frequent use of heroin (or illegal methadone[b]) and weekly or greater use of other narcotics. Next, a heroin-weekly pattern was formed; clients who used heroin (but not other narcotics) made up this second pattern classification. Then an "other narcotics"-weekly pattern was created that included clients who reported at least weekly use of other narcotics (but not heroin). Collectively these three patterns accounted for everyone who reported weekly or more frequent use of heroin or other narcotics.

The next pattern (labeled "multiple nonnarcotics") included clients who reported

[b] Because the properties of methadone are quite similar to those of heroin and there are few weekly users who did not also use heroin (n = 117, 1979 cohort), illegal methadone users are considered together with heroin users. Future references to heroin in connection with drug-use pattern should be assumed to include illegal methadone.

**TABLE 4.** Drug Use Patterns among White, Black, and Hispanic Males Aged 21–30 Admitted to TOPS Treatment Programs in 1979–1981

| Pattern Class | White ($n$ = 1994) | Black ($n$ = 1013) | Hispanic ($n$ = 572) |
|---|---|---|---|
| Heroin and narcotics | 14.8 | 14.0 | 6.5 |
| Heroin | 17.8 | 42.5 | 57.2 |
| Other narcotics | 15.3 | 11.8 | 3.3 |
| Multiple nonnarcotics | 9.9 | 3.2 | 2.3 |
| Single nonnarcotic | 17.0 | 9.7 | 5.9 |
| Alcohol/marijuana | 20.7 | 13.2 | 17.1 |
| Minimal | 4.6 | 5.7 | 7.7 |
|  | 100.1 | 100.1 | 100.0 |

using two or more of the following drugs at least weekly: minor tranquilizers, barbiturates/sedatives, amphetamines, and cocaine. The fifth pattern comprised the remaining clients who used one nonnarcotic at least weekly from the four drug types listed for the prior pattern. Note that both of the latter two patterns emphasize use of nonnarcotics without consideration of alcohol or marijuana use.

The next pattern classification "alcohol/marijuana," was created to describe the remaining clients, who reported using marijuana or alcohol (or both) and no other drugs on at least a weekly basis. Clients still unclassified by the foregoing rules constituted a residual minimal-use pattern (no drugs used weekly or more often).

It should be noted that the defining characteristics of the pattern classifications do not describe all of the drugs used by the clients. Rather, they focus on specific drugs at the weekly-use levels.

TABLE 4 summarizes the ethnic differences in the patterns. As can be seen, black and Hispanic 21–30-year-old male clients tend to be predominantly heroin (only)-users (43 and 57%, respectively). Blacks tend to be heroin- and other narcotic-users to a greater extent than Hispanic males in the TOPS programs.

The white drug-users are widely distributed among the seven patterns. Five of the seven pattern classes contain 15 percent or more of the white clients. These major differences in distribution of the ethnic groups among the drug-use patterns reinforce the argument for analysis within drug-use patterns.

*Alcohol Use*

In TABLE 5 we show the level of daily use of absolute alcohol within the patterns. The proportion of clients using 2.5 ounces per day is highest among multiple-nonnarcotic-users. More than 40 percent of the white and black multiple-nonnarcotic-users report the use of more than 2.5 ounces of absolute alcohol per day. Because of the extensive use of other drugs, these users would appear to be at risk for very serious problems.

The lowest level of alcohol use is found among the heroin-users who do not use other narcotics. There is a high proportion of abstainers among blacks with this pattern. Use of more than 2.5 ounces of absolute alcohol is also less common in this group. More than one-third of black clients who use other narcotics either with or without heroin also use 2.5 ounces of absolute alcohol. This is somewhat higher than white and Hispanic clients with the same patterns.

Patterns of some ethnic differences are observable within drug-use pattern classes,

**TABLE 5.** Average Daily Consumption of Alcohol by Type of Drug Use for White, Black, and Hispanic Males Aged 21–30 Admitted to Drug Treatment Programs in 1979–1981

| Daily Absolute Alcohol (oz) | White (n = 1865) | Black (n = 942) | Hispanic (n = 511) |
|---|---|---|---|
| *Heroin and Narcotics* | | | |
| 0 | 21.7 | 32.1 | 27.0 |
| 0.01–0.99 | 36.4 | 25.7 | 29.7 |
| 1.00–2.49 | 16.8 | 7.9 | 16.2 |
| 2.50+ | 25.1 | 34.3 | 27.0 |
| | 100.0 | 100.0 | 99.9 |
| | (n = 291) | (n = 140) | (n = 37) |
| *Heroin (No Other Narcotics)* | | | |
| 0 | 24.9 | 37.4 | 20.6 |
| 0.01–0.99 | 43.9 | 28.7 | 37.0 |
| 1.00–2.49 | 10.2 | 15.2 | 15.8 |
| 2.50+ | 21.0 | 18.7 | 26.6 |
| | 100.0 | 100.0 | 100.0 |
| | (n = 342) | (n = 428) | (n = 316) |
| *Other Narcotics* | | | |
| 0 | 24.5 | 31.6 | 21.1 |
| 0.01–0.99 | 35.9 | 24.8 | 31.6 |
| 1.00–2.49 | 11.1 | 7.7 | 15.8 |
| 2.50+ | 28.5 | 35.9 | 31.6 |
| | 100.0 | 100.0 | 100.1 |
| | (n = 298) | (n = 117) | (n = 19) |
| *Multiple Nonnarcotics* | | | |
| 0 | 17.9 | 25.0 | 7.7 |
| 0.01–0.99 | 27.0 | 18.8 | 38.5 |
| 1.00–2.49 | 14.8 | 9.4 | 23.1 |
| 2.50+ | 40.3 | 46.9 | 30.8 |
| | 100.0 | 100.1 | 100.1 |
| | (n = 196) | (n = 32) | (n = 13) |
| *Single Nonnarcotic* | | | |
| 0 | 13.8 | 32.3 | 29.4 |
| 0.01–0.99 | 38.3 | 34.4 | 41.2 |
| 1.00–2.49 | 18.6 | 10.4 | 8.8 |
| 2.50+ | 29.3 | 22.9 | 20.6 |
| | 100.0 | 100.0 | 100.0 |
| | (n = 334) | (n = 96) | (n = 34) |
| *Alcohol and/or Marijuana* | | | |
| 0 | 14.6 | 27.1 | 21.7 |
| 0.01–0.99 | 42.6 | 31.0 | 39.1 |
| 1.00–2.49 | 19.1 | 15.5 | 19.6 |
| 2.50+ | 23.8 | 26.4 | 19.6 |
| | 100.1 | 100.0 | 100.0 |
| | (n = 404) | (n = 129) | (n = 92) |

but it is difficult to discern any clear structure for the results. Some complex interactions may exist. However, it seems premature to conclude that there are ethnic differences within the use categories. In general, it appears that the type of drug use is a more important predictor than ethnic differences of level of alcohol use.

### Alcohol-Related Problems

Drug-use pattern differences again rather than ethnicity seem to be more descriptive of differences in the nature and extent of alcohol-related problems. As might be

**TABLE 6.** Number of Alcohol-Related Problems by Type of Drug Use for White, Black, and Hispanic Males Aged 21–30 Admitted to TOPS Treatment Programs in 1979–1981

| Number of Problems | White | Black | Hispanic |
|---|---|---|---|
| | *Heroin and Narcotics* | | |
| 0 | 76.8 | 74.1 | 67.6 |
| 1–2 | 9.2 | 9.4 | 21.6 |
| 3 or more | 14.0 | 16.5 | 11.8 |
| | 100.0 | 100.0 | 100.0 |
| | *Heroin* | | |
| 0 | 82.2 | 84.9 | 83.5 |
| 1–2 | 9.6 | 10.3 | 11.3 |
| 3 or more | 8.2 | 4.8 | 5.2 |
| | 100.0 | 100.0 | 100.0 |
| | *Other Narcotics* | | |
| 0 | 63.9 | 71.8 | 66.7 |
| 1–2 | 7.7 | 15.4 | 11.1 |
| 3 or more | 28.4 | 12.8 | 22.2 |
| | 100.0 | 100.0 | 100.0 |
| | *Multiple Nonnarcotics* | | |
| 0 | 48.5 | 60.6 | 61.5 |
| 1–2 | 20.2 | 12.1 | 15.4 |
| 3 or more | 31.3 | 27.3 | 23.1 |
| | 100.0 | 100.0 | 100.0 |
| | *Single Nonnarcotic* | | |
| 0 | 47.4 | 73.7 | 68.6 |
| 1–2 | 23.7 | 10.1 | 11.4 |
| 3 or more | 28.9 | 16.2 | 20.0 |
| | 100.0 | 100.0 | 100.0 |
| | *Alcohol and/or Marijuana* | | |
| 0 | 56.0 | 67.7 | 75.5 |
| 1–2 | 22.0 | 15.8 | 10.2 |
| 3 or more | 22.0 | 16.5 | 14.3 |
| | 100.0 | 100.0 | 100.0 |

**TABLE 7.** Types of Alcohol-Related Problems for White, Black, and Hispanic Males Ages 21–30 Admitted to Drug Treatment Programs in 1979–1981

| Pattern of Drug Use | Sample Size | Type of Problem | | | | | |
|---|---|---|---|---|---|---|---|
| | | Medical | Psychological | Family | Legal | Job | Financial |
| *White* | | | | | | | |
| Heroin and narcotics | 295 | 10.5 | 11.6 | 17.4 | 12.6 | 10.6 | 10.9 |
| Heroin | 355 | 5.9 | 8.5 | 12.7 | 8.2 | 5.6 | 6.2 |
| Other narcotics | 305 | 16.1 | 20.4 | 27.8 | 22.1 | 16.1 | 15.1 |
| Multiple nonnarcotics | 198 | 19.7 | 22.2 | 38.4 | 30.3 | 27.3 | 27.3 |
| Single nonnarcotic | 342 | 19.3 | 26.6 | 35.7 | 34.2 | 21.1 | 25.7 |
| Alcohol/marijuana | 414 | 10.6 | 21.0 | 27.8 | 26.3 | 17.4 | 20.4 |
| *Black* | | | | | | | |
| Heroin and narcotics | 142 | 14.2 | 12.2 | 16.5 | 10.1 | 13.7 | 10.9 |
| Heroin | 433 | 4.9 | 5.1 | 7.5 | 4.7 | 4.9 | 7.0 |
| Other narcotics | 119 | 12.6 | 13.7 | 20.5 | 12.0 | 12.0 | 16.2 |
| Multiple nonnarcotics | 33 | 27.3 | 27.3 | 27.3 | 21.2 | 18.2 | 21.2 |
| Single nonnarcotic | 99 | 11.1 | 14.1 | 17.1 | 15.1 | 11.1 | 14.1 |
| Alcohol/marijuana | 134 | 16.5 | 13.5 | 23.3 | 15.8 | 14.3 | 18.0 |
| *Hispanic* | | | | | | | |
| Heroin and narcotics | 37 | 8.1 | 10.8 | 16.2 | 16.2 | 10.8 | 5.4 |
| Heroin | 328 | 5.2 | 7.9 | 10.1 | 3.4 | 5.5 | 6.1 |
| Other narcotics | 19 | 5.6 | 16.7 | 27.8 | 27.8 | 22.2 | 22.2 |
| Multiple nonnarcotics | 13 | 23.1 | 15.4 | 30.8 | 7.8 | 15.4 | 15.4 |
| Single nonnarcotic | 35 | 20.0 | 14.3 | 28.6 | 8.6 | 2.9 | 14.3 |
| Alcohol/marijuana | 98 | 5.1 | 6.2 | 14.3 | 17.3 | 5.2 | 10.2 |

NOTE: Each cell percentage is independently calculated. Among white heroin pattern clients, for example, 5.9 percent report medical problems related to alcohol use.

expected, TABLE 6 shows that multiple-nonnarcotic-users report the highest level of alcohol-related problems. Almost one-third of the multiple-nonnarcotic-using white clients and one-fourth of the black and Hispanic clients report three or more alcohol-related problems. Three or more problems are also reported by a somewhat lower proportion of those in all other pattern classes except for heroin-uers. Less than 10 percent of heroin-users in all three ethnic groups report three or more alcohol-related problems. Whites in all except heroin and narcotics groups are more likely to report three or more alcohol-related problems.

TABLE 7 confirms a similar pattern of results regardless of the type of problem. High percentages of multiple-nonnarcotic-users consistently report each type of problem. High rates of each problem are reported for four types of white nonheroin-users. For black clients, the multiple-nonnarcotic-users have clearly the highest rates on each problem. Among the Hispanic clients the types of problems are more specific to a particular user group. For example, 29 percent of the single-nonnarcotic-users report family problems, but only 9 percent report legal problems.

*Alcohol Treatment*

TABLE 8 shows a surprisingly consistent pattern of history of alcohol treatment. Again we see that drug-use pattern is the key predictor of a history of alcohol treatment. The only ethnic variations are found in the high proportion of black multiple-nonnarcotic-users (24.2%) and Hispanic single-nonnarcotic-users (22.9%) who have had alcohol treatment. Typically, whites in all types of use patterns were more likely to have had alcohol treatment.

An expression of the current need for treatment was highest for white and black clients in four pattern classes. Only between 10 and 15 percent of Hispanic clients in five of the six pattern classes reported a current need for alcohol treatment. Among

**TABLE 8.** Drug-Use Patterns of White, Black, and Hispanic Male Drug Treatment Clients Aged 21–30 with a Past History of Alcohol Treatment and Currently Wanting Treatment for Alcohol Abuse

| Drug-Use Pattern | Past History of Alcohol Treatment | | |
| --- | --- | --- | --- |
| | White | Black | Hispanic |
| Heroin and narcotics | 9.5 | 8.6 | 8.1 |
| Heroin | 8.2 | 4.2 | 3.7 |
| Other narcotics | 15.2 | 11.9 | 16.7 |
| Multiple nonnarcotics | 18.3 | 24.2 | 7.7 |
| Single nonnarcotic | 23.5 | 16.3 | 22.9 |
| Alcohol and/or marijuana | 18.4 | 13.5 | 13.3 |
| | Currently Wanting Alcohol Treatment | | |
| | White | Black | Hispanic |
| Heroin and narcotics | 14.0 | 25.5 | 10.8 |
| Heroin | 9.1 | 11.5 | 10.4 |
| Other narcotics | 21.6 | 28.1 | 15.8 |
| Multiple nonnarcotics | 36.9 | 42.4 | 15.4 |
| Single nonnarcotic | 37.6 | 25.2 | 32.3 |
| Alcohol and/or marijuana | 26.7 | 30.3 | 15.6 |

NOTE: Each cell is independently calculated. Among black heroin pattern clients, for example, 11.5 percent currently felt a need for treatment of alcohol abuse.

blacks at least a quarter of the clients in all pattern classes except heroin-only needed treatment. More than 20 percent of all types of white nonheroin-users also needed alcohol treatment.

These results support the concept that Hispanics either do not perceive the need for treatment or feel the available treatment programs will not benefit them. Black clients, on the other hand, seem to want treatment most. This appears to be at odds with observations for the general black population, which suggest that alcoholism and the need for alcohol treatment are not generally recognized (King, 1982). It may be that exposure to the treatment system results in a recognition of alcohol problems among black drug-treatment clients.

*Influence of Family and Friends*

A final factor that may differentially affect alcohol use and problems among ethnic groups is peer group and familial influences. The general orientation of the TOPS survey precluded any detailed assessment of peer group relationships and family structure and support networks. We did, however, ask some questions and construct some scales that might provide some insight into possible relationships between these variables and alcohol use. TABLE 9 presents some data for three of these measures.

We chose four types of households to examine in TABLE 9: clients who lived alone in a dwelling (not on the street or in an institution), in a nuclear family (spouse and children), and in an extended family (other family members), and clients living with friends. The data in TABLE 9 show that clients living with friends had the highest rates of heavier alcohol use. The patterns did not appear to differ greatly among the ethnic groups.

There is a clear relationship between heavier drinking and having family or friends who "drink alcohol on a fairly regular basis." Heavier drinking is lower for clients in all ethnic groups who report having no friends who drink regularly. About one-fourth of the clients report having no friends who drink regularly.

A more global index of peer group influence may be indicated by involvement in

**TABLE 9.** White, Black, and Hispanic Male Drug Treatment Clients Aged 21–30 with Heavier Alcohol Use Patterns by Household Composition, Friends or Family Who Drink Regularly, and Involvement in Drug-Use Network

|  | White | Black | Hispanic |
|---|---|---|---|
| *Household composition* | | | |
| Live alone | 36.9 | 37.6 | 37.0 |
| Nuclear family | 35.2 | 29.7 | 32.8 |
| Extended family | 37.2 | 33.9 | 33.9 |
| Friends | 44.1 | 41.7 | 48.6 |
| *Friends or family who drink regularly* | | | |
| Yes | 43.9 | 39.4 | 40.4 |
| No | 17.8 | 15.1 | 15.3 |
| *Drug-use network* | | | |
| Low | 27.8 | 23.5 | 21.7 |
| Medium | 35.5 | 30.4 | 38.0 |
| High | 47.5 | 45.0 | 47.3 |

NOTE: Percentages are calculated in the same manner as noted in TABLES 7 and 8.

a drug-use network. The drug-use network index is a composite indicator based on a factor analysis of potential social-support variables. The index is composed of items on drug use among family and friends and involvement in sale and/or manufacturing of drugs. Again we see that higher proportions of heavier drinkers are found among the groups with more involvement in the drug-use network. Almost half of the clients heavily involved in the drug-use network report heavier drinking. There is no evidence of ethnic differences.

In summary, we examined three possible indicators of social influence on alcohol use. Although each of the measures appeared to be related to alcohol use among drug treatment clients, we found little evidence that these influences affected the ethnic groups differently.

## SUMMARY AND CONCLUSIONS

In this paper we have sought to identify differences in alcohol consumption patterns and problems among young adult males from white, black, and Hispanic ethnic groups entering drug treatment programs. In overall consumption patterns we found results similar to those obtained in general population studies. However, about one-third of the clients in all ethnic groups could be classified as heavier drinkers (drinking at least once a week and 4 or more drinks per drinking occasion) in the period immediately prior to treatment. About one-fourth of the clients in each ethnic group consumed a daily average of 2.5 ounces of absolute alcohol.

Compared with the other ethnic groups, blacks were the most likely to be abstainers and reported regular alcohol use and drunkenness at later ages. Regardless of the pattern of development, similar proportions of the clients in all ethnic groups reported heavier drinking levels by age 21–30.

Consistent with the current hypotheses in the literature, whites reported much higher levels of alcohol-related problems and prior treatment. Despite having similar levels of drinking, black and Hispanic ethnic groups did not appear to recognize alcohol as a problem or to report alcohol-related problems to the extent that whites did.

Examination of drug-use patterns showed great variation in the nature and extent of drug use among the three ethnic groups. Whites were distributed among the seven patterns of use. Heroin use with cocaine, marijuana, and alcohol was the predominant pattern for blacks and Hispanics. Although the patterns of drug use differed greatly, these patterns were not differentially related to alcohol consumption or alcohol-related problems within ethnic groups. On the contrary, the drug-use patterns appeared to be a stronger predictor than ethnicity of use and problems. Multiple-nonnarcotic-users reported the highest levels of alcohol consumption and the greatest numbers of alcohol-related problems. This group typically reported the highest number of alcohol-related problems. Expression of a current need for treatment and a history of prior alcohol treatment were highest for black multiple-nonnarcotic-users.

Our examination of the influences of family and friends was based on a limited number of questions available in the data. Heavier drinking was reported by clients who (1) lived with friends, (2) had family or friends who drank regularly, or (3) had extensive involvement in the drug-use network, including drug sales. No ethnic differences were found.

In general, this analysis revealed that the ethnic differences in the patterns of alcohol consumption and alcohol-related problems for drug treatment clients are similar to those for the general population. However, what may be more revealing is the strong relationship of drug-use patterns with alcohol consumption and alcohol-related problems. This relationship seems much stronger than the relationship with ethnicity. Because drug-use patterns are also strongly related to ethnicity, multivariate techniques are necessary to examine the relationship more completely. Such models may suggest that a more complex relationship exists between ethnicity, drug use, and alcohol use and problems. Rather than being determined by cultural factors, the nature of alcohol consumption and problems may be determined more by other features of the social environment, including socioeconomic factors and the availability of drugs other than alcohol.

## REFERENCES

ALCOCER, A. 1982. Alcohol Use and Abuse among the Hispanic American Population. Alcohol and Health Monograph 4. Special Population Issues (DHHS Publication No. [ADM] 82-1193). National Institute on Alcohol Abuse and Alcoholism. Rockville, MD.

BRAY, R. M., R. L. HUBBARD, J. V. RACHAL, E. R. CAVANAUGH, S. G. CRADDOCK, J. J. COLLINS, W. E. SCHLENGER & M. ALLISON. 1986. Client Characteristics, Behaviors, and Intreatment Outcomes of Clients in TOPS—1979 Admission Cohort (RTI/1500/04-04F). Research Triangle Institute. Research Triangle Park, NC.

BRAY, R. M., W. E. SCHLENGER, S. G. CRADDOCK, R. L. HUBBARD & J. V. RACHAL. 1982. Approaches to the Assessment of Drug Use in the Treatment Outcome Prospective Study (RTI/1901/01-05S). Research Triangle Institute. Research Triangle Park, NC.

CLARK, W. B. & L. MIDANIK. 1981. Alcohol use and alcohol problems among US adults. In Draft Report on the 1979 National Survey. Social Research Group, School of Public Health, University of California. Berkeley, CA.

CRADDOCK, S. G., R. L. HUBBARD, R. M. BRAY, E. R. CAVANAUGH & J. V. RACHAL. 1982. Client Characteristics, Behaviors, and Intreatment Outcomes: 1980 TOPS Admission Cohort (RTI/1901/01-01F). Research Triangle Institute. Research Triangle Park, NC.

GELB, A.M., B. L. RICHMAN & O. P. ANAND. 1978. Quantitative and temporal relationships of alcohol use in narcotic addicts and methadone maintenance patients undergoing alcohol detoxification. Am. J. Drug Alcohol Abuse 5(2): 191–198.

GREEN, J. & J. H. JAFFE. 1977. Alcohol and opiate dependence. J. Stud. Alcohol 38(7): 1274–1293.

GREEN, J., J. H. JAFFE, J. A. CARLISI & A. ZAKS. 1978. Alcohol use in the opiate use cycle of the heroin addict. Int. J. Addictions 13(7): 1021–1033.

JOHNSTON, L. D., J. G. BACHMAN & P. M. O'MALLEY. 1981. Student Drug use in America, 1975–1981 (DHHS Publication No. [ADM] 82-1221). National Institute on Drug Abuse. Rockville, MD.

KING, L. 1982. Alcoholism: Studies Regarding Black Americans. Alcohol and Health Monograph 4. Special Population Issues (DHHS Publication No. [ADM] 82-1193). National Institute on Alcohol Abuse and Alcoholism. Rockville, MD.

LOWMAN, C., R. L. HUBBARD, J. V. RACHAL & E. R. CAVANAUGH. 1982. Facts for Planning No. 5. Adolescent Marijuana and Alcohol Use. In Alcohol and Health Research World. : 69–75.

SCHLENGER, W. E., M. E. MARSDEN, J. V. RACHAL, E. R. CAVANAUGH & R. L. HUBBARD. 1984. Alcohol Use among Drug Treatment Clients. (RTI/1901/01-135.) Research Triangle Institute. Research Triangle Park, NC.

STIMMEL, B. 1979. Drug and alcohol treatment. In Handbook on Drug Use. R. L. DuPont, A. Goldstein & J. O'Donnell, Eds. U.S. Government Printing Office. Washington, DC.

# Personality, Cognitive, and Neuropsychological Correlates of Harmful Alcohol Consumption: A Cross-National Comparison of Clinical Samples

TOR LØBERG

*University of Bergen*
*Bergen, Norway*

WILLIAM R. MILLER

*Department of Psychology*
*University of New Mexico*
*Albuquerque, New Mexico 87131*

Research from the past three decades points to wide variation in the response of individuals to alcohol, both within and across societal samples. The consequences of both acute and chronic intoxication appear to depend in part on the social context of the drinker.

Yet to the extent that alcohol-related impairment is mediated by consistent organic changes resulting from overdrinking, a certain universality of deficits should be observed cross-culturally, at least on measures more directly tied to such changes. Whereas social behavior after drinking has been shown to be highly influenced by expectancy factors, the influence of set and setting on cognitive and motor performance measures appears to be less marked. It would be expected, then, that profiles of problem drinking patients on indices of enduring deficit would show similarities regardless of the nation in which assessment was conducted. Personality, cognitive, and neuropsychological performance measures would be logical dimensions for investigating such cross-national consistencies.

Of course cultural, ethnic, and national differences in drinking practices would be expected to contribute to differential consequences in central nervous system impairment as measured by neuropsychological tests. Thus cross-population dissimilarities in impairment level may still be observed in spite of consistency of the sequelae of specific drinking histories. Dimensions such as duration, amount, and frequency of excessive drinking have been found to be related to neuropsychological impairment severity among problem drinkers (Løberg, 1986), and cross-national differences in gross consumption level are also likely to be of importance. Population differences in drinking practices may even contribute to the *pattern* of deficits observed. Culture- and subculture-related differences in beverage congener content (Greizerstein, 1981) could result in differential impairment on certain measures. Nutrition likewise is an important potential confounding variable because malnutrition is known to be linked to patterns of impairment on tests of learning and memory in alcoholics (e.g., Guthrie and Elliott, 1980). Even if other consumption variables (amount, frequency, beverage) are consistent across populations, the drinking practices of groups may vary with regard to the spacing of drinks and thus the peak blood alcohol concentration (BAC) achieved on average drinking occasions. Differential peak BACs in the regular drinking pattern may in turn create varying patterns or levels of neuropsychological impairment even though total consumption appears consistent across groups. High BAC, for example, appears to be associated with a higher frequency of memory "blackouts," which in turn predict greater neuropsychological impairment levels among alcoholics (Løberg, 1986). Of course both blackouts and greater impairment could be accounted for by pre-existing differences in central nervous system vulnerability and sensitivity to alcohol. Findings on the Oriental flushing response to alcohol exemplify the potential importance of ethnic differences in neurochemical responsiveness to ethanol. All of these as well as other factors could account for dissimilarities across national groups with regard to neuropsychological impairment observed among excessive drinkers.

A first step in exploring this issue is to ask the question, "To what extent *are* there consistencies in neuropsychological impairment of alcoholics across national boundaries?" This raises still other complicating factors: discrepancies in criteria for diagnosing alcoholism, differences on crucial sample characteristics such as age and education, variation in tests and procedures employed for evaluating adapative abilities. Aware of these limitations, we have attempted here to take a first step by looking for similarities that may obtain across national samples in spite of (or controlling for) these confounding variables.

An immediate problem is that the empirical research to date on neuropsychological deficits among alcoholics has been predominantly American. We were able, however, to identify a number of investigations using standardized objective assessment procedures to study impairment in adaptive abilities among alcoholics from various other nations, including studies from *Sweden* (Bergman & Ågren, 1974; Carlsson *et al.* 1973; Claeson and Carlsson, 1970), *Denmark* (Lee, *et al.*, 1979), the *Netherlands* (Boeke, 1970), *Germany* (Köhler, 1974), *Ireland* (Miglioli, *et al.*, 1979), *England* (Ron *et al.*, 1979), *Scotland* (Fleming and Guthrie, 1980; Guthrie, 1980; Guthrie and Elliott, 1980), *Australia* (Cala *et al.*, 1978; Korboot *et al.*, 1977) and *Canada* (Long and McLachlan, 1974; Wilkinson and Carlen, 1980a, 1980b, 1980c).

In comparing such diverse studies it is important to rely as much as possible on assessment procedures that have general international applicability and known empirical validity. Some tests fulfill these requirements better than others, and international conventions have developed in the direction of using a more or less consistent battery of measures for the purpose of making clinical inferences. Although consensus is less than complete, the Wechsler intelligence tests (Wechsler-Bellevue or WAIS), the Wechsler Memory Scale, the Minnesota Multiphasic Personality Inventory (MMPI), and the Halstead-Reitan Neuropsychological Test Battery for Adults have been commonly used. Numerous reports have appeared attesting to the validity and reliability of these instruments and their sensitivity to various types of brain disorder (e.g., Kløve, 1974; Matarazzo, *et al.*, 1976; Reitan and Davison, 1974). In addition there has been a cross-national validation study on the diagnosis of brain lesions using these measures (Kløve, 1974). This battery of measures has also dominated the U.S. literature on impairment in alcoholism. Miller and Saucedo (1983) identified 37 studies using the Halstead-Reitan battery to study cognitive deficits among alcoholics and 17 controlled comparisons of Wechsler intelligence performance of alcoholics versus normal subjects.

Our central discussion here will focus on the comparability of deficits observed in two samples of alcoholic patients, one tested in the the United States (Miller and Orr, 1980) and the other in Norway (Løberg, 1980a). In comparing our findings on the assessment battery outlined above, we will also consider the extent to which consistencies that emerge are likewise reflected in studies of alcoholics from other nations.

## DESCRIPTION OF COMPARISON SAMPLES

The larger of our two samples consisted of 111 Norwegian men diagnosed and being treated for alcoholism. Their mean age was 39.6 ± 10.6, and mean education was 11.0 ± 3.2 years. They had had an average of 1.4 prior inpatient alcoholism treatment experiences and on the average reported 11 years of excessive drinking. They were tested on the average at 25.8 ± 11.1 days after admission, or about 34 days after termination of drinking. Further details regarding this sample have been reported by Løberg (1980a).

Miller and Orr (1980) studied a smaller sample of 36 right-handed men with a primary diagnosis of alcoholism and undergoing inpatient treatment. These men were more selected than Løberg's sample, having been referred for special neuropsychological evaluation. Those with evidence of brain pathology (head injuries, specific lesions, and so forth) were eliminated from the study, as in Løberg's sample. Mean age was 46.6, and mean education was 12.1 years. These patients were tested at least 8 days after the completion of detoxification, and they had had 2.6 previous inpatient admissions on the average. Their mean duration of alcohol abuse was 12.7 years.

In both studies complete neuropsychological assessment data were obtained including the Halstead-Reitan battery, the Wechsler intelligence and memory scales, and the MMPI. This permitted a rather complete comparison of these two samples of alcoholics, and a consideration of the similarities between our findings and those reported in the international literature.

## COMPARATIVE FINDINGS

### WAIS Patterns

Subscale patterns of Norwegian and American alcoholics on the WAIS showed marked similarities. In both samples, substantially greater deficits were apparent on Performance IQ (PIQ) relative to Verbal IQ (VIQ). In the U.S. sample, alcoholics performed significantly more poorly than controls on all five Performance subscales and on PIQ, precisely the same pattern as in the Norwegian sample with the exception of a nonsignificant difference on Picture Completion. Verbal subscale differences proved more discrepant: In the Nowegian sample, alcoholics showed a relative deficit only on Digit Span and superior scores on both Information and Similarities; whereas in the American sample, control subjects outperformed alcoholics on Comprehension, Arithmetic, Similarities, and VIQ.

Mean subscale profiles of our two samples are shown in FIGURE 1. Verbal performance in both samples is relatively even across subscales, except for an unusually poor score on Digit Span in the Norwegian sample and an atypically high Vocabulary score in the U.S. sample. The pattern of Performance scales is more consistent, with Digit Symbol representing the lowest and Picture Completion the highest mean score.

To what extent is this pattern consistent with other reported WAIS profiles of alcoholics? One directly comparable investigation using the entire WAIS with a sample of U.S. alcoholics was reported by Smith and Smith (1977). These investigators found deficits among alcoholics relative to controls on both VIQ and PIQ and on all sub-

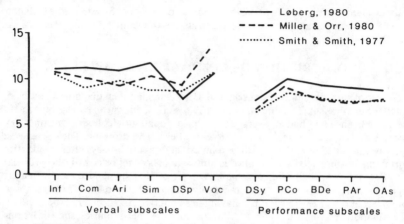

**FIGURE 1.** Wechsler Adult Intelligence Scale scores for alcoholic samples.

scales except Information and Vocabulary (the only two subscales also found to be without deficit in both of our own studies). In profile configuration, Digit Symbol was again the lowest scale score and Picture Completion the highest score on the Performance side of the WAIS. On the Verbal side, Vocabulary was highest, with Digit Span and Similarities tied for lowest. These data are also shown in FIGURE 1.

Three other studies reporting entire profile patterns of alcoholics relative to controls have used the Wechsler-Bellevue rather than the WAIS: Long and McLachlan's (1974) study of 22 Canadian alcoholics, the report of O'Leary *et al.* (1979b) on 38 U.S. alcoholics, and that of Plumeau *et al.* (1960) of 23 unremitted U.S. alcoholics of primarily Irish descent. As would be expected, mean scores on the Wechsler-Bellevue are higher than those from WAIS studies, but as shown in FIGURE 2 the profile configurations are similar. Digit Symbol is the low point in all three, and again Picture Comple-

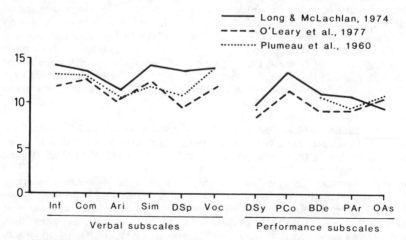

**FIGURE 2.** Wechsler-Bellevue Intelligence Scale scores for alcoholic samples.

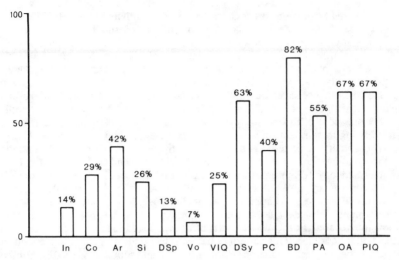

**FIGURE 3.** Percentage of investigations finding significant impairment among alcoholics relative to normal controls on scales of the Wechsler Intelligence tests.

tion is the highest Performance scale (except in Plumeau *et al.*, who did not report this scale). Verbal scales in general and the "hold" subscales in particular (Information and Vocabulary) show higher scores relative to Performance scales.

Still other studies have used certain portions of the WAIS or Wechsler-Bellevue to compare alcoholics with control subjects. In total we collated data from 15 U.S. studies (Blusewicz, 1975; Butter *et al.*, 1977; Fabian *et al.*, 1981; Fitzhugh *et al.*, 1960, 1965; Hewett and Martin, 1980; Miller and Orr, 1980; O'Leary *et al.*, 1977, 1979b; Plumeau *et al.*, 1960; Ryan and Butters, 1980; Schau and O'Leary, 1977; Silberstein and Parsons, 1980, 1981; Smith and Smith, 1977), two Canadian investigations (Long and McLachlan, 1974; Wilkinson and Carlen, 1980a), one Irish study (Clarke and Haughton, 1975) and Løberg's Norwegian investigation. Using all studies reporting data on each respective subscale, we calculated the percentage of investigations reporting impairment among alcoholics relative to controls. These percentages are shown in FIGURE 3.

Comparing this summary of published findings to date with the individual studies reported above (FIG. 3), we venture a few generalizations: (1) Performance IQ and subscales are more likely to be impaired in alcoholics relative to controls than are Verbal measures. (2) Although Digit Symbol is usually the lowest point in the profile, Block Design is most likely to be impaired relative to controls, followed by Object Assembly and Digit Symbol. (3) Of Performance scales, Picture Completion is least likely to be impaired. (4) Of Verbal scales, Arithmetic is most likely to be impaired relative to controls, followed by Comprehension and Similarities. (5) Information, Digit Span, and Vocabulary show comparatively little impairment, and Verbal measures in general are poor indicators of degree of neuropsychological deficit among alcoholics. Information and Vocabulary scores may, however, be useful in judging the degree of impairment relative to premorbid level of functioning.

Because these generalizations are based primarily on U.S. data, it is worthwhile to examine how existing studies from other nations deviate from these trends. Løberg's Norwegian sample is unique in its pattern of Verbal scores: Digit Span is impaired, a finding shared by only one other controlled study (Smith and Smith, 1977), and alcoholics showed superior scores relative to controls on Information and Similarities, a result unparalleled in U.S. studies, although several have found a complete absence of verbal impairment in alcoholics (Butter et al., 1977; Fitzhugh et al., 1960, 1965; Long and McLachlan, 1974; Ryan and Butters, 1980). This is not attributable to a lesser degree of overall impairment in the Norwegian sample, because Løberg's findings with regard to Performance scales are wholly consistent with U.S. studies: substantial overall impairment with the greatest deficit on Digit Symbol and least on Picture Completion. The only controlled Irish study (Clarke and Haughton, 1975) employed just four scales, finding impairment on Similarities, Block Design, and Object Assembly but not on Vocabulary — a pattern again consistent with data from U.S. studies. Both Canadian investigations (Long and McLachlan, 1974; Wilkinson and Carlen, 1980a) reported no impairment on VIQ but significant deficit on PIQ in alcoholics relative to controls.

This consistency of Wechsler profile configurations across national samples is noteworthy. Regardless of nationality, alcoholics appear to show consistent deficits on Performance subscales relative to control subjects and to their own scores on Information and Vocabulary, the two subscales often interpreted as indicative of premorbid intellectual functioning. This pattern of deficit is by no means unique to alcoholism. Greater deficits on Performance measures in general and suppression of Digit Symbol in particular are characteristic of global impairment from a wide variety of sources. Although sometimes interpreted as supporting a selective right hemisphere deficit in alcoholics, this pattern is consistent with global deterioration typical of toxic syndromes and dementias in general (Miller and Saucedo, 1983)

### Wechsler Memory Scale Patterns

FIGURE 4 compares Verbal, Performance, and Full-Scale intelligence quotients from the WAIS with Wechsler Memory Scale (WMS) quotients, as reported in four investigations of deficits in alcoholics (Butters and Cermak, 1980; Løberg, 1980a; Miller and Orr, 1980; Wilkinson and Carlen 1980a). Although the level of impairment again varies across studies, the pattern is one of normal and intact verbal intelligence with nonverbal intelligence impaired relative to verbal. Memory as assessed by the WMS appears to be mostly intact, with memory quotients more resembling VIQ than PIQ. It should be noted, however, that the WMS was "normed against" the Wechsler-Bellevue rather than the WAIS. An exception to the trend toward seeing no differences on the WMS is the Miller and Orr (1980) study, in which alcoholics were found to be significantly more impaired than psychiatric controls. In all of the studies reviewed, however, the degree of impairment in memory is moderate as compared with the specific and severe deficits found among patients with Korsakoff's Syndrome (Miller and Saucedo, 1983).

### Neuropsychological Patterns

FIGURE 5 presents neuropsychological findings from our two samples. Also presented are comparable data reported by Adams et al. (1980) for 23 diagnosed alcoholics with mean age of 36 and mean education of 12.9 years, tested 3 weeks after admission. This study was chosen as a third comparison sample because of the extensive data reported, including full neuropsychological batteries, psychometric intelligence quotients, and MMPI profiles. This latter investigation employed extensive exclusion criteria, eliminating all individuals showing any sign of brain damage or having ever taken

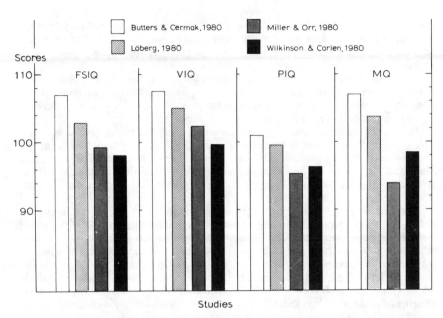

**FIGURE 4.** Illustration of WAIS Full-Scale, Verbal, and Performance intelligence scores and Wechsler Memory Scale quotients from U.S., Canadian, and Norwegian studies of alcoholics.

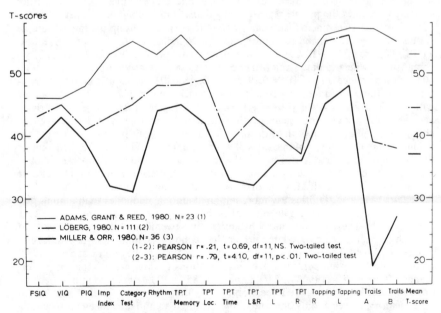

**FIGURE 5.** Comparison of three studies (from San Diego, California; Palo Alto, California; and Bergen, Norway). Samples of alcoholics were assessed with an extensive neuropsychological test battery.

a neuropsychological test as well as those being concurrently diagnosed or treated for any other psychiatric disorder or abuse of drugs other than alcohol. This study has been unique in the literature in its finding of comparatively little impairment among alcoholics, perhaps because its rigorous exclusion criteria may have ruled out in advance those patients showing alcohol-related impairment (Miller and Saucedo, 1983). The data in the study of Adams *et al.* are quite complete, however, and we have included them here, reasoning that even if these patients showed a less severe *level* of impairment, instructive similarities in *pattern* might be observed.

In order to make comparisons across studies, mean sample scores for each test were converted into $T$ scores from the $T$-score distribution of unpublished norms provided by the Neuropsychological Laboratory of the University of Wisconsin in Madison. This normative distribution was based on a total of 120 subjects without brain disorders. Test scores in each sample were converted to $T$ scores based on the closest age-group norms.

The superior performance level of the subjects reported by Adams *et al.* is evident in Figure 5, even compared with the normative level of performance ($T = 50$) of the Wisconsin sample. Overall the Adams sample performs better than nonalcoholic normal subjects. By contrast, both of our samples show poorer performance relative to norms, with somewhat greater impairment evident in the group reported by Miller and Orr (1980). It should be recalled that patients in Miller and Orr's study were selectively referred for neuropsychological evaluation, and although they were screened for other evidence of brain pathology these subjects were more likely to have been showing overt impairment as a referring concern. Løberg's sample occupies an intermediate position in degree of impairment.

Visual inspection of the composite profiles presented in Figure 5 suggests similarity of impairment pattern between our Norwegian and U.S. samples, although neither strongly resembles the profile reported by Adams *et al.* As a crude statistical index of similarity, $T$ scores across subscales were intercorrelated using the largest sample (Løberg) as a reference, and eliminating redundant indices (FSIQ, Impairment Index, TPT-L, TPT-R, TPT-L + R). A modestly high correlation was observed between Løberg's composite profile and data from Miller and Orr's sample, accounting for more than 60% of the variance [$r (n = 11) = 0.79, t = 4.10, p < 0.01$]. No significant intercorrelation of profiles was found, however, when comparing patterns in the Løberg sample with data from Adams *et al.* [$r (n = 11) = 0.21, t = 0.69$, NS]. The subjects of Adams *et al.* show remarkably good neuropsychological performance in spite of average psychometric intelligence. In both of the other samples, alcoholic patients show substantial impairment on a range of measures of adaptive abilities. With use of Reitan's cutoff scores to judge impaired performance, the following tests showed significant impairment in both of our samples: Categories Test, Tactual Performance Test (TPT) time and location scores, Trail Making forms A and B. In the Miller and Orr study, all of these tests were also significantly more impaired among alcoholics than among psychiatric controls. In both samples alcoholics showed normal performance on the TPT memory scale. These findings are substantially in agreement with the larger body of research on neuropsychological impairment in alcoholics. Summarizing 37 studies employing Halstead-Reitan measures to study alcoholics, Miller and Saucedo (1983) reported the following percentages of investigations finding mean impaired performance: Categories Test (96%), TPT total time (85%; 100% reported impairment on nondominant-hand time), TPT location (85%), Trails A (84%), Trails B (92%). On TPT memory, however, only one study (6%) reported an impaired mean score among alcoholics, a trend that is in agreement with our findings.

Mean test scores and $T$ scores for Halstead-Reitan measures are reported in TABLE 1 for these three investigations plus two Canadian and one Swedish study. Wilkinson and Carlen (1980b) described a sample of 68 chronic alcoholics, excluding amnestic patients with the Wernicke syndrome admitted to a Canadian inpatient alcoholism treatment facility. This sample was similar in age (47.0) and problem duration (10 years) to the Miller and Orr sample, and was tested between 2 and 4 weeks of abstinence. Another Canadian sample of similar age (44.6) but more education (13.9 years) and higher social status was described by Long and McLachlan (1974). Mean duration of heavy drinking was reported to be 8.9 years, and testing was conducted at an average of 11.4 days after admission. Finally a comparable Swedish sample has been studied by Bergman et al. (1980c).

$T$ scores in TABLE 1 were again computed in reference to the Wisconsin norms. Wilkinson and Carlen (1980b) found mostly normal psychometric intelligence but substantial impairment on Halstead-Reitan measures. Like Miller and Orr, they found exceptionally poor performance on the Trail Making Test in both forms A and B. Very similar findings are reported by Bergman et al. (1980c) for the Swedish sample: normal intelligence but impaired neuropsychological performance. An interesting exception is the Finger Oscillation (Tapping) test, where alcoholic subjects performed better than did Wisconsin normal subjects. Løberg reported similar findings for the Tapping test, representing an unusual finding in the larger literature, where 73% of studies have found impairment on dominant hand tapping and 86% on nondominant hand speed (Miller and Saucedo, 1983). Scandinavians (or at least Scandinavian alcoholics) appear to be top-rate tappers!

Long and McLachlan report data more similar to those of Adams, Grant, and Reed (1980). Their sample shows unusually high psychometric intelligence (>120), but by contrast surprisingly mediocre neuropsychological performance. Unlike the Adams and Grant group, Long and McLachlan reported significant impairment of alcoholics (compared to controls) on Category errors, TPT nondominant hand time and total time, tapping speed in both hands, Trails A and B, and overall impairment index.

Using Løberg's sample as a reference, we compared each of the other studies from TABLE 1 using two crude statistical indices: the mean $T$-score difference between profiles, and the Pearson product–moment correlation between $T$ scores of profiles. The results of these comparisons are reported in TABLE 2. As indicated earlier, the Miller and Orr (1980) and Wilkinson and Carlen (1980b) samples showed similar levels of impairment, somewhat more severe than those in Løberg's patients. Intercorrelations with the Løberg profile were 0.79 and 0.58, respectively. By contrast the Long and McLachlan (1974) and Adams et al. (1980) samples showed a relative absence of impairment and these profiles were statistically unrelated to Løberg's mean pattern ($-0.30$ and 0.21, respectively). This highest degree of agreement in both level and pattern was found with three Swedish samples ($r$ = 0.89, 0.89, and 0.96) reported by Bergman and colleagues (1980a, 1980b, 1980c).

The fact that studies have focused mainly on clinical groups of alcoholics raises the question of whether we have been measuring the effects of alcohol-related impairment or of more general dysfunctioning and malaise characteristic of individuals seeking treatment and perhaps suffering from problems and illnesses not typical of heavy drinkers outside treatment facilities. Bergman et al. (1980c) studied excessive drinkers drawn from the general population, Swedish men between the ages of 20 and 65 with a daily consumption of at least 40 g of ethanol and reporting loss of control but never treated for alcoholism. As indicated in TABLE 2, their test data strongly resembled the Løberg clinical sample in both level and pattern of impairment.

**TABLE 1.** Comparison of Comprehensive Neuropsychological Studies of Alcohol Dependence: Test Scores and $T$-Score Conversions

| | Loberg (1980) | | Miller & Orr (1980) | | Wilkinson & Carlen (1980b) | | Long & McLachlan (1974) | | Bergman (1980c) | | Adams et al., (1980) | |
|---|---|---|---|---|---|---|---|---|---|---|---|---|
| | Test Score | $T$ Score | Test Score | $T$ Score | Test Score | $T$ Score | Test Score | $T$ Score | Test Score | $T$ Score | Test Score | $T$ Score |
| Full-scale IQ | 102.9 | 43 | 99.3 | 39 | 98.1 | 38 | 125.1 | 63 | 102.4 (SRB-IQ) | | 107.4 | 46 |
| Verbal IQ | 105.0 | 45 | 102.4 | 43 | 99.7 | 41 | 125.9 | 60 | | | 107.1 | 46 |
| Performance IQ | 99.6 | 41 | 95.3 | 39 | 96.3 | 37 | 120.3 | 61 | | | 107.3 | 48 |
| Impairment index | .48 | 43 | .69 | 32 | | | | | .49 | 43 | .28 | 53 |
| Category test | 57.9 | 45 | 90.0 | 31 | 71.3 | 40 | 57.3 | 46 | 63.7 | 43 | 36.3 | 55 |
| TPT (right hand) | 8.8 | 37 | 9.0 | 31 | | | 6.9 | 46 | | | 6.0 | 51 |
| TPT (left hand) | 6.9 | 40 | 7.6 | 36 | | | 5.2 | 49 | | | 4.5 | 53 |
| TPT (both hands) | 4.1 | 45 | 6.3 | 32 | | | 3.1 | 51 | | | 2.3 | 56 |
| TPT total | 19.8 | 39 | 22.9 | 33 | 16.6 | 46 | 15.0 | 50 | 22.0 | 35 | 12.6 | 54 |
| TPT memory | 7.1 | 48 | 6.8 | 45 | 5.8 | 39 | 7.6 | 51 | 6.4 | 43 | 8.4 | 56 |
| TPT location | 4.0 | 49 | 2.4 | 42 | 1.8 | 39 | 4.2 | 50 | 4.0 | 49 | 4.6 | 52 |
| Finger Tap (right) | 48.6 | 55 | 38.1 | 45 | | | 38.3 | 45 | 52.6 | 58 | 50.9 | 56 |
| Finger Tap (left) | 45.0 | 56 | 36.7 | 48 | | | 35.0 | 46 | | | 46.0 | 57 |
| Trails A | 42.5 | 39 | 61.3 | 19 | 59.9 | 20 | 39.0 | 43 | | | 26.6 | 57 |
| Trails B | 117.1 | 38 | 150.0 | 27 | 176.7 | 19 | 74.0 | 52 | | | 63.3 | 55 |
| Rhythm | 24.8 | 48 | 23.6 | 44 | 24.0 | 45 | 26.0 | 52 | 24.2 | 46 | 26.3 | 53 |

**TABLE 2.** Comparisons of Outcome in Comprehensive Neuropsychological Studies of Alcohol Dependence with the Results from Løberg's Sample ($n = 111$): Mean T-Score Differences, Pearson Correlation Coefficients, Two-Tailed Test of Significance

|  | Miller & Orr (1980) | Wilkinson & Carlen (1980b) | Long & McLachlan (1974) | Bergman et al. (1980a) | Bergman et al. (1980b) | Bergman et al. (1980c) | Adams et al. (1980) |
|---|---|---|---|---|---|---|---|
| Mean T-score difference | 8.33 | 7.33 | −4.92 | −2.17 | 1.33 | 1.67 | −8.09 |
| Pearson r | 0.79 | 0.58 | −0.30 | 0.89 | 0.89 | 0.96 | 0.21 |
| t | 4.10 | 1.90 | .98 | 4.12 | 4.03 | 7.74 | 0.69 |
| df | 11 | 8 | 11 | 5 | 5 | 5 | 11 |
| p < | 0.01 | NS | NS | 0.01 | 0.01 | 0.001 | NS |

## MMPI Profiles

The MMPI was administered in both of our studies, permitting evaluation of similarities in personality characteristics. Data from our two samples and from the original Grant *et al.* (1979) sample are reported in FIGURE 6. Profile configuration similarity is apparent, particularly between the Løberg and Grant samples. This pattern is also similar to other group profiles found in alcoholics as reported by Hoffman (1976). Greater overall pathology is evident in the Miller and Orr sample, and is especially marked on Pt, Sc, and Ma scales — again perhaps contributing to the reasons for referral in this study. The Miller and Orr patients had also received more prior treatment than

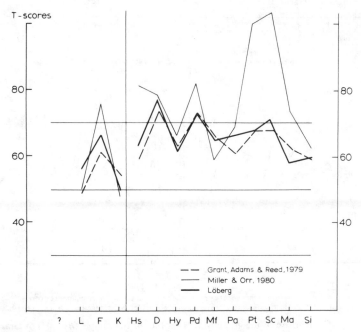

**FIGURE 6.** MMPI comparisons of alcoholic samples from San Diego, California; Palo Alto, California; and Bergen, Norway.

the other two groups, suggesting the possibility of greater severity of alcoholism. Bean and Karasievich (1975) have observed that the stage of inpatient alcoholism treatment is related to differences in personality functioning.

Mean profile configuration does not tell the whole story. It is rather clear that the search for a single dominant "alcoholic personality" has failed to yield very fruitful results (Miller, 1976), but there may be meaningful subtypes embedded within the general diagnosis of alcoholism and the search for such empirical clusters has intensified in recent years (Morey and Blashfield, 1981).

In prior research Løberg (1981, 1986) has compared MMPI protocols from his Norwegian sample with those from Veterans Administration hospital alcoholism treatment programs in Seattle, Washington (Donovan *et al.*, 1978) and Temple, Texas (Bean and Karasievich, 1975). Four meaningful subtypes were identified by cluster analysis in all three of these samples, and cluster configurations across the samples showed striking similarities. Correlations of cluster loadings between the Norwegian and Seattle samples for the first four clusters were found to be 0.87, 0.77, 0.91, and 0.94 (all *p*

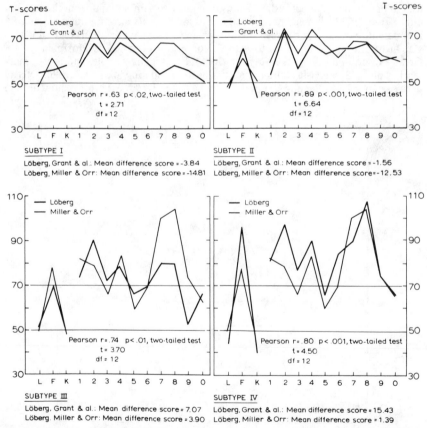

**FIGURE 7.** Comparison of the group MMPI profile for the sample (*n* = 43) of Grant *et al.* (1979) and the group MMPI profile for the sample (*n* = 21) of Miller and Orr (1980) with the most similar subtypes from Løberg's (1981) sample (*n* = 109).

< 0.005). Correlations with the Temple sample were also high: 0.76, 0.64, 0.88, and 0.85. This correspondence of profiles suggests the possibility of highly similar personality subtypes among alcoholics in different countries when admission criteria, demographic characteristics, and stage of treatment are comparable.

Because not all subjects provided complete MMPI protocols in the comparison studies ($n = 21$ in Miller and Orr and 43 in Grant et al.), the total sample size prevented meaningful cluster analysis for comparison with Løberg's data. The mean profiles for these studies did, however, resemble certain of Løberg's cross-culturally validated subtypes. In FIGURE 7 it can be seen that the Grant et al. profile showed closest resemblance to the least deviant subtypes (Subtype I: $r = 0.63$, $t = 2.71$, $p < 0.02$; Subtype II: $r = 0.89$, $t = 6.64$, $p < 0.001$). The Miller and Orr profile, on the other hand, was most similar to Subtypes III ($r = 0.74$, $t = 3.7$, $p < 0.01$) and IV ($r = 0.80$, $t = 4.5$, $p < 0.001$). This is consistent with Løberg's earlier report of increasing neuropsychological impairment from Subtypes I and II through III and IV, because the patients of Grant et al. and Miller and Orr are clearly differentiated in degree of cognitive deficit.

### The Broader Cross-National Data Base

Thus far we have compared findings of studies that have reported more extensive assessment of clinical samples of alcoholics, encompassing cognitive, personality, and neuropsychological tests. We have pointed to similarities on all three of these dimensions across national samples, and have indicated that these trends are generally consistent with the larger literature based mostly on U.S. studies (Miller and Saucedo, 1983).

There are many more reports employing smaller and selected sets of measures in a variety of national settings. In our reading of these studies we have found very little to contradict the patterns of alcoholic impairment identified here. One general finding is that a high percentage of individuals being treated for alcoholism — often about two-thirds — show significant deficits on cognitive and neuropsychological measures. This has been reported not only in North American studies (Miller and Saucedo, 1983), but also in Sweden (Carlsson et al., 1973; Claeson and Carlsson, 1970), Denmark (Lee et al., 1979) Germany (Köhler, 1974), Ireland (Draper et al., 1978), Italy (Miglioli et al., 1979), and Australia (Cala et al., 1978).

There is also reasonable cross-national agreement that alcoholics show marked improvement on certain neuropsychological dimensions over the early weeks of recovery, although some abilities remain impaired even at long periods of follow-up. This has been reported in studies conducted in the Netherlands (Boeke, 1970), Ireland (Clarke and Haughton, 1975), Sweden (Berglund and Risberg, 1980; Jonsson et al., 1962), Scotland (Fleming and Guthrie, 1980; Guthrie, 1980), Canada (Carlen, et al., 1978); Long & McLachlan, 1974; Sanchez-Craig, 1980), and the United States (Miller and Saucedo, 1983).

It is also rather universal to report relatively normal verbal intelligence as contrasted with poorer scores on nonverbal/performance measures such as Object Assembly, Block Design, Digit Symbol, Trail Making, and TPT. This trend has been reported in Sweden (Bergman and Ågren, 1974; Claeson and Carlsson, 1970), Germany (Köhler, 1974), Ireland (Clarke and Haughton, 1975), and Australia (Cala et al., 1978) as well as in the American and Norwegian research reviewed earlier. Other studies, which include investigations in Italy (Miglioli et al., 1979), England (Ron et al., 1979), and the U. S. (Miller and Saucedo, 1983), have found deficits on both verbal and nonverbal dimensions.

If such deficits indeed result from excessive alcohol consumption, then one would expect to find a consistent relationship across national samples between severity of impairment and quantitative indices of alcohol consumption. Studies in Australia (Cala et al., 1978), Canada (Long and McLachlan, 1974), Scotland (Guthrie & Elliot, 1980), Norway (Løberg, 1980a), and Germany (Götze et al., 1978) as well as numerous U.S. Studies (Miller & Saucedo, 1983) have reported relationships between duration of alcoholism and severity of impairment on a wide range of measures, although this finding is by no means universal and other studies have failed to find such a relationship (Bergman and Ågren, 1974; Wilkinson and Carlen, 1980a). Other research has pointed to severity of alcoholism, regardless of duration, as a predictor of neuropsychological deficits (Fleming and Guthrie, 1980; Guthrie, 1980; Korboot et al., 1977).

## SUMMARY AND DISCUSSION

We set out to determine the extent to which patterns of impairment following excessive drinking are consistent across national samples. Although our two comparison samples differed in overall level of impairment as well as in demography and selection criteria, we observed consistencies in the patterning of deficits. The following appeared to be characteristic of the WAIS profiles in both samples:

1. Greater impairment on Performance than Verbal subscales;
2. Relatively normal Verbal intelligence;
3. Digit Symbol as a profile low point;
4. Impairment on Block Design, Object Assembly, and Picture Arrangement;
5. Picture Completion least impaired of the Performance scales;
6. Digit Span low relative to the "hold" scales (Vocabulary and Information).

A comparison of these data with seventeen other control investigations of WAIS performance in alcoholics (FIG. 3) confirmed all of these assertions, except that impairment on Digit Span relative to controls is rather infrequent (13% of studies), whereas Arithmetic is more often found to be impaired among the Verbal subscales (42% of studies). Relative to controls, the subscale most likely to show deficit in alcoholics is Block Design, followed by Object Assembly and Digit Symbol.

Normal performance is often observed on Memory Quotient of the Wechsler Memory Scale, suggesting that this scale as well as Verbal IQ measures may be relatively poor indicators of the extent of cognitive impairment in alcoholics.

Our Norwegian and American samples also showed good convergence on scales of the Halstead-Reitan battery. In both samples the following were observed:

1. Impairment of abstract learning on the Categories Test;
2. Spatial learning and memory impairment on the TPT, with normal recall for shapes but impaired recall for their location;
3. Impaired psychomotor speed on Trails A and B.

All of these findings are corroborated in the larger neuropsychological literature, crossing national boundaries. Out most discrepant finding was on the Finger Oscillation (Tapping) test on which Norwegian alcoholics performed significantly better than Wisconsin normals, whereas our U.S. alcoholic sample showed significant impairment in both hands. Likewise Seashore Rhythm performance was impaired in the U.S. but not in the Norwegian sample of alcoholics. These scales may be less consistent indicators of alcoholic impairment cross-culturally, or may at least require reference to specific national norms.

A very interesting consistency has emerged from cluster analysis of large samples of MMPI protocols of alcoholics in Norway and the U.S. The first four clusters resulting from such analyses have shown strong similarities in samples from Washington, Texas, and Norway. Comparison of two other mean profiles with these types revealed marked resemblance. It appears that although the total composite profile for a diverse sample of alcoholics may be relatively uninformative, the examination of subclusters may be fruitful. There seems to be no single "alcoholic personality," but there may be meaningful subtypes or "personalities" within the general diagnostic domain of alcoholism, and these may retain consistency across national samples.

It is clear that some samples of alcoholics appear to show surprisingly little impairment. Data from the Adams and Grant group are a case in point, representing a reasonably flat and normal neuropsychological profile. It is interesting that both these data and the protocols of the Miller and Orr study were obtained from patients of Veterans Administration hospitals in California, yet are so discrepant in degree of impairment shown. Indeed the Miller and Orr data bear much greater resemblance to those of Norwegian alcoholics than to the Adams data obtained from a similar hospital in the same state (see FIGURE 5 and TABLE 1). Differences can be greater within the same nation or state than those observed across national boundaries.

### Factors Contributing to Diversity

This suggests that diversity in level of impairment among alcoholic samples may be generated more by selection factors than by national or cultural differences per se. Examination of the study at greatest variance with the overall literature (Grant et al., 1979) reveals unusually stringent exclusion criteria that may account for the atypical absence of impairment in this sample. This data set is further unique in failing to correspond to other studies not only in level but in pattern of impairment. Data from two other studies in which fewer significant deficits were observed (Long and McLachlan, 1974; Smith et al., 1973) nevertheless conform to the same relative patterning of subscale performance observed in other studies (Miller and Saucedo, 1983). The interesting point made by the Grant study, then, is not that alcoholics are unimpaired, but rather that with sufficiently stringent screening it is possible to identify a group of individuals who do indeed show little or no neuropsychological impairment in spite of the fact that they meet diagnostic criteria for alcoholism and show other kinds of impairment. Why and how do such individuals seem to escape the deficits apparent in most alcoholics? One possible explanation is that these individuals may have started from a higher level of performance and *are* impaired relative to their own premorbid level of functioning, although not in relation to general norms. This would appear to be the case in the Long and McLachlan (1974) sample, where psychometric intelligence (>120) and the hold subscales are high relative to the mediocre performance on Halstead-Reitan tests. But in the Grant study this is not true, for current functioning and indicated premorbid level of adaptive abilities are quite equivalent. We are left with the conclusion that it is possible to identify a relatively unimpaired (neuropsychologically) sample of alcoholics who otherwise meet diagnostic criteria. This should be of little surprise, because although many studies (as reviewed earlier) have found a high percentage of brain impairment among chronic alcoholic populations, most studies also report a substantial percentage (often about one-third) who show no apparent deficits. This is a group that deserves further study.

When impairment *is* present in an alcoholic sample, however, it seems to follow a rather predictable pattern regardless of nationality. To be sure there are individual difference factors that influence the level and pattern of deficits. These include the duration of abstinence prior to testing, the duration of alcoholism, preexisting neurochemical differences, pattern of drinking, beverages of choice, age, gender, education, severity of consequences and dependence, and ethnicity. Each of these is a potential contributor to variance in impairment. Given such diversity of individual differences, the cross-national consistency of deficit patterning is still more striking.

The presence of these confounding factors makes it extremely difficult if not impossible to study "pure" differences among national or ethnic groups. Various investigators (English and Curtin, 1975 and Pattison *et al.*, 1979, 1969) have provided evidence that alcohol treatment programs even within the same geographic area can have different admission criteria and thus attract different types of patients. Page and Bozlee (1982) found very similar MMPI profiles, conforming to previously published alcoholic MMPI prototypes, when Caucasian, Hispanic-American, and American Indian alcoholics were compared. All were veterans in treatment at the same V.A. Medical Center, represented similar secondary diagnoses, and were of similar age and education. The authors argued that situational and demographic variables have contaminated some prior studies ostensibly investigating racial or cultural differences, and pointed to the importance of controlling for educational, socioeconomic, and age-related differences.

Reviewers who attempt to do this *post hoc* encounter considerable frustration in comparing neuropsychological studies of alcoholism either within or across national boundaries. Even when identical testing procedures have been employed, differences in the reporting of patient characteristics abound. Age, if reported at all, may be expressed as a range in one study, a median in another, or as a mean with or without an index of dispersion. Time elapsed since admission (let alone since the onset of abstinence) is often poorly specified as a range (e.g., Miller and Orr, 1980) or as a median or mean number of days "after detoxification" or admission, rendering direct comparison very difficult in a field where one week of abstinence can make a meaningful difference in degree of impairment (Miller and Saucedo, 1983). Drinking practices of patients are often unstated, span various periods prior to treatment ranging from one week to a lifetime, and vary greatly in the reliability and validity of measures employed. Years of education is a variable often reported, but it is less than clear how comparable these years of education may be across state and national boundaries. Sex of patients is sometimes omitted or loosely indicated in spite of findings of clear differences in neuropsychological performance between men and women with lateralized brain lesions (Inglis and Lawson, 1981) and the indication of sex differences in cognitive impairment among alcoholics (Silberstein and Parsons, 1981).

Another major interpretive problem hindering comparison of studies is the vast diversity in diagnostic criteria for alcoholism. Defining characteristics have included quantity/frequency of drinking, negative consequences of alcohol consumption, "loss of control," alcohol-dependence symptoms, or an unspecified procedure leading to a diagnostic label of alcoholism. It is increasingly clear that alcoholism is not a single entity and that concepts and criteria for alcohol problems vary widely within and across nations (Miller, this volume). The simple designation that patients were "diagnosed alcoholics" is no longer adequate for sample specification, for it leaves the reader at the mercy of an unreplicable diagnostic procedure that, although clinically convenient, is of questionable scientific validity.

### Recommendations to Improve Comparability of Studies

Having completed this review of cross-national research on impairment among alcoholics, we offer the following as recommendations for future studies reporting on alcohol-related deficits on cognitive, neuropsychological, and personality dimensions.

1. Demographic data including age and years of education should be reported separately for each subsample studied, including mean, standard deviation, and range. Where subsamples are being compared, analysis of the comparability of groups on these variables is desirable (e.g., multivariate analysis of variance) and covariance analysis of dependent measures is recommended.

2. Ethnicity should be specified carefully, including procedures used to classify. Where sample size permits, comparison of performance of ethnic subgroups is desirable, but in such cases the role of confounding variables should be addressed (e.g., age, education, socioeconomic status).

3. The percentage of males and females studied should be specified. Inclusion of both men and women in study samples is desirable, given that most past research has focused exclusively on males and too few data are available on women and on sex differences. Where sample size permits, sex differences should be analyzed, again with awareness of potential confounding variables.

4. A full and detailed description of all selection procedures should be given. How did individuals qualify for the study? How did participants differ from the total population from which they were drawn? In cases where the sample consists of patients referred for testing, the reasons and criteria for referral should be discussed as a selection factor.

5. Clear specification of the nature and extent of alcohol problems should be given. A statement that alcoholism was diagnosed is insufficient without specification of the minimum criteria for diagnosis that were met by all individuals. Even where diagnostic criteria are specified, it is essential that the investigators provide further data regarding the nature and extent of alcohol involvement because diagnostic criteria provide only the minimal qualifying conditions and fail to specify central tendency, dispersion, and range of crucial dimensions of deterioration. The following are recommended as variables to be carefully assessed and reported:

*5A. Drinking history.* Quantity/frequency indices of past drinking (e.g., Cahalan, 1970) have been used in cross-national comparisons (Løberg, 1986). More detailed interview procedures for quantifying alcohol consumption have been described by Marlatt and Miller (1984). A still more heroic procedure attempts to tally the individual's full lifetime consumption of alcohol (Skinner, 1977), a variable of some promise in predicting neuropsychological impairment. An index of peak blood alcohol concentration reached during typical drinking episodes is also of value because the massing of drinks may be of more importance than the actual number of drinks consumed. This can be addressed by estimation procedures based on interview or questionnaire data (Marlatt and Miller, 1984; Matthews and Miller, 1979) or by multivariate analysis of both quantity and frequency data.

*5B. Negative consequences.* A meaningful measure of severity of alcohol problems is a cumulative measure of life problems encountered in relation to drinking. Several widely used instruments exist for this purpose (e.g., Selzer, 1971; Wanberg *et al.*, 1977), although the more common "laundry lists" of diagnostic questions typically confound negative consequences of overdrinking with symptoms of dependence. Miller and Marlatt (1984) have described an interview procedure for quantifying consumption and separating life problems from dependence symptoms.

*5C. Dependence symptoms.* Severity of dependence is increasingly recognized as an important index of deterioration in alcoholics. Past diagnostic criteria have confounded dependence with loss of control symptoms, with tolerance for ethanol, and with negative consequences of overdrinking. Scales for the direct assessment of dependence syndrome have been described by Skinner and Allen (1982), Stockwell *et al.* (1979), and Marlatt and Miller (1984).

*5D.  Duration of problems.*  Duration of alcohol-related problems is a measure of obvious interest in studying degree of neurophyschological impairment. Without specification of how this was measured and how "problems" were defined, however, the index is of little use. One useful procedure is to trace the first occurrence of negative consequences from drinking (5B). Another is to trace duration from the first occurrence of specific dependence symptoms (5C). Still another, albeit less reliable, procedure is to have the client specify the first occurrence of negative effects from drinking. In any event, the procedure used to identify duration should be specified clearly so that it could be replicated. Multiple measures of duration can also be used, permitting comparison of their predictive validity.

*5E.  Prior treatment.*  Still another index of severity is the amount of prior treatment received for alcoholism. The most common index is the number of previous inpatient admissions, but much additional treatment may have been received prior to the first admission. The number of different treatment contacts can be a useful index. Again the procedure used to specify prior treatment should be described.

*5F.  Collateral verification.*  In working with alcoholic patients it is desirable to verify the above data by contact with reliable collateral sources. These can include significant others (friends and relatives) as well as official records (such as hospital, or legal records). Procedures for reconciling self-report and collateral information vary, but generally it is prudent to accept the more pessimistic report as the more accurate. When multivariate analyses are employed, both self-report and collateral information can be entered for simultaneous analysis.

6. Duration of abstinence prior to testing is a crucial variable to report in neuropsychological research. There is clear improvement on several measures of impairment during the early days and weeks of abstinence. Thus the duration of pretesting abstinence is a critical variable both for cross-sample comparisons and for within-sample analysis of individual differences. Time since admission is inadequate for this purpose because patients enter treatment after varying lengths of abstinence.

7. Any additional terms used to characterize the sample should be carefully defined in a manner that allows replication. Examples from past literature include duration of "heavy drinking" and diagnosis of "loss of control."

8. Choice of dependent measures should be guided in part by their cross-cultural applicability and prior use. The measures described in this chapter (Wechsler, MMPI, and Halstead-Reitan) have been widely translated and applied in numerous nations.

9. Absolute as well as relative impairment data are desirable. Comparison with a control group is informative and provides one kind of information about level of impairment. Various studies have failed, however, to provide mean and dispersion data so that absolute impairment can be judged relative to appropriate norms or controls. This is vital in that *both* experimental and control groups in a given study may be impaired, a possibility that has sometimes been overlooked in past research (e.g., Templer *et al.*, 1975). Other investigators (e.g., Parker and Noble, 1977; Parker *et al.*, 1980) have employed correlational data to impute impairment among social drinkers without providing mean and dispersion data by which the absolute level of such impairment could be judged.

10. An adequate range of tests should be used if clinical inference of neuropsychological impairment (or its absence) is desired. Reliance upon a single index (e.g., Templer *et al.*, 1975) is inadequate. A reasonable range of adaptive abilities should be sampled. In the case of alcohol-specific deficits, prior research can be used as a guide in selecting a battery of measures mostly likely to reflect degree of impairment (Miller and Saucedo, 1983).

## Future Directions

Finally we would point to a few interesting directions for future research in this area. Some have already been mentioned: the exploration of sex and ethnic differences, a better understanding of differences in degree of impairment given apparently similar drinking histories and diagnostic pictures.

One challenge for the future is the development of early identification procedures. Neuropsychological impairment may be the first significant consequence of overdrinking, often appearing long before liver damage or even the development of life problems (Miller and Saucedo, 1983). This suggests that a simple but valid neuropsychological screening procedure would be of considerable value in evaluting high-risk groups without clear overt evidence of other alcohol problems (e.g., heavy "nonproblem" drinkers) or those with only minimal apparent problems (e.g., many drunk driving offenders). The assessment of developing neuropsychological impairment may also be a valuable aid in stimulating motivation for change (Miller, 1983).

Repeated testing of neuropsychological functioning in alcoholics is still in its early stages. It is clear that some deficits are reversed with extended abstinence, but others appear to be more stable. Future research could clarify the patterns of impairment that persist, and develop predictors of such long-term impairment. Another unresolved question is the extent to which improvement observed with abstinence also occurs (or fails to occur) when controlled drinking outcomes are maintained. Past research has tended to compare abstainers with *all* individuals who have continued to drink, with the predictable result that continuing drinkers show greater impairment (e.g., McLachlan and Levenson, 1974). Eckardt et al. (1980) found that "moderate drinking" defined in terms of frequency (drinking 1–6 times per week regardless of amount!) predicted greater impairment than was observed in abstainers, but that moderation defined by amount (up to 6 drinks per day regardless of frequency) was not associated with greater impairment than that observed in abstinence. Both definitions of "moderation" could be seen as excessively liberal.

Relatedly, it would be of value for public health reasons to know the minimum levels and patterns of alcohol consumption likely to result in significant or cumulative cognitive impairment. The research of Parker's group (Parker and Noble, 1977; Parker et al., 1980) has made a good start in this direction, but more data are needed to answer this vital question.

Another area of interest is the relationship between neuropsychological status and treatment outcome. Commonly observed deficits in abstraction among alcoholics may account in part for the rather universal observation that insight-based therapies show a poor rate of success (Miller and Hester, 1980). The extent and reversibility of cognitive deficits may be crucial variables to consider in selecting and implementing treatment (Miller and Saucedo, 1983; O'Leary and Donovan, 1979; O'Leary et al., 1979a).

Finally, careful neuropsychological assessment may contribute to a better diagnostic understanding of alcoholism. American thinking about alcoholism over the past few decades has tended to focus on a unitary disease conception that encompasses only a minority of problem drinkers (Miller, this volume). The major dimensions of deterioration observed following excessive drinking — life problems, biomedical sequelae, tolerance, dependence, neuropsychological deficits, personality and psychological problems — seem to proceed with surprising independence of one another. Are some individuals predisposed to rapid deterioration of cognitive functions with drinking or to the accelerated occurrence of addiction or liver disease? How is the development of tolerance or dependence symptoms related to deterioration on other dimensions?

Current data (e.g., Wanberg *et al.*, 1977) point to wide variation in patterns of impairment resulting from alcohol abuse rather than the final common pathway of a single and unitary disease. A better understanding of the "alcoholisms" (Jacobson, 1976) may be achieved by a truly multivariate assessment of these broad domains of deterioration across national boundaries.

## REFERENCES

ADAMS, K. M., I. GRANT & R. REED. 1980. Neuropsychology in alcoholic men in their late thirties: One-year follow-up. Am. J. Psychiatry 137: 928–931.

BEAN, K. L. & G. O. KARASIEVICH 1975. Psychological test results at three stages of inpatient alcoholism treatment. J. Stud. Alcohol 36: 838–852.

BERGLUND, M. & J. RISBERG. 1980. Reversibility in alcohol dementia. *In* Biological Effects of Alcohol. H. Begleiter, Ed. Plenum. New York, NY.

BERGMAN, H., S. BORG, T. HINDMARSH, C.-M. IDESTRÖM & S. MÜTZELL. 1980a. Computed tomography of the brain and neuropsychological assessment of alcoholic patients. *In* Biological Effects of Alcohol. H. Begleiter, Ed. Plenum. New York, NY.

BERGMAN, H., S. BORG, T. HINDMARSH, C.-M. IDESTRÖM & S. MÜTZELL. 1980b. Computed tomography of the brain and neuropsychological assessment of male alcoholic patients and a random sample from the general population. Acta Psychiat. Scand. 62: 77–88 (Suppl. 286).

BERGMAN, H., S. BORG, T. HINDMARSH, C.-M. IDESTRÖM & S. MÜTZELL. 1980c. Computed tomography of the brain, clinical examination and neuropsychological assessment of a random sample of men from the general population. Acta Psychiat. Scand. 62: 47–56 (Suppl. 286).

BERGMAN, H. & G. ÅGREN. 1974. Cognitive style and intellectual performance in relation to the progress of alcoholism. Quart. J. Stud. Alcohol 35: 1242–1255.

BLUSEWICZ, M.J. 1975. Neuropsychological Correlates of Chronic Alcoholism and Aging. Unpublished doctoral dissertation, Pennsylvania State University.

BOEKE, P.E. 1970. Some remarks about alcohol-dementia in clinically-treated alcoholics. Br. J. Addiction 65: 173–180.

BUTTERS, N. & L. S. CERMAK. 1980. Alcoholic Korsakoff's Syndrome: An Information Processing Approach to Amnesia. Academic Press. New York, NY.

BUTTERS, N., L. S. CERMAK, K. MONTGOMERY & A. ADINOLFI. 1977. Some comparisons of visuoperceptive deficits of chronic alcoholics and patients with Korsakoff's disease. Alcoholism Clin. Exp. Res. 1: 73–80.

CAHALAN, D. 1970. Problem Drinkers: A National Survey. Jossey-Bass. San Francisco, CA.

CALA, L. A., B. JONES, F. L. MASTAGLIA & B. WILEY. 1978. Brain atrophy and intellectual impairment in heavy drinkers: A clinical, psychometric and computerized tomography study. Aust. New Zealand J. Med. 8: 147–153.

CARLEN, P. L., G. WORTZMAN, R. C. HOLGATE, D. A. WILKINSON & J. G. RANKIN. 1978. Reversible cerebral atrophy in recently abstinent chronic alcoholics measured by computerized tomography scans. Science 200: 1076–1078.

CARLSSON, C., L. E. CLAESON & L. PETTERSON. 1973. Psychometric signs of cerebral dysfunction in alcoholics. Br. J. Addiction 68: 83–86.

CLAESON, L. E. & C. CARLSSON. 1970. Cerebral dysfunction in alcoholics: A psychometric investigation. Q. J. Stud. Alcohol 31: 317–323.

CLARKE, J. & H. HAUGHTON. 1975. A study of intellectual impairment and recovery rates in heavy drinkers in Ireland. Br. J. Psychiatry 126: 178–184.

DONOVAN, D. M., E. F. CHANEY & M. R. O'LEARY. 1978. Alcoholic MMPI subtypes: Relationships to drinking styles, benefits and consequences. J. Nerv. Mental Dis. 166: 533–561.

DRAPER, R. J., B. FELDMAN & H. HAUGHTON. 1978. Undetected brain damage in Irish alcoholics. Irish Med. J. 71: 353–355.

ECKARDT, M. J., E. S. PARKER, C. P. PAUTLER, E. P. NOBLE & L. A. GOTTSCHALK. 1980. Neuropsychological consequences of post-treatment drinking behavior in male alcoholic men in their mid-thirties. Psychiatry Res. 2: 135–147.

ENGLISH, G. E. & M. E. CURTIN. 1975. Personality differences in patients at three alcoholism treatment agencies. J. Stud. Alcohol 36: 52–61.

FABIAN, M. S., R. L. JENKINS & O. A. PARSONS. 1981. Gender, alcoholism, and neuropsychological functioning. J. Consult. Clin. Psychol. 49: 138–140.

FITZHUGH, L. C., K. B. FITZHUGH & R. M. REITAN. 1960. Adaptive abilities and intellectual functioning of hospitalized alcoholics. Q. J. Stud. Alcohol 21: 414–423.

FITZHUGH, L. C., K. B. FITZHUGH & R. M. REITAN. 1965. Adaptive abilities and intellectual functioning of hospitalized alcoholics: Further considerations. Q. J. Stud. Alcohol 26: 402–411.

FLEMING, A. M. M. & A. GUTHRIE. 1980. The electroencephalogram, psychological testing, and other investigations in abstinent alcoholics: A longitudinal study. In Biological Effects of Alcohol. H. Begleiter, Ed. Plenum. New York, NY.

GÖTZE, P., D. HÜHNE, J. HANSEN & H. P. KNIPP. 1978. Hirnatrophische Veränderungen bei chronischem Alkoholismus: Eine klinische und computertomographische Studie. Arch. Psychiat. Nervenkr. 226: 137–156.

GRANT, I., K. ADAMS & R. REED. 1979. Normal neuropsychological abilities of alcoholic men in their late thirties. Am. J. Psychiatry 136: 1263–1269.

GREIZERSTEIN, H. 1981. Congener contents in alcoholic beverages. J. Stud. Alcohol 42: 1030–1037.

GUTHRIE, A. 1980. The first year after treatment: Factors affecting time course of reversibility of memory and learning deficits in alcoholism. In Biological Effects of Alcohol. H. Begleiter, Ed. Plenum. New York, NY.

GUTHRIE, A. & W. A. ELLIOTT. 1980. The nature and reversibility of cerebral impairment in alcoholism: Treatment implications. J. Stud. Alcohol 47: 147–155.

HEWETT, B. B. & W. R. MARTIN. 1980. Psychometric comparisons of sociopathic and psychopathological behaviors of alcoholics and drug abusers versus a low drug use control population. Int. J. Addictions 15: 77–105.

HOFFMAN, H. 1976. Personality measurement for the evaluation and prediction of alcoholism. In Alcoholism: Interdisciplinary Approaches to an Enduring Problem. R. E. Tarter and A. A. Sugarman, Eds. Addison-Wesley. Reading, MA.

INGLIS, J. & J. S. LAWSON. 1981. Sex differences in the effect of unilateral brain damage on intelligence. Science 212: 693–695.

JACOBSON, G. R. 1976. The Alcoholisms: Detection, Diagnosis and Assessment. Human Sciences Press. New York, NY.

JONSSON, C.-O., B. CRONHOLM & S. IZIKOWITZ. 1962. Intellectual changes in alcoholics. Q. J. Stud. Alcohol 23: 221–242.

KLØVE, H. 1974. Validation studies in adult clinical neuropsychology. In Clinical Neuropsychology: Current Status and Applications. R. M. Reitan and L. A. Davison, Eds. Wiley. New York, NY.

KORBOOT, P. J., G. F. K. NAYLOR & A. SOARES. 1977. Patterns of cognitive impairment in alcoholics. Aus. J. Psychol. 29: 25–30.

KÖHLER, W. 1974. Kriterien verstandesmässigen Leistungsverlust chronisch Alkoholkranker in HAWIE. Z. Exp. Angew. Psychol. 21: 103–114.

LEE, K., L. MØLLER, F. HARDT, A. HAUBEK & E. JENSEN. 1979. Alcohol-induced brain damage in young males. Lancet 2: 759–761.

LONG, J. A. & J. F. C. MCLACHLAN. 1974. Abstract reasoning and perceptual-motor efficiency in alcoholics: Impairment and reversibility. Q. J. Stud. Alcohol 35: 1220–1229.

LØBERG, T. 1980a. Alcohol misuse and neuropsychological deficits in men. J. Stud. Alcohol 41: 119–128.

LØBERG, T. 1980b. Neuropsychological deficits in alcoholics: Lack of personality (MMPI) correlates. In Biological Effects of Alcohol. H. Begleiter, Ed. Plenum. New York, NY.

LØBERG, T. 1981. MMPI-based personality subtypes of alcoholics: Relationships to drinking history, psychometrics and neuropsychological deficits. J. Stud. Alcohol 42: 766–782.

LØBERG, T. 1986. Neuropsychologic findings in the early and middle phases of alcoholism. In Neuropsychological Assessment of Neuropsychiatric Disorders: Clinical Methods and Empirical Findings. I. Grant and K. M. Adams, Eds. Oxford University Press. New York, NY.

MARLATT, G. A. & W. R. MILLER. 1984. The Comprehensive Drinker Profile. Psychological Assessment Resources. Odessa, FL.

MATARAZZO, J. D., R. G. MATARAZZO, A. N. WIENS & A. E. GALLO. 1976. Retest reliability of the Halstead Impairment Index in a normal, a schizophrenic, and two samples of organic patients. J. Clin. Psychol. 32: 338–349.

MATTHEWS, D. B. & W. R. MILLER. 1979. Estimating blood alcohol concentration: Two computer programs and their applications in therapy and research. Addictive Behav. **4**: 55–60.

McLachlan, J. F. C. & T. Levenson. 1974. Improvement in WAIS Block Design performance as a function of recovery from alcoholism. J. Clin. Psychol. **30**: 65–66.

Miglioli, M., H. A. Buchtel, T. Campanini & C. DeRisio. 1979. Cerebral hemisphere lateralization of cognitive deficits due to alcoholism. J. Nerv. Mental Dis. **167**: 212–217.

Miller, W. R. 1976. Alcoholism scales and objective assessment methods: A review. Psychol. Bull. **83**: 649–674.

Miller, W. R. 1983. Motivational interviewing with problem drinkers. Behav. Psychother. **11**: 147–172.

Miller, W. R. & R. K. Hester. 1980. Treating the problem drinker: Modern approaches. *In* The Addictive Behaviors: Treatment of Alcoholism, Drug Abuse, Smoking and Obesity. W. R. Miller, Ed. Pergamon. Oxford, England.

Miller, W. R. & G. A. Marlatt. 1984. Manual for the Comprehensive Drinker Profile. Psychological Assessment Resources. Odessa, FL.

Miller, W. R. & J. Orr. 1980. Nature and sequence of neuropsychological deficits in alcoholics. J. Stud. Alcohol **41**: 325–337.

Miller, W. R. & C. F. Saucedo. 1983. Assessment of neuropsychological impairment and brain damage in problem drinkers. *In* Clinical Neuropsychology: Interface with Neurologic and Psychiatric Disorders. C. J. Golden *et al.*, Eds. : 141–195. Grune & Stratton. New York, NY.

Morey, L. C. & R. K Blashfield. 1981. Empirical classifications of alcoholism: A review. J. Stud. Alcohol **42**: 925–937.

O'Leary, M. R. & D. M. Donovan. 1979. Male alcoholics: Treatment outcome as a function of length of treatment and current adaptive abilities. Evaluation of the Health Professions **2**: 373–384.

O'Leary, M. R., D. M. Donovan & E. F. Chaney. 1977. The relationship of perceptual field orientation to measures of cognitive functioning and current adaptive abilities in alcoholics and nonalcoholics. J. Nerv. Mental Dis. **165**: 275–282.

O'Leary, M. R., D. M. Donovan, E. F. Chaney & R. D. Walker. 1979a. Cognitive impairment and treatment outcome with alcoholics: Preliminary findings. J. Clin. Psychiatry **40**: 397–398.

O'Leary, M. R., D. M. Donovan, E. F. Chaney, R. D. Walker & E. J. Schau. 1979b. Application of discriminant analysis of level of performance of alcoholics and nonalcoholics on Wechsler-Bellevue and Halstead-Reitan subtests. J. Clin. Psychol. **35**: 204–208.

Page, R. D. & S. Bozlee. 1982. A cross-cultural MMPI comparison of alcoholics. Psychol. Rep. **50**: 639–646.

Parker, E. S. & E. P. Noble. 1977. Alcohol consumption and cognitive functioning in social drinkers. J. Stud. Alcohol **38**: 1224–1232.

Parker, E. S., I. M. Birnbaum, R. A. Boyd & E. P. Noble. 1980. Neuropsychologic decrements as a function of alcohol intake in male students. Alcoholism: Clin. Exp. Res. **4**: 330–334.

Pattison, E. M., R. Coe & H. O. Doerr. 1973. Population variation among alcoholism treatment facilities. Int. J. Addictions **8**: 199–229.

Pattison, E. M., R. Coe & R. J. Rhodes. 1969. Evaluation of alcoholism treatment: A comparison of three alcoholism treatment facilities. Arch. Gen. Psychiatry **20**: 478–488.

Plumeau, F., S. Machover & F. Puzzo. 1960. Wechsler-Bellevue performance of remitted and unremitted alcoholics, and their normal controls. J. Consult. Psychol. **24**: 240–242.

Reitan, R. M & L. A. Davison, Eds. 1974. Clinical Neuropsychology: Current Status and Applications. Winston. Washington, DC.

Ron, M. A., W. Acker & W. A. Lishman. 1980. Dementia in chronic alcoholism: A clinical, psychological and computerized axial tomographic study. *In* Biological Psychiatry Today. J. Obiols, *et al.*, Eds. Elsevier. New York, NY.

Ryan, C. & N. Butters. 1980. Learning and memory impairments in young and old alcoholics: Evidence for the premature-aging hypothesis. Alcoholism: Clin. Exp. Res. **4**: 288–293.

Sanchez-Craig, M. 1980. Drinking pattern as a determinant of alcoholics' performance on the Trail Making Test. J. Stud. Alcohol **41**: 1082–1090.

Schau, E. J. & M. R. O'Leary. 1977. Adaptive abilities of hospitalized alcoholics and matched controls: The brain-age quotient. J. Stud. Alcohol **38**: 403–409.

SELZER, M. L. 1979. The Michigan Alcoholism Screening Test: The quest for a new diagnostic instrument. Am. J. Psychiatry 127: 1653–1658.

SILBERSTEIN, J. A. & O. A. PARSONS. 1980. Neuropsychological impairment in female alcoholics. In Currents in Alcoholism, Vol. 7. M. Galanter, Ed. Grune & Stratton. New York, NY.

SILBERSTEIN, J. A. & O. A. PARSONS. 1981. Neuropsychological impairment in female alcoholics: Replication and extension. J. Abnormal Psychol 90: 179–182.

SKINNER, H. A. 1977. Lifetime Drinking History Structure Questionnaire. Addiction Research Foundation. Toronto, Ontario, Canada.

SKINNER, H. A. & B. A. ALLEN. 1982. Alcohol dependence syndrome: Measurement and validation. J. Abnormal Psychol. 91: 199–209.

SMITH, H. H. & L. S. SMITH. 1977. WAIS functioning of cirrhotic and non-cirrhotic alcoholics. J. Clin. Psychol. 33: 309–313.

SMITH, J. W., D. W. BURT & R. F. CHAPMAN. 1973. Intelligence and brain damage in alcoholics: A study in patients of middle and upper social class. Q. J. Stud. Alcohol 34: 414–422.

STOCKWELL, T., R. HODGSON, G. EDWARDS, C. TAYLOR & H. RANKIN. 1979. The development of a questionnaire to measure severity of alcohol dependence. Br. J. Addiction 74: 79–87.

TEMPLER, D. I., C. F. RUFF & K. SIMPSON. 1975. Trail Making Test performance of alcoholics abstinent at least a year. Int. J. Addictions 10: 609–612.

WANBERG, K. W., J. L. HORN & F. M. FOSTER. 1977. A differential assessment model for alcoholism: The scales of the Alcohol Use Inventory. J. Stud. Alcohol 38: 512–543.

WILKINSON, D. A. & P. L. CARLEN. 1980a. Neuropsychological assessment of alcoholism: Discrimination between groups of alcoholics. J. Stud Alcohol 41: 129–139.

WILKINSON, D. A. & P. L. CARLEN. 1980b. Relationship of neuropsychological test performance to brain morphology in amnesic and non-amnesic chronic alcoholics. Acta Psychiat. Scand. 62: 89–101 (Suppl. 286).

WILKINSON, D. A. & P. L. CARLEN. 1980c. Relation of neuropsychological test performance in alcoholics to brain morphology measured by computed tomography. In Biological Effects of Alcohol. H. Begleiter, Ed. Plenum. New York, NY.

# Concepts of Alcoholism among American, French-Canadian, and French Alcoholics[a]

THOMAS F. BABOR,[b] MICHIE HESSELBROCK,[b]
SIMONE RADOUCO-THOMAS,[c] LUC FEGUER,[d]
J.-P. FERRANT,[d] AND KEITH CHOQUETTE[e]

[b]Department of Psychiatry
University of Connecticut School of Medicine
Farmington, Connecticut 06032

[c]Department of Pharmacology
Laval University
Québec, Canada G1K 7P4

[d]Centre Louis Sevestre
La Membrolle-sur-Choisille, 37390 France

[e]Dever State School
Taunton, Massachusetts 02780

To ponder the nature and meaning of alcoholism is not necessarily a frivolous academic exercise. To the extent that concepts of alcoholism influence social opinion, treatment philosophy, and, conceivably, alcoholic drinking patterns, such concepts may have important implications for society in general and for the excessive drinker in particular. The research described in this report was designed to explore the phenomenology of alcoholism from the viewpoint of diagnosed alcoholics, and how the alcoholic's perception of alcoholism varies in different cultural settings.

The role of sociocultural factors in structuring the meaning and definition of alcoholism has been noted by Jellinek (1960), who pointed out that acceptance or rejection of the "disease" concept may be influenced by deeply rooted drinking customs and by the nature of public education. In England, Scandinavia, and North America, the terms *alcoholic* and *alcoholism* tend to be associated with what Jellinek (1960, 1962) referred to as the "steady symptomatic excessive drinker," that is, a drinker whose loss of control over drinking is a consequence of an underlying psychological problem. This view of alcoholism may not be universal, however, as suggested by informal observation of public attitudes and medical concepts in the predominantly wine-drinking nations of southern Europe and South America. The French conception of alcoholism is considered to be typical of an alternative conception. According to Jellinek (1962,

[a] This work was supported in part by Grants 1K01AA00025 and 1P50AA03510 from the National Institute on Alcohol Abuse and Alcoholism.

p. 384): "There is in the French literature on alcoholism frequent mention of *l'alcoolisme sans ivresse* (alcoholism without drunkenness); that is, it is asserted that a drinker can become an alcoholic without ever showing signs of intoxication. This opinion is held by students of alcoholism as well as by the population at large."

The absence of intoxication is not the only characteristic distinguishing this "inveterate" drinker. Whereas psychological disturbance is presumed to underlie the excesses of Anglo-Saxon alcoholics, social customs and economic incentives are seen as the major influences in French alcoholism. That these drinking patterns and symptom clusters have some basis in fact has been demostrated in recent comparative studies of English-speaking and French-speaking alcoholics (Negrete, 1973; Babor *et al.*, 1974). Termed "gamma" and "delta" alcoholics, respectively, these alcoholics present varieties of alcoholism that are probably prevalent in every nation of drinkers. But because one variety or the other tends to predominate, the disease label brings with it a set of meanings consistent with the prevailing cultural view.

Of particular interest to the present investigation is the phenomenology of alcoholism in Québec, a French-speaking province within a predominantly English-speaking nation. A comparative study of Frnech-speaking and English-speaking Canadian alcoholics conducted by Negrete (1973) showed that Anglo-Protestants differed from French Catholics on indicators of poor social functioning, such as unemployment, marital adjustment, and legal problems. In addition to having poorer social performance, personality disorder seemed to be more prevalent among the Anglo-Protestants. These results suggest that by virtue of either their religion or ethnicity, French-speaking Catholics in Canada may be more like French alcoholics than American alcoholics.

It has generally been assumed by alcoholism treatment personnel in most industrialized countries that the disease-labeling process and the alcoholic's concomitant acceptance of the "sick" role would facilitate treatment and potentiate the chances of rehabilitation. Some writers (Roman and Trice, 1977; Steiner, 1969; Negrete, 1978), however, question the utility of indiscriminate application of the disease label, not only because it may not be appropriate for all varieties of alcohol-related problems, but also because it may influence the very behavior it attempts to describe. This could come about, according to Roman and Trice (1977), by altering the cognitive expectancies held by alcoholics and by those in their immediate social environment, such that the drinker no longer is seen as responsible for his or her behavior. In this view, loss of control over drinking may result more from learned expectations than from physical predispositions, and chronic alcoholism more from a dependency role than from physiological dependence.

Unfortunately, these provocative hypotheses have not been submitted to rigorous scientific evaluation, nor have cultural influences been examined as factors contributing to the definition of alcoholism and attitudes toward alcoholics. In order to explore how attitudes and beliefs are defined, learned, and in turn, influence the behavior of alcoholics, a cross-national study was conducted on treatment samples of diagnosed alcoholics in the United States, Canada (Québec), and France. These three countries were chosen to represent different points on a hypothetical continuum of opposing views of alcoholism. It was predicted that: (1) American alcoholics would endorse attitudes consistent with the gamma variety of alcoholism, the French would endorse attitudes consistent with the delta variety, while the Canadians would score between the two; (2) cross-national differences would be greater among males than among females, given the probability that generalized attitudes toward alcoholics and concepts of alcoholism apply primarily to the male alcoholic; and (3) the content of concepts as determined empirically by factor analysis would vary cross-nationally.

# METHODS

## Sample Selection and Patient Characteristics

TABLE 1 summarizes demographic and personal characteristics of the alcoholic patients who participated in this research. The male patients in each sample were comparable in mean age, but the French females (40.0 years) were significantly older than the Americans (37.2 years) and Canadians (36.5 years) ($t$ test, $p < 0.01$). There were significant differences among samples in the distributions of patients across marital status categories ($\chi^2$ (males) $= 39.8$, $p < 0.01$; $\chi^2$ (females) $= 9.7$, $p < 0.05$). The American alcoholics had a higher proportion of single, divorced and separated persons, while the French had the greatest proportion of married persons. There were no differences among female samples in the proportions within different occupational categories. Among the males, Canadians had a higher proportion of white collar workers, while the French had a higher number of blue collar workers ($\chi^2 = 71.7$, $p < .001$). There were also significant cross-national differences in educational achievement for both males ($\chi^2 = 85.1$, $p < 0.001$) and females ($\chi^2 = 29.1$, $p < 0.001$). The Americans had a greater proportion with postsecondary education and the French had greater representation in the technical/secondary category. These data indicate that the samples differ on a variety of personal and demographic characteristics that should be controlled in any attempt to evaluate cultural differences in attitude responses.

The sample of American patients ($n = 311$) was drawn primarily from the alcoholism treatment center at the University of Connecticut Health Center. Male patients were also recruited from a Veterans Administration facility and from an inner city treatment program.

The French-Canadian alcoholics ($n = 234$) were recruited from the inpatient and outpatient services of the Department of Alcology, Hôpital Saint-François d'Assise.

**TABLE 1.** Personal and Demographic Characteristics of American, French-Canadian, and French Alcoholics

| | American | | Canadian | | French | |
|---|---|---|---|---|---|---|
| | Male ($n = 231$) | Female ($n = 80$) | Male ($n = 184$) | Female ($n = 81$) | Male ($n = 259$) | Female ($n = 43$) |
| Age ($\bar{X}$) | 39.5 | 37.2 | 38.8 | 36.5 | 37.8 | 40.0 |
| Marital Status | | | | | | |
|   Single (%) | 30.3 | 22.2 | 29.3 | 28.7 | 28.2 | 13.3 |
|   Married (%) | 26.8 | 34.4 | 42.4 | 42.5 | 51.3 | 50.6 |
|   Separated/ divorced (%) | 42.9 | 43.3 | 28.3 | 28.7 | 20.6 | 36.1 |
| Education | | | | | | |
|   Elementary (%) | 34.2 | 24.4 | 20.7 | 17.5 | 16.1 | 9.5 |
|   Technical/ secondary (%) | 34.2 | 41.1 | 63.0 | 60.0 | 73.9 | 69.0 |
|   Post-secondary (%) | 31.6 | 34.4 | 16.3 | 22.5 | 10.0 | 21.4 |
| Occupation | | | | | | |
|   White collar (%) | 33.2 | 59.8 | 40.6 | 63.8 | 22.6 | 66.0 |
|   Blue collar (%) | 62.0 | 24.1 | 53.9 | 22.4 | 76.3 | 28.0 |
|   Unemployed/ housewife (%) | 4.9 | 16.1 | 5.6 | 13.8 | 2.0 | 6.0 |

NOTE: Percentages might not equal 100 because of rounding.

Approximately 1500 patients are admitted each year for treatment of alcohol-related disorders, making this facility the largest alcoholism treatment center in Québec.

The sample of French alcoholics ($n$ = 302) was drawn from Centre Louis Sevestre, one of the largest alcoholism treatment facilities in France. Randomly selected patients were asked to participate in a series of evaluations relating to their health and drinking behavior. More than 96% of the patients solicited agreed to participate, and of these, only 4% were screened out for reasons of psychological or physical impairment. Patients were referred from a large variety of social service agencies, with industrial health screening providing the greatest proportion of referrals. In general, the demographic profile of patients treated at Louis Sevestre is relatively similar to that emerging from epidemiologic studies of cirrhosis morbidity and heavy drinking in the French population.

### Procedure

Patients at each treatment center were given a self-report inventory consisting of 50 descriptive statements and a 7-point Likert-type rating scale. Each of the seven points was identified with a specific degree of agreement (7 = complete agreement) or disagreement (1 = complete disagreement). The rating scale, as well as the first 40 items, were adopted without modification from an instrument called the "Alcoholism Scale" (Marcus, 1980). Ten additional items were developed from statements found in the literature of Alcoholics Anonymous and in the writings of E. M. Jellinek. These were designed to measure aspects of alcoholism assumed to be peculiar to the French drinking pattern (e.g., *alcoolisme sans ivresse*) and to elaborate upon the "traditional" disease concept of alcoholism. The questionnaire was administered as part of a more extensive battery of assessments, usually during the first or second week of treatment.

As in all cross-national research, the problem of translating the instrument to achieve semantic equivalence was crucial. The task in this case was facilitated by the following considerations: (1) the words "alcoholic" and "alcoholism" were easily translatable; (2) no assumptions needed to be made about the semantic equivalence of these words because the object of our study was, in fact, to explore similarities and differences in the meaning of these concepts (3) the remaining content of the instrument was presented in sentence form that reduced the relative importance of individual words. Initially developed in English, all items were first translated into French by a bilingual native French translator. The first translation was then reviewed by a second bilingual French translator. The modified translation was then studied by three monolingual treatment personnel at the Centre Louis Sevestre. Appropriate modifications were again made to assure that the items were comprehensible to the target groups.

As described in TABLE 1, the three samples were diverse in terms of age distribution, marital status, educational achievement, and occupational status. While no claim can be made about the extent to which these patients are representative of the more general population of alcoholics in their respective countries, there seems to be sufficient variability in the sociological make-up of these samples to permit the application of statistical controls should any of these "noncultural" variables prove to be correlated with our dependent measures of attitude.

### Data Analysis

The ratings obtained from each sample were first summarized according to the composite-item scales developed by Marcus (1980) to measure nine dimensions of popular opinion about alcoholism. The first three scales pertain to general concepts of alcoholism; specifically, the concept that alcoholism is neither a disease nor illness, the belief that emotional difficulties and psychological problems are causes of alcoholism, and the notion that alcohol is an addicting substance responsible for the illness. The remaining scales measure attitudes toward alcoholics. For example, several scales describe alcoholics in terms of a negative stereotype, such as lacking in will power, having low social status, or indicating a poor prognosis for recovery. Other scales describe hypothetical alcoholic drinking patterns (impaired control of intake, periodic drinking), while a final set of items portrays alcoholics as having a harmless voluntary indulgence. Each of the Marcus scales served as dependent measures in a series of multivariate analyses that described their relationships to a set of predictor variables representing personal, cultural, and demographic factors. The statistical procedure employed was multiple classification analysis (MCA), a multivariate technique related to analysis of variance that assessed how several predictive factors simultaneously determine a dependent variable. In the series of MCAs described here, five categorical independent variables were used in each analysis. These were (1) nationality (American, Canadian, French); (2) gender (male, female); (3) marital status (single, married, divorced/widowed); (4) education (elementary, technical/secondary, post-secondary); and (5) occupation (white collar, blue collar, unemployed/housewife). In addition, age was used as a covariate in these analyses.

The reason for including variables other than nationality in the analysis was both statistical and heuristic. Given the fact that MCA examines the relationship between each predictor and the dependent variable (while adjusting for covariates and the remaining independent variables), it was considered desirable to include marital status, sex, education, and occupation so that potential differences in the predictive contribution of these variables could be controlled. Another reason for combining these variables in a single analysis was to compare the relative influence of each in explaining the variance in attitude scores. It was of interest, for example, to consider the extent to which sociological characteristics were independently associated with attitudes.

Within-sample correlational analysis was also conducted to determine the relation between attitude scale scores and self-report measures of alcohol dependence, alcohol-related problems, and average daily alcohol consumption. These measures assessed drinking behavior and problems during the 6 months prior to treatment and are described in greater detail in Hesselbrock et al. (1983) and Babor et al. (in press). In addition, the number of previous treatment experiences reported by the patient was also correlated with the attitude scales to assess the possible contribution of exposure to treatment ideology.

Finally, the ten supplemental items were factor-analyzed along with the 40 Marcus items in order to compare the multivariate patterning of concepts and attitudes within samples. The method of "parallel" factor analysis was chosen to summarize the findings because it offered a number of distinct methodologic advantages for cross-national comparisons of attitudes ratings. Factor analysis places items in relatively homogeneous groups on the basis of similar patterns of response, rather than on the basis of their receiving the same or similar ratings. To the extent that each item shares in the common variance of the general factor (item cluster), it can be assumed that items having the highest factor loadings represent most accurately the constituent elements of a more general concept. In the present analysis the general concept was unmistakably alcoholism, since almost all of the items used "alcoholism" or "alcoholic" as their referent. It can therefore be hypothesized that if Canadian and American alcoholics share similar concepts of alcoholism, their response patterns should yield similar item clusters. Such a procedure avoided the pitfalls involved in making direct comparisons of scale means that may be affected by several nationality-related response tendencies such as (1) acquiescence, the general tendency to agree with a statement, and (2) social desirability, the tendency to agree with statements which present the individual in a favorable light. Initial analysis of the frequency distributions indicated that while there was sufficient variance in the ratings of almost all items, the Americans, nevertheless, showed a greater tendency to agree *and* to disagree by using more extreme ratings. At present, it is difficult to determine whether these differences are "real" (in the sense that they derive from actual differences in the degree to which American patients endorse the same concept) or "false" (in the sense that they derive from cross-national differences in uses of the subjective rating scale). Fortunately, this issue can be clarified by factor matrix comparisons that emphasize cross-national differences in the empirical organization of responses, rather than absolute differences in scale ratings.

## RESULTS

TABLE 2 summarizes the results of the Multiple Classification Analyses. The $F$-statistics and beta coefficients (standardized partial correlation coefficients) are listed for each independent variable next to each attitude scale. The beta coefficients represent the relative degree of correspondence between dependent and independent variables. The table shows that nationality produced significant main effects on seven of the nine scales. Although education accounted for significant main effects on five scales, the beta-weights indicated that nationality was the most powerful correlate of the attitude measures. FIGURE 1 shows mean scale scores for each national group, expressed

**TABLE 2.** Summary Statistics of the Separate Multiple Classification Analyses Performed on Each Marcus Scale

| Scale | Nationality | | Sex | | Marital Status | | Education | | Occupation | |
|---|---|---|---|---|---|---|---|---|---|---|
| | $F$ | Beta | $F$ | Beta | $F$ | Beta | $F$ | Beta | $F$ | Beta |
| Alcoholism is not a disease | $56.19^a$ | 0.39 | 1.09 | 0.04 | $5.28^b$ | 0.12 | $6.58^a$ | 0.16 | 0.92 | 0.07 |
| Emotional difficulties cause alcoholism | $20.73^a$ | 0.23 | 0.30 | 0.02 | $3.53^c$ | 0.10 | 0.63 | 0.05 | 0.32 | 0.04 |
| Alcoholism is a harmless indulgence | $35.72^a$ | 0.32 | $7.78^b$ | 0.10 | 0.04 | 0.01 | $8.44^a$ | 0.19 | 0.45 | 0.05 |
| Alcoholics lack will power | $40.32^a$ | 0.33 | 1.76 | 0.05 | 0.10 | 0.02 | $14.62^a$ | 0.25 | 1.01 | 0.08 |
| Alcoholics have impaired loss of control | $9.11^a$ | 0.17 | 0.29 | 0.02 | 0.00 | 0.00 | 2.47 | 0.10 | 1.88 | 0.10 |
| Alcoholics can be periodic drinkers | $65.80^a$ | 0.42 | 0.01 | 0.00 | 0.85 | 0.05 | 0.42 | 0.04 | 2.29 | 0.11 |
| Alcohol is highly addicting | 0.28 | 0.03 | 2.80 | 0.07 | 1.86 | 0.07 | 0.82 | 0.06 | 0.93 | 0.08 |
| Alcoholics have low social status | 2.99 | 0.10 | 0.95 | 0.04 | 0.46 | 0.04 | $6.64^a$ | 0.17 | 1.55 | 0.09 |
| Alcoholics have poor prognosis | $8.30^a$ | 0.16 | 0.17 | 0.02 | 0.24 | 0.02 | $5.44^b$ | 0.16 | $3.78^b$ | 0.16 |

$^a$ $p < 0.001$.
$^b$ $p < 0.01$.
$^c$ $p < 0.05$.

as deviations from the neutral point of the rating scale. The means have been adjusted for age and for the effects of the other independent variables (sex, education, occupation) included in the MCA analysis. The differences portrayed in FIGURE 1 therefore reflect the independent effects of nationality when the influence of the other variables has been taken into account. The following discussion of scale means will highlight the results of *post hoc t* tests used to determine differences between specific groups.

FIGURE 1 shows that while all groups disagreed with the notion that alcoholism is not a disease, the Americans disagreed more strongly than the Canadians, who in turn scored closer to the neutral point. To the extent that disagreement with these

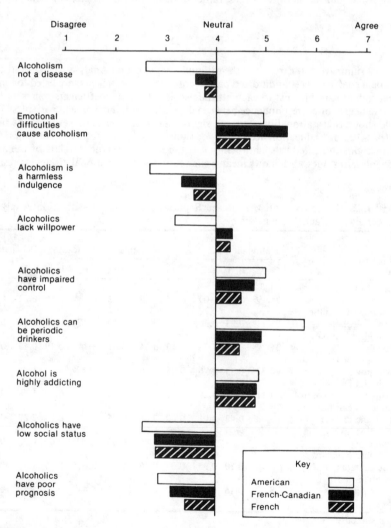

**FIGURE 1.** Mean scale scores for each national group expressed as deviations from the neutral point of the rating scale.

items implies acceptance of the "disease concept," it can be assumed, then, that the Americans endorsed the disease notion more than did the Canadians and the French.

The second scale refers to the role of emotional and psychological factors in the etiology of alcoholism. Here the Canadians are most extreme in their agreement. The Americans and French, while providing less endorsement than the Canadians, are nevertheless significantly different from each other ($t = 1.95$, $p < 0.05$) in the degree of their ratings, thereby supporting the hypothesis that the prototypical gamma alcoholics attribute psychological problems to alcoholism more than do the prototypical delta alcoholics.

The third scale, which portrays alcoholics as having a benign voluntary indulgence, invited consistent disagreement from all three samples. As in the case of the previous scales, however, the differences in degree were statistically significant, with the Americans disagreeing most and the Canadians least.

The next scale epitomizes the negative stereotype of the alcoholic as lacking will power and moral fortitude. Interestingly, the Americans disagreed moderately with these items, while the Canadians and the French agreed moderately. The differences between the latter two samples are negligible.

The next two scales describe characteristics of gamma alcoholics, specifically, that alcoholics have a condition making them incapable of controlling their drinking, and that alcoholics can be periodic excessive drinkers with periods of abstinence between drinking bouts. As predicted, the Americans agreed with these attitudes most, and the French endorsed them the least.

The seventh scale contains statements describing alcohol as a highly addicting substance that can result in problems regardless of beverage type. Interestingly, this was one of the only scales where cross-national differences were not evident.

The final two scales epitomize two aspects of the popular negative stereotype of alcoholics: that they are generally less educated and occupy low status occupations, and that their prognosis for recovery is poor. Both scales invited disagreement, which was strongest from the Americans and weakest from the French.

In an effort to determine whether various alcohol-related problems influenced the observed response patterns, the scale scores within each sample and gender group were correlated with self-report measures of alcohol dependence, alcohol-related problems, and daily alcohol consumption. This analysis was not performed on the Canadian sample because the necessary data were not collected. Alcohol dependence correlated significantly with several of the attitude measures, but the correlations were not of sufficient magnitude to suggest that this factor could account for the differences across samples. For example, the higher the level of alcohol dependence, as measured by a brief, self-report alcohol-dependence scale, the higher the endorsement of the impaired control concept by both American ($r = 0.17$, $p < 0.05$) and French ($r = 0.18$, $p < 0.05$) male alcoholics. Similarly, the scale measuring the concept that alcoholism results from emotional problems was correlated significantly in both the American and French male samples with measures of alcohol dependence (Americans, $r = 0.15$, $p < 0.01$; French, $r = 0.19$, $p < 0.01$) and alcohol-related problems (American, $r = 0.18$, $p < 0.01$; French, $r = 0.15$, $p < 0.05$). These relationships were not replicated in the female samples, nor was there any indication that exposure to previous alcoholism treatment was associated with a greater endorsement of the traditional disease concept or a rejection of any of the negative stereotypes.

The final part of the data analysis consisted of a comparison of the factor pattern matrices extracted from the full, 50-item data set through independent factor analyses conducted within each of the male samples. A principal components factor analysis program was used with orthogonal rotation of factor matrices. After examination of the eigenvalues, it was decided to extract five factors from each sample. The results of interest to this study are shown in TABLES 3 and 4, which summarize the common items loading on the first and second factors extracted from each nationality group. The content of subsequent factors were unique to each sample group and will be described only briefly.

TABLE 3 indicates that there was considerable overlap in the item content of the first factor in all three sample groups. The common items portray a negative stereotype of the alcoholic as having low social status, lacking in will power, and being unconcerned about his problem and unwilling to give up alcohol. As suggested by the peripheral items that are common to only two of the sample groups, the Americans and the Canadians share more of the stereotype than do the French. In general, these items were the ones inviting the most consistent disagreement by the respondents in each sample.

The second factor extracted from each sample contained only two items common to the three groups. These items, shown in TABLE 4, depict the essence of the classical disease concept: that alcoholism is a progressive disease with well-defined stages, and that once a person becomes an alcoholic, he remains an alcoholic whether drinking or not. The peripheral items on this factor show some items common to the Americans and the Canadians (craving and loss of control) and other items common to the Canadians and the French (*alcoolisme sans ivresse*, past history, family problems, weekend drinking).

## DISCUSSION

The findings indicate a rather consistent pattern of cross-national differences both in terms of the way in which alcoholics conceptualize the term "alcoholism," and how

**TABLE 3.** Verimax Rotated Factors and Major Factor Loadings Obtained from Separate Factor Analyses of American ($n = 259$), French-Canadian ($n = 183$), and French ($n = 152$) Male Alcoholics: First Principal Factor

|  | Factor Loadings | | |
|---|---|---|---|
|  | Americans | Canadians | French |
| Items Common to All Three Samples | | | |
| Alcoholics usually lack will power | 0.30 | 0.57 | 0.59 |
| Alcoholics are not found in important business positions | 0.41 | 0.57 | 0.41 |
| Alcoholism is a sign of character weakness | 0.53 | 0.43 | 0.66 |
| Alcoholics are unconcerned about their problems | 0.51 | 0.61 | 0.48 |
| Alcoholics drink because they enjoy drinking | 0.43 | 0.42 | 0.42 |
| Alcoholics are morally weak persons | 0.59 | 0.42 | 0.54 |
| Alcoholics are spineless people | 0.56 | 0.33 | 0.37 |
| Alcoholics don't want to stop drinking | 0.40 | 0.31 | 0.49 |
| Items Common to Two Samples | | | |
| Alcoholics seldom harm anyone but themselves | 0.61 | 0.48 | |
| Alcoholics have less education than most people | 0.43 | | 0.47 |
| Alcoholics drink or are drunk daily | 0.40 | 0.42 | |
| The average alcoholic is unemployed | | 0.41 | 0.50 |
| Psychological or medical treatment seldom helps | 0.32 | 0.40 | |
| Little warning occurs before becoming an alcoholic | 0.32 | 0.37 | |
| Alcoholics have only themselves to blame | 0.45 | 0.31 | |

**TABLE 4.** Verimax Rotated Factors and Major Factor Loadings Obtained from Separate Factor Analyses of American ($n$ = 259), French-Canadian ($n$ = 183), and French ($n$ = 152) Male Alcoholics: Second Principal Factor

| | Factor Loadings | | |
|---|---|---|---|
| | Americans | Canadians | French |
| Items Common to All Three Samples | | | |
| Alcoholism is a progressive disease | 0.54 | 0.44 | 0.61 |
| Even with cessation of drinking a person remains an alcoholic | 0.44 | 0.34 | 0.35 |
| Items Common to Two Samples | | | |
| Strong craving is indicative of alcoholism | 0.44 | 0.34 | 0.35 |
| Any alcohol in system precipitates loss of control | 0.55 | 0.60 | |
| One can become alcoholic without ever having been drunk | | 0.51 | 0.60 |
| Something in his past drives the alcoholic to drink | | 0.50 | 0.42 |
| Family problems lead to alcoholism | | 0.35 | 0.45 |
| Heavy weekend drinking can be indicative of alcoholism | | 0.31 | 0.41 |

they perceive its generalized victim, the alcoholic. Explaining these differences may be considerably more difficult than documenting them, given the diversity of factors that can influence an individual's concept development and attitude change.

The most direct explanation that can be invoked to explain the findings is the cultural differences among the three samples. This explanation is consistent with observations that concepts of alcoholism differ between France and the U.S., and it is supported by the results showing the female alcoholics respond more like their male counterparts within each culture than like their female counterparts across cultures. The difficulty with the cultural explanation lies as much with the complexity of the concept of culture as with the nature of alcoholism. Because culture is often used as a generic explanation for phenomena that cannot be explained by more specific causes, its value is limited by the meaning attached to it. In the present discussion, the notion of culture will be used broadly to describe socially learned behaviors and attitudes common to a group of people. Culture may be mediated through a variety of channels to account for the development of attitudes and concepts. Some are rather direct, such as the direct tuition or socialization an individual receives from his or her social environment. In the case of alcoholics, attitudes and concepts may be learned from more general stereotypes communicated in the media or through the process of socialization. Here one would predict that the psychological disease concept would be more prominent in the U.S., where there has been an organized attempt to change public attitudes about alcoholism and to improve the image of alcoholics. Another source of influence on alcoholics is the treatment process itself, since a major goal of treatment, especially in the U.S., is to convince the alcoholic of the validity of the disease concept, and to remove the personal stigma associated with the negative stereotype of the alcoholic (Roman and Trice, 1977). To the extent that the general public and specialized treatment personnel within a given country share specific concepts, attitudes, and perceptions concerning alcoholism, this might account for the observed differences among our treatment samples.

Several other factors related to culture may mediate the differences in attitudes and concepts observed in the comparisons. One of these is culturally patterned alcoholic drinking patterns. A number of studies have shown that alcoholics in different countries prefer different beverages, experience different drinking problems, and develop different types of alcohol-related disability (Babor *et al.*, 1974; Park, 1962; Negrete, 1973, 1978). In the present study, there was some evidence to suggest that male patients scoring high on measures of recent alcohol dependence and alcohol-related problems also believed that alcoholics are incapable of controlling their consumption after the first drink. These data suggest that alcoholics' concepts of alcoholism may be influenced by their own personal drinking styles and experiences. To the extent that these beliefs are mediated by cultural factors, such as socially learned beverage preferences, alcoholics in different nations may endorse different beliefs about the nature of alcoholism. This hypothesis is consistent with the finding that the Americans agreed most with the notion that alcoholics have impaired control, and that alcoholics can be periodic drinkers. However, these findings did not apply to females.

Certainly, this explanation is similar to that invoked by Jellinek in his references to cultural variations in the meaning of alcoholism (Jellinek, 1960, 1962). In his own discussions Jellinek also suggested that the meaning of alcoholism may be related to cultural differences in the way alcoholics drink, the symptoms they develop, the consequences they experience, and the various etiologic contributions to their disorder. Thus, one would expect that attitudes toward alcoholics would be colored by cultural stereotypes, to the extent that those stereotypes represent oversimplified generalizations from social reality.

Yet another possible culturally mediated explanatory variable is response bias, that is, the distortion that results from different styles of responding to questionnaire items. Response bias may be associated with national differences in the tendency to agree or disagree with general propositions, or from differences in the semantic equivalence of key words used in the rating scale and response items. This could explain why the Americans manifested the greatest degree of agreement as well as disagreement on almost every scale. However, response bias would not account for the corroborating evidence from the parallel factor analysis, where culturally mediated response tendencies were held constant.

A final explanation that should be considered in the interpretation of results is the effect of exposure to different treatment ideologies in the respective countries. Data available from the French and American samples concerning number of previous treatment experiences did not provide any support for this hypothesis.

Given the likelihood that the observed cross-national differences are best explained by culturally mediated differences in popular conceptions or personal experiences regarding alcoholism, it is important to consider the relevance of these findings to such issues as the role of attitude change in the treatment process, and international communication about alcoholism. For example, the results are interesting in light of a recent study of how alcoholics and treatment personnel attribute responsibility and blame for alcoholism (Stafford, 1982). In general, treatment personnel regarded alcoholics responsible, but not to blame, for their problems, while the reverse is true for their patients. Differences were also observed in the degree to which alcoholics were seen as being in control of their drinking and in the direction of their lives. Because these attitudes are socially learned and culturally mediated, it would seem important to investigate how they influence the alcoholic's acceptance of, and response to, treatment. Does belief in the impaired control construct, for example, either influence the rapidity with which alcoholics relapse after resuming drinking, or the degree to which they attempt to control their drinking after relapse? Is treatment differentially effective in different countries, and could this be related to culturally mediated attitudes? Does international communication about alcoholism suffer because of different connotations attributed to the term? These are just a few of the questions that might be pursued in future research.

## REFERENCES

BABOR, T. F., C. MARTINAY, J. Y. BENARD, J. P. FERRANT & A. WOLFSON. Homme alcoolique, femme alcoolique: Etude comparative sur l'alcoolisme feminin. [Male alcoholic, female alcoholic: A comparative study on female alcoholism]. Bull. Soc. Fr. Alcool. In press.

BABOR, T. F., T. R. MCCABE, P. MASANES & J.-P. FERRANT. 1974. Patterns of alcoholism in France and America: A comparative study. *In* Alcoholism: A Multilevel Problem. M. E. Chafetz, Ed. U.S. Government Printing Office. Washington, DC.

HESSELBROCK, M., T. F. BABOR, V. HESSELBROCK, R. E. MEYER & K. WORKMAN. 1983. "Never believe an alcoholic? On the validity of self-report measures of alcohol dependence." Int. J. Addictions **18**: 593–609.

JELLINEK, E. M. 1962. Cultural differences in the meaning of alcoholism. *In* Society, Culture and Drinking Patterns. Pittman and Snyder, Eds. Southern Illinois University Press. Carbondale, IL.

JELLINEK, E. M. 1960. The Disease Concept of Alcoholism. College and University Press. New Haven, CT.

MARCUS, A. M. 1963. The structure of popular beliefs about alcoholism. *In* Studies in Alcohol Education, Project 2: Report 1. Addiction Research Foundation. Toronto, Canada.

NEGRETE, J. C. 1973. Cultural influences on social performance of alcoholics: A comparative study. Q. J. Stud. Alcoholism **34**: 905–916.

NEGRETE, J. C. 1978. Disability from alcoholism: A cross-cultural perspective. Paper presented at World Psychiatric Association Meeting.

PARK, P. 1962. Drinking experiences of 806 Finnish alcoholics in comparison with similar experiences of 192 English alcoholics. Acta Psychiat. Scand. **38**: 227–246.

ROMAN, P. M. & H. M. TRICE. 1977. The sick role, labeling theory and the deviant drinker. *In* Emerging Concepts of Alcohol Dependence. Pattison, Sobell and Sobell, Eds. Springer. New York, NY.

STAFFORD, R. A. 1982. Locus of drinking problems as perceived by alcoholics and treatment personnel. J. Stud. Alcohol **43**: 593–598.

STEINER, C. M. 1969. The alcoholic game. Q. J. Stud. Alcoholism **30**: 920–938.

# Haunted by the *Zeitgeist:*
# Reflections on Contrasting Treatment Goals and Concepts of Alcoholism in Europe and the United States

WILLIAM R. MILLER

*Department of Psychology*
*University of New Mexico*
*Albuquerque, New Mexico 87131*

## AMERICAN ALCOHOLISM

On the surface it seems that we have come a long way in the United States toward understanding alcoholism. There is remarkable consistency of belief and opinion to be found in the American press and media, in government publications, and in articles and books written by experts on the subject. We have consensus in the U.S. about what alcoholism is and what it is not, a consensus so nearly complete that to question its basic assumptions is to be either rejected as a dangerous heretic or pitied as misguided and misinformed. Advising his colleagues on how to deal with dissenters from the traditional view of alcoholism, Lovern (1982) recently recommended: "Understand how they think, have some compassion for their position, and lovingly teach them what alcoholism really is." Failing this, Lovern advises, "If they don't respond to a caring, educational approach, consider the possibility . . . that they may be alcoholics themselves. Practice loving detachment, and if you are close to them, consider doing an intervention." (p. 39).

So what *is* alcoholism, really? If you ask most any informed American you are likely to have it explained to you that alcoholism is an irreversible disease that causes a person to lose control over drinking. Broken down into its component assumptions, the elements of this traditional American conception of alcoholism are as follows:

1. Alcoholism is *a* disease. It is recognizable as a unitary syndrome with certain symptoms and a predictable progression.

2. Alcoholism is a *disease*. Although the etiology is not completely known at present, it probably has a physical cause as well as psychological and spiritual elements.

3. Loss of control is the central symptom. An alcoholic loses the ability to control his or her drinking. "One drink, one drunk."

4. Alcoholism is irreversible. One can never become a recovered alcoholic, only a recovering alcoholic. Return to drinking causes resumed deterioration. "Once an alcoholic, always an alcoholic."

From these four assumptions which constitute the traditional American conception of the problem, there follow two additional assumptions commonly accepted in the U.S.:

5. The only possible hope for an alcoholic is total and permanent abstinence from alcohol.

6. Far and away the most effective means for achieving this is through the fellowship of Alcoholics Anonymous (AA), although certain other methods such as group therapy and the use of disulfiram have also been shown to be helpful.

The origin of these assumptions lies not in scientific data, nor (as is often mistakenly asserted) in the writings of E. M. Jellinek (1960), but rather in the philosophy and historic antecedents of Alcoholics Anonymous (Levine, 1978). The pervasiveness of this view in the U.S. is difficult to explain to those living in other nations, where wholly different assumptions may be held.

The perspectives expressed in this paper emerged during a sabbatical leave in 1982, during which it was my privilege to visit a wide range of professionals and alcoholism treatment facilities in seven European nations and to work intensively for 6 months with the staff of the Hjellestad Clinic near Bergen, Norway. This experience led me to reexamine the above mentioned assumptions, which are nearly universal in the U.S., and to place them in the context of the differing treatment goals and concepts of alcoholism that I encountered. This, in turn, led me to consider anew the basic research available to us on the nature and treatment of alcoholism and to ask what assumptions, if any, would be drawn if we were *starting* from the scientific evidence.

# 1. ALCOHOLISM IS *A* DISEASE

There have not always been alcoholics. Prior to Magnus Huss's introduction of the term in 1849, there was chronic intoxication or drunkenness (the subject of biblical injunctions) but no "alcoholism." Anthropologists remind us that there are entire societies where the concept of alcoholism does not exist. Indeed in my home state of New Mexico I have visited communities where acute intoxication to the point of nausea and unconsciousness accompanied by subsequent memory blackouts and disabling hangovers is accepted as ordinary drinking, a norm rather than a disease. When the term "alcoholism" was introduced by Huss in 1849 (and for some time thereafter) it was used to summarize the adverse *consequences* of chronic intoxication. This meaning was retained in the World Health Organization's first definition of alcoholism, which included virtually any pattern of drinking that leads to adverse personal or social consequences (WHO, 1952), a meaning similar to Cahalan's (1970) use of the term "problem drinker." This approach, which for present purposes will be termed the *generic* definition of alcoholism, is retained in the majority of diagnostic practices in the U.S., which look for any evidence of adverse sequelae of alcohol use. Such definitions-by-consequence range from the simplistic but popular checklists such as the "Johns Hopkins 20 questions" and the Michigan Alcoholism Screening Test to the more sophisticated indications approach of the National Council on Alcoholism (1972).

This much is relatively uncontroversial. To be sure, there are huge national differences in what is recognized to be a harmful amount of alcohol consumption. I observed this in presenting the same research data in various countries. The U.S. samples that I have defined as "problem drinkers" in my treatment studies have reported, at intake, an average consumption of 40–50 drinks per week (20–25 ounces or 0.6 to 0.75 of a liter of absolute alcohol). In Norway and Sweden, the audiences tended to be shocked by this amount of drinking and argued that my samples must consist of chronic addicted alcoholics. In Scotland and Germany, by contrast, audiences evidenced skepticism as to whether these clients had a real problem at all because such drinking, albeit heavy, seemed within normal limits. Nonetheless, all were willing to recognize the pragmatic classification of problem drinking made on the basis of adverse consequences, although perceived thresholds differed. The generic definition of alcoholism seems to have cross-cultural applicability.

Advocates of the traditional American conception of alcoholism want to go beyond this generic definition, however, and assert that there is *a* (one) syndrome with particular symptoms and a predictable progression, qualitatively different from normality. Alcoholism, then, becomes not a generic term for the consequences of overdrinking, but a unitary syndrome that one can "have" (or not have). Here the split from the rest of the world begins to appear. Scandinavians, for example, seem much more concerned about the adverse consequences of alcohol consumption for the population as a whole than about finding and treating an exceptional category of "alcoholic" individuals. Although we all employ the term "alcoholism," thereby giving the illusion of consensus, Europeans and Americans often mean something quite different by it.

What is the reason for America's departure from the original recognition of problems (plural) with drinking toward a postulation of a unitary syndrome? The answer is complex, and probably found in some combination of: (*a*) the requirement for a single primary diagnosis within older versions of the Diagnostic and Statistical Manual of the American Psychiatric Association, (*b*) political expediency in seeking third-party reimbursement for treatment and funding for research, (*c*) solidarity of identity within AA, and (*d*) western binary thinking in general. Current American attitudes about alcoholism may also, in part, be vestiges of attitudes towards drinking in general during the prohibitionist period of U.S. history (e.g., Thompson, 1915).

Certainly the justification for this departure is not to be found in the writings of Jellinek, who endorsed a generic definition and hypothesized a number of different kinds of alcoholism rather than a unitary syndrome. He recognized the trend in the U.S. toward singling out the gamma subtype as *the* definitive description of alcoholism, and he warned that gamma alcoholism "is what members of Alcoholics Anonymous recognize as alcoholism to the exclusion of all other species. . . . There is every reason why the student of alcoholism should emancipate himself from accepting the exclusiveness of the picture of alcoholism as propounded by Alcoholics Anonymous" (Jellinek, 1960; p. 38). Other writers have alluded to "the alcoholisms" (e.g., Jacobson, 1976; Winokur *et al.*, 1971), but the American conception continues to imply a single disease.

## Evidence on the Issue

Existing data on alcohol-related impairment point to anything but a monolithic entity (Goldman, 1979). Various dimensions of deterioration such as dependence symptoms, alcohol-related life problems, biomedical disorders, and neuropsychological impairment are continuous rather than discrete variables and are modestly intercorrelated at best (e.g., Miller and Saucedo, 1983). The search for an alcoholic personality, now spanning more than five decades, has failed to produce a consistent cluster of traits among alcoholics in general (Miller, 1976), although the search for a consistent *set* of clusters may prove more fruitful (Løberg and Miller, this volume). Multivariate investigations of alcohol problems have pointed to numerous orthogonal dimensions of impairment rather than a single principal factor or cluster (Horn, 1978; Skinner, 1981).

Have Americans perhaps been fixating on a particular but real *subtype* of alcoholism? Preliminary findings in several studies point toward the possibility of a more severe form of alcoholism that is partially influenced by genetic and family history variables (Goodwin, 1976; Tarter *et al.*, 1977; Winokur *et al.*, 1970, 1971). If such a subtype exists, however, we seem to be far from identifying differential markers in spite of extensive efforts. Existing biomedical indicators of "alcoholism" are restricted to measures of the generic physical sequelae of heavy drinking (e.g., Morse and Hurt, 1979; NCA, 1972; Skinner et al., 1980), useful variables to be sure, but substantially different from markers of a unitary or hereditary disease.

Nonetheless this assumption of a unitary disease is a pervasive one, influencing our language and thinking about alcoholism. It is customary in the U.S. to employ singular articles, referring to "the" disease of alcoholism and averring that it is indeed "a" disease. In my own writings I have referred to less dependent individuals showing adverse consequences as "early-stage problem drinkers." Only recently did I ask myself the question, "Early stage of what?"

## 2. ALCOHOLISM IS A *DISEASE*

A second assumption of the American conception of alcoholism is that it is a *disease* (emphasis here on the noun rather than on the article). In the most generic sense, the term "disease" is sufficiently vague as to be almost meaningless, as Jellinek recognized: a disease is whatever the medical profession chooses to claim as a disease. Few would question the biomedical deterioration that regularly accompanies excessive drinking, and such may reasonably be termed disease. But again Americans seem to want to say *more* in asserting the disease nature of alcoholism: that not only is it *a* disease (assumption #1), but also that it has a specific etiology.

There is not yet a consensus about what this etiology might be, but there does seem to be reasonable agreement on several points in the U.S.: (*a*) True alcoholism is a primary disease rather than being secondary to other problems. (*b*) The cause of the disease is not alcohol itself, because many people drink without having problems. (*c*) Alcoholism likely has a biomedical etiology not yet fully identified but involving hereditary perdisposition, biochemical abnormality, and/or brain disease rendering the individual incapable of self-control.

It is clear that these assumptions are not shared throughout Europe. While Americans pour tax monies into the search for the biochemical basis of alcoholism, European nations often place greater emphasis on psychosocial determinants (and again do not necessarily accept, in the same sense, the concept of a unitary disease for which a unitary cause must be found). Social policy in Sweden focuses on the control of alcohol consumption and the unhealthy consequences of overdrinking, seeking social causes and solutions to harmful drinking. The assertion that alcoholism (read: negative consequences of overdrinking) is not caused by alcohol would be met there with puzzled bemusement. In Germany and surrounding nations the psychodynamic tradition remains strong, attributing alcoholism to underlying pathology and thus viewing problematic drinking as a secondary symptom. In the U.S., interest in this latter perspective has warmed slightly via the concept of "secondary alcoholism," a subtype deriving from other problems such as affective disorder and presumably distinct from the primary disease of alcoholism (e.g., Schuckit, 1979).

### Evidence on the Issue

As indicated earlier, there is increasing evidence that family history factors and, by inference, genetic transmission can influence the probability of developing alcohol-related problems (Goodwin, 1976). Individual differences in tolerance for alcohol may influence one's ability to discriminate levels of intoxication and thus the potential for self-control (Lipscomb and Nathan, 1980; Nathan, 1980a). Tarter and his colleagues

(1977) have presented evidence pointing to a link between minimal brain dysfunction in childhood and alcoholism in adulthood, an interesting convergence with earlier findings (e.g., Jones, 1968) that childhood behavior problems may predict adult alcoholism (Miller, 1976). Interest has increased (accompanied by extensive U.S. research funding) in biochemical substrates of addiction and the desire for alcohol (e.g. Myers and Melchior, 1977; Triana *et al.*, 1980). Findings from all of these sources have been interpreted in the U.S. as definitive evidence for the American conception of alcoholism.

What is unclear at the present time is the *relative* importance of biomedical determinants of drinking when combined with other known influential factors such as modeling and social norms, operant reinforcement, and expectancies (Nathan, 1980a). To date no etiologic variable or combination of variables has enabled robust prediction of adult alcoholism within the general population, and assignment of "primary" importance to one class of determinants, be it chromosomes or personality traits, is a matter of faith rather than evidence. There is, as yet, no single circumscribed disease entity and no unitary etiology based on definitive scientific data.

## 3. LOSS OF CONTROL

The idea that certain individuals mysteriously lose self-control upon ingesting alcohol can be traced at least as far back as the nineteenth-century European concept of *dipsomania*, which historically has blended two kinds of loss of control: inability to stop drinking once started, and acute lack of volitional control over social behavior when drinking. The latter has now been crystallized into the syndrome of pathological or idiosyncratic intoxication, but it is to the former type of loss of control that the American conception of alcoholism usually refers. Best expressed in the AA slogan, "One drink, one drunk," the contention is that alcoholics react to the chemical alcohol in a unique fashion that causes them to become incapable of resisting further drink. Thus the taking of one drink and the availability of additional alcohol are believed to necessarily result in a drinking binge. It is fair to say that this belief is a cornerstone of the current American conception of alcoholism.

If there is any assumption about alcoholism that may be common between the U.S. and Europe, it is probably this one, perhaps because of the European origins of the idea of dipsomania, but even here there is wide variation. In Germany I was told that any treatment program permitting an alternative goal to permanent abstinence would likely be closed by the government through revocation of funding. In Britain, on the other hand, I encountered clinics where loss of control was regarded as a rather outdated assumption, disproved long ago by scientific research. The Norwegian clinic where I worked took an intermediate view: that loss of control occurs in some problem drinkers, but certainly not in all. The latter poses a tempting compromise: to conclude that "true alcoholics" do manifest loss of control whereas other problem drinkers ("prealcoholic" or "prodromal"?) do not. This is at least a somewhat stable détente for the U.S. professional trying to live with his or her colleagues while still making sense of the existing data.

### Evidence on the Issue

Yet existing research findings, if we are to take them seriously, require us to reach somewhat different conclusions. In the most thorough review of this issue to date, Scottish psychologists Heather and Robertson (1981) summarized the findings of the now numerous studies examining loss-of-control phenomena, including: (*a*) laboratory studies on intoxication in alcoholics, (*b*) experiments on factors controlling drinking behavior of alcoholics, (*c*) explorations of the effects of a priming dose of alcohol, and (*d*) expectancy research employing balanced placebo designs. From this large body of evidence they conclude:

> When allowed to determine the volume and pattern of their own drinking, alcoholics do *not* drink to oblivion but *do* clearly demonstrate positive sources of control over drinking behaviour. . . . In rejecting a chain-reaction type of loss of control, it is not being denied, of course, that alcoholics never drink until they pass out or get arrested, etc.; some frequently do and this is one of the most damaging and perplexing aspects of their behaviour. The point is, however, that this extreme drunkenness cannot be accounted for on the basis of some internally located inability to stop (p. 122).

They further reject more recent "watered down" versions of the loss of control belief (which assert merely that alcoholics cannot be sure of stopping once started; e.g., Keller, 1972), pointing out that such an assertion only restates what is already known without explaining it: that alcoholics are *more likely* than others to continue drinking once started.

Are there data to help us in constructing a less simplistic basis for understanding loss of control? One interesting line of research was initiated by Marlatt *et al.* (1973), who employed a balanced placebo design in which some alcoholics were led to believe they would be drinking alcohol, whereas others were told they would receive a nonalcohol drink. Within each of these two groups, half actually received alcohol disguised in a mixer and half did not. Thus there were alcoholics drinking alcohol and knowing it, others drinking alcohol without knowing it, others drinking a beverage they falsely believed to contain alcohol, and still others drinking only mixer and knowing it. Alcoholics drank more of the beverage when they believed it to contain alcohol, whether or not it actually did. These findings have been confirmed and extended in several studies: drinking and experienced craving appear to be triggered not by alcohol itself but by the belief that it is present. The plausible conclusion is that loss of control and craving, whatever they may be, are triggered by "psychological" rather than "physiological" stimuli. Marlatt has postulated a cognitive "abstinence violation effect" as one possible explanation (Cummings *et al.*, 1980).

A further experiment, however, suggests that this, too, is too simple. Repeating the Marlatt design, British researchers distinguished between severely dependent alcoholics and those showing only moderate levels of dependence, and they employed more sensitive measures of craving, including hand tremor (Stockwell *et al.*, 1982). For subjects with, at most, moderate dependence, Marlatt's findings were confirmed: drinking and craving were determined mostly by alcohol itself. For the severely dependent group, however, a craving effect was demonstrated in the group receiving alcohol without their knowledge.

What these important data may mean is that for the more severely dependent alcoholics, a physiological craving response appears if the individual drinks alcohol even without knowing it. This is consistent with the AA notion of an abnormal physical response to alcohol among alcoholics. Still several caveats must be noted before the celebrations begin: (*a*) Craving is not the same as loss of control. (*b*) The aforementioned findings regarding volitional control of drinking among alcoholics still stand: continued drinking is not a necessary consequence of a priming dose. (*c*) These findings can be interpreted equally well from a learning perspective (Hodgson *et al.*, 1979). (*d*) It may be possible to teach alcoholics to resist further drinking in spite of experienced craving, whatever its origin. The strategy of "cue exposure," although still unproved, may prove useful in helping alcoholics resist relapse when faced with high-risk situations (Hodgson and Rankin, 1976; Rankin and Hodgson, 1976). (e) Finally, the alcohol-triggered craving response was obtained only for severely dependent individuals, and does not apply to the vast majority of less dependent individuals who would be diagnosed in the U.S. as "alcoholic" according to generic criteria (cf. Hansen and Emrick, 1983).

Cue exposure represents an interesting avenue of research that may ultimately help us to understand the craving response in dependent drinkers and, perhaps, to develop an effective treatment program for overcoming it. This type of research would be very difficult to conduct within the U.S., where it is nearly unthinkable to administer alcohol to an alcoholic (particularly for therapeutic purposes). Although this has been done in some American experiments, the *Zeitgeist* requires that it be defended as an extraordinary and dangerous procedure. Yet the first question regarding such a proposed treatment procedure ought not be "Is it ethical?" but rather "Is it helpful?", for the former can hardly be answered without information about the latter. Should alcohol administration turn out to be one component of a highly effective method for combatting alcohol dependence and relapse, then it may be unethical *not* to use it. In Britain research is progressing on such questions (e.g., Is it possible to "decondition" craving for alcohol?). Recent evidence suggests that in spite of our best efforts for abstinence, more than 90% of alcoholics treated in U.S. public facilities drink again within 4 years, and most of them sooner rather than later (Polich *et al.*, 1981). Might it be possible to prepare them so that if a "slip" should occur, it would not turn into a disastrous full-blown relapse? Might it even be that teaching alcoholics *that they have no control* after the first drink (an assertion based on no scientific evidence) is harmful, increasing the risk of relapse (Cummings *et al.*, 1980; Miller, 1983b)? Such ideas are likely to be regarded in the U.S. as dangerous nonsense, primarily because of our unswerving commitment to the loss-of-control assumption.

## 4. ALCOHOLISM IS IRREVERSIBLE

Americans almost universally endorse the adage that alcoholism is irreversible: Once an alcoholic, always an alcoholic. AA members call themselves "recovering," not "recovered." The meaning of this assertion is not that it is impossible to return to health. Rather the meaning is that it is impossible ever to drink again and remain healthy. The assertion is absolute: not that it is *inadvisable* to drink, or that it is *unlikely* that an alcoholic could maintain nonproblem drinking, but that it is *impossible*. Heather and Robertson (1981) point out that in its absolute form, this assertion is essentially unverifiable in that only a single exception is required to refute it, and adherents must therefore discredit every reported case of moderate and nonproblem drinking in a diagnosed alcoholic.

Jellinek, to whom this assumption is sometimes attributed, never asserted the irreversibility of loss of control or alcoholism, warned against the restrictive definition that it implies, and specifically argued for a multiplicity of types of alcoholism requiring different kinds of treatment. Many of the clinics that I visited in Europe seemed to take a pragmatic approach more consonant with a generic view of alcoholism, working toward the general goal of minimizing future alcohol-related problems among their patients.

### Evidence on the Issue

Stated in its most extreme (although not unrepresentative) form, the irreversibility assumption asserts that "No true alcoholic has ever been or will ever be able to maintain nonproblem drinking." One can, of course, quibble about the meaning of "true alcoholic" and the length of time necessary to demonstrate "maintenance." Still, to any reasonable reader of the scientific research on alcoholism treatment outcome, this assertion must be regarded as soundly refuted. Numerous studies have documented sustained nonproblem drinking outcomes in individuals who were, by any criteria, diagnosable alcoholics. These studies have been reviewed in detail elsewhere (Heather and Robertson, 1981; Pattison et al., 1977). Suffice it to say that there is no scientific basis for maintaining the impossibility of nonproblem drinking outcomes, and that there is substantial evidence to the contrary. Such outcomes have been reported since the earliest treatment studies (e.g., Gerard and Saenger, 1966; Wallerstein et al., 1957; Shea, 1954), and continue to appear in virtually every investigation where adequate follow-up procedures are employed with a large sample of treated alcoholics (e.g., Polich et al., 1981).

## 5. NECESSITY OF ABSTINENCE

If one accepts the preceding four assumptions of the American conception of alcoholism, it follows logically that there is no alternative to total and lifelong abstinence for the alcoholic. American professionals who advocate any alternative to abstinence are likely to be (and have been) attacked as naïve fools, misguided intellectuals sadly misinformed about the "reality" of alcoholism, unwitting murderers, or perhaps themselves alcoholics denying their own disease. Scientific evidence inconsistent with this assumption is dismissed as invalid, fraudulent, and dangerous. Lovern (1982), writing in the national magazine *Alcoholism*, proclaimed that he "had undergone a conversion experience" and confessed his renunciation of scientific research, protesting that "the kind of science and technology that tries to teach alcoholics to drink is, in my mind, a warped Frankensteinian thing" (p. 39). The tone of his remarks is not atypical of the emotional confrontations that have surrounded the controlled drinking controversy in the U.S., some of the most intense conflicts in the alcoholism field since the rise and demise of prohibition (Miller, 1983a). Indeed, the total proscription of drinking for the special class of people called "alcoholic" is reminiscent of arguments from the prohibitionist period, except that during that time they were leveled against all drinkers. For example, Thompson (1915) proclaimed:

> Moderate drinking is a stage; it is not a fixed point . . . . There is no moderate drinker who is not going on to the next stage of his journey. . . . Few, of those who drink can be classed as moderate drinkers. Few, or you might say, none; for the moderate drinker is either coming or going. He is coming back toward the norm of sobriety, or he is going on toward drunkenness. One or the other. (p. 45).

The argument for inevitable progression is the same, except that currently it is reserved for "alcoholics" and no longer applied to all drinkers.

Nevertheless as a treatment issue, the controlled drinking controversy is of recent vintage. During the 1950s North American treatment outcome studies routinely reported nonpoblem drinking outcomes without apology, regarding them as successes. Wallerstein et al. (1957), for example, described a broad conception of improvement in their major treatment study at the Winter Veterans Administration Hospital:

> We have not defined abstinence in an absolute either-or manner but in terms of a state, admitting of degree and difference. Nor have we been committed to the proposition that complete abstinence is the only or necessary psychiatric goal of therapy for alcoholism. Our primary focus was on degree of change, and therefore we wanted to know how much the patient was drinking now as compared to the amount consumed prior to hospitalization. (p. 17).[1]

It was not until shortly after the publication of Jellinek's (1960) treatise on the disease conception of alcoholism that the first major tremors of the treatment controversy were felt, arising in response to the Davies (1962) report of nonproblem drinking among "recovered alcohol addicts." In Britain this report had been regarded as only modestly interesting, and the American outcry against it took Davies quite by surprise (Davies, 1979). Since then the conflict has become increasingly heated, to the point that moderation is now denied as being a possibility for anyone labeled "alcoholic" (Miller, 1983a). Because Americans still largely use the generic definition to *diagnose* alcoholism, this includes everyone with significant alcohol-related impairment. Prior to 1960, moderation outcomes were recognized and usually regarded as noncontroversial, and we are witnessing a conflict that has emerged in the U.S. with the ascendance of the current American conception of alcoholism.

Although this conflict of paradigms is not uniquely American, nowhere is there apparent the same degree of widespread and emotional clamor over the issue (cf. Saslow, 1969). The clearest demonstration of this for me was in observing audience responses as I presented my research on controlled drinking treatments. In the U.S. such talks are almost invariably met with resistance ranging from skepticism to overt hostility. European audiences who chose to attend my talks, by contrast, addressed pragmatic and methodological issues and expressed interest in learning the techniques and limitations of this approach: for whom would it be effective, and for whom not? I was challenged (quite rightly) on my sharp distinction between "addicted" and "nonaddicted" individuals, given that dependence is a continuous rather than discrete variable. In Britain I was astonished to find my ideas regarded as "a bit old-fashioned," particularly my defense of total abstinence as "the only realistic alternative for the addicted alcoholic." To be sure one could argue that my audiences were self-selected; yet a recent survey of alcoholism treatment units and of councils on alcoholism in Britain reflected an overall attitude markedly different from that in the U.S.: 93% of British programs regarded controlled drinking to be an appropriate goal, and 76% of the units reported that they were offering treatment aimed at controlled drinking for some patients (Robertson and Heather, 1982). Although some U.S. professionals now recommend controlled drinking for some clients, the percentage remains small (Perkins *et al.*, 1981).

It is perhaps no coincidence that much of the important progress on this issue of treatment goals has occurred outside of the United States. The American debate was sparked by British research (Davis, 1962). Controlled drinking therapies originated in Australia (Lovibond and Caddy, 1970) and continue to be evaluated there (Brown, 1980; Lovibond, 1975). In Japan, Arikawa and Inanaga (1973) reported that "A forced abstinence by persuasion or threat is an ineffective method in controlling alcoholism. It makes the alcoholic patient 'escape' further toward drinking. Therefore, we do not maintain any negative attitude toward the patient resuming drinking" (p. 11). Important studies have emerged from Canada (Alden, 1978; Popham and Schmidt, 1976; Sanchez-Craig, 1980, in press) and England (Orford, 1973; Orford *et al.*, 1976). Many U.S. researchers who have ventured into the arena of controlled drinking have found it difficult to sustain a program of research or obtain funding, and the controversy regarding the Sobell and Sobell (1973) study (Pendery *et al.*, 1982) is likely to discourage further U.S. research on this topic for some time to come. Meanwhile active research is progressing in England and Scotland, Norway and Denmark, Ontario and British Columbia.

A related and interesting difference between nations is in public response to programs offering controlled drinking. Virtually every investigation of this kind in the U.S. has had difficulty in recruiting clients. In a well-established research clinic after

7 years of work in Albuquerque (population 400,000), we still struggle to recruit 40 clients for a study offering free treatment. In California we advertised a similar program in the newspapers of San Francisco and San Jose, which reach over a million people. In the end we obtained a total sample of 28 (Miller et al., 1981). This pattern has persisted over seven clinical studies conducted over 9 years in three different states. Never have we been flooded with applicants, nor has any U.S. program of which I am aware. More than one clinic attempting to offer controlled drinking has closed the program for lack of referrals (e.g., Nathan, 1980b), and two U.S. attempts to establish self-help organizations based on moderation concepts have failed. Similar difficulties in client recruitment have been encountered in Scotland (Cameron and Spence, 1976; Heather, 1983). I was surprised, therefore, to learn from Oslo psychologist Fanny Duckert that she receives hundreds of calls from a single announcement and has to turn applicants away. Similar response followed announcement of a program at the Hjellestad Clinic in Bergen, under the direction of psychologists Arvid Skutle and Geir Berg. In Copenhagen, psychiatrist Andreas Sørensen began an experimental treatment program with a goal of moderation and has had more applicants over a period of 3 years than could possibly be treated by his four program staff. The texts of news media announcements for these programs were quite similar to those used in U.S. programs. Whatever the reason for this cross-national difference, it is a striking one.

### Evidence on the Issue

Evidence presented in regard to the irreversibility assumption was focused on the occurrence of nonproblem drinking outcomes after treatment which, in almost all cases, had advocated abstinence. These were therefore "accidental" or "incidental" moderation outcomes, unintended byproducts of a system designed to encourage abstention. The usual observed rates of controlled and nonproblem drinking range between 5% and 20% in such studies, when no direct training in moderation is provided (Miller and Hester, 1980; Polich et al., 1981).

But what is the result when problem drinkers are treated with the explicit goal of moderate drinking and are taught appropriate skills for maintaining nonproblem drinking? At least 24 investigations have been published to date, the findings of which have been reviewed elsewhere (Heather and Robertson, 1981; Miller, 1983a; Miller and Hester, 1980). Several findings have been quite consistent across these studies: (a) When the population being treated consists of problem drinkers with no more than moderate dependence on alcohol, successful outcomes range between 60% and 80% at follow-up studies at 1 to 2 years. (b) Success with more highly dependent drinkers is less impressive, although no study has yet demonstrated that moderation training is less effective than abstinence training overall. (c) Probability of maintaining controlled drinking can be predicted from the severity of alcohol problems, with less severe (and less dependent) problem drinkers achieving and maintaining nonproblem drinking outcomes, and more severe cases tending toward abstinence.

It has been argued that controlled drinking therapies are "experimental" and "unproven" treatments. This may be true, in that much research remains to be done. If this is asserted, however, then the same must certainly be said of every other alcoholism treatment method in existence because the total volume of controlled research confirming moderation methods by far exceeds that supporting any other approach (Miller and Hester, 1980). This leads directly to a discussion of the sixth and final assumption of the American conception of alcoholism.

## 6. SUPERIOR TREATMENT APPROACHES

If there is one assertion on which American experts seem to agree, it is that Alcoholics Anonymous is far and away the most effective hope for recovery. Madsen (1974) has called AA "the only continuing and successful group dealing with alcoholism" (p. 156) and, while acknowledging that it is not for everyone, has asserted that, in comparison with other therapies, its success rate is nearly miraculous" (p. 195). Father Joseph Martin (1980), outspoken advocate of the American conception of alcoholism, has proclaimed AA to be "medicine's crowning glory" and "the world's greatest therapy." Such praise continues to be echoed by the most eminent researchers in the U.S. alcoholism field. Vaillant, for example, recently stated in *Time* magazine that "AA is the most effective means of treating alcoholism" (O'Reilly, 1983, p. 89). The official "big book" of AA (1955) proclaims that 50% of those coming to AA and "really trying" became sober at once and remained so, 25% more had a few relapses and then became abstinent, and the remaining 25% showed improvement, further asserting that two-thirds of AA dropouts eventually return to the fellowship. Even major psychology textbooks (e.g., Coleman *et al.*, 1980) have echoed the "considerable success" of AA in treating alcoholism.

Clearly AA is the most favored and ubiquitous approach in the U.S. today, and has been for some time (Moore and Buchanan, 1966). There is, in fact, no other nation in which the influence of this organization is so strongly felt. In Norway, AA has never obtained a strong foothold and the American conception of alcoholism is not a dominant view. The relative absence of AA groups in Norway may, as several alcoholism professionals indicated to me, be due to the fact that "AA is simply not Norwegian." The public confessional aspects, overt religiosity, open revelations of personal feelings and problems in a group setting, intense social support and intentional intervention in the lives of others all fit much better in the American than in the Norwegian culture. A loosely related organization known as "the Links" has achieved greater acceptance, in part by adapting its format to local cultural norms and practices. Alcoholics Anonymous groups are more numerous in southern Europe and Britain, but nowhere does it dominate treatment ideology and practice as it does in the United States.

Beyond this there are other noteworthy differences among nations with regard to intervention approaches. The socialized medicine prevalent in Europe and Canada affords each government the opportunity to selectively favor certain treatment methods over others by certifying them as reimbursable interventions for alcoholism (a privilege held by private third-party insurers in the U.S.). In Scandinavia and Britain there is a clear trend away from expensive and extensive inpatient treatment and a movement toward the outpatient polyclinic as the primary source of care. In Germany, by contrast, alcoholism treatment proceeds within inpatient programs of a duration almost unthinkable in the United States. It encountered one system with an average inpatient stay of 6 months, where continuous inpatient treatment of 12 months or more was not unusual. Still another difference concerns the type of professional deemed appropriate for delivering treatment to alcoholics. The American emphasis on the recovering alcoholic paraprofessional was not apparent in any other country I visited. In Germany, alcoholism treatment is heavily entrusted to the medical community. In Holland, social workers appeared to be the more prevalent primary professional group involved in care of alcoholic patients. In Norway I found the psychologist to be regarded as a primary therapist, with medical and social work staff serving in collegial consulting roles. Nowhere did I encounter a special importance placed on whether or not the professional had had a personal history of alcoholism.

## Evidence on the Issue

The AA "big book" claim of 75% permanent sobriety plus additional improved cases would certainly be a miraculous recovery rate in a field where the average success rate of treatment programs has been estimated at 26% at 1 year (Miller and Hester, 1980). Unfortunately the claims of extraordinary success within AA are based on no data that have been published for scientific scrutiny. Questionnaire surveys of AA members have been plagued by inherent selection bias and the absence of any method for confirming anonymous self-reports, but even the most optimistic of these point to sobriety rates around 50% over 1 year among regular AA attenders, excluding from consideration less faithful members (Miller and Hester, 1980). Of the only two controlled studies published to date, one (Ditman and Crawford, 1966; Ditman et al., 1967) reported a 31% rate of success (no new arrests) for those randomly assigned to AA versus a 44% success rate in the probation-only control group. The other (Brandsma et al., 1980) reported a 68% drop-out rate in AA, and after random assignment the AA-treated patients were found to be significantly more likely to binge at 3-month follow-up than were the untreated control group or patients assigned to any of the three other treatment programs studied; otherwise no differences were found. Although both of these studies contain methodologic weaknesses, they represent the only current controlled investigations of the effectiveness of AA, and their findings are less than encouraging.

Other commonly lauded treatment methods for U.S. alcoholics are similarly unsupported by data. Group psychotherapies, probably the second most popular intervention in the U.S. (Moore and Buchanan, 1966), are not approaches about which one would be enthusiastic on the basis of existing research. Two controlled studies have reported no differences between patients assigned at random to receive versus not receive group therapy, with observed differences favoring the untreated groups (Pattison et al., 1967; Zimberg, 1974). Studies comparing group therapy with alternative treatments similarly have failed to support superiority of group methods, and particularly lacking is any evidence of effectiveness of the popular confrontational-style group (Miller and Hester, 1980).

The usefulness of disulfiram, a drug widely prescribed and sometimes mandated for alcoholics, is likewise unsupported by controlled research. Gallant et al. (1968) found no differences in effectiveness between group therapy alone, disulfiram alone, group therapy plus disulfiram, and no treatment. Present data suggest that the effectiveness rates reported in uncontrolled studies are probably attributable to placebo effects or motivational characteristics of patients willing to accept the drug rather than to any specific effectiveness of disulfiram itself (Becker, 1979; Miller and Hester, 1980). One recent study supports disulfiram as an aid in sobriety for married persons, but only if the drug is accompanied by a behavioral compliance program (Azrin et al., 1982). In the absence of strong evidence for efficacy, caution in the use of this drug seems warranted, given emerging indications of potential carcinogenic (Lijinski, 1979) or other harmful effects (Burnett and Reading, 1970; Kwentus and Major, 1979; Van Thiel et al., 1979).

It appears, then, that treatment methods routinely employed in most American clinics and widely endorsed as superior in effectiveness are quite lacking in scientific support. The existing literature would, in fact, lead one to the conclusion that these treatment methods would be of little or no value beyond that inherent in placebo and spontaneous remission, and that they may even be harmful in some cases. Other treatment methods are now reasonably well supported by controlled and comparative research: family therapies, aversion therapies, social skills training, desensitization, community reinforcement approach, and behavioral self-control training (for review, see Miller and Hester, 1980). Yet these methods are rarely used in current American programs. Still other treatment methods loudly praised in the U.S. simply cannot be evaluated because of a total absence of adequately controlled investigations of their efficacy. These include mandated "employee assistance" programs (often claimed to have an 80% success rate), "alcohol education" programs such as those frequently mandated for drunk driving offenders, and the many alcoholism treatment programs offering expensive inpatient care. (Significant exceptions are the aversion therapy hospitals — Schick and Raleigh hills — which have published at least uncontrolled outcome data for scientific scrutiny.) There is, at present, no adequate evidence that inpatient programs are any more effective than less costly outpatient approaches, that longer programs are more effective than briefer programs, or that counselors who are themselves alcoholics have a better success rate than nonalcoholics in counseling people with alcohol problems (Miller and Hester, 1980).

## REFLECTIONS

All of this leads me to the conclusion that the American alcoholism treatment community could benefit substantially from exposure to professionals and models from other nations. There has developed in the U.S. a pervasive ideology that conceptualizes alcoholism as a unitary disease characterized by an irreversible loss of control. Single-minded adherence to this view has led otherwise rational and objective professionals to ignore existing scientific evidence and to endorse poorly substantiated treatment practices to the exclusion of other possible and promising interventions. The dominance of this ideology has further discouraged the development of new approaches to treatment and prevention that may depart from the central assumptions outlined earlier. Patients who disagree with the fundamental assumptions of this ideology are likely to be accused of "denial" (Miller, 1983b), and professionals who deviate from it are regarded as profligates either denying or unaware of the "reality" of alcoholism. We do, indeed, seem to have "lost control over the disease concept of alcoholism" (Robinson, 1972) and to have adopted the very exclusivism against which Jellinek (1960) so clearly warned. Is this condition irreversible?

Although slow in emerging, there have recently been signs of change in response to the data reviewed above. Goldman (1979) has opined, "If the recent tide of behavioral research on alcoholism has suggested anything, it is that alcoholics are best studied not as a uniform group, but instead as a heterogeneous population which can be subdivided" (p. 79). Pattison et al. (1977) reviewed "emerging concepts" of alcoholism, a trend also recognized by Jacobson (1976):

> There is another development taking place, slowly but steadily gathering momentum, which will increasingly demand a greater awareness of and attention to systematic and scientifically sound approaches to detection, assessment, and diagnosis. That development is the growing recognition and acceptance of valid and reliable scientific evidence suggesting that the current concept of alcoholism may be inadequate at best and misleading at worst.
>
> The concept of alcoholism as a single disease, a unitary clinical entity based on a medical model, believed to progress along a known or predictable continuum, and measurable in terms of a single common symptom may be an oversimplified representation of a complex multidimensional problem, and acceptance of that concept may lead to faulty understanding of etiology and treatment. Detection, assessment, or diagnosis based on such a concept may be analogous to a physician's including in a single diagnostic category all patients who have the symptom of fever.

By categorizing all people by the same label on the basis of a common symptom—
the presence of a fever or the excessive use of alcohol—there is a tendency to focus on
similarities to the neglect of what may be some significant differences. Consequently one
may overlook some important clues to a meaningful diagnosis, fuller understanding of
etiology, and application of effective treatment.

Rather than continue the chimerical pursuit of a 'typical alcoholic' or a unitary 'alcoholism,' it would seem more reasonable and prudent to entertain the idea that there may
be several *alcoholisms*, which, once detected, assessed, and diagnosed, may be amenable
to different treatments (pp. 15–16).

Such departure from the unitary disease conception has been adamantly opposed
by some. Seixas (1976), for example, defended the utility of a unitary diagnosis because it "protects treatment centers from a hugh influx of patients not really needing
their services, protects researchers from falsely thinking they have arrested a disease
when they have only observed the incidental change of drinking pattern of an ex-
perimenter or a reactor, and it protects society from giving the benefits as well as
the penalties of the presumption of alcoholism to many citizens" (p. 412). Pursuing
this logic, Seixas argued for the delimiting of the term "alcoholism" to those individuals truly possessing the disease as he conceived it: "If we now should limit what we
mean by alcoholism to those who have developed cell tolerance, withdrawal states on
stopping, and the diseases associated with alcoholism (which recent research has shown
require such amounts of alcohol over periods of time as to bespeak cell tolerance),
we have delimited a disease which we know to be present in our alcohol-dependent
people" (p. 411).

Seixas thus does not fail to recognize the existence of different types of alcohol-
related impairment, but only advocates a special status for a dependent "disease" subtype and reservation of the term "alcoholic" for that subtype, a recommendation also
made by others (Miller and Caddy, 1977) and indirectly reflected in the current diagnostic standards of the American Psychiatric Association (1980). What is troubling,
however, is the implication that problem drinkers who are not fully qualified disease-
type alcoholics do not "really need" treatment or deserve the privileged status atten-
dant on the alcoholism label. It is unclear why society should reserve status and services only for those problem drinkers who have practiced excess sufficiently long to
establish dependence, cell tolerance, and physical deterioration.

Can we have it both ways? American fixation on this particular conception of
alcoholism did, after all, arise in part from the personal experience of alcoholics, and
Jellinek did postulate gamma alcoholism as one subtype within a larger spectrum of
alcohol-related problems. Would it be possible for us to recover the more generic perspective of alcoholism that arose in Europe (and still survives there), while still re-
taining our interest in the particular severe kind of alcoholism that currently occupies
center stage in U.S. alcoholism politics?

The answer, needless to say, is yes. Acknowledgment and exploration of the bigger
picture does not require the denial or erasure of any particular part. It is not necessary, for example, to insist that alcoholics have never experienced loss of control. Experienced loss of control is a fascinating phenomenon and one well deserving of further study. It is merely necessary to stop insisting that all alcoholics must or will
experience it. It is not necessary to deny the reality of craving. Craving does occur
and can be measured and experimentally manipulated. But *why* does it occur? The
vague attribution of this experience to a mysterious allergic-like disease was only a
beginning, and not one that has been very helpful in advancing our understanding
of how it arises and how it can be reversed (if it can). It is not necessary to deny the
importance of abstinence as a treatment goal for many alcoholics. Abstinence remains
a wise choice, and for some the only healthy choice. It is only necessary to stop in-

sisting that there is no other possibility for anyone with alcohol-related problems. It is not even necessary to deny denial! The phenomena that we have called "denial" have long been regarded as major stumbling blocks in the process of treatment. But what is denial? Is there a way in which we can help alcoholics to increase their motivation for treatment, rather than blaming them for not having enough? It should be possible to apply known principles of motivation and experimental social psychology in helping individuals with this difficult struggle of deciding whether to do something about their drinking, and indeed a large body of research exists to guide us in this process (Miller, 1983b, 1985).

A major obstacle, if we wish to understand different types of alcoholism more fully, is that at present we have few adequate diagnostic criteria. American efforts at diagnosis and early identification have focused largely on detecting the presence versus absence of a unitary disease, guided by the AA ideology (Miller, 1976). Assessment has been regarded as a problem in signal detection, in binary classification: individuals with the disease of alcoholism should be detected and treated as early as possible—others may drink as they please.

The "reality" of alcohol-related impairment seems to be much more complicated than this. Deterioration may occur in any or all of a wide variety of organ systems of the body, in neuropsychological capabilities, in social functioning, in work productivity, in family relations, in economic stability, in sexual functioning, in personal mood. Any one of these may show deleterious effects of drinking without more general deterioration appearing on other dimensions. Impairment on one or more of these domains may occur with or without personal awareness, family awareness, a family history of alcoholism, physical dependence on alcohol, or an official diagnosis of alcoholism. The generic definition of alcoholism—the original definition—encompasses all of these patterns. If it is too confusing for Americans to refer to all of these as "alcoholism," then perhaps we should adopt a different generic term such as "problem drinking" (Miller and Caddy, 1977). The danger in this, however, is thereby to imply an as yet unjustifiable *qualitative* distinction between "true alcoholics" and other problem drinkers (e.g., Seixas, 1976).

It is just possible, though, that somewhere in this generic tangle of multiple alcohol-related problems there are some meaningful syndromes or clusters. There may be, for example, a severe form of alcoholism that is partially inheritable and characterized by rapid development of dependence. The kind of research required to sort out such differential subtypes is only in infancy at present. Such efforts could certainly be accelerated by cross-national collaboration. If indeed there are "disease" entities with biochemical or genetic etiologic components, these should appear with some consistency across national boundaries. Syndromes that retain integrity across cultures are excellent candidates for study. To be sure, consistency should appear in the sequelae of excessive drinking (cf. Løberg and Miller, this volume). It was to this that Huss (1849) referred in introducing the term "alcoholism." But if we wish to validate the present American conception of alcoholism, the challenge is to find not only differentiated syndromes of impairment, but also distinct etiologic factors that predispose to these syndromes. They may well exist, but we are unlikely to find them if we continue looking for them by trying to differentiate between "normal" individuals and "alcoholics" diagnosed according to the generic definition.

There are several good reasons to move in this direction of jointly broadening our conception of alcoholism while continuing to seek subtype entities. First, it will allow us to understand and perhaps treat a broader spectrum of individuals with alcohol-related problems. At present almost anyone diagnosed as alcoholic in the U.S. is likely to be told that he or she has the disease of (gamma) alcoholism and must abstain for life. For *many* people with alcohol-related problems this simply is not true. Many problem drinkers, probably the vast majority, are not significantly dependent on alcohol and do not experience an inability to stop drinking. Kaprio (1981) has recently observed "that many alcohol problems cannot be conceptualized as manifestations of an underlying entity, that of alcohol dependence. Alcohol dependence, while widespread and worrying, constitutes only a small part of the total of alcohol-related problems" (p. xi). To treat the less dependent problem drinker as if he or she were a gamma alcoholic is inappropriate, and likely to result in either drop-out or unsuccessful outcome. To broaden our conception of alcoholism is to enable the process of identification, motivation, and treatment of a broader range of problem drinkers.

Second, if one or more etiologic entities do exist within the broad spectrum of alcoholism, it is vitally important to identify and more fully understand them. What are the cardinal markers, and what are the optimal treatment interventions for each? What are the earliest possible identifying signs?

Relatedly, a differential understanding of alcohol problems permits a more differentiated approach to intervention, both at the level of treatment and at a preventive level. Canadian researchers Schmidt and Popham (1980) have observed:

> The emphasis that has been placed, during the post-war period, on the treatment of alcoholics as the main remedial measure flowed logically from the disease concept. On the other hand, the concept seems to preclude any measure of primary prevention until the unique predisposing factor is discovered . . . One must emphasize that to challenge the classical disease concept is not to deny that those now labeled alcoholics are usually very sick people in need of help. Rather one challenges the usefulness of the assumption that the illness is the product of a unique susceptibility to alcohol . . . [A]lcoholics, as we know them from clinics, constitute only a minority among the drinkers who consume quantities that are liable to produce illness and early death (p. 2).

Three decades earlier, Jellinek (1952) warned that "an unwarranted extension of the disease conception can only be harmful, because sooner or later the misapplication will reflect on the legitimate use too and, more importantly, will tend to weaken the ethical basis of social sanctions against drunkenness" (p. 674).

Jellinek's description aptly captures what has been occurring in the United States, where social policy has focused on identifying "alcoholics" and dealing with them. This leaves "nonalcoholics" with the illusion that they can drink with impunity, and focuses public policy on "diagnosis" and "treatment" of a unique disease rather than on controlling alcohol consumption. Less bridled by a unitary disease conception, many European nations employ social policy to control alcohol use and misuse within the population at large (Mäkelä et al., 1981). What are the relative merits of these alternative approaches? What impact does each have on overall problem incidence levels? Departure from the limited conception of alcoholism as a unitary disease enables the development and evaluation of alternative strategies for reducing the incidence of harmful alcohol consumption.

Perhaps our best guiding principle through all of this is to remain close to the data. The current American conception of alcoholism and the treatment system that has been perpetuated by it exemplify how far it is possible to stray when a particular theory becomes more important than evidence itself. Each nation is likely to have its vested interests, its practiced conceptions of the problem. To reject and deny existing evidence because it is inconvenient or inconsistent with a cherished ideology, although not at all uncommon, is a disservice most of all to those we propose to help. It is premature to claim to have the answers when we are still searching for the right questions. With so many loose ends, so many questions unanswered and still to be asked, and so many possibilities at hand, we can scarcely afford to discard the few empirical maps that we have and set off across the uncertain terrain in pursuit of mirages, even though the vision on the horizon be that of the great American dream of how alcoholism ought to be.

## REFERENCES

ALCOHOLICS ANONYMOUS. 1955. Alcoholics Anonymous: The Story of How Many Thousands of Men and Women have Recovered from Alcoholism. AA World Services. New York, NY.

ALDEN, L. 1978. Evaluation of a preventive self-management programme for problem drinkers. Can. J. Behav. Sci. **10**: 258–263.

AMERICAN PSYCHIATRIC ASSOCIATION. 1980. Diagnostic and Statistical Manual of Mental Disorders, 3rd ed. Washington, DC.

ARIKAWA, K. & K. INANAGA. 1973. The therapeutic mechanism of the double medication technique with cyanamide for alcoholism. Folia Psychiatr. Neurol. Jpn. **27**: 9–15.

AZRIN, N. H., R. W. SISSON, R. MEYERS & M. GODLEY. 1982. Alcoholism treatment by disulfiram and community reinforcement therapy. J. Behav. Ther. Exp. Psychiatry **13**: 105–112.

BECKER, C. E. 1979. Pharmacotherapy in the treatment of alcoholism. *In* The Diagnosis and Treatment of Alcoholism. J. H. Mendelson & N. K. Mello, Eds. McGraw-Hill. New York, NY.

BRANDSMA, J. M., M. C. MAULTSBY & R. J. WELSH. 1980. The Outpatient Treatment of Alcoholism: A Review and Comparative Study. University Park Press. Baltimore, MD.

BROWN, R. A. 1980. Conventional education and controlled drinking education courses with convicted drunken drivers. Behavior Therapy **11**: 632–642.

BURNETT, G. B. & H. W. READING. 1970. The pharmacology of disulfiram in the treatment of alcoholism. Br. J. Addiction **65**: 281–288.

CAHALAN, D. 1970. Problem Drinkers: A National Survey. Jossey-Bass. San Francisco, CA.

CAMERON, D. & M. T. SPENCE. 1976. Lessons from an outpatient controlled drinking group. J. Alcoholism **11**: 44–45.

COLEMAN, J. C., J. N. BUTCHER & R. C. CARSON. 1980. Abnormal Psychology and Modern Life, 6th ed. Scott, Foresman. Glenview, IL.

CUMMINGS, C., J. R. GORDON & G. A. MARLATT. 1980. Relapse: Prevention and prediction. *In* The Addictive Behaviors: Treatment of Alcoholism, Drug Abuse, Smoking, and Obesity. W. R. Miller, Ed. Pergamon. Oxford.

DAVIES, D. L. 1962. Normal drinking by recovered alcohol addicts. Q. J. Stud. Alcohol **23**: 94–104.

DAVIES, D. L. 1979. Conversation with D. L. Davies. Br. J. Addiction **74**: 239–249.

DITMAN, K. S. & G. G. CRAWFORD. 1966. The use of court probation in the management of the alcohol addict. Am. J. Psychiatry **122**: 757–762.

DITMAN, K. S., G. G. CRAWFORD, E. W. FORGY, H. MOSKOWITZ & C. MACANDREW. 1967. A controlled experiment on the use of court probation for drunk arrests. Am. J. Psychiatry **124**: 160–163.

GALLANT, D. M., M. P. BISHOP, M. A. FAULKNER, L. SIMPSON, A. COOPER, D. LATHROP, A. M. BRISOLARA & J. R. BOSSETTA. 1968. A comparative evaluation of compulsory (group therapy and/or Antabuse) and voluntary treatment of the chronic alcoholic municipal court offender. Psychosomatics **9**: 306–310.

GERARD, D. L. & G. SAENGER. 1966. Out-patient Treatment of Alcoholism: A Study of Outcome and its Determinants. University of Toronto Press. Toronto, Ontario, Canada.

GOLDMAN, M. S. 1979. Reversibility of psychological deficits in alcoholics: The interaction of aging with alcohol. *In* Cerebral Deficits in Alcoholism. D. A. Wilkinson, Ed. Addiction Research Foundation. Toronto, Ontario, Canada.

GOODWIN, D. 1976. Is Alcoholism Hereditary? Oxford University Press, New York, NY.

HANSEN, J. & C. D. EMRICK. 1983. Whom are we calling "alcoholic"? Bull. Soc. Psychol. Addictive Behav. **2**: 164–178.

HEATHER, N. Personal communication, May 5, 1983.

HEATHER, N. & I. ROBERTSON. 1981. Controlled Drinking. Methuen. London.

HODGSON, R. & H. RANKIN. 1976. Cue exposure in the treatment of alcoholism. Behav. Res. Ther. **14**: 305–307.

HODGSON, R. J., H. J. RANKIN & T. R. STOCKWELL. 1979. Alcohol dependence and the priming effect. Behav. Res. Ther. **17**: 459–466.

HORN, J. L. 1978. Comments on the many faces of alcoholism. *In* Alcoholism: New Directions in Behavioral Research and Treatment. P. E. Nathan, G. A. Marlatt & T. Løberg, Eds. Plenum. New York, NY.

HUSS, M. 1849. Alcoholismus Chronicus. Chronisk Alkoholisjukdom: Ett Bidrag till Dyskrasiarnas Känndon. Bonnier/Norstedt. Stockholm, Sweden.

JACOBSON, G. R. 1976. The Alcoholisms: Detection, Diagnosis and Assessment. Human Sciences Press. New York, NY.

JELLINEK, E. M. 1952. Phases of alcohol addiction. Q. J. Stud. Alcohol **13**: 673–684.

JELLINEK, E. M. 1960. The Disease Concept of Alcoholism. Hillhouse Press. New Haven, Conn.

JONES, M. C. 1968. Personality correlates and antecedents of drinking patterns in adult males. J. Consult. Clin. Psychol. **32**: 2–12.

KAPRIO, L. A. 1981. Preface. *In* Alcohol, Society, and the State, Vol. I. K. Mäkelä, R. Room, E. Single, P. Sulkunen & B. Walsh, Eds. Addiction Research Foundation. Toronto, Ontario, Canada.

KELLER, M. 1972. On the loss-of-control phenomenon in alcoholism. Br. J. Addiction **67**: 153–166.

KWENTUS, J. & L. F. MAJOR. 1979. Disulfiram in the treatment of alcoholism. J. Stud. Alcohol **40**: 428–446.

LEVINE, H. G. 1978. The discovery of addiction: Changing conceptions of habitual drunkenness in America. J. Stud. Alcohol **39**: 143–174.

LIJINSKI, W. 1979. N-nitrosamines as environmental carcinogens. *In* N-Nitrosamines. J.-P. Anselme, Ed. American Chemical Society. Washington, DC.

LIPSCOMB, T. R. & P. E. NATHAN. 1980. Blood alcohol level discrimination: The effects of family history of alcoholism, drinking pattern, and tolerance. Arch. Gen. Psychiatry **37**: 571–576.

LØBERG, T. & W. R. MILLER. Personality, cognitive and neuropsychological correlates of harmful alcohol consumption: A cross-national comparison. Ann. N.Y. Acad. Sci. (this volume).

LOVERN, J. 1982. Moderation to abstinence: A confession. Alcoholism Sept/Oct:38–39.

LOVIBOND, S. H. 1975. Use of behavior modification in the reduction of alcohol-related road accidents. *In* Applications of Behavior Modification. T. Thompson & W. S. Dockens, Eds. Academic Press. New York, NY.

LOVIBOND, S. H. & G. CADDY. 1970. Discriminated aversive control in the moderation of alcoholics' drinking behavior. Behav. Ther. **1**: 437–444.

MADSEN, W. 1974. The American Alcoholic: The Nature-Nurture Controversy in Alcoholic Research and Therapy. Charles C Thomas. Springfield, IL.

MÄKELÄ, K., R. ROOM, E. SINGLE, P. SULKUNEN & B. WALSH, Eds. 1981. Alcohol, Society, and the State, Vol. I. Addiction Research Foundation. Toronto, Ontario, Canada.

MARLATT, G. A., B. DEMMING & J. B. REID. 1973. Loss of control drinking in alcoholics: An experimental analogue. J. Abnorm. Psychol. **81**: 233–241.

MARTIN, J., FR. 1980. Too few counselors effective. U. S. J. Drug Alcohol Dependence 3 (12): 9.

MILLER, W. R. 1976. Alcoholism scales and objective assessment methods: A review. Psychol. Bull. **83**: 649–674.

MILLER, W. R. 1983a. Controlled drinking: A history and critical review. J. Stud. Alcohol **44**: 68–83.

MILLER, W. R. 1983b. Motivational interviewing with problem drinkers. Behav. Psychother. **11**: 147–172.

MILLER, W. R. 1985. Motivation for treatment: A review with special emphasis on alcoholism. Psychol. Bull. **98**: 84–107

MILLER, W. R. & G. R. CADDY. 1977. Abstinence and controlled drinking in the treatment of problem drinkers. J. Stud. Alcohol **38**: 986–1003.

MILLER, W. R. & R. K. HESTER. 1980. Treating the problem drinker: Modern approaches. *In* The Addictive Behaviors: Treatment of Alcoholism, Drug Abuse, Smoking, and Obesity. W. R. Miller, Ed. Pergamon. Oxford.

MILLER, W. R., T. F. PECHACEK & S. HAMBURG. 1981. Group behavior therapy for problem drinkers. International Journal of the Addictions **16**: 829–839.

MILLER, W. R. & C. F. SAUCEDO. Assessment of neuropsychological impairment and brain damage in problem drinkers. *In* Clinical Neuropsychology. C. J. Golden *et al.*, Eds.: 141–195. Grune & Stratton. New York, NY.

MOORE, R. A. & T. K. BUCHANAN. 1966. State hospitals and alcoholism: A nation-wide survey of treatment techniques and results. Q. J. Stud. Alcohol 27: 459–468.

MORSE, R. M. & R. D. HURT. 1979. Screening for alcoholism. J. Am. Med. Assoc. 242: 2688–2690.

MYERS, R. D. & C. L. MELCHIOR. 1977. Alcohol drinking: Abnormal intake caused by tetra-hydropapaveroline in brain. Science 196: 554–556.

NATHAN, P. E. 1980a. Etiology and process in the addictive behaviors. In The Addictive Behaviors: Treatment of Alcoholism, Drug Abuse, Smoking, and Obesity. W. R. Miller, Ed. Pergamon. Oxford.

NATHAN, P. E. 1980b. Ideal mental health services for alcoholics and problem drinkers: An exercise in pragmatics. In Behavioral Medicine: Changing Health Lifestyles. P. O. Davison, & S. M. Davison, Eds. Brunner/Mazel. New York, NY.

NATIONAL COUNCIL ON ALCOHOLISM, CRITERIA COMMITTEE. 1972. Criteria for the diagnosis of alcoholism Am. J. Psychiatry 129: 127–135.

O'REILLY, J. 1983. New insights into alcoholism. Time, April 25: 88–89.

ORFORD, J. 1973. A comparison of alcoholics whose drinking is totally uncontrolled and those whose drinking is mainly controlled. Behav. Res. Ther. 11: 565–576.

ORFORD, J., E. OPPENHEIMER & G. EDWARDS. 1976. Abstinence or control: The outcome for excessive drinkers two years after consultation. Behav. Res. Ther. 14: 409–418.

PATTISON, E. M., M. B. SOBELL & L. C. SOBELL. 1977. Emerging Concepts of Alcohol Dependence. Springer. New York, NY.

PENDERY, M. L., I. M. MALTZMAN & L. J. WEST. 1982. Controlled drinking by alcoholics? New findings and a reevaluation of a major affirmative study. Science 217: 169–175.

PERKINS, D. V., W. M. COX & L. H. LEVY. 1981. Therapists' recommendations of abstinence or controlled drinking as treatment goals. J. Stud. Alcohol 42: 304–311.

POLICH, J. M., D. J. ARMOR & H. B. BRAIKER. 1981. The Course of Alcoholism: Four Years After Treatment. Wiley. New York, NY.

POPHAM, R. E. & W. SCHMIDT. 1976. Some factors affecting the likelihood of moderate drinking by treated alcoholics. J. Stud. Alcohol 37: 868–882.

RANKIN, H. & R. HODGSON. 1976. Cue exposure: One approach to the extinction of addictive behaviors. In Alcohol Intoxication and Withdrawal. M. Gross, Ed. Plenum. New York, NY.

ROBERTSON, I. H. & N. HEATHER. 1982. A survey of controlled drinking treatment in Britain. Br. J. Alcohol Alcoholism 17: 102–105.

ROBINSON, D. 1972. The alcohologist's addiction: Some implications of having lost control over the disease concept of alcoholism. Q. J. Stud. Alcohol 33: 1028–1042.

SANCHEZ-CRAIG, M. 1980. Random assignment to abstinence or controlled drinking in a cognitive-behavioral program: Short-term effects on drinking behavior. Addictive Behav. 5: 35–39.

SANCHEZ-CRAIG, M., H. M. ANNIS, A. R. BORNET & K. R. MACDONALD. 1985. Random assignment to abstinence and controlled drinking: Evaluation of a cognitive-behavioral program for problem drinkers. J. Consult. Clin. Psychol. 52: 390–403.

SASLOW, G. 1969. New views of the alcoholic. Rehabil. Rec. 10(1): 22–26.

SCHMIDT, W. & R. E. POPHAM. 1980. Alcohol Problems and Their Prevention: A Public Health Perspective (revised edition). Addiction Research Foundation. Toronto, Ontario, Canada.

SCHUCKIT, M. A. 1979. Alcoholism and affective disorder: Diagnostic confusion. In Alcoholism and Affective Disorder: Clinical, Genetic, and Biochemical Studies. D. W. Goodwin & C. K. Erickson, Eds. SP Medical and Scientific Books. New York, NY.

SEIXAS, F. A. 1976. Afterword. In The Alcoholisms: Detection, Diagnosis and Assessment. G. R. Jacobson, Ed. Human Sciences Press. New York, NY.

SHEA, J. E. 1954. Psychoanalytic therapy and alcoholism. Q. J. Stud. Alcohol 15: 595–605.

SKINNER, H. A. 1981. Primary syndromes of alcohol abuse: Their measurement and correlates. Br. J. Addiction 76: 63–76.

SKINNER, H. A., S. HOLT, B. A. ALLEN & N. H. HAAKONSON. 1980. Correlation between medical and behavioral data in the assessment of alcoholism. Alcoholism Clin. Exp. Res. 4: 374–377.

SOBELL, M. B. & L. C. SOBELL. 1973. Individualized behavior therapy for alcoholics. Behav. Ther. 4: 49–72.

STOCKWELL, T. R., R. J. HODGSON & H. J. RANKIN. 1982. Alcohol dependence, beliefs and the priming effect. Behav. Res. Ther. 20: 513–522.

TARTER, R. E., H. MCBRIDE, N. BUONPANE & D. U. SCHNEIDER. 1977. Differentiation of alcoholics: Childhood history of minimal brain dysfunction, family history, and drinking pattern. Arch. Gen. Psychiat. **34**: 761–768.

THOMPSON, V. 1915. Drink and be Sober. Moffat, Yard. New York, NY.

TRIANA, E., R. J. FRANCES & P. E. STOKES. 1980. The relationship between endorphins and alcohol-induced subcortical activity. Am. J. Psychiatry **137**: 491–493.

VAN THIEL, D. H., J. S. GAVALER, G. M. PAUL & W. I. SMITH. 1979. Disulfiram induced disturbances in hypothalamic-pituitary function. Alcoholism Clin. Exp. Res. **3**: 230–234.

WALLERSTEIN, R. S., J. W. CHOTLOS, M. B. FRIEND, D. W. HAMMERSLEY, E. A. PERLSWIG & G. M. WINSHIP. 1957. Hospital Treatment of Alcoholism: A Comparative Experimental Study. Basic Books. New York, NY.

WINOKUR, G., T. REICH, J. RIMMER & F. N. PITTS, JR. 1970. Alcoholism. III. Diagnosis and familial psychiatric illness in 259 alcoholic probands. Arch. Gen. Psychiatry **23**: 104–111.

WINOKUR, G., J. RIMMER & T. REICH. 1971. Alcoholism. IV. Is there more than one type of alcoholism? Br. J. Psychiatry **118**: 525–531.

WORLD HEALTH ORGANIZATION, EXPERT COMMITTEE ON MENTAL HEALTH. Report on the First Session of the Alcoholism Subcommittee. (Technical Report Series No. 48). Geneva, Switzerland.

ZIMBERG, S. 1974. Evaluation of alcoholism treatment in Harlem. Q. J. Stud. Alcohol **35**: 550–557.

# Drinking Patterns among Black and Nonblack Adolescents: Results of a National Survey

THOMAS C. HARFORD

*Laboratory of Epidemiology*
*National Institute on Alcohol Abuse and Alcoholism*
*Rockville, Maryland 20857*

Alcohol abuse is regarded as one of the greater health problems of the black community in the United States (Bourne and Light, 1979; Harper, 1976). Cirrhosis mortality rates are disproportionately high among black Americans. Rates among black men and women, aged 25 to 34, are several times higher than for white men and women of the same age. For all age groups up to 65 years of age, the cirrhosis mortality rate for black Americans is nearly twice that for white Americans. When racial differences in cirrhosis mortality rates are examined, it is important to acknowledge the potential contributions made by such factors as nutritional and genetic differences, bias in recording information on death certificates, and psychosocial differences. While alcohol is not the exclusive cause of cirrhosis of the liver, prolonged heavy drinking is recognized as a major contributor.

High cirrhosis rates in the black population are a historically new phenomenon. They did not begin to exceed rates in the general population until the late 1950s. Herd (1983) has shown that the abrupt rise in cirrhosis mortality among blacks in the late 1950s and 1960s was in part a reflection of a transformation in black drinking patterns initiated at the turn of the century and the massive population shifts which began at that time. The increase in cirrhosis mortality among black cohorts born in the early decades of this century are strongest in the highly urbanized areas, which were the major centers of black migration over the past century.

Although cirrhosis mortality rates are disproportionately high among black Americans, in another important segment of the black population — high school students — alcohol abuse and even use are at relatively low levels.

In a review of the literature appearing between 1960 and 1975, Blane and Hewitt (1977) noted that the majority of studies of alcohol use among black adolescents were derived from surveys of high school students. These surveys indicated lower rates of lifetime as well as current alcohol use among black high school students compared to nonblack students. While many of these surveys are limited by small subgroup sizes and nonrandom samples of students, several national surveys support these findings. The 1974 national survey of junior and senior high school students (Rachal *et al.*, 1975) indicated that black students had the smallest proportion of current drinkers when compared with white and other ethnic/racial groups of students. Blacks also had the lowest proportions of moderate and heavy drinkers. These findings were also replicated in the 1978 national survey of senior high school students (Rachal *et al.*, 1980). In a national household survey on drug abuse, Fishburne, Abelson, and Cisin (1979) reported that approximately 38 percent of white respondents, aged 12–17 years, were current drinkers compared with 20 percent among black and other races. Similar findings were reported for the years 1972, 1974, 1976, and 1977.

Several explanations may be offered to account for the lower prevalence of alcohol use among black high school students. Surveys of adolescent alcohol use, while indicating that older students drink more than younger students and that boys drink more than girls, also have shown that other demographic variables relate to alcohol use in this population (Rachal et al., 1975). Lower levels of alcohol consumption have been reported for teenagers living in southern geographic regions, those affiliated with Protestant religious denominations, and those that attain higher academic status in school work (Rachal et al., 1975; Blane and Hewitt, 1977). The conservative or fundamentalist Protestant upbringing of many blacks, for example, may be an important factor in accounting for the differences in drinking levels among black and nonblack youth. These and other demographic variations in the samples of black and nonblack students may account for the differences in alcohol use reported by these students in surveys. A few studies, however, indicate that differences between black and nonblack youth in drinking prevalence persist when demographic factors are controlled (Backman et al., 1981; Harford et al., 1982).

A second explanation for differences in drinking prevalence between these two groups of students relates to differences in underreporting of alcohol consumption. Blacks, as members of a minority group, may withhold or underreport their use of alcohol in national surveys. This is a reasonable point, especially for black students in predominantly white schools or white neighborhoods. The national surveys on drug abuse, however, revealed little variation in the use of illicit drugs among white and black respondents aged 12 to 17 years. It seems unlikely that blacks would conceal the use of alcohol but not other illicit drugs. Moreover, Harford, Lowman, and Kaelber (1982) examined the drinking patterns of black students in predominantly white schools and black students in predominantly black schools. It was hypothesized that black students in predominantly black schools would be less likely to withhold information on drinking practices than would black students in predominantly white schools. Statistical analyses of beverage-specific consumption were not significant. There was no evidence of selective underreporting of alcohol consumption. Nor was there evidence of variations in the self-reports of the frequency of the use of marijuana between black and white students.

A third explanation relates to the fact that surveys of school populations exclude the school dropouts, and these dropouts have been shown to have higher levels of problems associated with alcohol (Cockerham, 1975; MacKay, Phillips, and Bryce, 1967). Studies of institutionalized, delinquent, and school dropout populations, however, are inconsistent with respect to patterns of alcohol use among white and black teenagers— some reported lower rates of problem drinking among blacks, others reported higher rates, and others reported no differences (Blane and Hewitt, 1977). In addition, the U.S. Bureau of the Census (1981) figures indicate that white dropout rates are similar to or slightly higher than black rates up to 18 years of age. At 18, school dropout rates for black males and females begin to increase steeply and to exceed rates for white students.

A fourth explanation may be found in variables that differentiate exposure to and involvement with alcohol among black and nonblack students. Harford, Lowman, and Kaelber (1982) noted that the onset of drinking was grade-related among black students, but was characterized by a later onset relative to that of nonblack students. A delay in the exposure to alcohol may underlie the reported differences in drinking prevalence. Other studies, however, suggest a commonality of drinking correlates among both black and nonblack students. Jessor and his colleagues have developed a comprehensive network of variables encompassing personality, the perceived environment, and behavior patterns that account for more than 50 percent of the variance in adolescent involvement in problem drinking and marijuana use (Donovan and Jessor, 1978; Jessor and Jessor, 1977; Jessor, Chase, and Donovan, 1980). Their system of variables has been shown to reveal a psychosocial risk for problem behavior in subsamples of adolescents differing in gender and ethnic background. Despite the fact that similar predictors of drinking may apply to both racial groups, little is known about the processes underlying the differences in drinking prevalence for these two groups.

The overall objective of this study was to identify factors that relate to the use of alcohol within each of these racial/ethnic student groups. The 1978 national survey (Rachal et al., 1980) was limited to senior high school students and the overall sample of black students was 496. The present study draws upon the earlier 1974 national survey (Rachal et al., 1975) which encompassed a wider age spectrum and a larger sample of black students.

## MATERIALS AND METHODS

Data for the present study were obtained from a 1974 cross-sectional survey of a nationwide probability sample of all junior and senior high school students in grades 7–12 in the contiguous 48 states and in the District of Columbia (Rachal et al., 1975). A stratified two-stage sample was used. The primary sampling frame was stratified by census regions, by community size, and by ethnic characteristics. A sample of 50 primary sampling units (PSUs) consisting of counties or groups of counties was chosen. Within each selected PSU the number of homerooms and the number of students enrolled were determined for each of the six grades, either for all schools (rural areas) or for a sample of schools (metropolitan area). The homerooms were stratified into three grade strata: grade 7–8, 9–10, 11–12. A sample of approximately five homerooms per grade stratum was selected within each of the 50 PSUs. A self-administered, 35-page questionnaire was completed by students in the cooperating classes in the sample during the regular school hours at the school facilities. Useable questionnaires were completed by 13,122 students from 643 classrooms. Of the original 717 classes in the sample, 223 (31.1%) were lost because cooperation could not be obtained from state or local school officials. The overall response rate was 72.7 percent, including replacement classrooms.

The present analysis compared students who indicated in the questionnaire that they were "black" but not of Hispanic origin ($n = 930$), and all other nonblack students ($n = 12,192$).

Measures of alcohol consumption were obtained from beverage-specific estimates of the typical frequency of alcohol use (every day, 3–4 days a week, 1–2 days a week, 3–4 days a month, once a month, less than once a month but at least once a year, less than once a year, never) and from beverage-specific estimates of the number of drinks consumed per typical occasion (12 or more, about 9, 6, 5, 4, 3, 2, 1, less than 1, do not drink).

The beverage-specific quantity-frequency information was used to estimate overall frequency (most frequently used beverage) and overall quantity (highest beverage amount).

In addition to alcohol information, the questionnaire contained several items of relevance to alcohol use. The items are organized into the following sets of variables: demography, drinking models, attitudes, and behaviors. Item descriptions and mean scores for the samples of nonblack and black students are presented in TABLE 1.

**TABLE 1.** Variable Description and Mean Scores for Samples of Black and Nonblack Students

| Item Description | | Nonblacks ($n$ = 12,192) | Blacks ($n$ = 930) | Student's $t$ Test |
|---|---|---|---|---|
| *Demographic features* | | | | |
| Gender | Boys = 1; girls = 2 | 1.52 (0)[a] | 1.52 (0) | 0.49 |
| Grade in school | 7th through 12th | 9.35 (0) | 9.28 (0) | 0.95 |
| Socioeconomic index | Low = 0; high = 9 | 6.23 (0) | 5.44 (0) | 10.40[b] |
| Region | Nonsouthern = 1; southern = 2 | 1.27 (0) | 1.35 (0) | 5.48[b] |
| Religious affiliation | Baptist/Methodist = 1; other = 2 | 1.74 (916) | 1.33 (123) | 25.56[b] |
| Family intactness | Both parents = 1; other = 2 | 1.21 (312) | 1.41 (65) | 14.26[b] |
| Number of older siblings | None = 2; twelve = 14 | 3.97 (1150) | 4.89 (99) | 12.04[b] |
| Number of younger siblings | None = 2; twelve = 14 | 3.66 (1755) | 4.34 (153) | 10.18[b] |
| Number of peers | None = 1; nine or more = 10 | 5.99 (98) | 5.95 (5) | 0.50[b] |
| Number of older peers | None = 1; older = 2 | 1.14 (197) | 1.19 (22) | 4.05[b] |
| *Drinking Models* | | | | |
| Parental drinking | Both = 1; one = 2; none = 3 | 1.83 (416) | 1.95 (79) | 5.07[b] |
| School peers' drinking | None = 1; all = 5 | 3.24 (268) | 2.77 (76) | 12.71[b] |
| Friends' drinking | None = 1; all = 5 | 3.05 (263) | 2.54 (77) | 10.57[b] |
| *Attitudes* | | | | |
| Social effects | Not important = 1; important = 4 | 2.71 (449) | 2.37 (96) | 9.54[b] |
| Status reasons | Not important = 1; important = 4 | 1.87 (494) | 1.96 (108) | 2.84[c] |
| Personal effects | Not important = 1; important = 4 | 1.88 (501) | 1.99 (107) | 3.86[b] |
| Conforming reasons | Not important = 1; important = 4 | 1.94 (559) | 1.85 (113) | 2.51[c] |
| *Behavior* | | | | |
| Academic grades | A's = 1; D's and F's = 7 | 3.32 (0) | 3.79 (0) | 9.45[b] |
| Religiosity | Low = 5; high = 20 | 13.54 (670) | 14.70 (182) | 8.00[b] |
| Access to alcohol | No = 1; always = 4 | 2.34 (1242) | 1.77 (151) | 14.14[b] |
| Amount of spending money | None = 1; more than $11 = 5 | 2.99 (85) | 3.09 (4) | 2.28[c] |
| Extent of deviant behavior | Low = 12; high = 48 | 17.61 (705) | 16.80 (139) | 3.94[b] |
| Marijuana frequency | None = 1; 11 or more = 12 | 2.97 (718) | 2.82 (116) | 1.13 |

[a] Figures within parentheses indicate number of missing cases.
[b] $p < 0.001$.
[c] $p < 0.01$.

Demographic factors included gender, grade in school, an index of socioeconomic status using a combination of parents' occupation and education, geographic region, religious affiliation, family intactness (both parents in household), number of older siblings, number of younger siblings, size of peer network ("How many kids do you hang around with?"), and number of older peers.

The influence of drinking models was assessed by three items which included parental drinking (1 = one or both drink regularly, 2 = one or both drink sometimes, 3 = parents do not drink), number of students who drink (1 = none to 5 = all of them), and number of kids you hang around with drinking (1 = none to 5 = all of them).

Attitudes related to drinking assessed the overall importance of drinking in each of the following areas: (1) social effects ("to have a good time"; "it's a good way to celebrate"); (2) status functions ("people think you've been around if you drink"; "it's part of becoming an adult"); (3) personal effects ("when there are too many pressures on me"; "makes things like doing well in school seem less important"; "keeps my mind off problems"); (4) conforming functions ("not to be different from the rest of the kids"; "to be a part of the group").

Behavioral factors include academic grades, religiosity (determined by a five-item scale of the importance placed upon religious teachings, practice, and counsel for the direction of daily life developed by Rohrbaugh and Jessor, 1975), ease of access to alcohol, amount of spending money, extent of deviant behavior (determined by a twelve-item scale developed by Jessor and Jessor, 1977, assessing involvement in stealing, fighting, property destruction, truancy and other transgressions), and number of times the student reported using marijuana in the previous 6 months.

## RESULTS

Among the sample of black students, 33.3 percent of the boys and 43.2 percent of the girls reported that they either abstained from the use of alcohol or drank less than once a year. Abstinence and infrequent drinking were lower for nonblack students who reported that about 23 percent of the boys and 30.8 percent of the girls abstained or drank less than once a year. Overall, 38 percent of black students and 27 percent of nonblack students abstained or drank less than once a year.

While the proportion of abstainers is high among black students, Harford *et al.* (1982) have indicated that alcohol use is grade-related among both black and nonblack students. FIGURE 1 presents the proportions of students in the 1974 survey who reported drinking once a month or more by grade and ethnic/racial group. The figure indicates that the onset of drinking among black students is grade-related, as it is among nonblack students, but that the onset of drinking is delayed among blacks in grades 7 through 9. It is important, then, to examine the nature of the differences both within and between each of the two ethnic/racial groups.

Statistical analyses of the variables under study in TABLE 1 indicated that the sample of black students differed significantly from the nonblack sample on most of the variables.

Comparisons between the two groups revealed that blacks did not differ from nonblacks with regard to gender or grade in school. Blacks were of lower socioeconomic status, of Baptist/Methodist affiliations, from less intact families, from families with greater numbers of both older and younger siblings (larger families), and older peer networks.

In addition to differences in demographic characteristics associated with socioeconomic status, there were significant differences with respect to the alcohol-related vari-

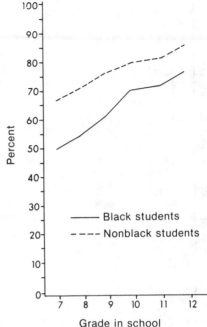

**FIGURE 1.** Proportion of students who report drinking alcohol once a month or more by grade and racial group.

ables. Blacks, when compared with nonblacks, reported less parental drinking and less drinking among both school peers and friends.

With regard to the importance of attitudes related to drinking, blacks rated social and conforming factors as less important reasons for drinking and status and personal effects as slightly more important than did nonblacks.

Blacks did less well academically and were higher on religiosity scores. They had less access to alcohol, slightly more spending money, and less deviant behavior patterns. The overall direction of these differences are such as to expect a lower drinking prevalence among black students. Blacks, for example, reported fewer drinking models, placed less importance on reasons for drinking, and had less access to alcohol than did nonblacks. Black students, while indicating poorer academic performance than nonblack students, had higher religiosity scores and less involvement in deviant behavior patterns. Consistent with other studies, however, black students did not differ from nonblack students with regard to the use of marijuana.

TABLE 2 presents the mean scores by drinker status (abstainer versus drinker) within each of the two samples for each of the variables under investigation. One-way analyses of variance for the four groups (drinker status by racial/ethnic group) were significant ($p < 0.01$) on every variable. TABLE 2 also indicates significant differences associated with planned comparisons within the four groups. Of initial concern are the differences within each of the two ethnic/racial groups.

Among the nonblack sample, the majority of variables were significantly related to drinker status. Drinkers, compared to abstainers, were more likely to be boys, older, of higher socioeconomic status, from nonsouthern regions and of non-Baptist/Methodist religious affiliation. Drinkers tended to be from less intact families (one or more

**TABLE 2.** Mean Scores on Demographic and Alcohol-Related Variables for Samples of Black and Nonblack Students

| | Nonblack Students | | Black Students | | Comparisons | | | |
|---|---|---|---|---|---|---|---|---|
| | Abstainers (1) | Drinkers (2) | Abstainers (3) | Drinkers (4) | (1)(2) | (3)(4) | (1)(3) | (2)(4) |
| *Demographic features* | | | | | | | | |
| Gender | 1.59 | 1.49[a] | 1.59 | 1.48 | a | a | NS | NS |
| Grade in school | 8.81 | 9.55[a] | 8.88 | 9.55 | a | a | NS | NS |
| Socioeconomic index | 5.94 | 6.34[a] | 5.31 | 5.51 | a | NS | a | a |
| Region | 1.35 | 1.24[a] | 1.38 | 1.34 | a | NS | NS | a |
| Religious affiliation | 1.64 | 1.78[a] | 1.31 | 1.35 | a | NS | a | a |
| Family intactness | 1.19 | 1.21[b] | 1.39 | 1.42 | b | NS | a | a |
| Number of older siblings | 4.02 | 3.95 | 5.18 | 4.71 | NS | b | a | a |
| Number of younger siblings | 3.75 | 3.62[a] | 4.49 | 4.24 | a | NS | a | a |
| Number of peers | 5.53 | 6.17[a] | 5.84 | 6.03 | a | b | NS | NS |
| Number of older peers | 1.09 | 1.16[a] | 1.16 | 1.22 | a | b | a | a |
| *Drinking Models* | | | | | | | | |
| Parental drinking | 2.17 | 1.70[a] | 2.13 | 1.84 | a | a | NS | a |
| School peers' drinking | 2.69 | 3.44[a] | 2.36 | 3.04 | a | a | a | a |
| Friends' drinking | 1.96 | 3.46[a] | 1.88 | 2.96 | a | a | NS | a |
| *Attitudes* | | | | | | | | |
| Social effects | 2.09 | 2.93[a] | 2.01 | 2.59 | a | a | NS | a |
| Status reasons | 1.85 | 1.88 | 1.91 | 2.00 | NS | NS | NS | NS |
| Personal effects | 1.85 | 1.89[b] | 2.01 | 1.98 | NS | NS | b | NS |
| Conforming reasons | 1.83 | 1.98[a] | 1.83 | 1.86 | a | NS | NS | NS |
| *Behavior* | | | | | | | | |
| Academic grades | 3.11 | 3.40[a] | 3.63 | 3.89 | a | b | a | a |
| Religiosity | 15.21 | 12.93[a] | 15.47 | 14.20 | a | a | NS | NS |
| Access to alcohol | 1.53 | 2.66[a] | 1.47 | 2.19 | a | a | NS | a |
| Amount of spending money | 2.61 | 3.14[a] | 2.85 | 3.24 | a | a | a | NS |
| Extent of deviant behavior | 14.50 | 18.70[a] | 14.90 | 18.09 | a | NS | NS | b |
| Marijuana frequency | 1.20 | 3.60[a] | 1.32 | 3.79 | a | NS | NS | NS |

[a] $p < 0.001$.
[b] $p < 0.01$.

parents absent), had fewer younger siblings, a greater number of peer networks, and more older peers.

Drinkers, compared to abstainers, reported greater models for drinking, placed greater importance on social and conforming reasons for drinking, and had greater access to alcohol, greater involvement in general deviant behavior and marijuana use, and less involvement in religion and school performance. These findings are consistent with the results obtained by Jessor and his colleagues in studies of adolescent problem drinking.

Within the sample of black students, black drinkers tended to be boys and older in age. Unlike nonblack drinkers, however, there were few other demographic differences between black abstainers and drinkers. There was a tendency for black drinkers to have fewer older siblings and to have a greater number of older companions in their peer group.

A pattern similar to that of nonblacks emerged with respect to drinking models, attitudes and behaviors. Black drinkers, compared with black abstainers, reported greater models for drinking, placed more importance on the social effects of drinking, had greater access to alcohol, greater involvement in general deviant behavior and marijuana use, and less involvement in religion and school performance.

These results indicate a similar pattern of the correlates of drinker status among both black and nonblack students with respect to the alcohol-related variables.

**TABLE 3.** Standardized Discriminant Function Coefficients among Samples of Black and Nonblack Students

| | Nonblack Students ($n = 9,268$) | Black Students ($n = 530$) |
|---|---|---|
| *Demographic features* | | |
| Gender | −06 | −10 |
| Grade in school | NS | 0.20 |
| Socioeconomic index | 0.03 | NS |
| Region | −12 | NS |
| Religious affiliation | | |
| Family intactness | | |
| Number of older siblings | | |
| Number of younger siblings | | |
| Number of peers | 04 | NS |
| Number of older peers | NS | 0.13 |
| *Drinking Models* | | |
| Parental drinking | −29 | −28 |
| Friends' drinking | 41 | 41 |
| *Attitudes* | | |
| Social effects | 32 | 42 |
| Status reasons | NS | NS |
| Personal effects | −09 | NS |
| Conforming reasons | −05 | −27 |
| *Behaviors* | | |
| Academic grades | 02 | NS |
| Religiosity | −09 | −13 |
| Access to alcohol | 32 | 0.09 |
| Amount of spending money | 07 | 25 |
| Extent of deviant behavior | 20 | 26 |
| Marijuana frequency | −07 | NS |

In order to assess the relative contributions of these variables with respect to drinker status, particularly those associated with demographic factors related to socioeconomic class, a discriminant function analysis was conducted separately for each student group. Because of the larger number of missing cases associated with some of the variables, their inclusion would drastically reduce the sample size for multivariate analysis. This is especially critical in view of the number of black students in the sample. For this reason, several of the variables were omitted from the analysis. The majority of these variables related to demographic factors, factors shown to be nonsignificant in the univariate tests with black students. The one exception to the demographic factors was access to alcohol. Because of its theoretical content, the discriminant analyses were conducted with this variable included. Its inclusion reduced the sample size of black students available for analysis from 594 to 530. Comparable results were obtained with the "access to alcohol" variable. The standardized discriminant function coefficients for black and nonblack students are presented in TABLE 3. These coefficients reflect the relative contributions of each variable controlling for the effects of all other variables. The canonical correlations in both analyses were highly significant ($p < 0.001$), both for blacks (0.569) and nonblacks (0.540). The results from the two analyses yield very similar findings. Among both black and nonblack samples, the major variables distinguishing abstainers and drinkers were parents' drinking, friends' drinking, importance of social effects of drinking, extent of deviant behavior, and

**TABLE 4.** Standardized Regression Coefficients (Beta) Predicting Drinking Frequency and Drinking Quantity among Nonblack and Black Students

| | Frequency | | Quantity | |
|---|---|---|---|---|
| | Nonblack | Black | Nonblack | Black |
| *Demographic features* | | | | |
| Gender | $0.07^a$ | $0.08^a$ | $0.12^a$ | $0.06^a$ |
| Grade in school | $0.04^a$ | 0.00 | $-04^a$ | $-10^a$ |
| Socioeconomic | 0.00 | 0.04 | $05^a$ | 0.02 |
| Region | 0.00 | $-0.04$ | $-01$ | $-03$ |
| Number of peers | $-0.04^a$ | $-0.03$ | $-04^a$ | $-05$ |
| Number of older peers | $-0.01$ | $-0.05$ | $-01$ | $-02$ |
| *Drinking Models* | | | | |
| Parental drinking | $0.10^a$ | 0.05 | 01 | 01 |
| School peers' drinking | | | | |
| Friends' drinking | $-0.23$ | $-0.19^a$ | $-22^a$ | $-16^a$ |
| *Attitudes* | | | | |
| Social effects | $-0.12^a$ | $-0.19^a$ | $-18^a$ | $-19^a$ |
| Status reasons | 0.00 | $-0.03$ | $06^a$ | $-04$ |
| Personal effects | 0.01 | $-0.03$ | $-01$ | 02 |
| Conforming reasons | $0.03^a$ | 0.09 | 01 | 03 |
| *Behaviors* | | | | |
| Academic grades | $-0.05^a$ | $-0.03$ | $-09^a$ | 01 |
| Religiosity | $0.03^a$ | 0.07 | $02^a$ | 06 |
| Amount of spending money | $-0.07^a$ | $-10^a$ | $-05^a$ | $-04$ |
| Extent of deviant behavior | $-0.14^a$ | $-13^a$ | $-16^a$ | $-18^a$ |
| Marijuana frequency | $-0.12^a$ | $-18^a$ | $-12^a$ | $-15^a$ |
| Number of subjects | 9247 | 527 | 9247 | 527 |
| Total variance (%) | 48.6 | 39.0 | 53.3 | 38.0 |

$^a$ $p < 0.01$.

amount of spending money. Grade in school, conforming reasons for drinking, and amount of spending money made relatively high contributions in the black student sample. Access to alcohol made a substantial contribution in the nonblack sample.

In order to assess the relative contributions of these factors with regard to the frequency of drinking and the number of drinks per typical occasion, the same set of variables used in the discriminant analysis was used in multiple regression.

Measures of the typical frequency of alcohol use and of the number of drinks consumed per typical occasion were regressed in a step-wise fashion on the set of predictor variables. The regressions were done separately for nonblack and black students, and the standardized regression coefficients (beta) are presented in TABLE 4.

Each coefficient reflects the effects of a particular variable after the effects of the others are controlled. Among black students, the following variables were related to the frequency of drinking: gender, friends' drinking, social effects, access to alcohol, amount of spending money, extent of deviant behavior, and frequency of marijuana use. More frequent drinking occurred among boys and among students with drinking friends, access to alcohol, greater involvement in deviant behavior and use of marijuana, more spending money, and attitudes viewing the social effects of alcohol as important. These same variables were significant among nonblack students. In addition, the following variables were also significant for nonblack students: grade in school, number of peers, parental drinking, conforming reasons for drinking, academic grades, and religiosity.

Among both samples of nonblack and black students, the following variables were significantly related to the amount of consumption: gender, grade in school, friends' drinking, social effects, access to alcohol, extent of deviant behavior, and marijuana frequency. Heavier consumption occurred among boys and older students and students with drinking friends, attitudes viewing social effects of alcohol as important, access to alcohol, greater involvement in deviant behavior and more frequent use of marijuana. In addition, the following variables were significantly related to the amount of consumption among nonblack students: social class, number of peers, status reasons, academic grades, religiosity, and amount of spending money.

An examination of the beta coefficients for alcohol quantity in TABLE 4 reveals a pattern similar to that of drinking frequency. Among black students, however, grade in school (age) predicts amount of consumption but not the frequency of consumption.

With regard to both samples of students, the regression analyses would suggest that the factors associated with the use of alcohol are similar for both black and nonblack students alike.

In light of the similarity of predictor variables within both samples of students, comparisons between both black and nonblack abstainers may reveal factors associated with the later onset of drinking among black students. TABLE 1 summarizes the results of statistical comparisons between the two ethnic/racial groups within each drinker status group. For both abstainers and drinkers, there were significant differences with respect to demographic factors associated with socioeconomic status. It was noted earlier, however, that these variables did not significantly differentiate black abstainers from black drinkers. The results may be interpreted as reflecting more persuasive social class differences between blacks and nonblacks in general. Aside from socioeconomic status, one would expect that black and nonblack abstainers would not differ with regard to the alcohol-related variables. This is true for the most part, but some exceptions can be noted. Among abstainers, nonblack students reported higher proportions of school peers to be drinkers.

A second factor significantly differentiating these two groups relates to the importance of the personal effects of alcohol. Black abstainers, compared with nonblack abstainers, viewed the personal effects of drinking as more important reasons for drinking. Since both groups are nondrinkers, this variable may reflect basic differences in the perception of alcohol between these two groups of students.

In order to assess the overall contributions of these variables while controlling for the effects of demographic differences, a discriminant function analysis was conducted with the two groups of abstinent students. The canonical correlation was .19 ($p < 0.001$) and the highest standardized coefficients were school peer drinking ($-0.61$) and personal effects (0.58). Next in magnitude of contribution were grade in school (0.31), socioeconomic status ($-0.31$), and academic grades (0.36). These findings indicate that both environmental exposure to drinking models and attitudes regarding the use of alcohol distinguish nonblack and black abstinent students.

## SUMMARY AND CONCLUSIONS

The overall objective of this study was to identify factors that relate to the use of alcohol among black and nonblack students and that might serve to explain the lower prevalence of drinking among black students.

Black students were shown to differ from nonblack students with respect to both demographic variables associated with social class and variables associated with exposure to and involvement with alcohol. Multivariate analyses, controlling for the effects of demographic status, yielded several predictors of the frequency and quantity of alcohol consumption. Among the major predictors of alcohol use were exposure to friends as drinking models, attitudes emphasizing the importance of social effects of alcohol, ease of access to alcohol, and behavior patterns of social transgressions and illicit drug use. While degree of religiosity and attainment of good school grades were inversely related to frequent and heavier use of alcohol among nonblack students, they were not related to patterns of alcohol use by black students. For the most part, however, there were more similarities than differences in the predictors of alcohol use among black and nonblack students. These findings suggest that environmental factors associated with the use of alcohol are similar for black and nonblack students.

While the overall use of alcohol is lower among black students, the onset of drinking is grade-related but later in onset relative to nonblack drinkers. Despite the fact that the same predictors of drinking are common to both black and nonblack students, there is need to identify the environmental factors that delay exposure to a more extensive network of peer drinking models and access to alcohol.

Comparisons between black and nonblack abstainers revealed that black abstainers reported lower proportions of school peers to be drinkers. This differential exposure to drinking models between black and nonblack abstainers may be implicated in the delay of onset of drinking among black students.

A second factor that may be implicated in the delay of onset of drinking among black students related to differences in the perception of alcohol between blacks and nonblacks. Black abstainers, compared to nonblacks, viewed the personal effects of drinking as more important reasons for drinking. These reasons stress the use of alcohol as a coping mechanism to deal with personal stress and problems.

Future studies need to address the status of these variables with regard to their implications in delaying the onset of drinking among black students.

## REFERENCES

BACHMAN, J. G., L. D. JOHNSTON & P. M. O'MALLEY. 1981. Smoking, drinking and drug use among American high school students: Correlates and trends, 1975–1979. Am. J. Public Health 71: 59–69.

BLANE, H. T. & L. E. HEWITT. 1977. Alcohol and Youth: An Analysis of the Literature 1960–75. Report No. PB-268-698. U.S. National Technical Information Service. Springfield, Va.

BOURNE, P. & E. LIGHT. 1979. Alcohol problems in blacks and women. *In* The Diagnosis and Treatment of Alcoholism. J. H. Mendelson & N. K. Mello, Eds. : 83–124. McGraw-Hill. New York, NY.

COCKERHAM, W. C. 1975. Drinking patterns of institutionalized and noninstitutionalized Wyoming youth. J. Stud. Alcohol **36**: 993–995.

DONOVAN, J. & R. JESSOR. 1978. Adolescent problem drinking: Psychosocial correlates in a national sample study. J. Stud. Alcohol **39**: 1506–1524.

FISHBURNE, P. M., H. I. ABELSON & I. CISIN. 1979. National Survey on Drug Abuse: Main Findings: 1979 (Contract No. 271-78-3508. National Institute on Drug Abuse. Rockville, MD.

HARFORD, T.C., C. LOWMAN & C. T. KAELBER. Current prevalence of alcohol use among white and black adolescents. Paper presented at the National Council on Alcoholism Conference, Washington, D.C., April 1982.

HARPER, F. 1976. Alcohol Abuse and Black America. Douglas Publishers. Alexandria, VA.

HERD, D. Migration, cultural transformation and the rise of black cirrhosis. Paper presented at the Alcohol Epidemiology Section, International Council on Alcohol and Addictions, Padova, Italy, June 1983.

JESSOR, R. & S. L. JESSOR. 1977. Problem behavior and psychosocial development: A longitudinal study of youth. Academic Press. New York, NY.

JESSOR, R., J. A. CHASE & J. E. DONOVAN. 1980. Psychosocial correlates of marijuana use and problem drinking in a national sample of adolescents. Am. J. Public Health **70**: 604–613.

MACKAY, J. R., D. L. PHILLIPS & F. O. BRYCE. 1967. Drinking behavior among teenagers: A comparison of institutionalized and noninstitutionalized youth. J. Health Soc. Behav. **8**: 46–54.

RACHAL, J. V., L. L. GUESS, R. L. HUBBARD, S. A. MAISTO, E. R. CAVANAUGH, R. WADDELL & C. D. BENRUD. 1980. Adolescent Drinking Behavior. Volume 1: The Extent and Nature of Adolescent Alcohol and Drug Use: The 1974 and 1978 National Sample Studies. Research Triangle Institute. Research Triangle Park, NC.

RACHAL, J. V., J. R. WILLIAMS, M. L. BREHM, B. CAVANAUGH, R. P. MOORE & W. C. ECKERMAN. 1975. A national study of adolescent drinking behavior, attitudes, and correlates. Report No. PB-246-002; NIAAA/NCALI-75/27. U.S. National Technical Information Service. Springfield, Va.

ROHRBAUGH, J. & R. JESSOR. 1975. Religiosity in youth: A personal control against deviant behavior. J. Pers. **43**: 136–155.

U.S. BUREAU OF THE CENSUS. May 1981. School enrollment — Social and Economic Characteristics of Students: October 1980 (Advance Report). Current Population Reports Series P-20, No. 362. U.S. Department of Commerce. Washington, DC.

# Cultural Factors in the Etiology of Alcoholism: A Prospective Study

GEORGE VAILLANT

*Dartmouth College Medical School*
*Hanover, New Hampshire 03756*

In Western societies one of the most obvious but least useful means of combating alcoholism has been to forbid drinking. Stated differently, *proscriptions* against alcohol use have rarely been as effective as social *prescriptions* for alcohol use. First, cultures that teach children to drink responsibly, cultures that have ritualized when and where to drink, tend to have lower rates of alcohol abuse than do cultures that forbid children to drink. Second, how a society socializes drunkenness is as important as how it socializes drinking. For example, both France and Italy inculcate in their children responsible drinking practices; but, in fact, public drunkenness is far more socially acceptable in France than in Italy—and France experiences a higher rate of alcohol abuse.

Because of an abundance of confounding variables, cross-cultural observations of this kind do not usually permit etiologic conclusions. Cultures and countries differ from each other in many ways besides socialization of alcohol use. They differ enormously in their means of reporting alcohol abuse and in the kind of alcohol available and its price structure. There may be racial differences that affect metabolism; there may be alternative recreational drugs. Finally, many of the anecdotal descriptions used to illustrate alcohol-related differences in other countries are not based upon longitudinal study. For example, what really happens to the 3-liters-of-wine-a-day French "social drinkers"? Does the "explosive relief drinking" by Finns *never* lead to alcohol dependence? Answers to these questions are not yet known.

By chance, the Core City sample originally studied in the 1940s by Sheldon and Elanor Glueck (Glueck and Glueck, 1950) offered unique controls for many of the confounding variables. Virtually all of the Core City men lived in an urban environment (Boston) where alcohol was readily available and was the principal recreational drug of choice. The Core City men shared the same schools and legal system; and they shared the same ethnically diverse peer group. The Core City men differed from one another in the cultural background of their parents. Sixty-one percent of their parents had been born in foreign countries, and ethnic intermarriage by their parents was rare.

## METHOD

The method and procedures employed in this study are described in detail in Vaillant (1983). Of the 456 men originally in the Gluecks' study, 400 men survived and were adequately studied after age 40 to be fully included in the follow-up sample. Of 400 individuals, 110 at some time met the criteria for alcohol abuse or problem drinking, and another 71 met the DSM-III criteria for alcohol dependence. Obviously, the defi-

142

nition of alcoholism is arbitrary. There is no one accepted definition of alcoholism any more than there is one definition for heart disease or hypertension. But the more one looks at the far end of the continuum, the more alcoholics look like other alcoholics, and the more they share the classic characteristics of alcoholism.

## RESULTS AND DISCUSSION

TABLE 1 illustrates the advantages of using the Gluecks' Core City sample to unravel important etiologic factors in alcoholism. In this sample, a large number of nonantisocial youths studied originally both for ethnicity and for family history of alcoholism were followed well into middle life by interview in a study that was deliberately prospective in design (Vaillant, 1983). The sample had little attrition and included both alcoholics who had and those who had not come to clinical attention.

TABLE 1 presents the critical relationships between premorbid and outcome variables. First, the table shows that parental social class correlates only in the most minimal way with a variety of adult outcome variables. Second, as the McCords (1960) and the Gluecks (1950) predicted, multiproblem families, measured here by the childhood environmental weaknesses scale, produced children who later were afflicted with sociopathy not alcoholism. For the purposes of this table, alcohol use was assessed on a 3-point scale: 1 = asymptomatic drinking; 2 = alcohol abuse by the criteria of the DSM-III (American Psychiatric Association, 1980); 3 = alcohol dependence. After 33 years, however, the effect of multiproblem family membership upon most adult outcome variables seems attenuated. Third, measured intelligence, besides being highly correlated with adult social class through its effect on attained education ($r$ = 0.38), was only modestly correlated with other outcome variables. In other words, parental social class, I.Q., and multiproblem family membership, variables whose importance has been suggested in cross-sectional studies, do not emerge as strong predictors in this study using a lifespan perspective.

As shown in TABLE 1, it was the childhood variables to which Freud, not Marx, would have us pay attention that made the greatest difference. Success at working, the absence of emotional problems, and the presence of strengths rather than weaknesses in the childhood environment correlated most highly with adult outcome. The boyhood competence scale probably comes as close as any childhood variable in this study to that ineffable, Platonic concept—ego strength. And ego strength undoubtedly is at the heart of what observers mean when they marvel at the "invulnerable child" who emerges seemingly unscathed from a multiproblem family.

Alcoholism, however, was most highly correlated with ethnicity and alcoholism in relatives, two premorbid variables that otherwise did not significantly predict adult outcome. As a means of assessing the effect of culture upon alcoholism, ethnicity was numerically ranked according to the degree to which the parental culture sanctioned drinking and proscribed drunkenness. Thus, a rank of 1 was assigned to the Irish, who tend to forbid alcohol before age 21, to admire drunkenness among men, and to drink outside the home and apart from meals. A rank of 2 was assigned to men of American, Canadian, or English descent, and 3 was assigned to men of Northern European countries, who occupy an intermediate position. A rank of 4 was assigned to men from Italy, Portugal, Spain, Greece, Syria, and Armenia. In most of these cultures, children are taught to drink by their parents, drinking occurs with meals, and drunkenness is taboo. For the purposes of classification, the six Jews in the Core City sample were assigned to the Mediterranean group. While such an arbitrary classification is controversial and in individual cases may be misleading, the intent was to assess

**TABLE 1.** Relationship of Childhood Variables to Adult Outcome[a]

| Childhood Variables | Adult Outcome Variables | | | | | |
|---|---|---|---|---|---|---|
| | Social Competence | Social Class (at age 47) | Sociopathy | Mental Health (HSRS) | % Adult Life Unemployed | Alcohol Use (DSM-III) |
| Boyhood competence | .23 | .28 | -.22 | .24 | -.23 | -.12 |
| Childhood environmental strengths | .12 | .21 | -.19 | .21 | -.17 | -.18 |
| Childhood emotional problems | -.20 | -.19 | .13 | -.19 | | |
| I.Q. | .13 | .35 | [b] | .15 | | |
| Childhood environmental weaknesses | [b] | .13 | .18 | [b] | .13 | .15 |
| Parental social class | [b] | .14 | | [b] | -.13 | |
| Alcoholism in heredity | [b] | [b] | [b] | [b] | [b] | .26 |
| Ethnicity[c] | [b] | [b] | -.14 | [b] | [b] | -.28 |

[a] Pearson product-moment correlation coefficient was the statistic used. Correlations greater than .15 are significant at $p < .001$.

[b] Since hundreds of correlations were obtained, many by chance would have been significant at $p = .05$; therefore, $r$'s smaller than .12 ($p < .01$) have been regarded as statistically insignificant.

[c] Ethnicity was arbitrarily scaled as follows: 1 = Irish, 2 = Anglo-American, 3 = Northern European, 4 = Mediterranean (Southern European). The rationale for this scaling is presented later in Vaillant (1983).

the probability that cultural attitudes toward alcohol might affect future problem drinking. Obviously, it would have been preferable to have obtained prospective data regarding parental attitudes rather than depending upon paternal ethnicity. (There was little intermarriage, and examining ethnicity in terms of maternal rather than paternal lineage did not alter the findings.)

TABLE 2 further illustrates the clear ethnic differences between men who became alcoholic and those who did not. There were also clear differences in the amount of alcohol abuse in their families.

TABLE 3 shows the dramatic effect of parental cultural background on the lifetime patterns of use and abuse of alcohol by the Core City men. In each ethnic group, roughly one man in five used alcohol less often than once a month; these 80 men (20%) were classified as teetotalers. In comparison, 4% of the French population and 50% of Protestant, middle-aged men in the rural southeastern United States are teetotalers.

The Core City men whose parents had grown up in the Mediterranean cultures were far less likely than men from other ethnic groups to develop alcohol dependence. Compared to men from other ethnic groups, men of Anglo-Irish background were somewhat less likely to drink regularly without problems. Each group seemed equally at risk for problem drinking without dependence (about 1 in 10).

Contrary to popular belief, when boys from similar neighborhoods were examined, the Irish were not at higher risk for alcohol dependence than other Northern Europeans. As TABLE 4 illustrates, however, the Irish were more likely to manifest multiple alcohol-related problems. Compared with the Anglo-Americans, men of Irish extraction were almost twice as likely to have scores over 8 on our Problem Drinking Scale. Yet they were no more likely to be diagnosed alcoholic, and the wives of Core City men of Irish extraction were rather less likely to be reported as objecting to their husbands' use of alcohol.

TABLE 5 underscores the prognostic power of classifying men according to the extent to which their culture sanctioned childhood drinking and proscribed intoxication. Alcohol dependence developed seven times more frequently in the Irish than in those Mediterranean descent. Late age of marriage has been postulated as enhancing the association between Irish ethnicity and a high incidence of alcoholism. However, in our sample Irish youth did not marry later than those in other ethnic groups. Drinking by Irishmen in Ireland, however, is undoubtedly different from that by Irish-Americans in Boston.

Certainly, the interrelationships of drinking practices and culture are far more complex than can be encompassed by the reductionistic TABLE 5. But the table's findings nevertheless bear out observations made from much more detailed study of Irish and Italian drinking practices. The Italians provide children with a long education in

**TABLE 2.** Childhood Differences between Men Who Never Abused Alcohol and Those Who Became Dependent

| | Asymptomatic Drinkers (n = 254) (%) | Alcohol-Dependent (n = 69) (%) |
|---|---|---|
| Irish ethnicity | 17 | 30 |
| Italian ethnicity | 35 | 6 |
| Alcoholism in 2+ ancestors | 9 | 21 |
| Alcoholism in a parent | 18 | 34 |
| School behavior problems and truancy | 2 | 13 |

**TABLE 3.** Use and Abuse of Alcohol among Different Ethnic Groups

| | | Alcohol Use Classification[a] | | |
|---|---|---|---|---|
| Ethnic Group | Abstainer (n = 80; 20%) (%) | Asymptomatic Drinker (n = 210; 52%) (%) | Alcohol Abuse without Dependence (n = 40; 10%) (%) | Alcohol-Dependent (DSM-III) (n = 71; 18%) (%) |
| Irish (n = 76) | 21 | 43 | 8 | 28 |
| Old American (n = 35) | 20 | 40 | 13 | 27 |
| Polish, Russian (n = 17) | 18 | 53 | 11 | 18 |
| English, Anglo-Canadian (n = 98) | 21 | 45 | 11 | 23 |
| Northern Europe Other (n = 20) | 5 | 65 | 5 | 25 |
| French Canadian (n = 26) | 15 | 54 | 8 | 23 |
| Southern Europe Other[b] (n = 23) | 30 | 57 | 9 | 4 |
| Italian (n = 99) | 18 | 70 | 8 | 4 |
| Jewish (n = 6) | 50 | 33 | 17 | 0 |
| Chinese (n = 1) | 0 | 0 | 100 | 0 |

[a] Only the 401 men rated on the alcohol-use scale are included here.
[b] Lebanon, Syria, Turkey, Greece, Portugal, and Armenia.

**TABLE 4.** Ethnicity and Reported Drinking Problems

| Problem | Irish ($n$ = 76) (%) | U.S., English, Canadian ($n$ = 159) (%) | Other Northern European ($n$ = 37) (%) | Mediterranean ($n$ = 128) (%) |
|---|---|---|---|---|
| Wife complains | 22 | 27 | 32 | 10 |
| Multiple medical problems | 12 | 7 | 6 | 0 |
| Clinical diagnosis of alcoholism | 17 | 15 | 14 | 2 |
| Multiple drunkenness arrests | 26 | 17 | 14 | 5 |
| Multiple hospitalizations for alcoholism | 16 | 7 | 5 | 2 |
| 8+ problems | 26 | 16 | 17 | 3 |

moderate alcohol use and encourage drinking with family members. They inculcate drinking practices that diminish the alcohol "high"; these practices include using low-proof alcohol and drinking alcohol with food. One Core City social drinker whose Italian family had served him alcohol since he was 4 years old, described how his father gave him "the look" when he once came home drunk.

In contrast, the Irish forbid children and adolescents from learning how to drink, but they tolerate—and covertly praise—the capacity of men to drink large amounts of alcohol. Alcohol use is a guilty secret. An extreme example of this was the Core City alcoholic whose Irish mother had spoon-fed him whiskey at age 7 until he was drunk. The Irish prefer drinking in pubs, where alcohol intake is carefully separated from the family dinner table and often from food intake of any kind. If in Italy low-proof wine has greater mystique than distilled liquor, in Ireland high-proof whiskey is more highly revered than low-proof beer. (A little reflection will reveal that the drinking practices that occur on many of our native American reservations are an exaggeration of those in Ireland.)

Like any other form of education, teaching children to drink is not without risk. Unlike Ireland, Italy has a problem with alcoholism in children. Indeed, Italy is the only country I know of that has an alcohol unit associated with a department of pediatrics! It is also probably true that the number of alcohol-related traffic fatalities increased when American states lowered the drinking age to 18 and that traffic fatalities have declined when states have raised the drinking age to 21. But adolescent automobile fatalities and occasional childhood alcohol dependence do not necessarily correlate with an increased total population risk for alcoholism. Besides, is not the best

**TABLE 5.** Relationship between the Culture in Which Parents Were Raised and the Development of Alcohol Dependence in Their Sons[a]

| Alcohol-Use Classification (DSM-III) | Parents' Culture | | |
|---|---|---|---|
| | Irish (%) | Other[b] (%) | Mediterranean (%) |
| No alcohol abuse | 59 | 58 | 86 |
| Alcohol abuse without dependence | 13 | 19 | 10 |
| Alcohol dependence | 28 | 23 | 4 |

[a] Significance $p < 0.001$ ($\chi^2$ test).
[b] Canadian, American, and Northern European.

way to reduce adolescent traffic fatalities to raise the minimum age for teenage driving —
not teenage drinking?

## REFERENCES

AMERICAN PSYCHIATRIC ASSOCIATION. 1980. Diagnostic and Statistical Manual of Mental Dis-
    orders (DSM-III), 3rd ed. Washington, DC.
GLUECK, S. & E. GLUECK. 1950. Unraveling Juvenile Delinquency. The Commonwealth Fund.
    New York, NY.
MCCORD, W. & J. MCCORD. 1960. Origins of Alcoholism. Stanford University Press. Stanford, CA.
VAILLANT, G. E. 1983. The Natural History of Alcoholism. Harvard University Press. Cambridge,
    MA.

# The Soviet Heavy-Drinking Culture and the American Heavy-Drinking Subculture

BORIS M. SEGAL

*Alcohol Dependence Treatment Program*
*FDR Veterans Administration Hospital*
*Montrose, New York 10548*

## THE ORIGINS OF RUSSIAN AND IRISH HEAVY-DRINKING

While the Russian culture is by and large uniformly heavy-drinking, American culture is not. Only some American subcultural groups (Irish-American, native American) tend to use alcohol to the point of severe intoxication and can be defined as heavy-drinking.

First, I shall try to show how various historical, sociocultural, and psychological factors have influenced the formation of Rusian and Irish patterns of heavy drinking. These findings are to a certain degree applicable, however, to the origins of heavy drinking among other groups, such as American Indians.

In the ninth and tenth centuries, the Vikings (the Norse, Varangians) "men of the bays," who were notorious alcohol-abusers, made settlements on the European continent, in particular in the regions populated by the Slavs and the Celts. In contrast to wine-producing peoples inhabiting the outskirts of the Mediterranean Basin, the ancient Vikings, the Slavs, and the Irish brewed drink from hops, wheat, or honey (McKinlay, 1948). Their descendents began to consume large amounts of fast-acting spirits. Distilled spirits affect behavior to a more considerable degree, producing more severe intoxication, altering consciousness more severely, and more frequently creating dependence. The introduction of distilled spirits (vodka and whiskey) coincided also with some dramatic changes in the history of the Russian and Irish people specifically, for that time was characterized by foreign invasions and by social and political turmoil (Riasanovsky, 1969; MacManus, 1972).

The psychological effect of exposure to spirits at the period of the formation of the nation (tribe, culture), or during a critical phase of its history, may be compared, to some degree, with imprinting (identification) at the early phase of individual growth. The development of social organization and civilization (that is, the sum of the behavioral norms, regulations, restrictions and achievements which serve, according to Freud, to increase security and to adjust mutual relations) tends to modify or control original "barbaric" patterns of alcohol abuse of the primitive tribes. The origin of ritualized drinking might be partially explained as a modification of the Pleasure Principle under the pressure of the Reality Principle. However, certain historical, social, economic and psychological events prevented some cultural (ethnic) groups from modifying their "wild" drinking style. In short, these events may be described as follows. In contrast to the experiences of such sober, or relatively sober, cultures as the Chinese, Indian and Jewish, which developed negative attitudes toward irrational drunken behavior and which were under pressure of powerful religious and moralistic concepts for a long period of time, the appropriate Slavic and Irish religious experience was too short. Besides, the Russian Orthodox Church and Irish Catholic Church alike have always been inconsistent in their sentiments toward the "vice of drunkenness," which they, in fact, tolerated, and sexual depravity, which they angrily condemned. Therefore, sobriety has never become a part of "decent" behavior among those cultures. It has also happened because Russian and Irish societies did not feel the influence of the Renaissance and its ideas of human harmony and individual potentialities (which influenced Italy, for instance), the ethical experience of the Protestant Reformation (which was accepted by all kinds of people in all parts of northern Europe and was characterized by puritanic ideals of moral duty and sobriety), and the cathartic effects of the nineteenth-century revolutions (which eventually brought political, legal, economic, and educational reforms to many European nations). Russia and Ireland were not involved in great discoveries and colonial adventures similar to those of Britain, Holland, Spain, and Portugal, whose ships crossed the oceans and whose people could release their suppressed energy and dissatisfactions in this manner. Finally, as opposed to the Muslim societies, the old Russian and Irish societies had never known effective prohibition and, as opposed to China, societies in Russia and Ireland have never accepted the notion of moderation with respect to alcohol. As a result, heavy drinking became the primary means of diminishing suppressed tension or substituting for the dissatisfied and frustrated desires of these nations, while other cultures tended to solve or sublimate their problems in less destructive ways (the Anglo-Saxon search for profit; Jewish dedication to success, children's education, and intellectual achievement; the Chinese cult of family life). It appears to be that the influence of the just-described historical factors, as well as economic backwardness, poverty of the majority of the population, and the relative isolation of Russia and Ireland from the mainstream of European development can be considered as factors analogous to certain important events in the infancy of the individual. It is known that due to certain unfortunate events, the psychosocial development of the individual may be partially arrested and fixated at any stage. Fixation may interfere with progress in subsequent developmental periods, or may cause the perpetuation of character traits associated with the developmental period in which the fixation occurred. Using a broad psychoanalytical approach to history, one may suggest that heavy-drinking nations may have experienced a similar kind of fixation. In other words, there is the temptation to assume that the Russian and Irish peasantry manifested a high incidence of "pregenital" traits, i.e., "oral," "anal," "phallic," and "latency-period" traits. These traits are related to a dependence-independence conflict, such as conflict between passivity and strivings toward automony, disturbances of capacity for giving and receiving affection, and of the balance between pessimism and optimism, with tendencies toward depression ("oral" traits). Other traits are related to ambivalent attitudes toward authorities (characterized by a mixture of hostility and submissiveness); ideas of order and revolt; an unresolved Oedipus complex and a feeling of inferiority and insecurity under the façade of self-confidence; and repression of erotic impulses with a tendency to close friendship with persons of the same sex and participation in structured group activities (the latency-period traits).

Paraphrasing Erikson (1950), one may suggest that national identity resulting in psychological strength depends on a total process which regulates cultural (national) development, the sequence of generations, and the structure of society simultaneously. Disruption of any of the components of this process leads to distress and identity confusion of a whole cultural (national) group.

However, is this assumption correct? Is it possible to talk about identity confusion or arrest of psychological development of a whole nation? In order to consider this question we shall discuss the relationships between child-rearing practices and an external structure. Child-rearing practices of the old Russian and Irish societies contributed to the persistence of mechanisms of splitting and arrest of emotional maturation. Lack of care and attention, physical abuse and neglect, and paternal rejection disturbed the psychosocial development of the child. We reported elsewhere that a contradiction between the Russian and Irish farmers' tendency to encourage their children's early self-reliance and at the same time to discourage their social independence had frequently contributed to the formation of traits resembling indeed some manifestations of the borderline personality organization (Segal, 1983). However, this psychological predisposition remained in most cases insignificant or latent. Only relatively small segments of Russian and Irish societies manifested overtly the signs of maladaptive behavior. These traits became more common during periods of the decline of social organization and the weakening of the patriarchal family, which were accompanied by marital role confusion and a breakdown of social mechanisms controlling behavior of the descendents of the Russian serfs and the Irish farmers. For these people excessive drinking was a desperate attempt to diminish emotional tension, identity confusion, and anxiety in interpersonal relations, and to overcome, at least temporarily, such feelings as mistrust, shame, guilt, insecurity, inferiority, isolation and boredom. As a result of the abolition of serfdom in 1861, the development of capitalism, and the decline of the joint family, the Russian peasant lost external structure, and simultaneously emotional tension and the rate of drunkenness increased (Segal, 1983). Similarly, immigration to the United States affected deeply the stability of the Irish family and traditional norms of Irish life. It resulted in the growth of disappointment due to loss of social status and dissatisfied expectations, and an increase in drunkenness (Bales, 1959; Segal, 1976). In other words, more and more Russian peasants and Irish-Americans demonstrated a set of traits resembling so-called prealcoholic personality traits. Predisposition to these patterns of behavior, in particular drinking behavior, has been transmitted to generations to come. This process has also been determined by social learning through identification with the frequently frustrated and drunk father. The Russians as well as the Irish-Americans do not constitute homogeneous groups, however. As individuals, they represent different personality types and manifest traits derived from different stages of psychosocial development. Any "traditional" national characteristic tends to be shaped, modified, "melted," or significantly inhibited by individual experience, family upbringing, and social demands, that is, environmental pressure. Besides, the communicative values of the words, "arrest of psychosocial development," "fixation at the pregenital stages," "splitting," "identity crisis," or "confusion" are limited and even distorted once one speaks of cultural and ethnic groups rather than individuals. Finding the terms "national character" or "national psychology" too static and therefore misleading, and such psychodynamic concepts as "fixation at the pregenital stages," "identity confusion," "splitting," or "borderline level of personality organization" not applicable to a whole nation, we have proposed concepts of "cultural" (or "national") and "social" styles and a "level of cultural (national) dissonance." Cultural (national) style may be characterized as a hypothetical curve describing a general mode of functioning *prevailing* in a particular culture. Cultural style becomes a factor determining the content of behavioral patterns of various social groups within a framework of a culture. However, behavioral patterns of these social groups — which we designate social styles — might be different to a considerable degree since various socioeconomic conditions may trigger various mechanisms of the general cultural style. The "level of dissonance" can be measured by examining the intensity of opposite intrapsychic forces, which are produced by a contradiction between old cultural traditions and old child-rearing practices, on the one hand, and a new social reality, on the other hand, as well as by the breakdown of the family and other social institutions supporting the stability of the old social structure. True, no representative studies on the prevalence of these inconsistent attitudes, feelings, and behavioral patterns among the members of various cultural or ethnic groups have been conducted to date. Yet a number of historical, psychological and sociological observations indirectly confirm our hypothesis that a "level of dissonance" among different cultural and national groups has been varied from one historical period to

**TABLE 1.** Common Historical, Sociocultural, and Psychobiological Variables Contributing to the Origin and Maintenance of Russian and Irish Heavy-Drinking Patterns (in Chronological Order)

1. Exposure to distilled spirits during critical periods of national development. Formation of the pattern to drink to intoxication ("imprinting").

2. Unresolved conflict between hedonistic ("pagan") attitudes and puritanical values of the Church.

3. Constant threats to food supply; substitution of drink for food.

4. Drinking as a symbol of virility and male solidarity. Mixed attitudes toward intoxication as both a virtue and a sin.

5. A shift from ceremonial to utilitarian drinking. Attitudes toward alcohol as a habitual means of consolation and escape; using distress-reducing and power-inducing functions of alcohol.

6. Isolation from the mainstream of European social and cultural development; cultural and socioeconomic backwardness.

7. Missed historical experiences that modified patterns of heavy drinking in some other European regions.
   a. Socially acceptable ways of self-actualization (e.g., profit, education);
   b. The Renaissance and its ideas of human harmony and individual potentiality;
   c. The Reformation and its ideals of sobriety, asceticism, and individual responsibility;
   d. Involvement in the great discoveries and colonial adventures which released suppressed energy in some nations;
   e. Cathartic effect of the nineteenth-century revolutions that brought legal, economic and educational reforms to some European countries.

8. No history of effective prohibition (as in the Muslim world) or doctrine of moderation (as in China), and failure to internalize the ethical principle of sobriety and to accept abstinence socially.

9. Child-rearing practices frustrating the child's early dependency needs; dependence/independence conflict; pressure toward early self-reliance versus lack of autonomy.

10. Cultural (national/or social) "style" similar to a set of "prealcoholic" personality traits ("alcoholic style") characterized by a high level of "dissonance": a mixture of passive ("oral") traits and hostility toward authority figures; affective instability; difficulties in interpersonal relationships; low self-esteem and sexual anxiety behind a façade of strong masculinity; feelings of boredom and loneliness followed by orgiastic feasts.

11. Destabilization of the family and the decline of the community and family support in the nineteenth and twentieth centuries. Consequently, there was a release and reinforcement of the suppressed positive attitudes toward frequent intoxication among the Russian peasants and the Irish immigrants to the United States.

12. Social learning: imitation of parental heavy drinking.

13. Effects of frequent intoxication on heredity (a possible biological predisposition among members of heavy-drinking groups).

another and has played an essential role in the origins of many psychosocial problems, in particular, the growth of drinking and alcoholism.

Comparative study of Russian and Irish drinking behavior suggests that there is a definite operational potentiality for concepts of "cultural" and "social" styles and a "level of dissonance." We found that despite significant differences between Russian and Irish cultures, drinking styles of both "distressed" nations have been quite similar. According to our assumption, this similarity was due to high levels of Russian and Irish cultural dissonance, which in its turn resulted from certain historical and social events and a contradictory nature of child-rearing practices in both societies.

The role of the most essential variables contributing to the origin and maintenance of heavy drinking among the Russian Orthodox and the Irish Catholic population is summarized in TABLE 1.

According to our hypothesis, the higher the level of distress (dissonance) due to sociocultural and psychological problems, the stronger the predisposition to heavy drinking. As long as society controls the individual's behavior, this predisposition might be manifested only on culturally approved occasions; but as soon as society becomes less structured and less restrictive and child-rearing practice becomes more indulgent, the cultural "dissonance" and consequently the frequency of heavy-drinking bouts in such alcoholism-prone societies tend to increase sharply. Alternatively, those cultures, subcultures and societies that tend to emphasize the pleasure-amplifying rather than the displeasure-reducing properties of alcohol, provide other means for relief of "dissonance," and that have had enough time and opportunity to internalize sanctions against irrational (hence dangerous and socially unacceptable) manifestations of severe intoxication would not develop persistent patterns of heavy drinking and high rates of alcoholism.

Finally, there is also a strong possibility that racial (ethnic) groups vary in their neurohumoral responses to ethanol, and consequently some of those groups are more alcoholism-prone than others. Although a biological predisposition for heavy drinking cannot be excluded, the impact of cultural and social factors is, however, much more important. The multidimensional model described in TABLE 1 implies also an interaction between historical, cultural, social, psychological, and biological determinants.

Needless to say the existence of heavy-drinking cultures and subcultures presents an intriguing challenge to virtually every student of human behavior and human civilization. The higher the incidence is of heavy drinking among members of a particular culture, the higher the incidence of alcohol-related problems, such as suicide, violence, accidents, divorces, medical complications and economic losses, and the higher the possibility is of psychological and biological damage to new generations. In contrast to the moderate use of alcohol, which sometimes has value for individuals, tribes, and cultures, heavy drinking and alcoholism seem to be a manifestation of a self-destructive instinct that may be turned on individual members of society and on a society at whole.

## ALCOHOL ABUSE AND ALCOHOLISM IN AMERICAN AND SOVIET SOCIETIES

Despite the differences in historical, cultural and social conditions between the Soviet Union and the United States, heavy drinking and alcoholism are, at present, a very serious problem for both societies (TABLE 2).

Both the United States and the Soviet Union have considerable differences in the incidence of alcoholism among various social and cultural population groups. Spe-

**TABLE 2.** Alcohol Abuse and Its Consequences in the United States and the USSR: A Comparison of Estimated Average Annual Rates (the 1970s)

|  | United States[a] | USSR[b] |
|---|---|---|
| 1. Consumption of alcohol (1970–76) (per capita per person over age 15) | 10.26 liters of absolute alcohol | 20 liters of absolute alcohol |
| 2. Alcohol taxes: federal, state, city | $11.0 billion | $30.6 billion |
| 3. Average family spending for alcohol | 1.3 percent of family budget | 18 percent of family budget |
| 4. Prevalence of heavy drinking among the population 15 years or older | 9–10 percent | 24 percent |
| 5. Prevalence of "classic" alcoholism (dependence) among the population 21 years and older | 2–3 percent | 11 percent |
| 6. Annual deaths in alcohol users and abusers | 200,000 | 900,000 |
| 7. Alcohol-related traffic accidents  Alcohol-related traffic injuries | 10 percent[c]  34 percent[c] | 25 percent[c]  50 percent[c] |
| 8. Alcohol-related suicides (1977) | 36 percent[c] | 50 percent[c] |
| 9. Arrests for drunkenness (percentage among total population) (1979) | 0.4 percent | 8 percent |
| 10. Alcohol-related murders (1973) | 30–65 percent[c] | 67 per cent[c] |
| 11. Alcohol-related assaults (1973)  Alcohol-related sexual assaults (1973) | 30–60 percent[c]  24–35 percent[c] | 90–95 percent[c]  69–76 percent[c] |
| 12. Alcohol-related economic losses | $43. billion (3.1 percent of 1974 GNP) | $278. billion (31.7 percent of 1976 GNP) |

[a] Sources for figures for the United States:
   1. U.S. Department of Health, Education and Welfare 3rd Special Report to the Congress, 1978.
   2. U.S. Department of Health, Education and Welfare, 4th Special Report to the Congress; Alcohol and Health, 1981.
   3. U.S. Department of Commerce, Expenditures for Beer, Wine and Distilled Spirits, 1979.
   4. Statistical Abstract of the U.S., Bureau of the Census, 1981.
   5. National Center for Health Statistics, 1978.
   6. National Clearing House for Alcohol Information.
   7. Consumer Expenditure Survey, Total Expenditure and Income for the U.S., U.S. Department of Labor, 1972, 1973.
   8. Berry, Boland, et al., The Economic Costs of Alcohol Abuse and Alcoholism, 1977.
   9. The publications of the NIAAA (1974–1980).
[b] The projected figures and estimates for the USSR are based on the following sources:
   1. Annual Statistical Reports and the National Census (1973–1979). Moscow.
   2. The Reports of The Regional Mental Health Centers and the Emergency Stations.
   3. Statistics of the Ministry of Health and the Ministry of Justice.
   4. The National Epidemiological Study on Alcohol Abuse and Alcoholism, 1969–1972.
   5. The Classified Information of the Soviet Ministry of Internal Affairs and the Police.
   6. The Classified Information of the Central Statistical Administration (Ts. S.U.).
   7. The Reports of the Institute of Studies on the Causes of Crime, Moscow.
   8. A number of the Soviet publications (see the bibliography in Segal, 1976).
[c] Of the total number.

cifically, the rates of alcoholism are lowest in the Soviet Union among the Jews, Muslims, and in the Caucasus, and highest among blue-collar male workers in the Slavic and Baltic regions (Segal, 1976), while in the U.S. they are highest among Irishmen, American Indians, and in the urban ghettos. Drinking in the middle classes is usually more controlled in both countries. But the social status and the reference group, rather than "class" affiliation, exert an especially marked effect on drinking behavior. At the same time the tendency toward a gradual lessening of differences conditioned by cultural background and social and sex factors, especially among youth, is observed in both societies. In Russia, the growth of drinking occurred first of all as a result of the increase in the urban population, the adoption of the ethnic Russian urban drinking patterns by the peasantry and the minorities, and alcohol abuse of a significant number of young men. Although in the Soviet Union the number of female heavy drinkers has also been growing, the greater conservatism of Russian society has made the proportion of female to male alcoholics still somewhat lower than in the United States.

Alcoholism, in a very real sense, threatens the health of the population and does great damage to the social and economic lives of both countries. But the situation is especially dangerous in the USSR. According to our estimations, in 1973 the incidence of alcoholism in the USSR increased in comparison with the pre-Revolutionary (1913) rates by a factor of five and the per capita consumption of alcohol increased more than five times; more than one-fourth of the contemporary Soviet adult population (over 21 years of age) may be classified as heavy drinkers and more than one-fifth and one-ninth of the adult population may be regarded as problem drinkers and alcoholics, respectively. These figures are two and four times as much as the most reliable corresponding American indices. Soviet people consume much more distilled spirits per capita than any other nation. Estimated per capita consumption of alcoholic beverages in the USSR in 1985 was 8 times as much as before the 1917 Revolution and 3 times as much as in the United States. The Soviet Union has also by far outdistanced the United States in the number of accidents, crimes, suicides, and deaths connected with intoxication. According to our findings the rate of violent alcohol-related crimes against persons (assaults, rapes and murders) is 10.5 times as high as that of the United States. The growth of heavy drinking has also affected productivity. The Soviet legal system cannot cope with illegal production of "moonshine." An estimated total amount of Soviet economic losses due to use and abuse of alcoholic beverages was 6.5 times higher than that of the United States. The ratio of these Soviet losses to the index of the Soviet GNP was 10.2 times as much as the corresponding American ratio. Soviet alcohol-related losses have exceeded the annual Soviet state budget. These losses are in fact equivalent to half the Soviet national income and nine times as much as the governmental net profit from the sale of alcoholic beverages. Alcohol abuse is an important contributing factor to economic shortcomings, low productivity, and the shortage of supplies in that country.

The disruption of family relations, morbidity, and decline of mores are also, at least in part, due to the enormous rise in Soviet drinking (Segal, 1967, 1976; Tkachevsky, 1966). However, it must be remembered that the rates of drug abuse and drug-related problems in the USA are much higher than those in the USSR.

## COMMON CAUSES OF ALCOHOL ABUSE IN SOVIET AND AMERICAN SOCIETIES

Let us now generalize about the common causes of alcohol abuse shared by American and Soviet societies. Both societies no longer recognize the three original functions of alcohol, namely, the religious, the medical, and the nutritional (although some Russians still harbor beliefs in the latter two). The loss of social restrictions against alcohol abuse and the decline of ritualistic drinking are closely related to dramatic social and psychological changes in the contemporary world. The similarities in these changes in both capitalistic and socialistic societies are more pronounced than are the differences caused by specific historical, cultural, and political experiences between the two societies.

The most essential variables influencing alcohol and drug abuse in the contemporary world are related to the crisis of our culture. Lasch points out that "the sense of an ending, which has given shape to so much of twentieth-century literature, now pervades the popular imagination as well. The Nazi holocaust, the threat of nuclear annihilation, the depletion of natural resources, well-founded predictions of ecological disaster have fulfilled poetic prophecy, giving concrete historical substance to the nightmare, or death wish, that avant-garde artists were the first to express" (1979, p. 28). The following explanations for this despair seem to be most crucial:

(1) The breakdown of the family is accompanied by a dramatic increase in the number of separations and divorces in both societies. Disorganization of the family, leading to the loss of its protective functions, and an unfavorable home environment provide the seedbed in which alcohol abuse grows. Both American and Soviet writers reported that those children who had been brought up in "broken homes" or in families where the level of tension was high tend to develop later emotional disorders and alcoholism. Frustration of the early dependency needs, overprotection or overindulgence, which are frequent consequences of intrafamily conflicts, lead to the disruption of psychosocial development and produce emotional immaturity, anger, disappointment, inability to cope with stress, ambivalent attitudes to authority figures, and difficulties in dealing with persons of the opposite sex. Children from such families turn to alcohol as the means of escape from emotional problems and maladjustment.

(2) Societal changes such as urbanization, migration, social disorganization and loss of community support and control, have always been conducive to the growth of excessive drinking.

(3) The inability of our civilization to control technological and scientific progress creates feelings of anxiety, powerlessness and escapist tendencies.

(4) The decline of traditional beliefs and values, and the spiritual vacuum created by the loss of a theological outlook and the rise of secular belief all undermine the intellectual authority of the Church. The disappearance of the religious (Judeo-Christian) foundations of society has had a far-reaching impact on human behavior, facilitating the loss of restrictions, taboos, and social norms, especially those proscribing nonritualistic drinking. Both American and Soviet societies have also experienced the downfall of nonreligious ideologies and ethics. Disillusionment in ideology leads to escapist reactions that include alcohol and drug abuse.

(5) Capitalistic society is *gradually* losing the sense of historical continuity, whereas the Communist revolution in Russia *abruptly* interrupted societal development. In both cases this disruption of continuity is associated with a decline of the traditional mores and "prejudices," including those that limited alcohol, drug use, and promiscuity.

(6) The Renaissance created the concept of personality, which replaced the medieval corporate or class consciousness. However, humanism eventually gave birth to anti-humanism, which has been accompanied by the mushrooming of various cults that abuse human dignity and by the explosion of violence. Denying immortality, an alienated individual is intolerant of any delay in gratification. He experiences feelings of emptiness and boredom and is anxious to get here on the earth all possible pleasure. (An advertisement for Schlitz beer says: "You only go around once in life, so you have to grab all the gusto you can," while the Russians say "drink and be merry, we live

only once.") In the United States and in Russia, a growing number of individuals exist who display social indifference and who are extremely selfish and exploitive in their relationships with other people. Of course, such attitudes are formed during childhood, but society itself can play the role of a confused, ambivalent, vain and cold parental figure and thus participate in the formation of narcissistic and borderline personality traits which predispose to the use of alcohol and drugs.

By reviewing the origins of alienation and loneliness we may also be able to understand better the role that alcohol plays in our time. We must deal today with an impersonal and sometimes hostile world. Alcohol appears to lessen that pain by helping people to establish, at least temporarily, casual emotional relationships with drinking companions. Drinking is thus one means of coping with a feeling of isolation, creating an illusion of friendship.

## ALCOHOL ABUSE AMONG YOUTH AND WOMEN

Age and sex are two important variables which all societies use in prescribing accepted behavior and role performances for their members. One of the factors determining the general rise in the use of alcohol in any contemporary society is the inclusion of even larger segments of young people. The high level of drinking among American adolescents confirms the notion that in the United States drinking is learned in adolescence (Maddox, 1971).

The same type of social learning in adolescence (rather than during childhood, as in France and Italy) predominates in Soviet society (Segal, 1967, 1976). The drinking patterns of society are extremely important in the origin of this learning.

The increase in drinking among youth is a consequence of their aspiration to self and social identification. Drinking is a social act symbolizing membership in the youth culture. Alcohol is also a means of self-assertion, a means of overcoming identity crisis and a lack of self-confidence, and a step on the road to sexual maturity and adulthood.

Drinking among youth is also an expression of hedonistic tendencies and the desire to gain life's pleasures through any means. Alcohol and drug abuse reflect also the turning of some segments of Soviet and American youth toward violence and the criminal world. The increase of drinking among youth is also influenced by escapism, the desire for emotional experience, dissatisfaction, frustration, and disillusionment with official ideology.

For some Russian and American adolescents drinking is still a form of protest, against the hypocrisy of society or an attempt to avoid social responsibility. Both in the United States and in the Soviet Union, youthful and adolescent behavior was much more strictly controlled in the past. This could explain the excessive drinking of youths who have broken away from their fathers' control (in Russian and Anglo-Saxon Protestant families) or their mothers' overprotection (in Irish families). At present, however, the role of the family is growing weaker both in the Soviet Union and in the United States. Thus, the spread of drinking among youth can no longer be completely attributed to protest. Maddox (1971) pointed out that drinking among teenagers in American society is not primarily a response to tensions resulting from an inferior position in social structure or an expression of hostility toward adult authority. Rather, the opposite is much more likely to be a causative factor: the role of permissiveness and overindulgence during childhood, which is a consequence of the decline of the father-centered family.

Some American observers see the preoccupation with self, incapacity to give and receive love, escapism, and the decline of interest in public life and social goals as evidence of a growing narcissism among young Americans. But the same tendency can be detected in contemporary Russian society. To feel responsible for society's problems was a characteristic of the pre-revolutionary Russian young people. Now there is a growing feeling of social indifference among Soviet youth.

Differences in male and female alcoholism have been explained, from a sociological point of view, by different role expectations. These sexual differences, however, are gradually diminishing in both American and Soviet societies. The reduction in the ratio of male to female alcoholics is connected not only with the fact that more women turn to physicians for medical help, but also with the real rise in the number of female drinkers. The number of known American women alcoholics has doubled since World War II, while in the USSR, according to my estimates, the corresponding rate has been increased five times.

## SPECIFIC CAUSES OF EXCESSIVE DRINKING IN THE SOVIET UNION

In addition to the factors that favored drinking in prerevolutionary Russia and still maintain alcohol abuse in capitalistic countries, there are a number of problems specific to Soviet society that are conducive to excessive drinking. Basic human needs are frustrated; the individual cannot satisfy his need for self-realization and self-actualization. Alcohol abuse, neurosis, and violence are the result of these frustrations. In the USSR the person has fewer choices for activity than he or she does in the West. Each Soviet citizen feels that he or she is only a powerless cog in a gigantic state mechanism, while in American society such a sense of powerlessness is observed only among the uneducated, the poor, and the older population groups. The Soviet government controls not only the economy, trade, and mass media, but also the private life of the individual. Although the terrible repressive measures of Stalin's time are no longer in effect, civil rights are completely lacking as before. A majority of the population must be considered poor from the Western point of view. There is a chronic shortage of food and housing. Nonconformist approaches to cultural values are regarded as the result of "bourgeois ideology." Soviet literature and art are controlled by censorship. Alcohol becomes one of the permissible paths to the manifestation of suppressed activity. Today, in Soviet society drunkenness is also the result of disillusionment with Communist ideology and a protest against reality. Symbolically, one can say that the Soviet people drink so desperately because they are suffering from a severe postrevolutionary "hangover," following an intoxication by revolutionary enthusiasm.

The Soviet press formerly claimed that alcoholism, as the "remnants of capitalism in the people's consciousness," was rapidly vanishing from socialist society, but it is now forced to admit the growth of heavy drinking. At present, the Soviet, as well as American mass media are sounding the alarm and reporting the prevalence of drinking among youth, the growing amount of violence and accidents committed under the influence of alcohol, and the negative effect of alcoholism on mores, national health, family relations, and labor productivity. The Soviet leadership partially understood the harm that alcoholism causes the economy, although it never fully realized the scope of these losses. Soviet officials are against alcoholism, but retain sympathy for "normal" drinking because a drinking society is not so likely to organize resistance against the dictatorship. After alcohol abuse the individual is "discharged" and is more easily controlled. The Soviet authorities take this effect into account. Therefore, the Soviet government increased the production of alcoholic beverages not only with the aim of generating tax revenues and preventing the illegal production of "moonshine," but also with the goal of avoiding the mistake made by the Tsarist government when it introduced the "Dry Law" in 1914 thereby closing the safety valve which had hitherto prevented the Russian state from exploding. Drunkenness is an inalienable part of Russia's destiny. A long experience of alcohol abuse has affected Russian mentality and influenced national behavior deeply. Governmental restrictions on the sale of alcoholic beverages may cause more dissatisfaction and anger among the Russian population than political oppression or violations of human rights. Therefore, heavy drinking will remain an essential feature of Russian culture for an indefinite time in spite of the recent (1985–1986) antialcoholism campaign. But a drunken society cannot act in a sober, responsible and realistic manner. It is a danger to itself and to the rest of the world.

## CONCLUSION

In summary, there are several common social and psychological causes of excessive drinking in the Soviet and American societies. In both societies there are large segments of the population whose patterns of heavy drinking are rooted in their cultural heritage. Urbanization and industrialization in the Soviet Union had a more forcible and destructive impact than in the West, but consequences of these social changes in both societies were similar: the weakening of social control and patriarchal taboos, the decline of the protective role of the family and small neighborhood, and learning to drink in a nonritualistic and utilitarian fashion. The influence of these common factors primarily affects youth as well as dissatisfied groups whose expectations are greater than their real opportunities. Disillusionment with ideologies, old moral values, and bureaucracy are important motives for alcohol and drug abuse. Alcohol abuse is also a reaction to growing alienation, anxiety, boredom, narcissism, and the loss of a sense of belonging.

However, there are also a number of different factors contributing to alcohol abuse in both societies. One of these factors is conditioned by the historically determined traditional Russian drinking pattern, characterized by a tendency to drink to the point of manifest intoxication. This is accepted by the majority of the Soviet population, while in the United States the same pattern is shared only by certain subcultural groups. The second essential distinction is related to the totalitarian nature of the Soviet society, which frustrates basic human needs and makes drinking one of the most common and socially approved means of gratification and escapism.

### REFERENCES

ABLON, J. 1980. The significance of cultural patterning for the "alcoholic family." Family Process **19**: 127–144.
BALES, R. F. 1959. Cultural differences in rates of alcoholism. *In* Drinking and Intoxication. R. G. McCarthy, Ed. Yale Center for Alcohol Studies. New Haven, CT.
ERIKSON, E. 1950. Childhood and Society. Norton. New York, NY.
LASCH, C. 1979. Culture of Narcissism. Norton. New York, NY.
MACMANUS, S. 1972. The Story of the Irish Race. Devin-Adair. New York, NY.
MADDOX, G. L. 1971. Drinking prior to college. *In* The Domesticated Drug: Drinking Among Collegians. G. L. Maddox, Ed. College & University Press. New Haven, CT.
MCKINLAY, A. 1948. Ancient experience with intoxicating drinks: Non-classical peoples. Q. J. Stud. Alcohol **9**: 388–414.
RIASANOVSKY, N. 1969. A History of Russia. Oxford University Press. New York and London.

SEGAL, B. 1967. Alkogolizm [Alcoholism]. Meditsina. Moscow.

SEGAL, B. 1976. Drinking patterns and alcoholism in Soviet and American societies: A multidisciplinary comparison. *In* Psychiatry and Psychology in the USSR. S. A. Corson & E. O'Leary Corson, Eds. Plenum Press. New York, NY.

SEGAL, B. M. 1983. The Russian child-rearing practice and the national "character." Presented at the Sixth Annual Convention of the International Psychohistorical Association, June 8-10, 1983.

TKACHEVSKY, YU. M. 1966. Prestupnost'i alkogolizm [Crime and alcoholism]. Znanie. Moscow.

# An Experimental Detoxification Center in Helsinki from a Cross-National Perspective

SIRKKA-LIISA SÄILÄ

*Social Research Institute of Alcohol Studies*
*00100 Helsinki 10, Finland*

This paper describes the administrative and operational activities of detoxification ("detox") centers. An experimental detox center in Helsinki serves as an example. The activities of detox centers in Sweden, Poland, Great Britain, the United States, and Ontario, Canada, are also described.

## THE TÖÖLÖ EXPERIMENTAL DETOX CENTER IN HELSINKI

The Töölö experimental detox center was established for a period of 5 years at the end of 1981. The detox center applies the principles of social work and is administratively subordinate to the City of Helsinki welfare board. It operates in premises previously used as a jail in conjunction with a municipal clinic. The police, social welfare, and health care authorities bear responsibility for the internal functions of the detox center, and the State Alcohol Monopoly of Finland (ALKO) provides funding for the experimental project.

The Töölö experimental detox center is designed to offer further treatment mainly for 18–50-year olds who require shelter because of drunkenness and who are capable of returning to work and benefiting from treatment. Ten percent of the persons arrested for drunkenness in Helsinki end up in the detox center.

The detox center has 23 places and is open from Wednesday to Friday between the hours of 8 AM to 5 PM and on Saturdays and Sundays from 8 AM to 3 PM. The police select persons to be taken to the detox center from among those arrested and sobering up in the morning.

The detox center staff consists of a physician, nurses, social workers, and assistants. The police are charged with providing for the security and belongings of the sheltered as well as with maintaining public order in the center. Police officials also maintain records on persons entering the detox center, fill in an arrest form when a person is released, and see that no one is kept in custody or in the detox center for a period longer than 24 hours. The police do not assist in providing actual treatment to detox center clients.

Assistants and a nurse receive clients at the center. The nurse evaluates a client's condition and the immediate need for care. Assistants arrange showers and bedding, serve juice and food, and talk with clients in detox center facilities.

After the morning routine clients are taken in turn to a social worker and, if needed, to a nurse and/or physician. They are offered a cigarette in this context.

A social worker draws up background reports on clients, admits them to further treatment, and provides advice in the search for accommodation in a boarding house or in applying for social assistance. The nurse administers medication for hangover and minor ailments, measures the blood alcohol concentration, and refers clients to a physician. The physician conducts medical examinations, treats minor complaints, prescribes medicine and refers clients on to further medical tests or other treatment institutions.

This report describes the selection process of detox center clients from among those taken into custody in Helsinki jails as well as treatment provided at the center in February 1982. Data were collected from arrest forms filled in by police officials and from detox center records. A single visit served as the research unit. Study material consists of a sample of only those persons arrested who have been jailed and of all arrest cases referred to the detox center. The jail sample included 347 males and 29 females, while the detox center material consisted of 399 males and 49 females. Because the number of cases listed in the tables vary according to the data source and because detox center records have been inconsistently completed, the data remain incomplete.

## Selection of Detox Center Clients

Persons admited to the detox center ranged from 18 to 50 years of age. No upper age limit is applied in jailing persons in Finland, and individuals under the age of 18 may also be jailed. Against this backdrop, detox center cases naturally include persons between the ages of 18–50 years (TABLE 1). A closer look at age distributions reveals that two-fifths of the male clients in the detox center were between the ages of 31 and 40 and fewer than two-fifths were between 21 and 30 years of age. A full twentieth of the cases fell in the 18–20-year-old age group as opposed to a seventh in the group of 41–50-year olds. Less than a third of the men from the jail sample were aged 41–50 years, a quarter were 31–40-years old, a full fifth were 51–60-years old, a twentieth were 61 years of age or over, while as many were 20 years of age or under.

The situation was similar for women. Half of the cases involving women were 21–30 years of age, a third were 31–40 years old, a seventh 41–50 years of age, and a twentieth were girls 18–20 years old. Less than a third of the women included in the jail sample were 41–50 years of age, a quarter were 31–40 year olds, and less than a quarter were 17 years of age or younger, the same percentage being recorded for those 51 years of age or older.

**TABLE 1.** Age Distribution of Detox Center Clients and Jail Sample Arrestees in February 1982 by Sex

| Age (yr) | Men (%) | | Women (%) | |
|---|---|---|---|---|
| | Detox Center | Jail | Detox Center | Jail |
| . . . –17 | – | 1 | – | 18 |
| 18–20 | 7 | 5 | 6 | – |
| 21–30 | 38 | 13 | 50 | 11 |
| 31–40 | 41 | 24 | 31 | 25 |
| 41–50 | 15 | 28 | 14 | 29 |
| 51–60 | – | 22 | – | 4 |
| 61– . . . | – | 6 | – | 14 |
| Total | 101 | 99 | 101 | 101 |
| n | 399 | 344 | 49 | 28 |

Detox center cases in the main involved younger men and women than those in the jail sample, the only exception being those under the age of 18 in the jail sample.

A review of the marital status of detox center clients and arrest cases indicated that two-thirds of the men admitted to the detox center were single, one-quarter were married, and another quarter divorced. A full half of the men in the jail sample were single, a tenth were married, less than a third were divorced, and only 2 percent were widowed. A greater share of single men was found in the detox center than in the jail sample, where the number of married men was also somewhat lower. The share of divorced men was higher in the jail sample than in the detox center.

A similar distribution was observed among women. Half of the women registered in the detox center were single, a quarter were married, and another quarter divorced. Of women representing the jail sample, two-fifths were single, one-fifth married, and two-fifths divorced.

The same differences emerged in respect to marital status for men and women in comparing detox center with jail cases. Clients entering the detox center were single more often than in the jail sample, while divorced persons were more frequently found in the jail sample.

A client's address tells much about social involvement. More than two-thirds of the men in the detox center lived in private housing, and one-seventh lived in group accommodation, while less than one-seventh had no permanent address. Of the men in the jail sample, nearly one-half had private housing, while a quarter lived in group accommodation, and less than one-third were vagrant.

Housing inequalities were more noticeable for women than for men. Nine of ten detox center women lived in private accommodation and fewer than a tenth in group accommodation. Nearly three-fifths of women in the jail sample lived in private housing, less than a twentieth lived in group accommodation, and two-fifths were homeless.

If we regard address as an indicator, then clients of the detox center were socially stabler than those from the jail sample. On average, persons admitted to the detox center enjoyed a better social standing than jailed persons.

### Detox Center Treatment and Care

Persons entering the detox center are offered a shower, breakfast porridge, and a meal. In the last week of February 1982, 80 percent of clients showered and changed into hospital clothing. According to records kept by assistants, 96 percent of clients ate breakfast porridge and 77 percent had a daytime meal there.

TABLE 2 lists the kind and percentages of consultations clients had with the detox center staff. In varying treatment combinations, 94 percent of men and 96 percent of women asked to see a social therapist. The nurse was consulted by one-third of the men and nearly two-fifths of the women. The physician treated a quarter of the men and one-half of the women. Nearly all men and women consulted a social therapist. Nearly the same proportion of men and women used a nurse's services, while women consulted a physician twice as often as men.

Medication administered at the detox center was not specifically reported in detail. Prescribed medication ranged from medicine for hangover, vitamins, rash ointment, and medication corresponding to previously personally prescribed medicines. A quarter of the men and full two-fifths of women were prescribed medication, as were some of the persons who consulted the nurse and/or the physician (see TABLE 2).

Less than one-sixth of men admitted to the detox center willingly volunteered for treatment, compared to the vague willingness expressed by one-tenth and the unwilling participation in treatment by more than three-fifths of the men. A quarter of the women

**TABLE 2.** Consultations between Detox Center Staff and Clients in February 1982 by Sex

|  | Men (%) | Women (%) |
|---|---|---|
| Nurse | 1 | — |
| Physician | 3 | 2 |
| Social worker | 54 | 38 |
| Nurse and physician | 1 | 2 |
| Nurse and social worker | 19 | 10 |
| Physician and social worker | 9 | 23 |
| Nurse, physician and social worker | 12 | 25 |
| Consultation refused | 1 | — |
| Total | 100 | 100 |
| n | 390 | 48 |

willingly entered treatment, fewer than one-sixth were vaguely willing and a good half unwillingly participated in treatment. Women displayed more positive attitudes towards treatment than men. Nearly one-tenth of men and 2 percent of women required no treatment, and 2 percent of both men and women were treated elsewhere. Attitudes towards treatment can be understood to apply to a single detox center visit or to treatment and care in general.

More than half of the men and more than two-fifths of women registered at the center had received previous treatment for an alcohol problem. No immediately subsequent treatment measures were recorded for the majority of the men and women visiting the detox center in February 1982. Four percent of men and 2 percent of women were ordered to further treatment. Four percent of men and 6 percent of women were admitted to the Töölö A clinic or its outpatient ward.

A team consisting of a physician, nurse, social therapist and assistants decide upon a client's discharge from the center in their midday meeting. Clients have received the necessary treatment before discharge. Pressing reasons for early discharge or justification for extended treatment are discussed case by case. The usual order of discharging clients is that those taken into custody or to the detox center first are among the first to be released. The average length of stay at the center varies from 3 to 5 hours.

The frequency of visits to the detox center does not as such constitute an obstacle to admission, but the appearance of a client's name on a detox center blacklist may be since records are kept of persons considered unfit for treatment at the center because of mental health disorder or disorderly behavior. These lists are passed on to the police with the request that persons appearing on them not be brought to the detox center. In 1982, 70 percent of clients treated at the detox center were first-time visitors. When compared with arrestees, persons admitted to the center had fewer visits: In February 1982 there were 1.07 admissions per person to the detox center, compared with 1.14 jailings per person. The number of arrests was somewhat higher than the number of detox center admissions partly because so-called chronic alcoholics were not referred to the center.

Although the best arrest cases are selected for treatment in the detox center, the staff at the detox center remains dissatisfied with the police selection procedure. They have voiced the suspicion that the police have intentionally sent "bad" clients to the center and have kept the better cases in jail. The detox center staff regards "good" clients as those who brawl only at home, first-time visitors, and persons motivated for treatment, whereas "bad" clients are found among arrestees who suffer from mental health disorders, or who are aggressive or have criminal records.

Attitudes against compulsory treatment have been observed among the detox center staff. Staff members, with the exception of the assistants and the nurse, avoid entering the cell side of the center, because it is regarded as representing coercive treatment, while treatment on the reception side of the center represents voluntariness.

## DETOX CENTER ACTIVITY FROM A CROSS-NATIONAL PERSPECTIVE

This section includes data on the administration of detox centers in a number of countries, including Sweden, Poland, Great Britain, the United States, and Canada.

### Sweden

There are ten experimental detox centers in Sweden: three subordinate to the hospital administration and seven under the social welfare administration. The police can admit to a detox center any intoxicated person found in a public place in a condition posing a danger to himself or others or unable to fend for himself. Some detox centers also admit persons remanded by authorities other than the police or take in persons individually seeking treatment on their own. Treatment is voluntary and extends over 24 hours at a time. Detox center personnel consists of nurses, social workers, assistants, and a consulting physician. The aim is not to provide actual medical or nursing care, but to look generally after clients.

Clients can be admitted selectively; if a person has left the center after a short period of time against the advice and judgment of center personnel, he or she is not readmitted to a detox center for some time, nor are intoxicated and aggressive persons allowed in. The need for further treatment is assessed when a client leaves a center. Many persons treated at detox centers also receive social welfare assistance. Detox centers in Sweden have not operated at full capacity because of too few clients. Intoxicated persons have not been referred to detox centers because of inconvenient opening hours or too great a distance to a center (Johansson and Johansson, 1981).

### Poland

There are 35 detox centers operating under the supervision of the Ministry of the Interior of Poland. Detox centers have the right to detain for 24 hours those under the influence of alcohol who misbehave in public. The centers not only work to keep public order, but they also function in a medical, diagnostic and preventive way as well. In Poland, 70 percent of cases of drunkenness lead to referral to a detox center and the remainder to arrest and jail, since detox centers do not exist in all localities (Moskalewicz, 1981). Because there is no regular selection procedure, a person can repeatedly be admitted for treatment in a detox center, although in many cases clients treated in detox centers are referred yet again for further treatment (Bot eller böter, 1968).

### Great Britain

Detox centers in Great Britain function in a few cities in conjunction with mental hospitals or poison centers. A British detox center is primarily intended to serve as an alternative to the jail/fine/prison cycle by providing treatment on a voluntary basis. Habitual offenders form the largest client group. Intoxicated persons may be admitted to detox centers by officials other than the police alone. The average treatment period is 3 days. Making the stay at a detox center compulsory has been thought to remedy repeated visits and too-short stays in a center. Continued treatment is relatively common since 30 to 60 percent of clients are accepted for further treatment (Hamilton, 1979; Hore, 1982).

### United States

Detox centers have been established in more than 20 states in the U.S. to function as treatment facilities for skid-row alcoholics after the decriminalization of public drunkenness. Detox centers are either hospital wards or independent units engaged primarily in social work. Treatment at a detox center is based on voluntariness, and a client is requested to stay there at least for 1 day, which can be extended to 5 days when necessary. Refusal to readmit a client who leaves the center after a period shorter than a day is used as a means to restrict repeated visits. Thirty percent of detox center clients have been referred to various forms of further treatment (Fagan and Mauss, 1978; Regier, 1979).

### Ontario

Two parallel systems providing treatment to intoxicated persons are in operation in Ontario, Canada. Detox centers were established to function alongside the existing jail/fine/prison system. Detox centers are administratively subordinate to the hospital near which they are located. The centers apply the principles of social work and use no medicine in treatment. Treatment available at a detox center is based on voluntariness and offers an alternative to jail. Officials other than the police can turn a person in to a detox center. In some cases clients may be selected. If a client leaves too soon after entering the center and shortly thereafter volunteers for treatment, he or she is urged to seek treatment elsewhere. Readmissions are common and the share of first-time clients amounts to some 30 to 50 percent. Treatment provided at detox centers lasts on the average for four 24-hour periods to a maximum of one week. Ten percent of clients are referred on to further treatment (Säilä, 1980).

## DISCUSSION

The detox center was originally established to substitute medical treatment for incarceration or fines. In reality, a new activity was created, but the old one remains as well. Despite the different forms of administration of detox centers in Western countries, the difficulties in administration are similar throughout. According to our observations, detox centers (except in Poland) have similar problems with selection of suitable persons, readmissions, release of clients, and aftercare.

Except in Poland the goals of the police are different from those of the social/medical community. The main goal of the police is to maintain public order — a goal that is less important for social/medical authorities (Pastor, 1978). This creates difficulties in the handling of public inebriates.

Detoxification centers in Poland and Finland not only provide compulsory treatment, but also maintain public order. Problems are encountered in detox centers providing voluntary treatment in that treatment periods are too brief. In addition, persons other than arrestees are accepted so that facilities can operate at full capacity. Clients entering detox centers on their own initiative often enjoy a higher social status and are more motivated for treatment. Detox center staff members regard these so-called middle-class alcoholics as easier to work with than arrestees (Hore, 1982; Ogborne and Smart, 1982; Regier, 1979).

Treatment in detox centers remains beyond the reach of many intoxicated persons, because detox centers are not widely located, and not all intoxicated persons seek treatment in detox centers. In keeping public order, the police also prefer to take drunkards to jail rather than to detox centers (Daggett and Rolde, 1980; Hore, 1982; Ogborne and Smart, 1982).

Detox center treatment does not benefit socially alienated alcoholics, unless their living conditions are also improved since many of the detox center clients or arrestees have no source of income nor any place to live. The treatment offered for alcoholics is thus inappropriate for many public inebriates since it does not address their basic needs. Therapy is suitable for some, but many need food, shelter and a job (Regier, 1979). Differentiation of treatment services might correct this problem.

Only infrequently do intoxicated detox center clients need medical care (Annis, 1979; Hore, 1982). Policemen manning jails could be complemented by nurses or social workers, as in some jails in Finland and Sweden (Johansson and Johansson, 1981; Säilä, 1980), in place of costly detox centers. Treatment provided in jail is an obvious solution in that it would eliminate the problems of client selection and transport. Arrestees desiring and needing treatment could then easily be referred on to further treatment.

## REFERENCES

ANNIS, H. M. 1979. The detoxication alternative to the handling of public inebriates. The Ontario Experience. J. Stud. Alcohol 40: 196–210.

Bot eller böter, Del 1 [Treatment or Fines, Part 1]. Statens offentliga utredningar No 55. Stockholm, 1968.

DAGGETT, L. R. & E. J. ROLDE. 1980. Decriminalization of drunkenness. Effects on the work of suburban police. J. Stud. Alcohol 41: 819–828.

FAGAN, R. W. & A. L. MAUSS. 1978. Padding the revolving door: An initial assessment of the uniform alcoholism and intoxication act in practice. Soc. Probl. 26: 232–246.

HAMILTON, J. R. 1979. Evaluation of a detoxification service for habitual drunken offenders. Br. J. Psychiatry 135: 28–34.

HORE, B. D. 1982. The Manchester Detoxification Centre – An evaluation of its aims and results. Paper presented at the 28th International Institute on the Prevention and Treatment of Alcoholism, München, July 5–9, 1982.

JOHANSSON, A. & S. O. JOHANSSON. 1981. Försöksverksamhet med tillnyktringsenheter [Experimental Activity of Detox Centers]. Högskolan i Karlstad. Karlstad.

MOSKALEWICZ, J. 1981. Alcohol: Commodity and Symbol in Polish Society. In Alcohol, Society and the State, Vol. 2. E. Single, P. Morgan & J. de Lint, Eds. Addiction Research Foundation. Toronto, Ontario, Canada.

OGBORNE, A. & R. G. SMART. 1982. Reactions to research: The case of the evaluation of Ontario's detoxication centres. Br. J. Addiction 77: 275–282.

PASTOR, P. A. 1978. Mobilization in public drunkenness control: A comparison of legal and medical approaches. Soc. Probl. 26: 373–384.

REGIER, M. C. 1979. Social Policy in Action. Lexington, MA.

SÄILÄ, S.-L. 1980. Päihtyneiden käsittely Ontariossa ja Suomessa [Handling of inebriates in Ontario and Finland]. Alkoholipolitiikka 45: 258–261.

# Alcohol Treatment in American Indian Populations: An Indigenous Treatment Modality Compared with Traditional Approaches[a]

ROBERTA L. HALL

*Department of Anthropology*
*Oregon State University*
*Corvallis, Oregon 97331*

It has been known for many years that alcoholism poses significant community health problems for American Indian groups (Baker, 1977; Lewis, 1982; Brod, 1975). Alcoholic beverages were virtually unknown in North America before the arrival of European immigrants, and the tragedy of Indian alcoholism is a part of the history of domination which the native peoples experienced at the hands of Europeans. Although the historical, social, and medical aspects of Indian alcoholism have been studied in detail, less attention has been focused upon attempts by Indian people to free themselves of afflictions due to alcohol (Johansen, 1980; NIAAA, 1980; Mail and McDonald, 1980).

This paper reports on features of contemporary Indian alcohol treatment, with a focus on indigenous practices, especially the sweat lodge. Before presenting the data collected in this study, we will briefly review the research on Indian alcoholism and on native American social movements.

The fact that native Americans from many tribes with varied cultural, economic, and physical environments proved susceptible to the ravages of alcohol has led to speculation about the etiology of alcohol abuse in this population (Lewis, 1982). Persistent among biological theories has been the hypothesis that for Indian persons the metabolism of alcohol is somehow different — either faster or slower — than for other people. Although some research indicates that slight differences exist between Indian and other populations in the metabolism of alcohol or its first metabolic product, acetaldehyde, results have been neither strong nor consistent (Fenna *et al.*, 1971; Hanna, 1976; Reed *et al.*, 1976; Zeiner and Paredes, 1978; Schaefer, 1982). Nor has a link been found between differences in metabolism and unhealthful patterns of alcohol use.

Researchers who have emphasized environmental and behavioral aspects of the etiology of alcoholism have had somewhat more material to work with (Leland, 1976). Historically, Indian societies, which had developed highly structured ways of handling other problems of life, were first exposed to alcohol at a time when many other direct and indirect threats were leveled at them (Jilek-Aall, 1978). This situation made it unlikely that the new drug would be integrated in a positive fashion into Indian

[a] This work was supported in part by Grants 1-P50-AA-03510-01A1 and 1-T32-AA07290-01A1 from the National Institute on Alcohol Abuse and Alcoholism and by a postdoctoral research training program at the University of Connecticut Alcohol Research Center.

social life. Instead, alcohol became a symbol of Euroamerican domination and Indian subjugation. What Indian people received in exchange for their way of life and the unrestricted access to the resources of the country was a drink with which to forget the past, the present, and even the future. Carrying this symbol further, Indian drinking patterns have been called the world's oldest ongoing protest movement (Lurie, 1975).

Environmental hypotheses accounting for relatively high levels of alcohol abuse by Indians incorporate one or all of the following: (a) historical-symbolic explanations as presented above; (b) social modeling concepts based on the premise that children learn behavior patterns from the adults around them; thus, initial problems which Indians experienced with alcohol have been repeated through many generations; (c) socioeconomic explanations which relate levels of alcohol abuse to conditions which still characterize the Indian minority in this country: poverty, unemployment, and low access to status and power as it is conceived by the dominant population.

Some researchers who have examined differences in tribal rates of alcohol problems (Stratton et al., 1978) have concluded that cultural factors that existed at the time of initial exposure to alcohol have affected the subsequent incidence of alcoholism. While acknowledging the reality of regional and tribal differences in the prevalence of alcohol problems, this report will focus instead on common features of etiology and treatment.

# NATIVISTIC MOVEMENTS AND USE OF ALCOHOL

Over the past century several nativistic or revitalization movements have swept through Indian America as responses to cultural and material deprivation (Wallace, 1956). These movements incorporate aspects of traditional culture, but may alter ancient traditions and incorporate elements taken from the dominant culture or other societies as well. Several of these movements are millenarian; that is, they expect a miraculous release from current conditions and an immediate restoration of the ancient ways. Those termed *reformative nativism* (Voget, 1956) focus on restoration of native traditions, but do not expect magical transformations to occur. While emphasizing a return to behaviors practiced in the past, those in reformative nativistic movements expect a continuation of the dominant culture and they aid individuals in making personal accommodations. Many focus on physical healing and reform of such behavior as drunkenness and excessive gambling, often portraying alcoholism as the symbol of the Euroamerican culture. As an antidote, they offer a revival of native traditions.

## Previous Nativistic Movements

Probably the best known Indian nativistic movement is the Ghost Dance of 1890. This millenarian movement spread across much of the country, predicting the disappearance of Euroamerican culture, the return of the buffalo, and magical protection of Indians. Its influence ended in a massacre at Wounded Knee on December 29, 1890.

More pertinent to alcohol treatment are two reformative movements, the Religion of Handsome Lake, which was based in the East, and the Indian Shaker Church, which had origins and influence in the West. A Seneca Indian named Handsome Lake, who was given to excessive drinking, fell ill in 1799. While in a coma he experienced a series of visions in which the Creator appeared and sent instructions for proper living, with emphasis on the prohibition of alcohol. Almost a century later on the West Coast, near Olympia, Washington, a similar set of circumstances occurred to John Slocum, a Squaxim Indian (Barnett, 1957; Castile, 1982). John Slocum became ill and appeared to have died. During an unconscious period, he experienced visions, on the basis of which he preached personal reform and abstinence from alcohol. Since Slocum did not adhere to the reforms, he became ill again. In agitation, his wife began to shake; Slocum recovered, and the shaking was believed to be a sign of possession (Sackett, 1973).

Although these movements express native concepts, such as the belief in the importance of visions, they include some non-Indian elements as well. Speaking at a 1977 conference on native religious beliefs in Canada, Tom Porter, a Mohawk Indian, said: "Now we have religion whereas before we had a way of life. With the introduction of Handsome Lake our way of life became like the whiteman's where there is a separation between state and religion" (Waugh and Prithipaul, 1979, p. 37).

In terms of longevity and number of members, neither of these religions were as successful as the Native American Church, a syncretist sect which began in the late nineteenth century. In addition to using both Christian and North American native concepts, it incorporates the psychogenic drug, peyote, a drug formerly unknown north of Mexico (Slotkin, 1956; Aberle, 1966). Additionally, the church offers a strong social support system.

Like the Native American Church, the religion of Handsome Lake, and the Shaker Church, the sun dance ritual gives expression to the Indian concept that the individual can participate directly in the forces of the universe. In this ritual, participants pledge to tie their flesh to a tall pole placed in the center of a large gathering and to dance around the pole without food or water for three nights and days. Traditionally, dancers pledged in order to gain success in the hunt or in warfare, but in the twentieth century the focus has turned to concern over illness of friends and relatives and loss of tribal spirit (Shimkin, 1953). In preparation, sun dancers are admonished to give up alcohol, but some enter the dance to obtain help to stop drinking (Jorgensen, 1972).

### The Sweat Lodge

Unique, yet similar to all of these predecessors, is the recent revival of a traditional ritual and healing practice, the native American sweat lodge. The sweat lodge ceremony is neither a millenarian movement nor a religion, yet it has become the focus around which a pan-Indian resurgence is developing.

Therapeutic sweats probably were known in all areas of aboriginal America, although the purposes and practices differed regionally and culturally (Lopatin, 1960; Aaland, 1978). It is likely that the hot-rock form of the sweat lodge which is customarily used today was most common aboriginally, although some groups sweated with direct heat provided by burning logs in an enclosed lodge (Aaland, 1978). Today the sweat lodge is a small, circular dome-shaped structure made of 12 willow poles arched and tied together. This frame is tightly covered by blankets that prevent light from entering. In the center of the lodge are placed thoroughly heated rocks, on which water is poured to release steam. Steam in the enclosed space produces high levels of sweating in participants, who sit around the outside of the lodge's circle and face the center. Removing toxic metals, urea, lactic acid, and other wastes from the body, the sweat produces physical cleansing (Aaland, 1978) and a feeling of energetic serenity.

Sweats performed in the native American tradition usually last for several hours and are separated into sequences called rounds. After the sprinkling of water on the hot rocks, the sweat leader begins prayers, which are continued from person to person around the circle. At the end of a round, the blanket flaps through which participants have entered are opened and a brief cooling occurs. Flaps are secured before the next round.

The form of the ritual varies culturally but certain elements are found universally. The sweat lodge is considered to provide the means to bring the individual closer to the elemental forces of life. It expresses unity between humans and other living beings, inorganic matter, and physical forces — all components of the universe. In some belief systems, the lodge symbolically is the womb. Prayers are addressed to "Grandfather" but this term means the ultimate ancestor, not a specific person.

Indian people disagree as to whether in aboriginal times the sweat lodge was used principally for physical cleansing or for religious practices. However, native cultures did not make academic distinctions between spheres of life such as are common in technological societies. Nor do Indian people agree on specific ritual practices or their meaning (Waugh and Prithipaul, 1979). For example, women are cautioned not to enter the sweat lodge during the menstrual period, but whether this is due to fear of uncleanliness, the belief that women's cycles provide sufficient cleansing in themselves, or respect for the special powers of women at this time of the month, is in dispute. In some traditions, women and men sweat separately, while sweats are integrated in others.

Ritual regulations have continued to differ culturally and regionally. In some areas a medicine man or recognized spiritual leader is required to officiate at a sweat lodge ceremony, but in others each person is considered to be his own religious specialist. Differences also exist as to whether non-Indians or Indians who have no knowledge of ancient religious traditions should be encouraged to take part. No Indian religion is evangelistic in the sense that Western religions are, but differences do exist about how much to encourage or discourage interested outsiders from taking part.

The sweat lodge practice as described above differs from those of other nativistic movements and organized churches. In several important respects it has most in common with the sun dance, for it involves a serious commitment to Indian heritage but does not prevent, and may facilitate, accommodations to contemporary society. Many sun dance participants also are users of sweat lodges and in some regions participation in the sun dance is one of the means of qualification for sweat lodge leadership. In contrast to the sun dance, sweat lodge participation is not restricted to one season of the year, and it offers participation to a larger number of persons on a regular basis.

As a pan-Indian symbol the sweat lodge is effective because its original distribution was wide and because it makes both a physically and culturally powerful impression; it possesses a disarming simplicity. As an example of the extent to which the sweat lodge has become a symbol of Indian religion and identity, the Native American Rights Fund (1980) reports that most states that have Indian prisoners have sweat lodges available for Indian inmates, and recommends it for all. According to many Indian people, participation in the sweat is a symbol of a person's affirmation of Indian identity.

Given the background of revitalization movements in North America, it should not be surprising that the sweat lodge would be used in the context of alcoholism treatment. Because the sweat lodge produces a powerful physical and mental experience, it has been considered an antidote for alcohol, which also produces strong physical and mental reactions. As a ritual practice rather than a formal organization, the sweat lodge offers the added possibility of supplementing programs that use other medical and behavioral techniques for alcohol rehabilitation.

# METHOD

## *Purpose of the Study*

This study was begun to investigate the use of the sweat lodge as an indigenous treatment modality within established alcoholism treatment programs under contract to the Indian Health Service. The goal was to describe characteristics of current programs and to investigate the relationship of the sweat lodge to other treatment services which programs provide, as well as to their philosophic, demographic, and geographic features.

Programs under contract to the Indian Health Service (IHS) are not the only alcohol programs which serve Indian clients nor the only ones which utilize the sweat lodge (Otis and Katz, 1981). However, the Indian Health Service has the special mission of serving Indian clients, and since contracts are let on a nationwide basis and serve nonregistered as well as registered Indians, its programs appeared appropriate for the purposes of the present pilot study. A full study would include a larger sample, site visits in addition to telephone interviews, and comparison with alcohol treatment and prevention programs run by agencies other than the Indian Health Service.

## *The Sample*

The Indian Health Service's list of 190 contract programs was stratified into six regional areas from which a 20 percent sample was drawn randomly. Directors or other representatives of 39 projects in the random sample were reached for telephone interviews which averaged 40 minutes in length. Personnel from five other projects were interviewed, two at the request of the IHS Alcohol Program Director and three known to the author. Tabulations were made for the random sample of 39 as well as for the total sample of 44 to avoid biases which might have been introduced by the small selected component. Since the results of both analyses were highly consistent, the findings from the larger sample are reported here.

## *The Survey*

Basic data collected from each project included information on the staff, number of years of program operation, source of funds in addition to the IHS contract, services offered, client characteristics, and use of the sweat lodge and other traditional practices.

Modal number of staff members is six; most projects have staff members who predominantly are of Indian descent and are recovering alcoholics. Most programs include outpatient services and some educational programs in the community or schools. Many have an inpatient or halfway house component as well. Only one program offered a medical detoxification service, although many cooperated with county or other detox centers. Only one was a day-service crisis center. (A full tabulation of these variables will be sent upon request.)

# RESULTS

In the random sample, 50 percent of the programs either offered a sweat lodge at their site or provided access and encouragement for use of the sweat lodge at an-

**TABLE 1.** Sweat Lodge and Tribal Emphasis and Control of Alcoholism Programs: Random Sample

| | Tribal Control and Emphasis | | |
| Sweat Lodge | Single-Tribe Emphasis | Several-Tribe Emphasis | Nontribal or Pantribal |
| --- | --- | --- | --- |
| Present and encouraged on-site or off-site | 5 (23%) | 7 (32%) | 10 (45%) |
| Not present or not encouraged in the community or on site | 14 (64%) | 3 (13%) | 4 (23%) |

$\chi^2 = 7.52$; $p < 0.02$.

NOTE: Programs that use the sweat lodge are evenly distributed according to tribal emphasis, but those that do not use it are found predominantly in the single-tribe category.

other site in the community; 50 percent either did not have the sweat lodge or did not encourage use of those in the community. No program made sweat lodge participation mandatory. Eight programs in the random sample had their own sweat lodges at the treatment site, while 14 programs provided access to a sweat lodge maintained elsewhere in the community. Eight others made access to a community-run sweat lodge possible but did not actively encourage its use, particularly by clients to whom it was unfamiliar. Four programs were in areas that do not have a sweat lodge, but where interest in starting one exists among program personnel. Finally, the sweat lodge was unavailable in 10 programs. However, these include a northern Alaskan program in an area where sweating was not practiced aboriginally, but in which recently reinstituted village-elder "spirit committees" have been formed to deal with current problems such as alcoholism (see Vesilind [1983] for a discussion of the traditional revival in these areas). Except for the absence of active sweat lodges in all three of the programs sampled in the Eastern block, lodges were found in the same proportion in each region.

Cross-tabulations were made between the presence or absence of the sweat lodge and other program attributes. TABLE 1 shows the relationship between sweat lodges and the tribal emphasis of programs. Chi-square analysis indicates that a larger proportion of programs that were nontribal or were run by several tribes used the sweat lodge than did those run by single tribes. Secondly, more programs that used a medicine man also used the sweat lodge (TABLE 2). Two other program characteristics that were related less strongly to the sweat lodge were the presence of the Native American Church in the community and a client population composed of tribally mixed and nonstatus Indians (as opposed to a client population from a single tribe).

The following program characteristics were not related to sweat lodge use; geographic area; presence of inpatient unit, halfway house, educational program, youth group, family therapy, or job counseling service; strong emphasis upon Alcoholics Anony-

**TABLE 2.** Sweat Lodge Use Related to Use of Medicine Man in Alcohol Program

| Sweat Lodge | Medicine Man Used | Medicine Man Not Available |
| --- | --- | --- |
| Present and encouraged on-site or off-site | 12 (63%) | 7 (37%) |
| Not present or not encouraged in the community or on site | 4 (19%) | 18 (81%) |
| Missing observations: 3 | | |

$\chi^2 = 6.87$; $p < 0.01$.

NOTE: In this analysis a medicine man is a spiritualist healer, not an herbalist.

mous; staff composition in percentage of Indian employees or in recovering alcoholic status; and extent to which Antabuse is used.

## DISCUSSION

Most interesting of the statistically significant relationships is the one between the sweat lodge and the tribal emphasis. As a pan-Indian phenomenon, the sweat lodge appeals most to programs that are established and run by multitribe groups. Additionally, there appears to be a relationship between the tribal composition of clients and a program's use of the sweat lodge. It should be emphasized that not all non-tribal programs use the sweat lodge nor do all single-tribe programs lack them. Interviews with personnel in programs on reservations, however, indicate a greater conservatism in the handling of the sweat lodge and other traditional practices. These groups tend to be less accepting of rituals that are not native to their areas and are more likely to restrict the performance of traditional rituals to those known to have been practiced in the past. Because some practices are forgotten, through time rituals become reduced in number and less dynamic.

The Native American Church is not as widely distributed as the sweat lodge, but it is not surprising to find an association between the two practices. The roots of the church are eclectic and, like the sweat lodge and the sun dance, the church offers a means for native Americans to accommodate to some aspects of the dominant culture while still maintaining an Indian identity and value system. In several alcohol programs, a sweat precedes the peyote ceremony of the Native American Church.

The absence of a relationship between the sweat lodge and most program characteristics deserves attention. This finding seems to indicate the flexibility with which the sweat lodge can be applied, e.g., with resident or outpatient clients, in connection with Alcoholics Anonymous or separate from it, in programs involved in community education, and with those that are not. Except that the sweat lodge has been adopted most readily in programs that are run by and that serve Indians of diverse tribal backgrounds, its use appears to be dependent on factors that do not vary systematically— factors that may include such things as the personality of the director or the availability of a sweat lodge group in a nearby community.

In 1968, Leon argued that only the development by Indian people of a treatment program coupled with a new identity would offer a workable solution to the problem of Indian alcoholism (Leon, 1968). The current Indian Health Service practice of offering contracts for alcohol programs is consistent with his proposal, since it appears to offer a greater degree of local control than was previously known. Jilek-Aall (1978) found that AA groups that had been adapted to the Salish Indian culture were taking on some characteristics of an indigenous movement and she argued for more local control of treatment programs coupled with community development. The use of traditional cultural material in treatment has been investigated by a number of researchers in the past 10 years (Jilek, 1974, 1981, 1982; Jilek and Todd, 1974; Jilek-Aall, 1981; Nelson, 1977; Cohen et al., 1981; Miller and Wittstock, 1981; Otis and Katz, 1981; Otis, 1981; Stratton, 1981). Most researchers express the opinion that local control, cultural sensitivity, and the use of traditional cultural practices are positive steps (Haven and Imotichey, 1979; Andre, 1979; Beane et al., 1980; DHHS, 1981).

Many treatment personnel reported that in their areas a resurgence of interest in Indian culture has begun in the last 5 or 10 years. One indication of the resurgence was an increase in the number of pow-wows (gatherings for traditional dancing, games, and displays of other traditional arts and crafts). Formerly, pow-wows have been occasions for hard drinking and drug use, but in many areas recent attempts to enforce drug-free pow-wows have been successful. Accordingly, alcohol treatment staff in many regions make arrangements for clients to attend.

While none of the treatment personnel implied that the cultural resurgence will provide easy answers to the alcohol problems that Indian communities face, many suggested that it may help. Several observed that alcoholics have an identity problem to work out in the course of treatment, and Indian alcoholics have a group identity problem as well. Several treatment centers have developed preventive programs which use traditional arts and crafts in an effort to reinstate pride in an Indian heritage which excludes the use of alcohol. Other youth projects were focused upon psychological skill development and did not use culture-specific materials or themes, while still other programs combined these approaches. Particularly striking in the interviews was the ability of personnel to integrate contemporary psychological concepts and skills, such as family therapy and behaviorist techniques, with traditional arts and beliefs. The annual Tiyospaye Network workshop (Weeks, 1982), which I attended in the summer of 1982, has shown that family therapy is compatible with traditional values of Plains Indian people, in whose aboriginal home in western South Dakota the workshop takes place.

In general, tradition-enhancing programs were found less often in tribal areas that have remained isolated. Some program personnel in these areas said they did not emphasize cultural programs because the traditional culture was present in the area. For them, use of the material was considered redundant or distracting to clients. One staff member recommended that clients get involved after leaving the inpatient program, however. In other isolated areas, traditional practices have been lost; all that remains to remind people of their Indian heritage is a feeling of ethnicity and the problems of minority discrimination, economic underdevelopment, and alcoholism.

Whereas all of the treatment programs in this survey are sensitive to the ethnic needs and historical background of Indian clients, all do not rely upon indigenous healing methods or traditional cultural practices, nor are goals identical. Several treatment personnel said that their program provides traditional modalities in part so that clients cannot use the excuse that the program is not sensitive to their background to avoid serious involvement in rehabilitation. Several other persons noted that they always have to convince clients that Alcoholics Anonymous is not oriented to any one religion or to any one group of people. They said that AA can be ethnically sensitive, as Jilek-Aall (1978) found among the Salish, and other treatment methods have been altered to fit Indian culture also. Several staff members mentioned, for example, that their group therapy sessions are less confronting than are typical, in order to conform more closely to ideal patterns of interaction among Indians.

Use of the sweat lodge, a traditional medicine man, or the Native American Church, involves more than sensitivity to cultural background or appreciation of Indian history and art; it requires trust in another mode of healing and in a different philosophy of life as well as involving volunteers from the Indian community. Unlike AA, which also consists of volunteers, sweat lodge volunteers are not exclusively reforming alcoholics and their goals are broader than the specific goals of alcohol treatment. Although sweat lodge participants follow a code that is binding, it is not a written code which is readily understood in the medical community. The involvement of the general community in sweat lodges suggests that the sweat lodge program may integrate alcoholic clients into the wider community. Because many program personnel, sweat lodge leaders, and spiritual leaders are recovering alcoholics, their sobriety and reliance upon traditional culture may serve as a model for other Indian people, including youth. Westermeyer and Peake (1983) found that recovering alcoholics who worked with treatment programs had an improved chance at maintaining sobriety. Sweat lodge leaders, whether recovering alcoholics or not, also serve as role models who represent an alternative image to the "drunken Indian" stereotype, which many Indian young people still emulate, consciously or not. The questions raised by this study should be pursued in further field research.

The possibility exists that, fostered by but not controlled by or restricted to alcohol treatment programs, the sweat lodge may have a major role in the prevention of alcohol abuse and in the creation of a new Indian identity. Although the resurgence of this traditional practice has much in common with other nativistic social movements which have wrestled with alcoholism, the sweat lodge also has unique features. Neither orthodox nor nativistic remedies have solved the alcohol problem in Indian populations, but all have proved valuable in the rehabilitation of many individuals. While we may have confidence that the sweat lodge program will aid in rehabilitation, it is too much to expect that any one program will solve the problem of alcoholism. The sweat lodge resurgence has shown that native philosophy and practice still have power and beauty, but attempts to forecast the role of the sweat lodge in alcohol treatment or prevention programs, or its place in native American culture of the twentieth and twenty-first centuries, can only be speculative.

## ACKNOWLEDGMENTS

I want to thank Bud Mason and Mary Tyner of the Indian Health Service for providing the list of contract programs; Tom Babor, Victor Hesselbrock, Nancy Carter-Menendez, and Alison Otis for their interest and encouragement; Don Hall for editorial advice; and the Oregon State University Department of Anthropology for typing and computer assistance.

### REFERENCES

AALAND, M. 1978. Sweat. Capra Press. Santa Barbara, CA.

ABERLE, D. F. 1966. The Peyote Religion among the Navahos. Aldine. Chicago, IL.

ANDRE, J. M. 1979. The Uniqueness of Alcoholism among American Indians with some Thoughts on Prevention, Treatment, and Rehabilitation. Report Presented to the Senior staff of the NIAA, Albuquerque, New Mexico.

BAKER, J. M. 1977. Alcoholism and the American Indian. In Alcoholism: Developments, Consequences, and Interventions. N. J. Estes and M. E. Heinemann, Eds.: 194–203. Mosby. St. Louis, MO.

BARNETT, H. G. 1957. Indian Shakers: a Messianic Cult of the Pacific Northwest. Southern Illinois Press. Carbondale, IL.

BEANE, S., C. A. HAMMERSCHLAG & J. LEWIS. 1980. Federal Indian policy: Old wine in new bottles. White Cloud Journal of the American Indian 2: 14–17.

BROD, T. 1975. Alcoholism as a mental health problem of native Americans. Arch. Gen. Psychiatry 32: 1385–1391.

CASTILE, G. P. 1982. The "half-Catholic" movement: Edwin and Myron Eells and the rise of the Indian Shaker Church. Pacific Northwest Q. 73: 165–174.

COHEN, F. G., R. D. WALKER & S. STANLEY. 1981. The role of anthropology in interdisciplinary research on Indian alcoholism and treatment outcome. J. Stud. Alcohol 42: 836–845.

DEPARTMENT OF HEALTH AND HUMAN SERVICES. 1981. Fourth Special Report to the U.S. Congress on Alcohol and Health. U.S. Government Printing Office. Washington, DC.

FENNA, D., L. MIX, O. SCHAEFER & J. A. L. GILBERT. 1971. Ethanol metabolism in various racial groups. Can. Med. Assoc. J. 105: 472–475.

HANNA, J. M. 1976. Ethnic groups, human variation, and alcohol use. *In* Cross-Cultural Approaches to the Study of Alcohol. Everett, Waddell, and Heath, Eds.: 235–242. Mouton. The Hague.

HAVEN, G. A., JR. & P. J. IMOTICHEY. 1979. Mental health services for the American Indian: the USET program. White Cloud Journal of the American Indian **1**: 3–5.

JILEK, W. G. 1974. Indian healing power: Indigenous therapeutic practices in the Pacific Northwest. Psychiatr. Ann. **4**(11):13–21.

JILEK, W. G. & N. TODD. 1974. Witchdoctors succeed where doctors fail: Psychotherapy among Coast Salish Indians. Can. Psychiatr. Assoc. J. **19**: 351–355.

JILEK, W. 1981. Anomic depression, alcoholism and a culture-congenial Indian response. J. Stud. Alcohol (Suppl.) **9**: 159–170.

JILEK, W. G. 1982. Indian Healing. Hancock House. Surrey, British Columbia.

JILEK-AALL, L. 1978. Alcohol and the Indian-white relationship. Confinia Psychiatrica **21**: 195–233.

JILEK-AALL, L. 1981. Acculturation, alcoholism and Indian style alcoholics anonymous. J. Stud. Alcohol (Suppl) **9**: 143–158.

JOHANSEN, B. 1980. The teepees are empty and the bars are full. Alcoholism (Nov.–Dec.):33–38.

JORGENSEN, J. 1972. The Sun Dance Religion. University of Chicago Press. Chicago, IL.

LELAND, J. 1976. Firewater Myths. Rutgers Center of Alcohol Studies. New Brunswick, NJ.

LEON, R. 1968. Some implications for a preventive program for American Indians. Am. J. Psychiatry **125**: 232–236.

LEWIS, R. G. 1982. Alcoholism and the Native American: A review of the literature. *In* Alcohol and Health Monograph No. 4: Special Population Issues. :315–328. U.S. Government Printing Office. Washington, DC.

LOPATIN, I. 1960. Origin of the Native American steam bath. Am. Anthropologist **62**: 977–993.

LURIE, N. O. 1975. The world's oldest ongoing protest demonstration: North American Indian drinking patterns. Pacific Historical Rev. **40**: 311–322.

MAIL, P. D. & D. R. MCDONALD. 1980. Tulapai to Tokay: A Bibliography of Alcohol Use and Abuse among Native Americans in North America. Human Relations Area Files. New Haven, CT.

MILLER, M. & L. W. WITTSTOCK. 1981. American Indian Alcoholism in St. Paul. Center for Urban and Regional Affairs, Minneapolis, MN.

NATIONAL INSTITUTE ON ALCOHOL ABUSE AND ALCOHOLISM. 1980. Indian traditions offer alternatives to alcohol. Information Feature Service No. 69: 4. February 19, 1980.

NATIVE AMERICAN RIGHTS FUND. 1980. Indian Offender Project: An Indian Offender Needs Assessment. Native American Rights Fund. Boulder, CO.

NELSON, L. 1977. Alcoholism in Zuni, New Mexico. Preventive Med. **6**: 152–166.

OTIS, A. 1981. Traditional Medicine and Self-Determination in Resolving Mental Health Problems among Southwest Oregon Native Americans. Master's thesis, Oregon State University, Corvallis, OR.

OTIS, A. & S. J. KATZ. 1981. An Assessment of Mental Health Services to Native Americans in Southwest Oregon. Report prepared for the Oregon Mental Health Division, Department of Human Resources, Salem, OR.

REED, T. E., H. KALANT, R. J. GIBBINS, B. M. KAPUR & J. G. RANKIN. 1976. Alcohol and acetaldehyde metabolism in Caucasians, Chinese and Amerinds. Can. Med. Assoc. J. **115**: 851–855.

SACKETT, L. 1973. The Siletz Indian Shaker Church. Pacific Northwest Q. **64**: 120–126.

SCHAEFER, J. M. 1982. Ethnic and racial variations in alcohol use and abuse. *In* Alcohol and Health Monograph No.4: Special Population Issues. : 293–313. U.S. Government Printing Office. Washington, DC.

SHIMKIN, D. B. 1953. The Wind River Shoshone sun dance. Bureau of American Ethnology Bulletin 151, Anthropological Paper No. 41:397–484.

SLOTKIN, J. S. 1956. The Peyote Religion. Octagon Books. New York, NY. (Reprinted 1975.)

STRATTON, R. 1981. Indian alcoholism programs and Native American culture. *In* New Directions for Mental Health Services No. 10. A. Paredes, Ed. Jossey-Bass. San Francisco, CA.

STRATTON, R., A. ZEINER & A. PAREDES. 1978. Tribal affiliation and prevalence of alcohol problems. J. Stud. Alcohol **39**: 1166–1177.

VESILIND, P. J. 1983. Hunters of the lost spirit. National Geographic **163**(2): 151–197.

VOGET, F. 1956. The American Indian in transition: Reformation and accommodation. Am. Anthropologist **58**: 249–263.

WALLACE, A. F. C. 1956. Revitalization movements. Am. Anthropologist **58**: 266–281.

WAUGH, E. H. & K. DAD PRITHIPAUL, Eds. 1979. Native Religious Traditions. Canadian Corporation for Studies in Religion. Waterloo, Ontario, Canada.

WEEKS, M., Ed. 1982. The Tiyospaye Network Voice. Institute of Indian Studies, University of South Dakota. Vermillion, SD.

WESTERMEYER, J. & E. PEAKE. 1983. A ten-year follow-up of alcoholic Native Americans in Minnesota. Am. J. Psychiatry **140**: 189–194.

ZEINER, A. R. & A. PAREDES. 1978. Racial differences in circadian variation of ethanol metabolism. Alcoholism: Clin. Exp. Res. **2**: 71–75.

# Cultural Affiliation among American Indian Alcoholics: Correlations and Change over a Ten-Year Period[a]

JOSEPH WESTERMEYER AND JOHN NEIDER

*Department of Psychiatry*
*University of Minnesota*
*Minneapolis, Minnesota 55455*

## INTRODUCTION

Cultural affiliation has been identified as an important factor in maintaining mental health (Dean, 1977; Garrison, 1978; Westermeyer, 1973; Allison, 1968; Jilek, 1974). Its role in alcoholism is not known, however. On one hand it might be argued that, since ethnic origin is a major etiologic factor in alcoholism, greater ethnic affiliation (that is, one's current ethnic ties and behaviors) may be associated with greater pathologic disorder. Or, if it is the absence of ethnic affiliation (rather than only one's particular ethnic origin) that is pathogenic, perhaps greater ethnic affiliation is associated with less disorder. Alternatively, affiliation with a particular culture might have no influence on the course of alcoholism.

These hypotheses were tested among native American persons treated for alcoholism, using a sample from those admitted to University of Minnesota hospitals. This particular group has two advantages for such a study. First, the rate of alcohol-related problems among Indian people in Minnesota is high (Westermeyer and Brantner, 1972). Normative drinking involves ingestion of large volumes over many hours (Westermeyer, 1972). Second, it was possible to distinguish skills derived from specific Indian cultural affiliation from general coping skills in American society, given the unique characteristics of native American culture.

Data were collected on the same subjects at two points in time, 10 years apart. This permitted the assessment of cultural affiliation over time. Since some subjects continued to have alcohol-related problems while others did not, it was also possible to examine the association between ethnic affiliation and either continued alcoholic abuse or recovery.

## METHOD

### Sample

Forty-five native American alcoholics were admitted to University of Minnesota hospitals in 1970–71. About half of these patients were referred from hospital emer-

[a] This study was supported in part by Grant HP-78-75-3 from the State of Minnesota.

179

gency rooms and outpatient clinics, and about half from Indian alcoholism coun-selors, associations, and halfway houses. They have been described previously in the literature (Westermeyer, 1972).

A follow-up study on these 45 subjects was undertaken during 1980–81. Among the original 45, 33 were alive, 9 deceased, and 3 could not be located. This study has also been reported (Westermeyer and Peake, 1982).

*Instruments*

The Indian Culture Scale included 10 items: These are shown in TABLE 1 along with the scoring criteria. The total scale score range was 0 (minimum affiliation) to 16 (maximum affiliation). The actual range in the 1970–71 sample was between 4 and 14. The 1980–81 sample ranged from 5 through 15. Both distributions approached normality.

Other scales employed in this study are listed in APPENDIX A. These were com-pleted in 1970–71 on the basis of the person's life up to that time. Some of them were again completed in 1980–81 on the basis of the person's life between 1970–71 and 1980–81.

A self-rating scale for depression, the Zung, was administered in 1980–81. Sub-jects were requested to rate themselves as they presently felt; all had been abstinent from alcohol for at least 48 hours. While the Zung scale has not been standardized

**TABLE 1.** The Indian Culture Scale: Item Content and Scoring Criteria

| Items | Scoring Criteria and Weighting Values | | |
|---|---|---|---|
| | 0 | 1 | 2 |
| a. Contact with Indian relatives in the last year: | Some | Has visited them | Lives with them |
| b. Contact with Indian friends in the last year: | None | Some contact | At least weekly |
| c. Presence of Indians in area neighboring usual residence: | None | Some | Almost exclusively Indian |
| d. Comprehension of any Indian language: | None | Some | Fluency |
| e. Age at leaving reservation: | < 5 yr | ≥ 5–15 yr | > 15 yr |
| f. Last visit to home reservation: | ≥ 5 yr | 2–4 yr | ≤ 1 yr |
| g. Attendance at pow wows in last year: | None | Any | |
| h. Ricing, beading, other traditional activities last year:[a] | None | Any | |
| i. Active with Indian organization in last year:[b] | None | Any | |
| j. Practiced Indian religion in last year:[c] | None | Any | |

[a] These included making Indian bread, making dance costumes, fishing, hunting, and guiding.

[b] These included drum group, quilting group, American Indian Movement, and other local associations.

[c] This included either aboriginal religions (e.g., Midwinin among Chippewa) or more recent syncretic religion (e.g., Native American Church).

to Indian people, it has been applied widely among both clinical and nonclinical samples of various ethnic groups (Zung, 1973; Marsella *et al.*, 1974). A rating scale for alcoholism was also used, the Michigan Alcoholism Screening Test (Selzer, 1971). This was also completed in 1980–81 on the basis of the person's life-long drinking pattern.

## Statistical Analysis

Student's *t* test with a pooled analysis of variance was used for paired parametric comparisons. For bivariate comparisons Pearson's correlation coefficient test was used.

Data for 1970–71 include all 45 subjects. Analyses involving status at follow-up were also made for all 45 subjects. Data from 1980–81 was obtained from all those 33 living subjects who were located. Comparisons between the 1970–71 and the 1980–81 data were made only for these 33 subjects.

In order to assess the extent and direction of the bias from losing 12 subjects in 1980–81, a comparison was made between the 12 lost subjects and the 33 interviewed subjects using the 1970–71 data. The lost group had a significantly lower Cultural Affiliation score in 1970–71 as compared to the others ($t = 2.48$, 43 df, $p < 0.02$). The two groups were similar for all other variables in 1970–71.

# FINDINGS

## Cultural Affiliation in 1970–71

This analysis includes all 45 original subjects (see TABLE 2).

### Demographic Characteristics

Those who had ever been married (including divorced, separated, and widowed subjects) showed a significantly higher Indian Cultural Affiliation at the 0.02 level. Gender did not reveal a difference.

It had been anticipated that older age would be associated with greater Indian affiliation since older subjects had been more influenced by traditional culture (e.g., Indian language as first language) and less by majority influence (e.g., radio, TV, integrated schools). For the same reason, we considered that more education might be associated with less Cultural Affiliation. However, neither factor demonstrated a significant association.

Other variables included *employed* versus *unemployed*, and *living alone* versus *living with others*. Neither were associated with Cultural Affiliation.

### Other Rating Scales

Only one rating scale, the Psychiatric Problems Scale, was correlated with the Cultural Affiliation Scale in 1970–71 ($r = -0.33$, $p < 0.01$). Those with fewer psychiatric events reported greater Indian cultural affiliation.

Rating scales in 1970–71 that were not correlated with Cultural Affiliation included Alcoholism History, Withdrawal Severity, Liver Dysfunction, Malnutrition, Legal Problems, and Social Competence. Despite the absence of statistical correlation, there

**TABLE 2.** Cultural Affiliation among 45 Native American Alcoholics: 1970–71

| Characteristic | Number of Subjects | Cultural Affiliation Scores: Mean (and Standard Deviation) | Statistical Significance |
|---|---|---|---|
| *1. Demography* | | | |
| Gender | | | |
|   Male | 37 | 10.1 (2.2) | $t = -0.80$, 43 df |
|   Female | 8 | 9.4 (3.5) | $p =$ not significant |
| | 45 | | |
| Age (yr) | | | |
|   < 20 | 3 | 10.3 (3.1) | |
|   20–29 | 10 | 9.0 (3.4) | |
|   30–39 | 12 | 10.2 (1.7) | $r = +0.23$ |
|   40–49 | 11 | 9.4 (2.2) | $p =$ not significant |
|   50–59 | 8 | 11.6 (1.8) | |
|   ≥ 60 | 1 | 11.0 (0) | |
| | 45 | | |
| Education | | | |
|   ≤ 8 yr | 17 | 9.7 (2.4) | $r = 0.00$ |
|   9–10 yr | 13 | 10.5 (2.6) | $p =$ not significant |
|   11–12 yr | 13 | 10.0 (2.6) | |
|   > 12 yr | 2 | 9.5 (0.71) | |
| | 45 | | |
| Marital Status | | | |
|   Never married | 20 | 9.1 (2.7) | $t = -2.32$, 43 df |
|   Ever married | 25 | 10.7 (2.0) | $p < 0.03$ |
| | 45 | | |
| *2. Rating Scales* | | | |
| Psychiatric problems | | | |
|   None | 15 | 10.9 (1.6) | |
|   One | 11 | 10.7 (1.6) | $r = -0.33$ |
|   Two | 10 | 8.5 (3.2) | $p < 0.01$ |
|   Three | 9 | 9.3 (2.7) | |
| | 45 | | |

was a trend for those with greater Indian affiliation to have less severe disability, i.e., less severe alcoholism, fewer legal problems, and better social coping.

### Cultural Affiliation in 1970–71 versus Characteristics in 1980–81

This analysis includes outcomes for all 45 subjects, but only rating scales for the 33 subjects located in 1980–81 (TABLE 3). Comparisons were undertaken to assess the predictive influence that Cultural Affiliation in 1970–71 exerted on other variables 10 years later.

#### Outcome

Cultural Affiliation in 1970–71 strongly predicted outcome in 1980–81. Those who were judged improved reported the most cultural ties and activities, while those who were deceased or lost to follow-up reported the least (TABLE 3).

**TABLE 3.** Cultural Affiliation in 1970–71 and Characteristics after 10 Years

| Characteristics in 1980–81 | Number of Subjects | Cultural Affiliation: 1970–71 Mean (and Standard Deviation) | Statistical Significance |
|---|---|---|---|
| Outcome | | | |
| Improved | 7 | 11.4 (1.7) | |
| Same | 7 | 11.1 (1.2) | $r = -0.41$ |
| Worse | 19 | 9.9 (2.4) | $p < 0.002$ |
| Dead, lost[a] | 12 | 8.6 (2.8) | |
| | 45 | | |
| Michigan Alcoholism Screening Test score | | | |
| 21 to 34 | 8 | 11.3 (1.0) | |
| 36 to 39 | 7 | 11.7 (2.1) | $r = -0.45$ |
| 43 to 47 | 9 | 10.8 (1.2) | $p < 0.005$ |
| 48 to 54 | 9 | 8.7 (2.5) | |
| | 33 | | |
| Zung Depression score | | | |
| < 50 | 25 | 10.9 (1.9) | |
| 50–59 | 6 | 9.7 (2.5) | $r = -0.30$ |
| ⩾ 60 | 2 | 8.0 (1.4) | $p < 0.05$ |
| | 33 | | |
| Legal problems | | | |
| None | 6 | 11.77 (1.5) | |
| One | 6 | 11.17 (1.9) | $r = -0.30$ |
| Two | 16 | 10.5 (2.0) | $p < 0.05$ |
| Three | 5 | 9.0 (2.9) | |
| | 33 | | |
| Alcoholism history | | | |
| 3 yr | 6 | 11.8 (0.8) | |
| 4–5 yr | 11 | 11.1 (1.6) | $r = -0.43$ |
| 6–8 yr | 10 | 10.2 (1.7) | $p < 0.01$ |
| 9 yr | 6 | 8.5 (2.5) | |
| | 33 | | |

[a] This includes nine deceased persons and three not found during follow-up (two of the latter, both women, are presumed by their families to be dead).

*Rating Scales*

Subjects with the highest Cultural Affiliation in 1970–71 reported the following in 1980–81:
(1) lowest Michigan Alcoholism Screening Test results ($r = -0.45$, $p < 0.005$);
(2) lowest Alcoholism History score ($r = -0.43$, $p < 0.01$);
(3) fewest depressive symptoms on the Zung scale ($r = -0.30$, $p < 0.05$);
(4) the fewest legal problems in the decade between 1970–71 and 1980–81 ($r = -0.30$, $p < 0.05$).

Of interest, there was stability in the Cultural Affiliation scores over time, with a positive correlation at the 0.02 level ($r = 0.36$, $p < 0.02$) between 1970–71 and 1980–81.

The 1970–71 Cultural Affiliation scores failed to show any association with the following scales: Social Competence in 1980–81 and Psychiatric Disorders during the interim from 1970–71 to 1980–81.

## Cultural Affiliations in 1980–81

This analysis was done only for the 33 subjects interviewed in 1980–81. The Cultural Affiliation scores as well as the other scores were all obtained in 1980–81.

### Demography

The Cultural Affiliation Scale again revealed no association with gender, age, education, residence or employment. Marital status, which had been related to Cultural Affiliation in 1970–71, was no longer related to it in 1980–81.

### Outcome

On the basis of earlier observations in 1970–71, we expected that those with better clinical outcomes (among the 33 survivors) would report more Indian contacts and activities in 1980–81. This was not the case, however. Not only was Cultural Affiliation in 1980–81 unrelated to outcome, but it was also not related to duration of recent abstinence or duration of longest abstinence in the last decade.

### Rating Scales

The 1980–81 Cultural Affiliation score was not associated with any of the other 1980–81 scores, including Alcoholism History, Michigan Alcoholism Screening Test, Legal Problems, Psychiatric Problems, or Social Competence.

## DISCUSSION

### Protective Influence of Early Cultural Affiliation

These data support the notion that greater ethnic affiliation is associated with less impairment. Those reporting greater Indian Cultural Affiliation in 1970–71 were more likely to have ever been married and to have had fewer psychiatric problems in 1970–71. Both of these items were significant at the 0.02 level, although one would not have expected any significant relationships at the 0.02 level of the 14 demographic variables and rating scales which were compared with Cultural Affiliation (i.e., only 1 of 50 significant relationships would be expected at the 0.02 level). It is of interest that in 1970–71 increased Cultural Affiliation was associated only with psychosocial variables (i.e., more marriage, fewer psychiatric problems), but not with indices of alcoholism. Thus, if one had conducted only a cross-sectional study, no association between Cultural Affiliation and alcoholism would have been demonstrated.

High Cultural Affiliation in 1970–71 was a powerful predictor of better clinical outcome in 1980–81, and of less pathologic disorder on four rating scales (i.e., two alcoholism scales, a depression scale, and a legal problems scale). This strong relationship was unexpected: Five out of the seven variables studied showed a significant association at the 0.05 to 0.005 level. Unlike the concurrent comparisions, this prospective comparison demonstrated that increased Cultural Affiliation was associated with better clinical outcome with regard to alcoholism, but also with depression and legal problems.

What do these data mean? One possibility is that greater involvement with one's own kin, religion, social activities, and traditional crafts acts as a buffer against depression, psychiatric problems, legal problems, severity of alcoholism, and inability to acquire a spouse. Or alternatively, those who maintain greater ethnic affiliation may simply be constitutionally more able and/or less disturbed individuals. These data do not definitively answer the question of whether social or constitutional factors predominate, but they do provide some clues. Several indicators of competence were not associated with Cultural Affiliation (including level of education, employment, and the Social Competence scale), so that competence per se did not overlap closely with Cultural Affiliation. This suggests that constitutional competence was not an overriding factor accounting secondarily for the sociocultural finding. Moveover, other factors in 1970–71 were not nearly so powerful as Cultural Affiliation in predicting outcome, alcoholism scales, and depressive symptoms in 1980–81. This suggests that ethnic involvement also operated independently of social competence in influencing outcomes.

In conclusion, these data support the hypothesis that early ethnic affiliation alleviates the subsequent effects of alcoholism over time. It probably accomplishes this effect as an independent factor, rather than as an element of social competence.

## Cultural Affiliation and Recovery

While Cultural Affiliation in 1970–71 demonstrated several significant associations with other variables, the same scale repeated in 1980–81 was not related to any of the demographic characteristics, clinical outcome, or other rating scales. This was a surprising eventuality on two counts. First, the deterioration of significance for the same scale over time was unusual. And second, the Cultural Affiliation scores, when compared with themselves in 1970–71 and 1980–81, showed a significant correlation at the 0.02 level.

What might account for this? One factor could be the loss of 12 subjects by death ($n = 9$) or loss to follow-up ($n = 3$). However, this effect was minimal, since only the 33 located subjects were studied in the comparison of Cultural Affiliation in 1970–71 with the rating scales in 1980–81. Yet in the latter comparison, four of the six comparisons were statistically significant.

On further analysis of the cases, it became apparent that those seven subjects with improved outcomes tended to have minimal shift in their Cultural Affiliation scores, or even to move somewhat away from affiliation with the Indian community, while those with worse outcomes tended to move away from non-Indian society (especially work-related contacts, living in mixed Indian/non-Indian communities) and toward increased contact with Indians only (i.e., no work contacts, living back on the reservation). For example, four of the seven improved subjects moved their residence away from Indian communities during their recovery, and reduced their ethnic behaviors and affiliations. Among these four subjects (two men and two women), one returned to her Caucasian spouse (from whom she had been separated), and three married non-Indian spouses. The three latter subjects also took regular jobs, which reduced their contacts with Indian people and increased their contacts with non-Indians. Of the three remaining subjects, one married an Indian woman and two remained single. These latter three men remained in Indian communities, but two of them — for the first time in their lives — took training in majority (i.e., non-Indian) educational institutions. Both men later took jobs that involved Indian clients and employees, but also that brought them into daily contact with non-Indian clients, employees, coworkers, and employers. By contrast, the other subjects in the "same" and "worse" categories continued their ethnic associations at about the same level from 1970–71 to 1980–81. Anecdotal data from the nine deceased and three lost subjects also suggested that their ethnic associations continued at about the same level as in 1970–71 up to the time when they died or disappeared.

Are recovered Indian alcoholics lost to their communities? Do they abandon their ethnic roots? The answer is a qualified "yes." To some extent, especially during the first year or two after becoming abstinent, they moved away from former ethnic affiliations. It was during this time that the recovering subjects tended to acquire non-Indian spouses, to enter non-Indian training or educational programs, and/or to acquire jobs in the majority society. Interviews with these subjects also indicated some further data regarding ethnic behavior. About one to two years after assuming abstinence, six of the seven subjects increased their activities in the Indian community. These activities varied from person to person, but included the following: helping relatives with alcohol problems, taking more leadership in the family/clan/community, purchasing Indian art, using supervisory capacity to hire Indian employees. As noted in the Cultural Affiliation scale, these variables were not reflected in the rating scale that was employed. Another factor not detected by the Cultural Affiliation scale is the fact that social contacts and activities of all kinds increased among recovered persons, including both those in the Indian and non-Indian communities.

In sum, the Cultural Affiliation scores in 1980–81 showed no correlations because of the marked shift in the "improved" group. In 1970–71 the subjects had reported the more exclusively Indian activities, whereas many majority contacts and activities had been initiated by 1980–81. This shift occurred early in these persons' recovery. Of interest, recovered alcoholics in Missouri similarly reported decreased contact with their social network, whereas continuing drinkers did not (Favazza, 1983). This occurred since they had abandoned drinking friends, but had not yet replaced them.

Given the limitations in the Cultural Affiliation scale (as detailed above), did recovery actually involve a decrease in ethnic activities, or was this just an artifact of the scale? At least early recovery, ethnic contacts and activities did decrease. Later, certain ethnic activities not tapped by the scale did increase. To be sure, ethnic identity among these subjects at the time of the research interview was strong and apparently egosyntonic. However, activities determined by several subscales of Cultural Affiliation continued at a lower level, including pow-wow attendance, involvement with traditional crafts, and visits to the reservation. In part this was due to the fact that the regular jobs of these persons interfered with these activities. But in at least some of these cases the avoidance of Indian activities was due to the pressures towards heavy normative drinking in the tribal groups (mostly Chippewa, with a few Sioux and other groups). Any refusal of proffered alcohol was generally viewed as a personal rebuff, even an insult, and as an intent to "act superior" or "act like a white man" or otherwise create distance between one's self and the person or people making the drinking offer. It is in the local Indian style for drink to be shared, rather than for each person to attend to his own supply (which would be considered an indication of alcoholism, extremely selfish, or bizarre). Consequently, the decision to remain abstinent at many Indian social events led to repeated negative interpersonal experiences among former heavy drinkers. Thus, they opted not to continue certain social contacts in favor of maintaining abstinence and avoiding conflict.

### Implications

What practical implications are derived from these findings? First, resources that reaffirm or support Indian ethnic affiliation may alleviate the sequelae of alcoholism in Indian communities. These resources include Indian community centers, Indian self-help groups, and various Indian associations and cultural activities. While these are generally viewed as having only cultural enrichment value, they may also have positive effects on enhancing health and reducing social and behavioral problems.

Second, culturally sensitive treatment resources might attract the best treatment candidates. Those who subsequently do best have the most affiliation with Indian communities and activities. They may be the candidates least apt to enter majority or mainstream (i.e., non-Indian) programs.

Third, culturally sensitive or Indian-oriented programs should accept the possiblity that some recovering patients may need to move away from their cultural affiliation for a time during early recovery. To be sure, this will not be true in all cases. It may not be true in the future if and when normative drinking in certain tribal groups does not include a strong drinking imperative (i.e., "If you don't drink with me, you are against me").

And fourth, the deteriorated Indian alcoholics tended to drift back into Indian neighborhoods and reservations, and away from jobs and residence in the majority society. This observation suggests that Indian communities need resources to deal with such a highly morbid population. These resources include detoxification facilities, halfway houses, and residential treatment facilities. Otherwise reservations, already economically stressed, may be further burdened by the need to support those who have returned as social casualties from the majority society.

## ACKNOWLEDGMENTS

Data were collected with the assistance of Emily Peake, Trudell Starr, Arlene Dearing, Elwin Benton, and Leroy Strong.

## REFERENCES

ALLISON, V. 1968. Adaptive regression and intensive religious experiences. J. Nerv. Mental Dis. 145: 452–463.

DEAN, A. & N. LIN. 1977. The stress-buffering role of social support. J. Nerv. Mental Dis. 165: 403–417.

FAVAZZA, A. 1983. Psychosocial networks of alcoholism. Presented at the annual meeting of the American Psychiatric Association, New York.

GARRISON, V. 1978. Support systems of schizophrenic and nonschizophrenic Puerto Rican migrant women in New York City. Schizophrenia Bull. 4: 561–596.

JILEK, W. W. G. & N. TODD. 1974. Witch doctors succeed where doctors fail: Psychotherapy among Coast Salish Indians. Canad. Psychiatr. Assoc. J. 19: 351–356.

MARSELLA, A. J., K. O. SANBORN, V. KAMEOKA, et al. 1974. Cross-validation of depression among normal populations of Japanese, Chinese and Caucasian ancestry. J. Clin. Psychol. 31: 281–287.

SELZER, M. L. 1976. The Michigan Alcoholism Screening Test: The quest for a new diagnostic instrument. Am. J. Psychiatry 127: 1653–1658.

WESTERMEYER, J. 1972a. Options regarding alcohol usage among the Chippewa. Am. J. Orthopsychiatry 42: 398–403.

WESTERMEYER, J. 1972b. Chippewa and majority alcoholism in the Twin Cities: A comparison. J. Nerv. Mental Dis. 155: 322–327.

WESTERMEYER, J. 1973. Lao Buddhism, mental health, and contemporary implications. J. Religion Health 12: 181–188.

WESTERMEYER, J. & J. BRANTNER. 1972. Violent death and alcohol use among the Chippewa in Minnesota. Minn. Med. 55: 749–752.

WESTERMEYER, J. & E. PEAKE. 1983. A ten-year follow-up of alcoholic Native Americans in Minnesota. Am. J. Psychiatry **140**: 189–194.

ZUNG, W. W. 1973. A cross-cultural survey of symptoms in depression. Am. J. Psychiatry **126**: 116–121.

## APPENDIX A

### AMERICAN INDIAN STUDY SCALES

| Scale Name and Constituent Items | Item Weights and Weighting Criteria | | |
|---|---|---|---|
| *Alcoholism history scale* | *0* | *1* | |
| Presence of DTs | 0 | + | |
| Presence of seizures | 0 | + | |
| Experience of withdrawal symptoms | 0 | + | |
| Loss of control while drinking | 0 | + | |
| Use of emergency intoxicants | 0 | + | |
| Experience of blackouts | 0 | + | |
| Traumatic injuries (alcohol-related) | | + | |
| Previous chemical dependency therapy | | + | |
| Arrest record (alcohol-related) | | + | |
| Change in tolerance | | + | |
| *Mental health scale* | *0* | *1* | |
| Suicide attempts | 0 | + | |
| Outpatient psychiatric therapy | 0 | + | |
| General hospital, psychiatric ward | 0 | + | |
| State hospital | 0 | + | |
| *Withdrawal scale* | *0* | *1* | *2* |
| Temperature | < 99° | 99–100° | > 100° |
| Blood pressure | < 140 | Systolic > 140 | Systolic > 180 (?) |
| Pulse (resting) | Normal | > 100 | > 120 (?) |
| Hallucinations | 0 | + | |
| Tremulousness | 0 | + | |
| *Social problems scale* | *0* | *1* | |
| Arrest | 0 | + | |
| Jail | 0 | + | |
| Prison | 0 | + | |
| *Social competence scale* | *0* | *1* | *2* |
| Marital status | Never | Ever | Currently |
| Residence | None | Alone, with others | Own place with others |
| Employment history | None | Episodic | Regular |
| Current employment | None | Recent casual day labor | Stable job |
| Finances | < $20 | ≥ $20 | ≥ $20 + convertibles[a] |

[a] Such as furniture, car, trailer or home.

# Treatment and Recovery in Alcoholism: Contrast between Results in White Men and Those in Special Populations

FRANK L. IBER

*Alcoholism Service*
*Baltimore Veterans Administration Medical Center*
*Baltimore, Maryland 21218*

Alcohol dependence in North America has identifiable social, family, health and employment consequences that are largely reversible if abstinence is obtained and largely sustained. There is a large literature indicating favorable results if intervention is taken to avert destruction in the social, health and employment spheres of life (Emrick, 1974, 1975; Armor *et al.*, 1976). These data derive, in the majority, from information obtained from white males. Improvement is a common finding with programs of highly divergent emphasis and treatment philosophies and almost always occurs without a clear understanding of the factors that led the person to become dependent in the first place. It is the purpose of this paper to analyze aspects of alcoholism identification, treatment initiation, the treatment process and treatment retention. When information is available on special groups in alcoholism treatment, such as adolescents, women, blacks, Mexican-Americans or Native Americans, this will be illustrated.

## GENERALIZATIONS ON THE TREATMENT PROCESSES

Treatment is conducted by one or many individuals acting according to plan (Armor *et al.*, 1976). There is an agreement (often implied) between the treatment person or facility and the client as to what each will provide and for how long; there is usually some information available on what other similar clients have experienced with the treatment.

Most treatment programs feature a single philosophy of treatment and utilize only a few of many possible treatment modalities. The successfully treated alcoholics in any community usually require multiple methods of treatment based on several different philosophies (Armor *et al.*, 1976). Evaluation of treatment utilizes, most commonly, measurements of less drinking, days of complete sobriety, and resocialization in job or family. (Finney and Moos, 1979).

Many modalities are represented in alcoholism treatment (see Schuckit, 1979) and these vary widely in cost, exclusiveness, philosophy of treatment, and availability, but, curiously, evaluations of all of these indicate impressive improvements among the clients who utilize them (Lemere and Voegtlin, 1950). The key concept is that while those who utilize the program improve, all programs suffer from refusals to enter, rejection, and dropout. All programs calculate effectiveness of their treatment after defining a *minimal increment of exposure*, which allows elimination of the rejections and early dropouts. No program successfully appeals to all clients who need it. (Brandsma *et al.*, 1979; Gallant *et al.*, 1973; Baekeland and Lundwall, 1975; Smart and Grey, 1975).

Patients who perceive the treatment to be helpful or perceive their treatment environment positively have a better outcome (Cronkite and Moos, 1978).

The principle emerges from these many reviews that any form of alcoholism treatment that maintains contact with the client and is perceived as beneficial is, in fact, beneficial. Thus, factors that assure compliance with a treatment program assume great importance, and when issues of special groups are considered this may well be the major difference in programming for special populations (Feldman, 1982; McLellan *et al.*, 1982).

The treatment process cannot be entered until there is recognition for need to change a drinking pattern. Once this recognition occurs and treatment is sought, ease or complexity of entry into programs becomes important. Most programs feature (1) a more intensive early period, including detoxification, lasting from 7 to 60 days and (2) a much less intensive aftercare program (Neubuerger *et al.*, 1982).

## ENTRY INTO TREATMENT AND THE PROBLEMS ENCOUNTERED BY SPECIAL POPULATIONS

Among individuals who enter treatment programs for alcoholism there is a higher than expected proportion of men; black, Spanish-American, native American, separated or divorced persons, and those below the median income and occupational prestige levels (Armor *et al.*, 1976). It is likely that treatment for the white rich does not appear in the alcoholism literature. Recognition of destructive drinking is much more frequently likely to result from peer group or societal pressure than from within the individual him or herself. Entry into treatment occurs from intervention of family or friends sometimes, more often from intervention of employers, and increasingly from counselors or physicians who are consulted for a problem that the client believes is unrelated to drinking. Arrests for breaking public nuisance laws and court actions precipitated by driving while intoxicated and marital discord are quite frequently the reason for a client's entry into treatment (see Ferguson, 1970). In each of these paths toward the recognition and initiation of treatment activities there are strong ethnic, economic, and cultural considerations for which a few generalizations will be made.

Alcohol use in quantity is required for the "production" of substantial numbers of alcoholics. Jewish drinking patterns have featured control by the individuals and lead to less alcohol use and less abuse (Blane, 1980; Snyder, 1958; Stivers, 1976).

Special groups use alcohol in highly different ways; subsequently what constitutes abuse, and factors leading to recognition of abuse are different. Alcohol use by suburban high school students, by inner city school dropouts, by suburban singles, and by blacks, Irish men, and New York women have all been studied and differences identified. What constitutes abnormal use depends highly upon the norm for these groups and influences the support for changes by the individual and others from these peer groups (Ferguson, 1970). For example, white American alcoholics tend to have mean daily intakes of less than 250 grams in contrast to native Americans who drink nearly twice this amount. The native American tends to be more a binge drinker and more often drinks to unconsciousness than does his white counterpart. Blacks and native Americans have a greater incidence of epilepsy, unconsciousness, hallucinations, and delirium tremens than do white alcoholics, who have more liver disease (Gross *et al.*, 1972; Remmer *et al.*, 1971; Viamontes and Powell, 1974; Vitols, 1968; Baekeland

and Lundwall, 1975). In a study of alcoholism in four different cultural groups in New Mexico (Beigel *et al.*, 1974), Mexican-Americans and blacks who were alcoholics were much more commonly identified by social agencies than were white alcoholics; the latter were more readily identified from contact with physicians and ministers. Social class and nearness to alcoholism facilities influence entry into treatment (Hoffman, 1974; Westermeyer and Lang, 1974). Black alcoholics and native American alcoholics use treatment facilities run by white professionals much less frequently than do white alcoholics (Lowe and Hodges, 1972; Nathan *et al.*, 1968; Remmer *et al.*, 1971; Gross *et al.*, 1972; Bergel *et al.*, 1974; Vitols, 1968; Westermeyer, 1972). White alcoholics in Georgia were advised to seek alcoholism treatment, while black alcoholics needed to request these services (Gross *et al.*, 1972).

Strategies that correct underutilization by special populations include (*a*) locating the facility where the special population lives, (*b*) inclusion of a large number of the special population group on the treatment staff, (*c*) designing ethnic and ecological factors into the treatment program, (*d*) demonstrating sensitivity to ethnic differences.

A representative study was undertaken in Miami, Florida looking at ethnicity, sex, and age in those seeking assistance at an emergency room alcohol program. The population served in the alcoholism facility was 68 percent white, 80 percent male, and mostly in the age group from 35 to 49 years. Blacks, Spanish-speaking persons, women, and both the young and old were underrepresented in comparison to their proportions in the surrounding population. Analysis of the referrals indicated marked differences: Women were referred for subsequent services twice as often as men. Spanish patients had a significantly higher proportion of leaving without being seen (Westie and McBride, 1979).

It is apparent that entry into therapy and the availability of facilities for early treatment are highly different for special groups. The recognition, availability, and sensitivity to the needs of special groups are so different in the early accession to therapy that a large literature exists suggesting that only programs run by special groups can be effective for them. Although there is little question that programs run by special groups (women, blacks, native Americans) are effective for those groups, because of their limited value to the larger groups of alcoholics they often fail for lack of public support. A far more valuable strategy for longevity of these programs is to incorporate the needed availability, sensitivity and understanding into existing programs (Ferguson, 1970; Bourne and Light, 1979).

## DETOXIFICATION AND EARLY TREATMENT

Detoxification, the process that occurs in the initial week after alcohol use ceases, is a time of frayed nerves, physical and nutritional debility, and almost completely successful denial of problems that soon emerge as real (Schuckit, 1979). Sedative medications are usually needed in diminishing amounts for 1 or 2 weeks, as is food for the body and compassion for the self. Clearly, compassion can come from many, but is often more effective when coming from a deep knowledge of the many forces bearing on that individual's mind. Even the sedation and feeding are more effective if some small attention is paid to the background of the person. For example, an ardent and mostly successful, but recently slipped, member of Alcoholics Anonymous is helped most by minimal medication (if necessary by injection). In addition the provision of tantalizing, individualized food aids a patient's self-esteem. At this stage most staff members can be trained to be effective, and ongoing education can keep highly different clientele in treatment.

As detoxification is completed, counseling and discussions begin. The goal is to build self-esteem and to provide a variety of therapies or adjustments in lifestyle to encourage resocialization, to return the patient to employment and health, and to maintain sobriety. All counseling is educational and often gently directive. Clearly, understanding of the client's inner self is beneficial in program selection and influences eventual compliance with that program. A client's abruptly deciding to terminate is a great problem and all programs experience clients who leave treatment. This early withdrawal from treatment is greater for minority groups, and in programs that do not use medication or have limited personnel. In our experience staff education can regularly diminish the number who withdraw from treatment, but cannot eliminate it entirely. The skillful avoidance of confrontational situations and maintenance of some client self-esteem is necessary. These things are much easier when all clients are from a single sex, economic, racial, or employment background than when they are highly mixed. Almost always failures are more frequent among groups in whom the issues of self-esteem and confrontation are different. There grows from this a clamor for separate facilities for adolescents, blacks, women and native Americans run by persons of the same background who by lifetime experiences have the kind of understanding that is difficult to teach. The economy has long provided such persons and facilities for wealthy, prominent, and socially advantaged persons.

Although there are limited data, there do not seem to be substantial differences in programs usually used for whites when black or native Americans are included. The outcome is similar. Reviews on treatment of women conclude that there are no differences (Blume, 1980).

## SUCCESS IN TREATMENT

There is substantial agreement that successful treatment must be judged by many indicators of social adjustment and health retention as well as by the magnitude and duration of sobriety. It is quite evident that poverty or ethnic-related unemployment may render the special populations at far greater risk of failure to meet the success criteria than is the case with the white population in the United States.

There is wide agreement that less severe alcoholics and those in a less socially or physically deteriorated condition have a better outcome. Thus, programs aimed at employed clients whose health and marriages are intact have a better outcome. Self-paying patients had a better outcome than patients paid for by Medicare.

Strategies that are frequently beneficial in keeping patients in therapy include reducing anxiety, giving attention and support, providing models who have benefited from treatment, social skills training procedures, relaxation training, and assertiveness training (Feldman, 1982).

Clearly, cultural pertinence plays a large role in many of these strategies within families and within an ethnic group. Yet in employment, in interpersonal relationships across ethnic lines, and in everyday living all patients have deeper common features. Once treatment is undertaken, the available studies fail to show differences in outcome, suggesting that the more superficial factors of race and ethnicity are less important. Thus, Argeriou (1978) found that outcomes among black and white participants in a drunk driving program were similar.

## CONCLUSION

Entrance into alcoholism treatment and early retention in treatment are widely different when special populations are compared with white American males in the United States. However, experience and outcome of detoxification, counseling therapy, group therapy, or psychotherapy are remarkably similar if compassionate therapists are involved.

Maintenance of sobriety and social and health improvement are regular outcomes of therapy. Subjects with less physical and social deterioration have a better chance of recovery than do those with greater deterioration of health and social standing. Among similar persons, those who stick with a given treatment longer have a better outcome. The client's perception of an advantage in one treatment over another proves an excellent predictor of benefit.

The implications of these conclusions are summarized in the following five suggestions:

1. Programs addressed exclusively to special populations usually do not continue to enjoy public support and often have great difficulty in continuing services.

2. Ease of entry into programs and persistence in them after entry are two major problems for special populations. Both can be addressed effectively by increased sensitivity of programs to the needs of the special populations.

3. Each program can compare its clients with the ethnic and age and sex makeup of its constituent communities. Where there are discrepancies, these can be addressed through an adivsory board including representatives from the groups underserved.

4. Consideration for employment of members from special populations should be made.

5. Entry into and continuation in programs benefits special populations to about the same degree as white male populations.

## REFERENCES

ARGERIOU, M. 1978. Reaching problem-drinking blacks: The unheralded potential of the drinking driver programs. Int. J. Addiction 13: 443–459.

ARMOR, D. J., J. M. POLICH & H. B. STAMBUL. 1976. Alcoholism and Treatment. Report prepared for the National Institute on Alcohol Abuse and Alcoholism. Rand Corporation. Santa Monica, CA.

BAEKELAND, F. & L. LUNDWALL. 1975. Dropping out of treatment: A critical review. Psychol. Bull. 82: 738–783.

BEIGEL, A., E. J. HUNTER, J. S. TAMERIN, E. H. CHAPIN & M. J. LOWERY. 1974. Planning for the development of comprehensive community alcoholism services: I. The prevalence survey. Am. J. Psychiatry 131: 1112–1116.

BLAINE, A., Ed. 1980. Alcoholism in the Jewish Community. Commission on Synagogue Relations. New York, NY.

BLUME, S. B. 1980. Researches on Women and Alcohol. Casefinding, diagnosis, treatment and rehabilitation in alcoholism and alcohol abuse among women. Research Monograph No. 1 of the NIAAA, U.S. Department of Health, Education, and Welfare. Washington, DC.

BOURNE, P. G. & E. LIGHT. 1979. Alcohol problems in blacks and women. In J. H. Mendelson & N. K. Mello, Eds. The Diagnosis and Treatment of Alcoholism. New York: McGraw-Hill Book Co.

BRANDSMA, J. M., M. C. MAULTSBY & R. J. WELSH. 1979. The Outpatient Treatment of Alcoholism—A Review and Comparative Study. University Park Press. Baltimore, MD.

CADDY, G. R. 1982. Evaluation of behavioral methods in the study of alcoholism. In E. M. Pattison & E. Kaufman, Eds. Encyclopedic Handbook of Alcoholism. Gardner Press. New York, NY.

CRONKITE, R. C. & R. MOOS. 1978. Evaluating alcoholism treatment programs: An integrated approach. J. Consult. Clin. Psychol. 46: 1105–1119.

EMRICK, C. D. 1974. A review of psychologically oriented treatment of alcoholism: I. The use and interrelationships of outcome criteria and drinking behavior following treatment. Q. J. Stud. Alcohol 35: 523–549.

EMRICK, C. D. 1975. A review of psychologically oriented treatment of alcoholism: II. The relative effectiveness of different treatment approaches and the effectiveness of treatment versus no treatment. Q. J. Stud. Alcohol 36: 88–108.

FELDMAN, R. H. L. 1982. A guide for enhancing health care compliance in ambulatory care settings. J. Amb. Care 5: 1–15.

FERGUSON, F. N. 1970. A treatment program for Navaho alcoholics. Results after four years. Q. J. Stud. Alcohol 31: 898–919.

FINNEY, J.W. & R. H. Moos. 1979. Treatment and outcome for empirical subtypes of alcoholic patients. J. Consult. Clin. Psychol. 47: 25–38.

GALLANT, D. W., M. P. BISHOP, et al. 1973. The revolving door alcoholic: An impasse in the treatment of chronic alcoholics. Arch. Gen. Psychiatry 28: 633–635.

GROSS, M. M., S. M. ROSENBLATT, E. LEWIS, S. CHARTOFF & B. MALENOWSKI. 1972. Acute alcoholic psychoses and related syndromes: Psychosocial and clinical characteristics and their implications. Br. J. Addiction 67: 15–31.

HOFFMAN, H. 1974. County characteristics and admission to state hospital for treatment of alcoholism and psychiatric disorders. Psychol. Rep. 35: 1275–1277.

LEMERE, F. & W. L. VOEGTLIN. 1950. An evaluation of the aversion treatment of alcoholism. Q. J. Stud. Alcohol 11: 199–204.

LOWE, G. D. & H. E. HODGES. 1972. Race and the treatment of alcoholism in a southern state. Soc. Probl. 20: 240–252.

McLELLAN, A. T., L. LUBORSKY, C. P. O'BRIEN, G. E. WOODY & K. A. DRULEY. 1982. Is treatment for substance abuse effective? J. Am. Med. Assoc. 247: 1423–1428.

NATHAN, P. E., A. G. LIPSON, A. P. VETTRAINO & P. SOLOMON. 1968. The social ecology of an urban clinic for alcoholism: Racial differences in treatment entry and outcome. Int. J. Addiction 3: 55–63.

NEUBUERGER, O. W., S. I. MILLER, R. E. SCHMITZ, J. D. MATARAZZO, H. PRATT & N. HASHA. 1982. Replicable Abstinence Rates in an Alcoholism Treatment Program. J. Am. Med. Assoc. 248: 960–963.

RIMMER, J., F. N. PITTS, T. REICH & G. WINOKUR. 1971. Alcoholism: II. Sex, socioeconomic status, and race in two hospitalized samples. Q. J. Stud. Alcohol 39: 942–952.

SCHUCKIT, M. A. 1979. Treatment of Alcoholism in Office and Outpatient Settings. In The Diagnosis and Treatment of Alcoholism. J. H. Mendelson & N. K. Mello, Eds. McGraw-Hill. New York, NY.

SMART, R. & C. GRAY. 1978. Multiple predictors of dropout from alcoholism treatment. Arch. Gen. Psychiatry 35: 363–367.

SNYDER, C. R. 1958. Alcohol and the Jews: A Cultural Study of Drinking and Sobriety. Free Press. Glencoe, IL.

STIVERS, R.A. 1976. A Hair of the Dog: Irish Drinking and American Stereotype. Pennsylvania State University Press. University Park, PA.

VIAMONTES, J. A. & B. J. POWELL. 1974. Demographic characteristics of black and white male alcoholics. Int. J. Addiction 9: 489–494.

VITOLS, M. M. 1968. Culture patterns of drinking in Negro and white alcoholics. Dis. Nerv. Syst. 29: 391–394.

WESTERMEYER, J. 1972. Chippewa and majority alcoholism in Twin Cities: A comparison. J. Nerv. Ment. Dis. 155: 322–327.

WESTERMEYER, J. & G. LANG. 1974. Ethnic differences in use of alcoholism facilities. Int. J. Addiction 10: 513–520.

WESTIE, K. S. & D. C. McBRIDE. 1979. The effects of ethnicity, age and sex upon processing through an emergency alcohol health care delivery system. Br. J. Addiction 74: 21–29.

WILSNACK, S. C. 1976. The impact of sex roles on women's alcohol use and abuse. In Alcoholism Problems in Women and Children. M. Greenblatt & M. A. Schuckit, Eds. Grune & Stratton. New York, NY.

# The Public Health Perspective on Alcoholism

WILLIAM MAYER[a]

*Alcohol, Drug Abuse and*
*Mental Health Administration*
*Washington, D.C.*

Alcohol problems must be seen as one of the major public health issues in the world — a set of problems that reaches even to some of the least developed countries. The main focus of the American federal effort in this area has been on how to treat and, if possible, to prevent the adverse consequences of alcohol use. In the early years, the emphasis was on the delivery of services and on training. (It should be kept in mind that the mental health community itself was very small until the end of World War II.) Public health programs dealing with drugs and alcohol operated as minor parts of the mental health system until about 10 years ago. They were separated from mental health when it was discovered that people with substance-related disorders were not getting good services from mental health programs. It is notable that in states where alcohol and drug agencies were under mental health they were not well developed. In recent years there has been pressure for the federal programs to retreat to the National Institute of Health; but I have concluded that the Alcohol, Drug Abuse and Mental Health Administration (ADAMHA) should remain a separate agency, that the interests of these major public health programs could not "compete," for example, with support for research on cancer.

There are tremendous discrepancies between the social cost and human distress associated with the disorders with which we are concerned and those associated with many of the diseases dealt with by the National Institutes of Health. The use of alcohol and its misuse constitute a public health problem almost without parallel in history. When I was in medical school, the great disease was syphilis — it could mimic, interfere with, and increase the effects of almost every disease. Illinois provided for two years of mandatory treatment for it, treatment that was very painful. (The treatment of tuberculosis was coercive then also.) Now, in place of syphilis, we have alcohol problems — a remarkable product of our affluence and of the notion that perhaps adolescents are pushed to grow up before their time. Alcoholism is the leading cause of death in persons aged 15 – 24 years. It is a major factor in half of the homicides committed in this country. It is also a major factor in perhaps 50 percent of suicides, and in child and spouse abuse, cancer, myocardial heart disease, liver disease, and pancreatic disease. In terms of disease, alcohol is almost all things to all mankind.

In this paper I want to discuss alcohol problems from a public health point of view, in terms of host, agent, and environment. The actions in the host are complicated, but we are beginning to untangle the puzzle by means of neuroscience and other

[a] Address for correspondence: William Mayer, M.D., Assistant Secretary of Defense for Health Affairs, Department of Defense, Washington, D.C. 20301.

research. The agent is simple, at least chemically. But the environment — social, political, economic and cultural — is an immensely complicated subject.

My job is one of communicating: communicating between and among a marvelous variety of audiences such as the psychosocial and the biomedical research community. We need to converse and to foster communication among the National Institute on Alcohol Abuse and Alcoholism (NIAAA), the National Institute of Mental Health (NIMH), and the National Institute of Drug Abuse (NIDA), the groups among which there is relatively little commerce. My job is also one of communicating between the research network and the treatment community: these groups are themselves very diverse, holding intense and often conflicting opinions on such issues as controlled drinking and aversive conditioning. The differences among the various constituencies, such as the big hospital chains, the private entrepreneurs, the recovering alcoholics, and Alcoholics Anonymous, are great, and all the infighting in the field convinces the "power structure" that the field is disorganized and in its infancy. My job is also to communicate with the public at large. This public was moved by moral indignation, not so long ago, to abolish alcohol, which we have seen does not work in a pluralistic society (although it may succeed in some Middle Eastern countries). Mine is really a job of communicating with various publics, including policymakers. Policymakers are influenced by what they see around them in Washington, such as the perceived misuse of psychiatry at public expense (Washington has the highest per-capita concentration of psychiatrists in the country), and these perceptions are applied to other forms of putative misbehavior like alcohol abuse treatment schemes. We have an uphill struggle, even within the Public Health Service, to convince both the public and the government of the legitimacy of alcoholism as a major problem that can be alleviated by research and treatment. Here are the main messages that I am trying to get across, particularly to the government, but also to the public at large.

(1)   The problem of alcoholism is legitimate and deserving of attention (at least as much as syphilis!).

(2)   The problem is real and it is big. Compare it with polio in the 1950s, where we had a major epidemic, with 3000 deaths per year, including those of 2000 adolescents. Now we have 10,000 adolescents killed in drunk driving accidents alone. We can make other comparisons, for instance, with Vietnam war deaths. About as many adolescents are also killed in other accidents connected with alcohol. This is a major kind of epidemic, and it is literally fatal. One hundred times as many are injured as are killed. The message in this particular mortality and morbidity is not well understood, particularly by the medical profession. Alcohol is a very real destroyer of human life and health.

(3)   Alcoholism is treatable in many if not most instances, and it may be preventable, although we are a long way from that.

(4)   Our science has merit. It is hard for people to understand that we are doing good science. Because of the complexity of the topic, the research is, of necessity, multivariate and multidisciplinary.

(5)   A great many disciplines besides medicine must be involved in struggle to correctly apply knowledge to the action that is used to treat alcohol problems.

Now let me turn to prevention, a topic that is frustrating, at times defeating, and problematic. We are fairly good at *tertiary* prevention, thanks to Alcoholics Anonymous, rehabilitative medicine, and other forms of alcoholism treatment. *Secondary* prevention consists of early intervention and vigorous treatment, lengthening remission, and so forth, and we are not too bad at that. We have had a huge boost from private industry in this regard. There are 5000 Employee Assistance (EAPs) Programs in the country (many do not just deal with alcohol, although most started that way). The EAPs have spawned a large number of quite good treatment facilities: there are

4500–5000 alcoholism treatment centers or facilities in the country. As for *primary* prevention: we are really bad at that. We do not know of any means for primary prevention, although we may learn of effective ways if *you* do your work. The government has been taught not to expect quick results, but they do want *some* results down the line.

We cannot achieve primary prevention just by imitating the great victories of the past. Perhaps the greatest public health victory was the chlorination of water, which greatly reduced death and disability due to dysentery and other water-borne diseases. But we cannot detoxify ethanol, so we cannot imitate this strategy. Walter Reed's attack on yellow fever involved a war on the mosquito, that is, it interfered with the vector of the disease. (Presumably the parallel in alcohol would be to shoot all the liquor dealers—obviously not a strategy.) Another great public health advance was vaccination. In our field, the only vaccination is thought to be education—the great remedy in Western civilization, second only to scientific research—but there is no evidence that it works. Then there are "magic bullets" such as insulin for diabetes, a drug that controls an otherwise devastating metabolic disease. We do not see signs of any such miracle drug in the field of treatment for alcoholism. Even the best brain science is not going to come up with a full solution to the problem of alcohol abuse.

Instead the solutions may come from looking at such things as the causal relationships between cultural attitudes, family values, legal measures, and economic issues. (In our country's particular political system there is the problem of imposing controls on legitimate businesses.) There are economic barriers to changing our habits and patterns of drinking. We need to understand how families deal with alcohol both in terms of religion and of family life. We need to examine social controls (just talking about these is considered by the alcoholic beverage industry to be "Neo-Prohibitionist") and not only such issues as regulation of advertising, but also minimum drinking ages, labels on alcoholic beverages, and other such touchy issues. What about the provision that a liquor store must be 100 yards from a church? What about the effects of price on consumption? We do not know with certainty the relationships between such factors. (I remember from my own experience in college that our drinking was strongly affected by the available money.) We do not know how much we can manipulate the environment, particularly in a free society. Again, we have to seek the factors that have an effect on alcohol misuse.

Alcohol is the most fascinating of all public health problems. Solving the problem of alcoholism will call for participation by more elements of society than has any other problem in public health history. An answer to this problem demands our best social science as well as biomedical research, and it will call for a new understanding by the public. This is a period of enormous opportunity—alcohol and its problems have never been blessed by more benign attention in our country than they are today. In the last two years, there has been a 58 percent increase in NIAAA's research budget, with another 38 percent increase asked for this year. The support from the Administration and Congress is thus more than lip service, and is particularly remarkable in these hardpressed times. The effort to manage alcohol problems is receiving increased support, thanks to the fact that more scientists have come to the field. There are great challenges, and great opportunities for benefits to mankind. But it is also a time of great danger: we are looked at more critically than before. There is public outcry to try drunk drivers for homicide and to raise taxes on alcohol to astronomical levels; there is a real danger of an immoderate reaction. There is also worldwide pressure for the imposition of international controls on marketing. Such calls are bound to be seen by those legitimately making a living in the trade as a potential impairment to their livelihood. What I want to leave with you is a sense of the excitement, of the adventure of intellectual discovery, and of the goodwill towards our common endeavor that I see as marking the alcohol field today.

# Elusive Goals and Illusory Targets: A Comparative Analysis of the Impact of Alcohol Education in North America and Western Europe

MARCUS GRANT[a]

*Division of Mental Health*
*World Health Organization*
*1211 Geneva 27, Switzerland*

## INTRODUCTION

Even within industrialized countries, such as those of North America and Western Europe, educational opportunities are not equally available to all sections of the population. Nor, let it be said, is the desire to take up such opportunities as are presented equally distributed among all individuals in these countries. Some sections of the population have enhanced educational opportunities and some individuals are particularly eager to optimize the benefits that these opportunities bring. Other sections of the population are presented with very restricted educational opportunities and some individuals are resistant to becoming involved in formal education of any kind. This inequality of opportunity and disparity in demand, evident even in relation to the most basic skills such as literacy, are all the more striking when comparatively marginal educational areas, such as alcohol education, are considered.

Alcohol education is marginal, not in the sense of being irrelevant to the lives of those who might receive it, but in the sense of being perceived as distant from the more formal academic concerns which dominate, for example, curriculum design in the school system. Increasingly, however, issues to do with health, with personal relationships, and with social functioning are edging their way into the main body of what is being taught. Indeed, alcohol education has a longer tradition than do some other health-related topics. It is therefore important to assess whether, given the obstacles it has to overcome, there are lessons that can be learned from previous attempts at alcohol education that may be relevant to future planning. One way of exploring this issue is through an examination of the impact of alcohol education programs in different countries.

Young people have traditionally been the favorite target for alcohol education and there is no sign of this trend being reversed at present. Indeed, statements by international bodies, by individual governments, by trade associations and by alcohol researchers all indicate an increase rather than a dilution of interest in young people as the most frequent target for most alcohol education. This trend is confirmed by

[a] Address for correspondence: Alcohol Education Centre, Maudsley Hospital, 99 Denmark Hill, London SE5 8AZ, England.

a review of alcohol education impact studies published in North America and Western Europe between 1960 and 1980. Of a total of 145 identified studies, 57 (40%) describe programs directed exclusively towards young people and many others include young people within wider target populations. This paper looks specifically at those 57 studies concerned with evaluating alcohol education programs directed towards young people within the context of an educational institution, since those certainly represent the largest single category of alcohol education studies in the whole review.

If, as appears to be the case, young people are increasingly being selected as prime targets for alcohol education, the question that has to be asked is whether this represents the strategy that is likely to prove most beneficial to society in terms of minimizing alcohol-related morbidity and mortality and of deploying scarce resources in the most cost-effective way. While we do not deny the popularity of youth-targeted alcohol education among the adult population, there is little evidence that it is particularly popular with young people themselves or that it makes a great deal of impact upon them. The purpose of this paper is to attempt to use cross-national data in order to propose an approach to this area that may stand a better chance of being seen as relevant by its recipients and of encouraging them to reject drinking patterns associated with unacceptable levels of social and health damage.

## HISTORICAL ROOTS OF CURRENT CONCERN

One of the most immediately striking trends to emerge from this review is the overwhelming preponderance of data from alcohol education projects located in the United States. Of the total number of 57 studies of projects directed towards youth, some 46 (81%) originate in the U.S. The situation is, in fact, even more unbalanced than it appears at first sight, since of the remaining 11 studies, 6 describe projects in Canada, thus leaving only 5 (9%) from Western Europe. There can be no doubt that, in purely numerical terms, North America's current dominance of alcohol education cannot be challenged.

There are important historical reasons for the special emphasis given to alcohol education in the United States. Before the turn of the century, virtually every state required by law that instruction about alcohol be included in the public school curriculum. The earliest of these laws was passed in 1858 and legislative activity has continued this century, with several state provisions being revised in the 1930s after the repeal of Prohibition. The terms of these laws do, of course, vary considerably from state to state in relation to the specific subject matter to be taught, the length of time devoted to the instruction, the grades in which teaching is to take place, as well as many different special curriculum requirements and penalties for infringement. Roe (1942) reviewed these regulations and surveyed the content of textbooks in use in the United States at that time (Roe, 1943). Milgram's (Milgram, 1975, 1980; Milgram and Page, 1979, 1980) more recent annotated bibliographies of alcohol education materials confirm that there has been a proliferation rather than reduction in the sheer volume of alcohol education activity since the time when Roe was writing.

This contrasts very strikingly with the position in Western Europe, where there is scarcely any mandatory alcohol education in the school system. While the degree of autonomy regarding all curriculum matters does vary considerably between countries, the involvement of the state through legal provision only rarely extends to what are generally perceived as marginal subjects, such as health education or, within health education, alcohol education. Religious and cultural studies and the acquisition of basic skills in literacy and numeracy are generally given much higher status in Western

European educational provision than are essentially "nonexaminable" subjects to do with personal development. Where this is changing, it is more in response to shifts in practice at school level than as a result of statutory requirements. Within Western Europe, the Nordic countries (Finland, Norway, Sweden, Denmark and Iceland) have the strongest temperance traditions and this has resulted in more attention being devoted to alcohol control policies than to education. There seems, indeed, to have been an assumption in many Western European countries that alcohol education is simply an expendable curriculum option, to be fitted in instead of organized games on rainy afternoons. As a consequence, even where there is some evidence of educational activity in this area, it has rarely been evaluated.

At its simplest, therefore, the preponderance of evaluated alcohol education programs from the United States can be related to the general high level of alcohol education activity in that country. This is not merely to say that a constant proportion of all educational activity is likely to be evaluated and thus, the more activity, the higher the number of evaluated programs. Where a great deal of disparate educational activity is being sponsored, evaluation is likely to become particularly important as a means of distinguishing between individual programs. This has certainly proven to be the case in terms of federally funded U.S. programs, where the National Institute on Alcohol Abuse and Alcoholism has tended to demand an evaluative component as a criterion of eligibility for the receipt of funds. Staulcup et al. (1979) in their review of federal primary alcoholism prevention projects were able to rely heavily upon evaluative documentation produced *routinely* by these projects as part of their NIAAA contracts. Thus, given the uneven quality of much alcohol education, it was possible to see the emergence of the NIAAA Prevention Demonstration Projects as part of an attempt to introduce both higher quality and greater conformity to a relatively incoherent area of educational activity. This possibility is discussed by Wittman (1980), who also points to the extent to which these projects actually provide detailed instructions for the evaluation of any replications that may occur. The trend, it seems, is likely to continue.

On a more speculative level, it would be possible to argue that there is a higher level of acceptance in the United States of the importance of evaluation in a wide range of activities. Where society is organized upon competitive principles so that it is those who are perceived to be most effective who are valued most highly, then it is essential to be able to distinguish between competence and excellence. The principles of market justice, which can so clearly demonstrate commercial success, are less easy to apply in an area like education, yet the thirst still persists to identify those whose performance is deemed superior to their competitors. It is important, therefore, not merely to succeed. You must be *seen* to succeed and others must be seen to fail. Evaluation of impact, however defined, may therefore have both a symbolic and a practical importance in separating the sheep from the goats in American alcohol education.

When we turn to the actual studies included in this review, it is possible to plot them by date of publication in order to demonstrate the pattern that emerges within the two decades being examined. It is, unfortunately, not possible to undertake this excercise in terms of the actual date of the implementation of the programs they describe, since this information is frequently not available from the published data. No eligible studies were identified in the first five years, from 1960–1965. During the remaining three periods of five years, the growth in the number of evaluated studies is very striking. This information is summarized in FIGURE 1.

Some caution has to be exercised in interpreting this information. As pointed out above, the data relate to when the studies were published rather than when the programs were implemented. It might be, therefore, that what emerges is a publication

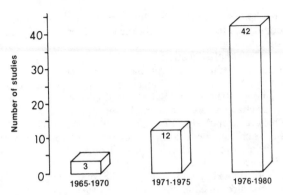

**FIGURE 1.** Studies of evaluated alcohol education in the school system (1960–1980) analyzed by date of publication.

trend rather than an educational trend. One cannot ignore the fact that the 1970s saw the emergence of specialist journals which provided an extended forum for discussion of issues to do with alcohol education and similar topics. Nevertheless, despite their probable role in stimulating an increase in educational activities, it is likely that the emergence of these journals can best be interpreted as a response to demands for vehicles of publication for a growing body of data. There has, of course, been an information explosion in many areas of science and scholarship during the past twenty years. On the other hand, alcohol education is not a new activity, nor are there, frankly, many technological or theoretical breakthroughs to communicate. What this trend most accurately demonstrates, therefore, may well be an increase in public concern.

## SEEKING AN OPTIMUM AGE

Given the high level of alcohol education in the United States public school system, given the dramatic increase in the evaluation of alcohol education, which begins in the mid 1960s and rises to its peak in the late 1970s, and given the extent to which, nearly 50 years ago, a real attempt was already being made to design constructive alcohol education curricula, it would be reasonable to suppose that the 57 studies included in this review could be analyzed in terms of the relative contributions they made to a coherent and systematic approach to minimizing alcohol problems. Unfortunately, as most people actually working as alcohol educators seem only too eager to agree, the last 15 years of alcohol education represent a frantic search for best practices rather than a development of acknowledged truths.

In their report on the status of drug education in Ontario in 1977, Goodstadt (1978) and his colleagues were able to demonstrate a relationship between exposure to drug education and frequency of reported drug use for tobacco education and tobacco use among some students, and marijuana education and marijuana use among rather more. They were, however, unable to find any relationship to speak of, either positive or negative, between alcohol education and frequency of drinking or between alcohol education and drunkenness. Similarly chastening conclusions have emerged from other reviews of attempts at alcohol and drug education (Schaps, 1978).

In order to give coherent shape to the sample of 57 disparate studies which are being considered here, a distinction has therefore been drawn on the basis of the age of the target population towards which the alcohol education programs were directed. The issue of optimum age is one that stimulates heated debate between proponents of rival models of alcohol education. From the Goodstadt study referred to above, it is clear that different educational approaches (in terms of content, format and intensity) were favored by students of different ages. Equally, survey data on the drinking habits of young people (Davies and Stacey, 1972; O'Connor, 1978) make it clear that drinking behavior changes very considerably during adolescence, whether or not the young people receive alcohol education. Given, therefore, the changing drinking practices and given the changing educational preferences of young people, the choice of the most appropriate age for the delivery of alcohol education programs has great potential significance.

It would be shortsighted to ignore the symbolic component in this debate. Choosing a particular age for alcohol education says a great deal about the view that is being taken of developmental stages in young people and of the level of personal social responsibility they are seen as exercising. It may also relate to the view that is taken of their vulnerability to alcohol problems and the extent to which they may, by their own efforts, aided presumably by the education they receive, be able to protect themselves from a potentially harmful influence.

Of the programs included in this review, it is probably not surprising to find that most were directed towards young people aged over 11 years. Since not all studies give detailed information about the precise age (or academic grades) of the young people in question, it was not possible to analyze very precisely the age distribution of the target audiences. It was, however, possible to distinguish three basic categories, namely, *primary school-age* children (defined as 11 years and below), *secondary school-age* children (defined as over 11 years, but still attending an institution in the school system), and those receiving *tertiary level education* (defined here as university, college or similar institution). On this basis, 8 of the 57 studies relate to educational program directed towards primary school-age children, 39 to studies directed towards secondary school-age children, and 14 to those in tertiary level educational establishments.

Of the 39 studies of projects directed towards secondary school-age children, four are concerned with all ages, and the remainder split almost equally between those concerned with children under the age of 14 and those concerned with the 14+ age group.

Of the 39 studies of projects directed towards secondary school-age children, four are concerned with all ages, and the remainder split almost equally between those concerned with children under the age of 14 and those concerned with the 14+ age group.

Of the eight studies of projects directed towards primary school-age children, none examines educational programs offered to children below the age of 8 years. The most popular age span for primary school alcohol education to be offered is 9-11 years.

Comparing North American and Western European studies, and bearing in mind the relatively small number of European examples, the only important distinction to emerge was the total absence of any European programs directed towards tertiary level students. It seems that there is a presumption in Europe that if students have not learned sensible drinking by the time they leave secondary school, then it is already too late. The fact that there is a minimum legal drinking age in many European countries which is as high as, or higher than, the age at which students leave secondary school is a paradox that does not seem to have affected educational planning. Of greater significance may be the general trend for a higher proportion of secondary level students in North America to transfer to tertiary educational establishments than do students in almost any European country. Tertiary education is more likely to be seen in North America as a continuation of an unbroken educational process, while in Europe, it remains in most countries the temporary alternative to employment or unemployment for a relatively small and elite minority of the secondary school-age student population.

## IMPACT OF ALCOHOL EDUCATION

Before proceeding to examine the results of this review, several notes of caution should be sounded. First, this summary of the spread of positive results between knowledge, attitudes, and behavior is based upon aggregate level data only. It obviously fails to take account of individual alcohol education programs that may have displayed remarkable levels of imagination, sensitivity, and intellectual rigor. Second, the quality of the evaluations applied to the 78 separate alcohol education programs discussed in the 57 studies included in this review was far from uniform. If the standards of strict experimental methodology had been applied, only a handful of these studies would have survived for inclusion here. Recognizing the unrepresentativeness of such a restricted sample and taking account of the reservations that have in any case been voiced (Wallack, 1980) regarding the inappropriateness of too slavish an adherence to an "effects-only" scientific evaluation in areas of social education such as this, we decided to include all programs that demonstrated a reasonably objective attempt to measure impact using some sort of control or comparison group that was roughly equivalent to the experimental group and/or that introduced some reasonably objective and comparable pre- and post-test, even where that test was not independently verifiable. The third note of caution relates to the process of scientific reportage and the extent to which individual programs that may well have been exceptionally impressive experiences for their recipients were written up in terms that were so distant from that experience as to be virtually impenetrable. It was, in some cases, impossible to determine what form the education took, who delivered it, or what they actually said. Sadly, there was a tendency for those programs with the most precise evaluative methods to be the least well documented educationally and for the most innovative and best-described programs to be the most poorly evaluated.

Bearing these caveats in mind, the results of the studies are most conveniently summarized in the three age categories described above, since some specific issues arise from each category. General issues, which are common to all three categories, are also discussed.

First, then, in relation to alcohol education directed towards primary school-age students, the eight studies describe nine separate programs (one study compared two programs). FIGURE 2 summarizes the results, comparing the number of programs that tested for change with the number in which change was actually found. Changes were sought in three distinct areas—knowledge, attitudes and behavior. Not every study tested for changes in all three areas. It is outside the scope of this paper to discuss the nature of the relationship between knowledge, attitude, and behavior variables. It should be noted, however, that no assumption is made of any causative or consecutive link between any of these variables.

As is apparent from FIGURE 2 every primary school-age alcohol education program that was tested for knowledge increase was found to have achieved that goal; those that were tested for positive attitude change were found to have rather more ambiguous results, with four of nine claiming certain success and another three doubtful success; and of those that were tested for behavioral change, only one of three claimed positive impact. Since these programs were directed towards students under the age of 11 years, it may be argued that it is inappropriate to seek a behavioral

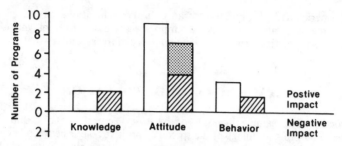

**FIGURE 2.** Impact of alcohol education upon primary school-age students. □ = programs which have been tested for change; ▨ = programs in which definite change was found; ▧ = programs in which change was doubtful, ambiguous, or not statistically significant.

outcome in terms of actual drinking behavior (few very young children are regular drinkers) or behavioral intentions (young children have more negative attitudes towards alcohol than do even early adolescents). Of greater value, therefore, may be changes towards more appropriate attitudes, where appropriate is defined as being consistent with the stated aims of the particular educational program that they experienced. If those studies that claimed unambiguous positive attitudinal change are examined, only one common characteristic emerges. The staff delivering the education had all received some form of special training designed to improve their skills in relation to this task. While it is true that staff delivering one of the less successful programs had also received such training, it seems reasonable to conclude that training is in general associated with more positive attitudinal impact. Other variables, such as intensity and duration of the educational experience and the content of the educational program (where known), did not relate to positive impact in this way.

The same tendency, although rather less marked, was apparent in terms of the studies of alcohol education directed towards secondary school-age students (FIG. 3).

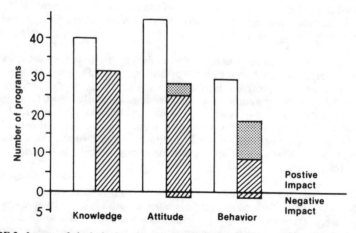

**FIGURE 3.** Impact of alcohol education upon secondary school-age students. □ = programs which have been tested for change; ▨ = programs in which definite change was found; ▧ = programs in which change was doubtful, ambiguous, or not statistically significant.

Although trained teachers did not always produce successful programs, few successful programs did not use either trained teachers or trained peer group leaders (a phenomenon absent from primary school-age programs and probably one that presumes specially trained teachers, even where this is not specifically noted in the study). There seemed, indeed, to be a high positive association between use of trained peer group leaders and successful outcomes, particularly where positive impact was found in both attitudinal and behvioral areas. It does seem, therefore, that positive impact is enhanced by the use of specially trained teachers or peer leaders rather than regular class teachers, visiting experts, or ex-addicts. There has, for some time, been a considerable amount of informal rhetoric surrounding the inadvisability of using either experts or ex-addicts because of their low level of sustained commitment to the educational establishments that they visit and also because of their possibly arcane or partisan points of view. Although no clear evidence emerges from this review to associate such visitations with especially low levels of positive impact or, as was sometimes suggested in the field of drug education (Goodstadt, 1978), with increases in experimental substance use, this may well be associated with the normative nature of teenage drinking as opposed to teenage drug taking. Equally, it may be that some schools were simply better at following up guest visitations with topic-centred discussion programs or other educational approaches. Certainly, those programs that offered only a single lesson, whoever gave that lesson, tended to show lower positive impact.

There is, therefore, particularly in the larger scale U.S. programs, an increasing insistence upon preliminary training for teachers and, in some cases, for peer leaders. This is obviously an encouraging trend, to the extent that it is an indication of careful planning and, possibly, of the "prioritization" of different levels of educational objectives. An additional benefit of such training programs, and one that is rarely measured, is the impact they may have upon those teachers and students selected to play key roles in the subsequent alcohol education programs. Evidence from the area of professional training (Cartwright, 1980) suggests that the increased motivation that is felt by those engaging in experiences that they perceive as enhancing their skills is itself a characteristic of higher positive outcome measures. It may well be that some of the principles of clinical training, with its insistence upon the pragmatism of its approach and the empiricism of its content, can be carried over to the area of youth-targeted alcohol education.

Another trend that emerges from secondary school-age alcohol education programs (and which is certainly not at odds with the data for primary school-age programs either) is that positive impact upon attitude and behavior variables tended to be associated with educational experiences that include discussions, project work, role-playing and audio-visual resources. Programs relying upon direct verbal instruction as the sole or principal means of communication, while relatively successful in enhancing knowledge, were not so successful in relation to changes in the other variables. The more passive the mode of communication, the less impact it tended to have on any variable other than knowledge.

This trend for the more active and varied programs to report greater successes may well be associated with a tendency for many students to view alcohol education and, indeed, most long-term health issues as irrelevant, or at best marginal, to the important priorities of their lives. Equally, more didactic health education approaches may seem to be reinforcing a rigid and authoritarian system of adult values which, certainly in the case of alcohol education, is at odds with young people's actual experience of the adult world. When, therefore, a more active and varied approach is adopted, the marginality and perceived hypocrisy of didactic education may be undercut in a way that encourages the students to be less rejecting of the substance of the program's message.

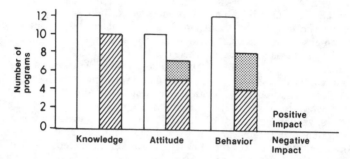

**FIGURE 4.** Impact of alcohol education upon tertiary-level students. □ = programs which have been tested for change; ▨ = programs in which definite change was found; ▩ = programs in which change was doubtful, ambiguous, or not statistically significant.

The disparity between active and passive educational approaches to alcohol problems was even more marked in relation to tertiary level students. It is clear that the minority of programs that included field trips, visits to local treatment centers and, in some casers, to drinking establishments, showed a greater proportion of positive behavioral and attitudinal changes (Fig. 4). The breaking down of the classroom walls between theoretical discussions of drinking and its consequences, on the one hand, and actual manifestations in daily life, on the other, may be something that has as yet unexploited implications for primary and secondary school-age education as well. If, indeed, the goal of the educational programs is to have an impact upon individual behavior, then those programs that are themselves conceived in terms that utilize behavioral (rather than cognitive or attitudinal) responses may be producing a kind of fusion between the educational goal and the educational method. Drinking is a complex behavior, loaded with symbolic meaning. Alcohol problems, too, are complex phenomena, producing various deeply felt reactions in those who encounter them. Educational programs that incorporate actual drinking situations or actual alcohol problems, rather than descriptions, simulations, or representations of those situations or manifestations may well be able to awaken a far more direct and impressive response from the target audience.

That increasing knowledge is a relatively simple goal, changing attitudes rather a more difficult one, and that influencing behavior is the most elusive goal of all are further emphasized by a comparison of the summary of the results of the studies of tertiary level students with the summary of results of secondary school-age children. As in the case of secondary school-age programs only half of the tertiary level programs that claimed positive behavioral impact were able to do so unequivocally. Indeed, in all three age categories, only a third of the programs that were tested for positive impact were able to claim that actual behavior had been altered as a result of the educational experience. Since many programs were not even tested for changes in this variable, a total of only 14 of the 78 programs (fewer than 18%) actually claim statistically significant behavioral impact. When the methodologic criticisms that could be leveled at virtually all those studies are taken into account, the case for supporting alcohol education as an important influence upon individual drinking behavior becomes exceedingly difficult to maintain.

## INDIVIDUAL CHANGE AND SOCIAL CHANGE

The extent to which it has proved possible to review the substance of the alcohol education programs that have been offered to young people during the last 20 years has been hampered by the failure of most research studies to provide any but the most meager details of the objectives of the programs, the curriculum that was followed, the interactive process of the exchange between teacher and students, or the theoretical assumptions underlying the educational models selected. An attempt to classify approaches to alcohol education by means of the dominant view of alcohol problems (such as disease concept, control of consumption, or moral flaw) had to be abandoned at a very early stage because of a lack of even inferential data. Equally, a later attempt to classify programs by means of clearly defined educational goals (Grant, 1980) led to a recognition of the frequency with which a general and unexceptionable aim, such as "to encourage moderation," could be used to justify educational experiences that seemed to have nothing at all by way of intelligent, imaginative, or even tolerably relevant content to communicate. This paper has therefore been based upon the modest proposition that it is probably useful, at least in terms of attempting to avoid repeating the more obvious mistakes of the past, to consider together those alcohol education programs directed towards the same target (in this case, young people) and having the same general goal (in this case, the minimization of future alcohol-related damage). It represents, therefore, an attempt to move away from the sad state of affairs which is summarized in the title of the paper. All too often, alcohol education is directed towards a target audience that simply melts away out of sheer boredom, inertia, and lack of footholds in the substance of what is being taught. Similarly, while the goal of knowledge increase appears relatively easily attainable, it is difficult to know how important it is in the face of the increasingly ambiguous results that are achieved, the closer an evlauation comes to actual day-to-day drinking behavior.

It may be that the crucial dilemma is one that is common to other areas of health education as well, namely, whether the educational process is seen as being directed primarily towards the goal of individual behavior change or whether a larger, more ambitious agenda is being considered, in which education is seen essentially as an instrument of social change (Partanen, 1982). Here, the Report of the Technical Discussions of the 1982 World Health Assembly (WHO, 1982) is illuminating. "It was appreciated," it states, "that education meant a great deal more than simply providing reasonably accurate information. In fact, it has to do with the creation of social awareness."

Since, therefore, successful school alcohol education programs are the exception, not the norm, it would seem that a great deal of effort (not to say time and money) has been expended in order to achieve comparatively little. If this situation is to be improved, then it is important to try to understand why it is that people have, for 20 years, continued to do something that has been repeatedly shown to have very low positive behavioral impact. Unterberger and Di Cicco (1968) contend that sharp emotional disagreements concerning overall goals and plans of action have resulted in a neglect of promising instructional programs or at best superficial coverage. It may be, however, that the problem lies at an even deeper level and has to do with whether it is, in any case, appropriate to use schools as the main arena for alcohol education.

Much confusion exists in the minds of educational theorists, in the minds of individual teachers, and in the minds of parents as to the way in which schools should guide pupils and prepare them for adult life. Society charges schools with the task of bringing new generations to full citizenship. It is for this reason, presumably, that nineteenth-century social reformers in the United States were so eager for the statutory inclusion of alcohol education in the public school curriculum. Yet, quite apart from relaying information and establishing a code of moral values, schools do have other social tasks to perform. Today, for example, particularly in Western Europe, it is impossible to ignore the role of schools in attempting to alleviate youth unemployment and in streaming young people for the inequality of their future working lives (Dorn, 1983). Such roles make it particularly difficult for schools to undertake the role of liberal nurturing which is implied in alcohol education. Partanen (1981), commenting on this dilemma, writes: "It is sometimes thought that the best way to alter prevalent drinking habits is to concentrate on children and young people whose behavioral patterns are as yet unformed. But one might justifiably maintain that alcohol attitudes and drinking habits are transmitted by the older to the younger, that the adult world influences its junior counterpart. Schools tend to conserve cultural values and habits, not reform them."

Thus, at an individual level, there may be a need to turn attention away from persistent consideration of the damaging effects of excessive drinking, particularly when these effects are predominately of a chronic nature and when the target of the educational program is young people who perceive such effects to be irrelevant to their lives. Leaving aside, as beyond the scope of this paper, the possible force of genetic and fetal influences, there remain well-documented accounts of those situational and interpersonal factors which exert the strongest influence upon young people's attitudes and behavior with respect to alcohol. Family and peer influence have been carefully analyzed by a number of researchers (Davies and Stacey, 1972; O'Connor, 1978; Strickland, 1982) who have related their conclusions to stages in emotional and educational development and to society's explicit and implicit values regarding drinking, intoxication, and marketing practice. Similarly, the role of media stereotyping (Cook and Lewington, 1979) and of advertising (Grant, 1982; Strickland, 1983) have been assessed.

What emerges certainly in societies like those of North America and Western Europe is that despite the ambivalence of the value systems, despite the pluralistic nature of the social networks, learning to drink is one important demonstration of the ritual passage from childhood into adulthood. Although occasionally this passage is associated with rebellion, with experimentation and with repeated excessive consumption, far more frequently it is sanctioned, even encouraged, by the adult population (Aitken and Leathar, 1981). Many children, probably the majority in all the countries considered here, are given their first drink by their parents. Later, perhaps, peer influences become more important determinants of drinking behavior than are parental models, but, as things stand currently, most youth-targeted alcohol education programs take little account of either parents or peers, thus ignoring what must appear to be, at least potentially, impressive opportunities for encouraging positive change.

These programs focus instead upon the consequential damage of excessive consumption, a lesson which, to judge from the pre-test evaluations examined in this review, is already quite well internalized by most of the young people towards whom these programs are directed. It comes as no surprise to them to learn that drunk people crash their cars or that alcoholics die of liver cirrhosis. More to the point, perhaps, would be an educational approach that could deal with the potent influences (parents, peers, the media) upon their drinking, instead of one which, flagrantly ignoring these influences, concentrates upon what may well be perceived by the target audience as depersonalized and irrelevant goals.

# CONCLUSIONS

What emerges finally is that the differences between alcohol education in North American and Western Europe are a great deal less impressive than the similarities. Whichever side of the Atlantic Ocean one is examining, good intentions clearly are not sufficient to justify token efforts. The results of this review certainly confirm the need for funding agencies to continue to press for evaluation as an integral component of educational program design. Further, however, it is clear that more of the same is not actually good enough. While better research design would be most welcome, what really matters is the ability to notice that alcohol education is not simply an arbitrary activity which happens to be worth evaluating. It is little wonder that results are so shabby, when the great majority of programs are directed towards illusory targets and pursue elusive goals. Alcohol education programs are all too often like firing quivers full of arrows into the night. Some of them, indeed, will hit home. Others may hit targets for which they were never intended. Most will be lost forever in the dense undergrowth and unmown grass of the school system. As it stands, this is a spectacularly wasteful enterprise. Yet, like many such enterprises, it remains popular with international organizations, governments, trade associations, and miscellaneous researchers. The rethinking that is proposed in this paper may make alcohol education a little less popular with all those worthy bodies. It stands a chance, however, of making it rather more popular with the young people themselves.

## REFERENCES

AITKIN, P. O. & D. S. LEATHAR. 1981. Adults' Attitudes towards Drinking and Smoking among Young People in Scotland. Her Majesty's Stationery Office. Edinburgh, Scotland.

CARTWRIGHT, A. K. J. 1980. The attitudes of helping agents towards the alcoholic client: The influence of experience, support, training and self-esteem. Br. J. Addiction 75: 413–431.

COOK, J. & M. LEWINGTON. 1979. Images of Alcoholism. BFI/AEC, London.

DAVIES, J. & B. STACY. 1972. Teenagers and Alcohol: a developmental study in Glasgow. Her Majesty's Stationery Office.

DORN, N. 1983. Alcohol in Teenage Culture, Croom Helm. London.

GOODSTADT, M. 1978. The Status of Drug Education in Ontario, 1977. Addiction Research Foundation. Toronto, Ontario, Canada.

GRANT, M. 1980. Aims, form and content: First stages in developing a taxonomy of preventive education in drug and alcohol use. Proceedings of 1st Pan-Pacific Conference on Drugs and Alcohol, Canberra, Australia.

GRANT, M. 1982. Alcohol advertising and young people: Ethical, legal and regulatory issues. In Child Health and Development, Vol. 2: Alcohol & Youth. D. Jeanneret, Ed. S. Karger, Basel.

MILGRAM, G. G. 1975. Alcohol Education Materials: An Annotated Bibliography. Rutgers Center for Alcohol Studies, Brunswick, NJ.

MILGRAM, G. G. 1980. Alcohol Education Materials, 1973–78. Rutgers Center for Alcohol Studies, Brunswick, N.J.

MILGRAM, G. G. & P. V. PAGE. 1979. Alcohol education materials, 1978–79: An Annotated Bibliography. J. Alcohol Drug Education 24: 4.

MILGRAM, G. G. & P. B. PAGE. 1980. Alcohol education material, 1979–80: An Annotated Bibliography. J. Alcohol Drug Education 25: 4.

O'CONNOR, J. 1978. The Young Drinkers. Tavistock Press, London.

PARTANEN, J. 1981. Teesejë valistukeesta. Alkoholipolitiikka 46: 161–168.

PARTANEN, J. 1982. The philosophy of alcohol education. Paper presented at 28th International Institute on the Prevention & Treatment of Alcoholism. ICAA. Lausanne, Switzerland.

ROE, A. 1942. Legal regulations of alcohol education. Q. J. Studies Alcohol 3: 433–464.

ROE, A. 1943. A survey of alcohol education in the United States. Q. J. Studies Alcohol 4: 574–663.

SCHAPS, E. 1978. Primary Prevention Evaluation Research: A Review of 127 Programme Evaluations. Pacific Institute of Research and Evaluation, California.

STAULCUP, H., K. KENWARD & D. FRIGO. 1979. A review of federal primary alcoholism prevention projects. J. Studies Alcohol 40: 934–968.

STRICKLAND, M. 1982. Parents, peers and problem drinking: An analysis of interpersonal influences on teenage alcohol abuse in the US. Paper presented at 28th International Institute on the Prevention & Treatment of Alcoholism, ICAA, Lausanne, Switzerland.

STRICKLAND, D. E. 1983. Advertising exposure, alcohol consumption and misuse of alcohol. *In* Economics and Alcohol: Consumption and Controls. M. Grant, M. Plant & A. Williams, Eds. Croom Helm, London.

WALLACK, L.M. 1980. Mass media campaigns: The odds against finding behaviour change. Paper F.111, Social Research Group, University of California, Berkeley.

WORLD HEALTH ORGANIZATION. 1982. Alcohol Consumption and Alcohol-Related Problems: Development of National Policies and Programmes. Report on Technical Discussions of 35th World Health Assembly. Geneva, Switzerland.

UNTERBERGER, J. & L. DE CICCO. 1968. Alcohol education re-evaluated. Bull. Natl. Assoc. Secondary School Principals 52: 25.

WITTMAN, F.D. 1980. Current status of research demonstration projects in the primary prevention of alcohol problems. Draft chapter prepared for Alcohol & Health, National Institute on Alcoholism and Alcohol Abuse. Rockville, MD.

# Alcohol-Control Policies in Latin America and Other Countries

REGINALD G. SMART

*Addiction Research Foundation*
*Toronto, Ontario, Canada*

MARIA-ELENA MEDINA MORA

*Institute of Psychiatry*
*101 Mexico 22 D.F., Mexico*

Alcohol-control policies reflect the concepts and philosophy behind governments' efforts to limit the availability of alcoholic beverages to the population. From a health and safety perspective, limits on availability are now designed to control such alcohol problems as alcoholism, alcohol-related violence, traffic accidents, lowered productivity, and family disorganization. In earlier eras controls on alcohol were imposed on religious grounds to limit possibilities for fun or immorality, but they now have a different purpose—to contribute to public health. Much empirical research has demonstrated that alcohol controls *do* have an effect on both drinking and drinking problems (see Popham *et al.*, 1975, and Smart, 1982, for reviews).

Debates about alcohol-control policies have been numerous in many North American and European countries in the past ten years. For example, proposals to limit the advertising of alcohol have been discussed by legislatures in Canada, the United States, and England, and actual bans on such advertising have been introduced in New Zealand, Poland, Finland, Sweden, and parts of Canada. Age limits for drinking have been raised in all Canadian provinces and in half of the states in the United States. Limited prohibition has been introduced into Northern areas of Canada and Poland. However, such debates are uncommon in Latin American countries. For example, a document prepared for the World Health Organization's technical discussions on alcohol-related problems showed that alcohol policies are not an important area of interest for most Latin American countries. Empirical studies of how alcohol controls actually work in these countries are almost impossible to find. In addition there appear to be few national or local policies about alcohol controls and those that do exist are often ignored.

The main purpose of this paper is to consider the issue of alcohol controls and policies in Latin America in relation to the extent of drinking there. A secondary purpose is to describe the types of research and policy initiatives relevant to alcohol controls which should be started. Information for this paper is drawn from a knowledge of research on alcohol problems and controls in Latin America and elsewhere, as well as recent World Health Organization (WHO) documents. It also contains experiences and observations drawn by the first author from his visits to most Latin American countries over the past 20 years for studies related to alcohol problems. In addition, the second author has lived in Mexico for many years and has close contacts with many alcohol researchers in other countries. To some extent this presentation depends upon personal experiences of life in Latin America which, although extensive, may not be unbiased or complete.

## DRINKING IN LATIN AMERICA

There is a shortage of officially collected data on alcohol consumption in Latin America. For example, the largest recent study, the World Alcohol Project (Sulkunen, 1973) contained data for 1950 to 1970 only on Peru and Cuba. Estimates of per capita alcohol consumption based on sales are difficult to find for most Latin American countries, in part because so much alcohol sold is home-produced or unregistered and authorized producers are unwilling to provide sales figures. No continuous statistics are available. Without such figures trends cannot be easily studied and countries lack an important tool for studying the need for new alcohol controls and how the existing ones are working.

Fortunately, we have numerous studies involving various communities and regions in Latin America. These have been very well summarized by Caetano (1982) and only a few highlights need to be pointed out here. Medina *et al.* (Caetano, 1982) found in a province of Chile that 20 percent of the urban and 12 percent of the rural population were alcoholics. A general population study by Grimson *et al.* (1972) in Buenos Aires found 16 percent to be excessive drinkers and 6.7 percent alcoholics. Several studies of general populations in Peru have found 10 percent to be alcoholics. Rates of problem drinkers in Brazil appear to be lower, for only 10 percent were reported to be problem drinkers. In the northern area of Mexico City, Cabildo *et al.* (1969) found that 12.5 percent and 11.7 percent were, respectively, excessive drinkers and alcoholics, and these figures are similar to those reported by Fromm and Maccoby (1973) in a rural area.

In general, community surveys in most Latin American countries indicate a high level of excessive and alcoholic drinking, especially among males. Many studies show a high level of tolerance of drunkenness among males and an association of heavy drinking with manliness or *machismo*. Often rates are highest in rural areas. High levels of abstention (up to 50 percent) and low levels of problems are typically found among women. Levels of survey-identified drinking problems in Latin American studies are usually higher than those in Canada, the United States, or England. However, surveys have not been done in countries with no generally recognized alcohol problem, e.g., Honduras, Panama or Colombia.

Fortunately, some alcohol-problem data are available for most Latin American countries. For example, the Pan American Health Organization (1978) has produced data on liver cirrhosis death rates per 100,000. The data are not perfect since the index year varies somewhat (1969–75) and there is some doubt about how complete liver cirrhosis reporting can be in developing countries with few hospitals and doctors. Nevertheless, the rates vary greatly from a high of 22.7 in Mexico and 22.6 in Chile to a low of 3.3 in Panama and 3.5 in Columbia. The rates in Mexico and Chile are higher than in France. They are 2.5 times as high as in the United States and three times as high as in Canada. About one-third of the countries of Latin America are above the average for North American countries and two-thirds are below. Those which are above include Mexico, Chile, Guatemala, Puerto Rico, Argentina, and the Dominican Republic.

Somewhat similar results are found when the percentage of alcoholics among admissions to mental hospitals are examined: Chile, Mexico and Argentina have rates varying from 36 percent to 20 percent, which are higher than in North America (8 percent of admissions in United States and 18.6 percent of admissions in Canada). These data clearly suggest that in many Latin American countries alcohol problems are sufficiently important to receive attention from government policymakers. However, there are several countries (for example, Panama and Colombia) where the rates are very low on the basis of a world-wide comparison, and hence alcohol policies could not be expected to be an important government priority. Nevertheless, many Latin American countries do have substantial alcohol problems when judged on a hemispheric or world-wide basis, and they should be taking an interest in alcohol-control policies as a method of prevention.

## SOME OBSERVATIONS ON THE AVAILABILITY OF ALCOHOL IN LATIN AMERICA

Alcohol availability includes all aspects of control of access to alcohol. Virtually all governments seek to closely control its sale and nowhere is alcohol treated like other consumer products. The most common aspects controlled are taxes regulating prices, the numbers of alcohol outlets, the hours and days of sale, and the ages of those allowed to purchase or drink alcoholic beverages. Methods have been established for rating alcohol availability and they have been used in studies in the United States and Canada (Smart, 1977). However, such scales have apparently not been developed for Latin America nor have those for North America been used in research there. A good availability scale for Latin America would require some indication of access to illegal or unregistered alcohol and hence those from North America would not be suitable.

Because of the lack of empirical research on alcohol availability, we are left with impressions and observations. Most travellers to Latin America from Europe or North America would see a high level of availability. In virtually all Latin American countries, alcoholic beverages are sold in grocery stores, something that is rarely seen in North America and Northern Europe. Age limits in Latin America for buying alcohol in closed bottles seem to be completely nonexistent and young children can often be observed buying alcoholic beverages. In most countries of Latin America, bars, cantinas and restaurants have long and flexible hours of sale. For example, in Chile bars now open at 8 AM and close at 2 or 3 AM. In many rural areas of Mexico, *pulque* is delivered to houses; it is probably purer than water, which has no delivery system. In Mexico, some authorized premises sell closed bottles of alcoholic beverages 24 hours per day. In almost all countries Sunday sales and drinking are allowed, even in Venezuela, where technically Sunday sales are forbidden. In Brazil at carnival time, municipalities give away thousands of gallons of *cachaça* (a sugar-cane-based spirit), so that people can have a good time.

In countries such as Mexico, Honduras, Chile and Costa Rica, illegal drinking establishments are very common, especially in smaller towns and rural areas. For example, in Costa Rica, researchers studied a community which had only one licensed premise to sell alcoholic beverages (Caetano, 1982). However, there were ten illegal ones located in private houses. In several countries (Caetano, 1982) illegal production of alcohol has been estimated to be as much as the legal production. In a rural area of Mexico Berruecos *et al.* (1982) estimated that two authorized establishments produced 100 liters of *aguardiente*, but six unauthorized ones produced 2100 liters per day. However, in a variety of European and North American countries estimates are that illegal production is only 6 to 10 percent of legal production (Mäkelä *et al.*, 1982).

It is difficult to compare real prices of alcoholic beverages from one country to another, but some observations can be made. Currently, in Mexico *pulque* is about the same price as a soft drink and the increase in prices from 1971 to 1977 has been less for alcohol than for milk and meat (Rosovsky, 1982). In Brazil, a liter of 40 percent *pinga* (a sugar-cane-based spirit) is the same price as a bottle of milk. However, in the United States spirits would usually be three to five times as costly and eight times as costly in Canada. In Costa Rican restaurants, beer and soft drinks have the same price and, in a few, beer is even cheaper. Illegally produced beverages are usually even cheaper than described here, depending upon where they are bought or how they are produced. In Chile and Brazil, taxes on domestic wine are no greater than for other drinks and hence both are very cheap compared to the price in North America, where the tax is often 200 percent of the real price.

Reference has already been made to the tendency to ignore existing alcohol-control laws in Latin America. Laws of opening and closing of drinking establishments are often loosely enforced. Public inebriates are rarely arrested in most countries. In sight of the Ministry of Health in Costa Rica, a group of derelicts were recently seen to be drinking commercial alcohol quietly in a park. The first author observed a serious three-car accident in Mexico City caused by an almost stuporously drunk driver. Police appeared to investigate the accident and assess damage to the cars, but no arrests were made and no charges laid for impaired driving. In fact, alcohol breath-testing equipment for use in investigating accidents is almost unavailable in Latin American countries, although in general use in almost all other Western countries (Gonzalez and Katatsky, 1978).

Both Heath (1982) and Negrete (1982) have noted the tendency of some Latin Americans to "beat the system" and to delight in "ignoring or circumventing established legal restrictions" (Negrete, 1981, p.169) as a justifiable reaction against "authorities." The folk culture of Mexico, Brazil, and Argentina includes admired characters who are experts at bypassing restrictions or legal hurdles and having their own way. Inconsistent observance of laws by the population certainly limits the impact of alcohol controls. There are many such controls, but they cannot be enforced if the population does not cooperate and accept their necessity and value. It may be that alcohol controls do not suit the predominant values and mores of many Latin Americans. Such controls limit access to an important beverage, frequently used in rituals and celebrations and frequently used by males whose concept of *machismo* is tied to the amount of drinking they do.

## CULTURAL AND ECONOMIC ASPECTS OF ALCOHOL CONTROL IN LATIN AMERICA

Alcohol controls and policies always have a unique history and are embedded in the society where they are found. Controls on alcohol consumption have complex historical and cultural roots, which require understanding in any country. Heath (1982) has pointed out the inconsistency of Spanish colonizers in Latin America in legal matters. In colonial times, it was claimed that laws were meant to be there but not necessarily kept. With regard to heavy drinking, the tradition in many countries is a very long one. For example, Calderon (1968) has described drunkenness among the Aztecs at the time of the Spanish Conquest. It is well known that pre-Colonial peoples in Latin America (e.g., Mexico) discovered and used alcoholic beverages, but the Indians in North America had no alcoholic beverages until the Europeans came.

Latin American countries lack strong traditions of temperance or religiously based abstinence movements. In North America, Europe and Scandinavia, there were historically strong temperance unions, clubs, political parties and societies associated primarily with Protestant religious movements. In varying years the sale of alcoholic beverages has been prohibited in the United States, in all but one province in Canada, and in all Scandinavian countries. The temperance movement has strong historical roots in Germany, Holland, Belgium, and especially England, although these countries have had no recent periods of official prohibition. Much of the alcohol-control machinery in these countries resulted from the efforts of temperance workers to ensure limited access to alcoholic beverages. In countries that have had official prohibition, the current control laws were largely enacted at the end of prohibition, although all have been liberalized since that time. Temperance sentiment seems never to have existed in Latin American countries except among a few Protestant missionaries. In some Latin American countries religion may help to keep people away from drinking as promises are made to God or the Virgin Mary to abstain. However, religious festivals are times of great drinking and drunkenness. There is no Latin American country that has had official prohibition, although local prohibition existed in a few areas of Mexico. The experience of prohibition in Mexico was negative, in that it led to a proliferation of drinking premises outside the prohibited areas.

Prohibition sentiment does exist in a variety of developing countries without Protestant traditions. The Islamic prohibition against drinking is well known. It has had a major impact in limiting the availability of alcohol in most Islamic countries as well as prohibiting its use in several others (e.g., Saudi Arabia, Pakistan). Traditional Hinduism also favors alcohol prohibition and a variety of prohibition edicts have been issued in countries such as India. Such traditions, along with fundamental Protestantism, are entirely foreign to Latin America and could never be expected to exert any influence. It is possible, however, that the relative lack of effective alcohol controls is related to the lack of a temperance or abstinence tradition in Latin America.

Another set of reasons underlying the lack of controls involves economics. In many Latin American countries alcoholic beverages are important products whose creation employs many agricultural and urban workers. Mexico and Costa Rica derive considerable funds from the export of spirits such as tequila and rum. Rum, cachaça and pisco are derived from plentiful sugar cane grown locally for which there is no other market. Chile and Argentina export large amounts of wine. It has been estimated that in Mexico about 50 percent of the sales of small grocery stores are from alcoholic beverages.

Of course, in all countries governments derive large amounts of taxes from the sale of alcoholic beverages and would be reluctant to lose them. About 7 to 10 percent of government revenues are currently derived from the sale of alcohol in the seven countries studied by Mäkelä et al. (1982), but the proportions of tax revenue are not known for Latin America. As stated by a Ministry of Health official in one Latin American country, "Alcohol is often seen as a solution to problems in that country, not a problem in itself. It provides taxes, jobs for people, a use for agricultural surplus products and a way for people to forget the economic hard times."

Several Latin American countries also have alcohol-control systems which favor the development of tourism. Countries such as Mexico, Costa Rica, Peru, and Venezuela have a large tourist industry, which is often the second or third largest source of income, especially of income in hard currency. Tourists are known to drink large amounts of alcoholic beverages, to frequent bars and taverns, and to prefer a "wide-open" policy about alcoholic beverages. They bring liberal drinking habits to the notice of people in the countries visited and probably contribute to the sentiment that alcohol should be generally available. In Mexico, certain restrictions on alcoholic beverages are not enforced in tourist areas. Introducing stricter measures about hours of sale, for example, would be likely to alienate tourists, increasing the already considerable economic problems of the Latin American countries. Of course, such economic concerns make strict controls less attractive than they might otherwise be for public health reasons.

## ASPECTS FAVORABLE TO ALCOHOL CONTROLS
## IN LATIN AMERICA

So far, we have emphasized factors hindering the development of alcohol controls, but a variety of recent events can be seen in a more positive light. A large number of Latin American countries (14 of 21) participated in the WHO technical discussions on alcohol consumption and alcohol-related problems. The technical discussions clearly showed the need for national alcohol policies and for "review [of] alcohol availability from a public health perspective."

Overall plans to renovate the alcohol-control system or to make major changes seem not to be under consideration anywhere in Latin America. However, Argentina, Peru and Mexico are taking steps to limit alcohol advertising. In addition, a few countries appear to recognize the need for better legislation on availability and are considering its development. Most countries describe the need for improved education and preventive measures related to alcohol use and a few recognize the need for new treatment activities (World Health Organization, 1982). Several countries, such as Costa Rica, Honduras and Mexico, have recently established institutes to deal with alcohol problems.

Women should be favorable to the development of controls on alcohol availability. Indeed, they might represent the abstinence or temperance sentiment lacking on a religious basis. For example, Medina-Mora (1980) found that 49 percent of females in Mexico City were abstainers. Azoubel Neto (1967) found that 36.5 percent of females in a town near São Paulo were abstainers. In a Costa Rican study (Caetano, 1982) abstention among women varied from 34 to 70 percent. In general, surveys of drinking in Latin America show abstention among women to be two to four times as high as among men and the average seems to be around 35 percent in recent studies. Women, of course, have far fewer problems when they do drink but are often the victims of the worst consequences of male drinking, such as violence or economic problems. They should then constitute a group that could lobby for better alcohol controls or at least support them when they are proposed or instituted.

There is also some indication that research and prevention efforts could be increased in Latin American countries. The Institute of Psychiatry in Mexico has conducted numerous epidemiologiç surveys of alcohol problems. This Institute is currently engaged in a project with the World Health Organization which examines the import and export of alcoholic beverages. The National Institute in Alcohol Research in Costa Rica has also conducted surveys of alcohol problems. Alcohol research in Chile has always been well developed, although it is mostly of a pharmacologic and epidemiologic nature. Also, plans have been made to create a new Institute on Alcoholism in Honduras to do both treatment and preventive work. Research relevant to policy development could be done in all these countries with established centers for prevention and treatment.

## FUTURE NEEDS

Alcohol controls must be given a larger place on research and policy development agendas. In many countries such controls are not even considered as part of the public health approach to alcohol problems. Current initiatives are mainly to create treatment and educational programs, which, although important, are not likely to have the same impact as stricter alcohol controls. The World Health Organization or other international agencies could sponsor policy development initiatives via conferences of ministers of health and by having the need for alcohol controls placed on the agenda of the World Health Assembly and the Pan American Health Organization. This would help to increase the visibility of controls as a public health issue and begin debate on the issues and problems involved.

An additional need is for research on existing alcohol controls in Latin America since there appears to be virtually no published research from Latin American countries. For example, several recent bibliographic reviews of research on availability and controls (Smart, 1982; Macdonald, 1982) found no Latin American research. At present, we do not know how well existing controls work in Latin America, which are the most effective, how often they are enforced, or how controls relate to availability and to rates of drinking. In addition, we do not know how much illegal or unregistered alcohol is sold in most countries nor how it could be better controlled. There is a clear need for alcohol researchers in Latin America to study issues relating to the functioning and effectiveness of alcohol controls in their own countries.

## REFERENCES

AZOUBEL NETO, D. 1967. Estado actual de la epidemiologia del alcoolismo y problemes del alcool en algunas paises de America Latina: Brasil. *In* Epidemiologia del Alcoholismo en America Latina. J. Horwitz, *et al*., Eds. Acta. Buenos Aries, Argentina.

BERRUECOS, L. 1982. La salud del joven rural. Rev. Estudios Juventud 2(7).

CABILDO, H. M., M. SILVA MARTINEZ & J. M. TUAREZ. 1969. Encuestra sobre habitos de ingestion de bebibas alcoholicas. *In* Salud Publica de Mexico 16: 759–769.

CAETANO, R. 1982. Manifestations and perceptions of alcohol-related problems in the Americas. *In* Legislative Approaches to Prevention of Alcohol-Related Problems. A. K. Kaplan, Ed. Institute of Medicine. Washington, DC.

CALDERON, N. G. 1968. Consideraciones acerca de alcoholismo entre los pueblos pre-hispanicos de Mexico. Rev. Instituto Nacional Neurologia (Mexico) 2: 5–13.

FROMM, E. & M. MACCOBY. 1973. Sociopsicoanalisis del Campesino Mexicano. Fondo de Cultura Economica. Mexico.

GONZALEZ, R. & M. KATATSKY. 1978. Epidemiological research in Latin America. *In* International Collaboration: Problems and Opportunities. B. Rutledge & E. Fulton, Eds. Addiction Research Foundation. Toronto, Ontario, Canada.

GRIMSON, W. R., A. C. DE BLANCO, M. ESTRAGAMON, E. LASTRES, S. NECCHI, E. PHILLPOT & A. M. TEISAIRE. 1972. Investigacion epidemiologica de entidades psiquiatricas. Bol. Of. Sanit. Panam. 73: 572–585.

HEATH, D. 1982. Historical and cultural factors affecting alcohol availability and consumption in Latin America. *In* Legislative Approaches to Prevention of Alcohol-Related Problems. A. K. Kaplan, Ed. Institute of Medicine. Washington, DC.

MACDONALD, S. 1982. A Bibliography and Summaries on the Relationship Among Alcohol Outlets, Alcohol Consumption, and Alcohol-Related Problems. Substudy No. 1224. Addiction Research Foundation, Toronto, Ontario, Canada.

MÄKELÄ, K., R. ROOM, E. SINGLE, P. SULKUNEN & B. WALSH. 1982. Alcohol, Society and the State: A Comparative Study of Alcohol Control. Addiction Research Foundation. Toronto, Ontario, Canada.

MEDINA-MORA, M. E. *et al*. 1980. El consumo de alcohol en la poblacion del D.F. Salud Publica Mex. 22(3):281-288.

MEDINA-MORA, M. E., J. G. GANDOLFO, B. L. POBLETE, M. T. VERSIN, H. C. VERSIN, J. A. FIGUEROA & S. R. NUNEZ. 1980. Prevalencia de distintos tipos de bebedores de alcool en Talcu. Cuadernos Med. Soc. 21: 26–40.

PAN AMERICAN HEALTH ORGANIZATION. 1978. Health Conditions in the Americas: 1973-1976. P.A.H.O. Scientific Publication No. 34. Washington, DC.

POPHAM, R. E., W. SCHMIDT & J. DE LINT. The effects of legal restraint on drinking. *In* The Biology of Alcoholism, Vol. 4. B. Kissin & H. Begleiter, Eds. Plenum Press. New York, NY.

Rosovsky, H. 1981. Panorama del impacto del consumo de alcohol en Mexico. Conferencia presentada en la Reunion Internacional "Las estrategias preventivas ante los problemas relacionados con el Alcohol" Mexico, July, 1981.

Smart, R. G. 1977. The relationship of availability of alcoholic beverages to per capita consumption and alcoholism rates. J. Stud. Alcohol **38**: 891–896.

Smart, R. G. 1982. The impact of prevention legislation: An examination of research findings. *In* Legislative Approaches to Prevention of Alcohol-Related Problems. A. K. Kaplan, Ed. Institute of Medicine. Washington, DC.

Sulkunen, P. 1973. On International Alcohol Statistics. Reports from the Social Research Institute of Alcohol Studies. Helsinki, Finland

World Health Organization. 1982. Background Documents for Technical Discussions on Alcohol Consumption and Alcohol-Related Problems. Geneva, Switzerland.

# International Collaboration on Alcohol-Related Problems: Perspectives from the U.S. National Institute on Alcohol Abuse and Alcoholism

LELAND H. TOWLE[a]

*International and Intergovernmental Affairs*
*National Institute on Alcohol Abuse and Alcoholism*
*Rockville, Maryland 20857*

## OVERVIEW OF THE NIAAA INTERNATIONAL PROGRAM

The International Program of the National Institute on Alcohol Abuse and Alcoholism (NIAAA) is guided by two major goals: (1) to further NIAAA domestic goals through international cooperation and collaboration with other countries and international organizations; and (2) to support U.S foreign policy objectives. Within the second goal is a third—namely, to enhance other countries' knowledge and capabilities to deal more effectively with their alcohol-related public health problems. This is consistent with the U.S. view of itself and other nations' view of the U.S. as a world leader. The program is also guided by relevant legislation in the Public Health Service Act (Sect. 301, 304, and 307), which provides an orientation toward research-related activities, including fellowships; authority does not exist for provisions of services or training of personnel.

The Institute's International Program embraces information exchange, the exchange of scientists, technical cooperation and collaboration, and research. Activities are carried out through bilateral agreements developed with other countries, multilaterally with the World Health Organization (WHO) and other international organizations, by support of worthy research grants and contracts, through a foreign visitors program, and through participation in significant international meetings and conferences.

• Current bilateral activities are being conducted under formal U.S. agreements with Finland, Poland, Yugoslavia, Japan, Mexico and Spain. Specific programs of scientific cooperation on alcohol problems exist between the NIAAA and Japan (signed in October 1980), the NIAAA and Mexico (signed in March 1982), and Israel (signed in March 1983). A specific program with Finland is being developed after execution of a Memorandum of Understanding between DHHS and Finland in October 1982. A specific program with Spain is also being developed, and a program with India is under discussion.

[a] Address for correspondence: L. H. T., Director, International and Intergovernmental Affairs, National Institute on Alcohol Abuse and Alcoholism, Room 16-95, Parklawn Building, 5600 Fishers Lane, Rockville, Maryland 20857.

- The World Health Organization, both through its parent headquarters in Geneva and through its regional offices (especially the Pan American Health Organization [PAHO] and affiliated agencies [specifically, the International Agency for Research on Cancer]), has become a major focus for NIAAA international cooperation and support since the Institute's establishment in 1971. This cooperation and collaboration have been carried out through NIAAA's network of recognized U.S. consultant experts and advisors, U.S. research scientists supported by NIAAA, and the Institute's own senior staff and research scientists. The NIAAA is closely aligned with the WHO program strategy and objectives on the public health aspects of alcohol-related problems, and over the last 5 to 6 years, the Institute has been a major contributor (in an advisory and technical assistance capacity) toward the planning and development of the WHO Expanded Program on Alcohol Problems.

- As a "member state" of the United Nations system and WHO, the U.S. has actively supported World Health Assembly resolutions dealing with increasing alcohol-related problems on a world-wide scale. The U.S. Surgeon General and Assistant Secretary for Health have endorsed an expanded WHO alcohol program, and they have expressed support through NIAAA on a specific project basis, and more recently in relation to the Institute's designation as a WHO Collaborating Center for Research and Training on Alcohol Problems.

- Currently, no foreign research grants are being supported by NIAAA, but there are a few domestic grants with a "foreign component," and a proposal is being developed for funding under the "Special Foreign Currency Program" with Yugoslavia.

- Each year, the Institute plays host to forty to fifty foreign visitors. These vistors include technical program staff, research scientists, intermediate- and high-level foreign government and international agency officials, and occasionally private individuals with an interest in alcohol problems. The focus for these visits may be on specific technical or research topics; program development or assessment methods /experience; policy issues and development; or general background on national, state, and local policies, programs, research, and evaluation data. The Institute assists in planning for these visits, arranges meetings with appropriate NIAAA staff and other agency staff, and provides pertinent information.

- Also each year the Institute participates in fifteen to twenty international workshops, meetings, or conferences both in the U.S. and in other countries. NIAAA provides partial support to several of these, both directly through the research grant mechanism and indirectly through funding of travel costs for staff and grantees to attend these events.

## A REVIEW OF NIAAA COOPERATION WITH WHO SINCE 1972

It is not possible in this short paper to cover all projects and activities that have been undertaken in cooperation with the WHO. Therefore, the paragraphs below outline briefly only some of them selected to indicate the wide variety and nature of NIAAA's support and cooperation.

The first funded project with WHO-Geneva (initiated in 1974) brought together several U.S. and U.K. experts to study and prepare a report in collaboration with WHO on criteria for identifying and classifying disabilities related to alcohol consumption (Edwards *et al.*, 1977). Definitions developed during this study, including that of the "alcohol dependence syndrome," were incorporated into the ICD 9th revision (1977) and have had a profound effect on initiating an extension of the earlier, more narrow definition of alcoholism to include other alcohol-related problems/disabilities.

The WHO project entitled Community Response to Alcohol-Related Problems, supported by NIAAA since 1976, is particularly significant because it is a cornerstone for the WHO Expanded Program on Alcohol Problems. This project was a multinational collaborative effort involving the participating countries of Mexico, Scotland, and Zambia and affiliated studies in the U.S. and Canada. The objectives of this project were to assist in development of a long-term multinational program on community response to alcohol-related problems; to develop basic epidemiologic and psychosocial data in a variety of settings; and to develop information on available community resources and community capability to deal with alcohol-related problems.

The WHO Phase I Final Report (WHO, 1981), in conjunction with a companion report reviewing "cross-cultural findings" and final reports from the three participating countries, provides a wealth of information on the patterns of alcohol-related problems, attitudes of the populations studied toward alcohol consumption and alcohol abuse, community response resources, and plans of action under way to improve both national and community response to alcohol-related problems.

Phase II of the project has just been completed and has resulted in a set of general guidelines (Rootman and Moser, 1984) for use by other countries in undertaking similiar research and planning studies, as well as a report (WHO, 1983) on follow-up actions taken in the three countries (Mexico, Scotland, and Zambia). During 1981 the Ministries of Health in both Mexico and Zambia held 2–3 day national meetings to present results and findings of the projects in their respective countries and to carry out planning workshops; this resulted in recommendations to national leaders for improving national and community response to alcohol problems. In Scotland, a similar meeting was held at the "community level" (Lothian Region) and a national meeting took place in early 1983.

The Institute has also supported alcohol epidemiological research at the International Agency for Research on Cancer (IARC) since 1973, the most recent 3-year study having ended in 1980. These studies on the relationship of alcohol to cancer and other diseases take advantage of the significant research capability at IARC coupled with the availability of disease registers (including alcoholism registers) which are unique to several of the European countries. Results of this research have been widely published in journals and in Special Reports to the U.S. Congress on Alcohol and Health. Among the results is a clear demonstration of a multiplier effect of the combination of tobacco smoking and alcohol consumption in their relationship to esophageal cancer (Tuyns et al., 1977). IARC's work was largely responsible for welding the linkage between the National Cancer Institute and NIAAA in the joint sponsorship of a major alcohol and cancer workshop on the NIH campus in October 1978 (Groupe and Salmoiraghi, 1979). This connection has been important for exploring and developing alcohol and cancer research opportunities between NCI and IARC.

The NIAAA, with cooperation from PAHO, planned and conducted a 5½-day international seminar program on alcohol abuse and its treatment (August 31–September 5, 1981) for 20 alcoholism professionals from 13 Latin American countries. The overall goals of this seminar were: (1) to provide participants with an orientation and medium for information exchange in the organization, treatment, and rehabilitation of the alcohol abuser, and (2) to give insight concerning U.S. Hispanic experience in the organization, establishment, and management of alcohol abuse treatment centers. Emphasis was provided on both nonmedical and medical approaches in a "working" seminar environment conducted almost entirely in Spanish and Portuguese. To stimulate group interaction, one-half of the participants (primarily psychiatrists and psychologists) were included as faculty. Other faculty were from NIAAA, PAHO, and the National Center for Alcohol Education. The program included visits to Hispanic treatment centers in Philadelphia and Washington, D.C. Representatives of Alcoholics Anonymous from the U.S. and Latin American countries also participated.

In collaboration with the WHO Regional Office for Europe (EURO), the NIAAA-funded Alcohol Research Center in Berkeley, California co-organized (with the Finnish Foundation for Alcohol Studies) and collaborated with six countries in the 3-year International Study of Alcohol Control Experiences (ISACE), which examined the structure of alcohol production, regulation, and policies; other participating countries included Canada, Finland, Ireland, Netherlands, Poland, and Switzerland. Several reports on this study have been published by the Addiction Research Foundation, Toronto, Canada (ARF, 1981; ARF, 1983; see also Österberg, this volume).

The Institute took an active advisory/consultation role in cooperation with the DHHS Office of International Health, WHO, and PAHO in the planning and organizing of an inter-American workshop conducted in March 1982 by the Institute of Medicine of the National Academy of Sciences entitled "Legislative Approaches to Prevention of Alcohol-Related Problems." An extensive report with this title was published (IOM, 1982), and a paper, "Consensus Views on Development of Alcohol Policies," was prepared and used as input by the U.S. Delegation at the World Health Assembly Technical Discussions in May entitled "Alcohol Consumption and Alcohol-Related Problems: Development of National Policies and Programmes" (IOM, 1982).

In September 1982, at the invitation of the World Health Organization, NIAAA participated in a 4-day WHO Advisory Group meeting of international experts entitled "Legislation in Relation to Treatment of Alcoholism and Drug Abuse," held at Harvard University. Prior to the meeting, materials on the U.S. situation and extensive guidance by key NIAAA staff were provided to the WHO consultant preparing a draft report on the subject. In addition to this report (WHO, in press), to be published in 1983 or 1984, a meeting report, including recommendations of the Advisory Group, was also prepared.

## CURRENT NIAAA INTERNATIONAL PROGRAM ACTIVITIES AND INITIATIVES

### Bilateral Activities

Since early 1980, the Institute has made a deliberate effort to both sustain and expand bilateral cooperation with other countries in recognition of the mutual benefits that could be derived. The signing of a specific Statement for Scientific Cooperation on Alcohol-Related Problems with the Japanese Ministry of Health and Welfare (National Institute on Alcoholism) in October 1980, was followed by a similar agreement with the Mexican Institute on Psychiatry in March 1982, and more recently with the Israeli Ministry of Labour and Social Affairs. Each of these agreements contains similar elements, which allow for information and/or data exchange, the exchange of scientific visits, the placement of individuals into work-study assignments in host-country institutions, and collaboration in the conduct of specific projects and research investigations, which in some cases may be joint projects. In the case of work-study assignments and the exchange of scientific visits, the "sending country" generally pays salary and travel costs and the "receiving country" covers "in-country" travel and subsistence cost, unless otherwise mutually agreed. Current NIAAA bilateral activities are described briefly by country below:

## Mexico

Collaboration in the analysis of comparable epidemiologic survey data on drinking patterns and related problems from the U.S., Mexico, Zambia, and Scotland initiated during 1982 is continuing; in addition, a Mexican Institute of Psychiatry scientist made a short-term visit to the University of Connecticut Alcohol Research Center, participating in the international conference entitled "Alcohol and Culture" in May and was introduced to a collaborative study on treatment and management of persons with harmful alcohol consumption being conducted in cooperation with the center and other WHO collaborating centers.

## Japan

Placement of Japanese scientists on 1–2-year work-study assignments is continuing, with two additions planned in 1983; a collaborative study of blood chemistries, as part of the NIAAA development of a technique for identifying heavy drinkers, is also continuing; and a joint cross-cultural community-based epidemiological study of drinking patterns and related problems in Japanese and Japanese-Americans is being developed for initiation in 1984.

## Israel

A plan for Mutual Cooperation between NIAAA and the Ministry of Labour and Social Affairs and an outline of activities for 1983 were developed in November 1982; execution of the plan called for technical cooperation in management of a residential treatment facility and study of the medical and psychiatric aspects of alcoholism, and development for a joint epidemiologic research project on drinking patterns, attitudes, and behavior.

## Finland

Under the November 1982 Health Memorandum of Understanding between the Finnish Ministry of Health and the U.S. Department of Health and Human Services, a cooperative program on alcohol abuse and alcoholism is being developed, emphasizing joint prevention and policy research and demonstration projects.

## India

The development of collaborative epidemiologic studies of alcohol drinking patterns, behaviors, and problems related to alcohol consumption is under discussion.

## Poland

In follow-up to exchanges in previous years, plans are being made to receive two

Polish scientists for short-term collaborative assignments, and to send two U.S. scientists for short-term assignments to the Psychoneurological Institute in Warsaw.

### Spain

A joint Alcohol Research Planning Seminar is being planned for early 1984 in Barcelona. The purpose of the Seminar is to present and discuss ongoing alcohol research of specific interest to scientists of both countries and to plan specific collaborative project proposals to the Joint Spanish-US. Committee for Cooperation in Science and Technology.

### Yugoslavia

In follow-up to previous exchanges and special Foreign Currency Program studies, a new study (under Joint Committee Funding) of the effectiveness of different family treatment techniques for alcoholism (including network therapy) is being developed; U.S. family experts will consult on this study to be undertaken in Belgrade.

### Multilateral Activities

To date, the Institute's prinicipal multilateral effort has been in relation to WHO, its regional offices, and affiliates as described in earlier sections of this paper. Thus, it seems very appropriate to signal as a major initiative the designation of NIAAA as a WHO Collaborating Center for Research and Training on Alcohol Problems.

Although the Institute's mission has shifted over the past year towards one that is predominantly research and research training, it is maintaining and strengthening its national leadership role not only in these areas, but also in the areas of research dissemination and utilization, information and statistical data, prevention and treatment demonstrations, and cooperative/collaborative linkages with other federal agencies, state and local governments, and the voluntary and private sectors. In view of current emphasis on improved economy and effectiveness, NIAAA's role as the national coordinating focal point for alcohol abuse and alcoholism has increased importance for partnership relations with WHO — for example, in dealing with teenage alcohol problems. As a Collaborating Center, the Institute will build upon the growing cooperation and collaboration with WHO over the last few years by fostering and facilitating WHO collaborative linkages with the National Alcohol Research Centers and individual research investigators funded by NIAAA, as well as Institute consultant experts, research scientists, and senior staff.

The nature of the work to be planned and carried out as a WHO Collaborating Center can be generally classified in the six categories described below:

1. Exchange of scientific information and statistical data.

2. Exchange of scientific research and professional personnel in work/study programs.

3. Training of personnel from developing countries, particularly in the area of epidemiologic studies and the treatment and management of alcohol-dependent persons.

4. Collaborative projects directed toward the development and application of research instruments and methods, especially in clinical and epidemiologic areas.

5. Collaboration in planning and carrying out seminars, workshops and conferences on alcohol-related problems; and in the preparation and publishing of reports and monographs of international interest.

6. Consultation in planning and developing the WHO program including participation in Advisory Groups convened by WHO for this purpose, as well as for the review of projects.

Within this framework, it is appropriate to cite a few examples of work that has already been initiated. One of the NIAAA-funded Alcohol Research Centers has taken the lead role in conducting 4–country cross-cultural analysis of data from Phase I of the study of Community Response to Alcohol-Related Problems, especially general population survey data from the studies in Mexico, Scotland, Zambia, and the U.S. (California). This project is being carried out by collaborators from the four countries, and will yield a manuscript suitable for publication in book form. Another of the NIAAA-funded Alcohol Research Centers is collaborating in the WHO-initiated project directed at developing and testing (1) a methodology for early identification of individuals at high risk for alcohol-related problems; and (2) low-cost early intervention strategies. The Institute is collaborating with WHO in the development of a system for reporting international statistics on alcohol-related problems and it has been proposed that NIAAA become the "focal point" for the collection, analysis, and publication of these statistics once a system has been developed and proved feasible. The knowledge and experience gained over the last six years in building the U.S. Alcohol Epidemiological Data System (AEDS) will be invaluable in extending this capability to a comparable set of global indicators on problems related to alcohol consumption.

To mark the designation of NIAAA as a WHO Collaborating Center, a 4-day international research seminar program on alcohol abuse and alcoholism was held in the Fall of 1983 at the Pan American Health Organization in Washington, D.C. This event included a 2-day technical workshop on early diagnosis of alcohol abuse, which will result in a "state-of-the-art" research monograph on this subject. This program also included an official designation ceremony and plenary presentation and discussions by recognized U.S. scientists in the alcohol field. It ended with a 2-day WHO project collaborators' meeting on the development and testing of methods for early identification of and intervention for persons at high risk for developing alcohol-related problems. Overall goals for the seminar program were (1) development of knowledge and (2) identification of opportunities for collaborative studies and future exchange among U.S. participants from the twelve or more institutions in other countries.

## FUTURE DIRECTIONS FOR INTERNATIONAL COLLABORATION

As reflected in the foregoing sections, a trend has emerged over the last two to three years toward international cooperation and collaboration on a joint project or activity basis, and away from the U.S. funding of specific research grant projects and contract studies with foreign investigators and international organizations. In part, this is a result of more stringent procedural requirements coupled with increased competition from domestic sources. It may also be a result of relatively greater resources being available in other countries for work in the alcohol field, in recognition of the magnitude of the health, economic, and social costs of alcohol-related problems. But perhaps more important, behind this growing trend, is the realization that greater benefits can accrue to all sides through the mutual exchange of information and scientists, and through the *joint* undertaking of research investigations and cooperative activities in the alcohol field.

It is expected that this trend in international cooperation and collaboration will continue. As a WHO Collaborating Center for Research and Training, the NIAAA will encourage the development of joint cooperative activities and collaborative projects through its network of consultant experts and advisors, U.S. research scientists supported by NIAAA, and the Institute's own senior staff and intramural research scientists. This encouragement will extend not only to the WHO Alcohol Program initiatives, but it will also extend to the existing "bilateral agreements" between the Institute and institutions of other countries, and to other international efforts in the alcohol field. In addition, opportunities will be explored for the development of new bilateral agreements and for cooperation with regional and international organizations.

The specific areas for future international collaboration no doubt will be varied, depending upon the mutual interests and priorities on both sides. Research and training will still be the principal focus for NIAAA within the biomedical, clinical, psychosocial, epidemiologic, prevention, intervention, and treatment areas. Within these areas, international collaboration is likely to reflect the promising new areas of alcohol research, for example, alcohol's effect on brain structure and function, biological markers, pharmacologic agents, treatment assessments, public policy aspects of prevention, cultural relationships, and alcohol problem statistics. More emphasis is also expected in the future on the convening of international technical workshops as a means for furthering the interchange of knowledge and the development of collaborative work in the alcohol field. This conference, on Alcohol and Culture is exemplary in that it has provided a forum for researchers from many countries in Europe and from North America to present the results of their work and to exchange their knowledge, experience, and viewpoints in an atmosphere that is highly conducive to future interchange. It is hoped that this endeavor will also have stimulated cross-cultural collaboration on one or more research studies that are planned or are under way.

This paper describes some of the current international activities of the U.S. National Institute on Alcohol Abuse and Alcoholism and provides a brief outlook for international cooperation and collaboration in the future. The Institute's program is based on the conviction that the benefits to be gained are mutual, and that the results will provide a significant contribution toward reducing the incidence and prevalence of alcoholism and other alcohol-related problems.

## REFERENCES

ADDICTION RESEARCH FOUNDATION. 1981. Alcohol, Society, and the State. Vol. 1: A Comparative Study of Alcohol Control *by* K. Mäkelä, R. Room, E. Single, P. Sulkunen & B. Walsh, Eds. and Vol. 2: The Social History of Control Policy in Seven Countries. E. Single, P. Morgan & J. deLint, Eds. Addiction Research Foundation. Toronto, Ontario, Canada.

ADDICTION RESEARCH FOUNDATION. 1983. Consequences of Drinking. Trends in Alcohol Problem Statistics in Seven Countries *by* N. Giesbrecht, M. Cahannes. J. Moskalewicz, E. Österberg & R. Room, Eds. Addiction Research Foundation. Toronto, Ontario, Canada.

CURRAN, W., A. ARIF & W. PORTER. The Law and Treatment of Drug and Alcohol Dependent Persons. World Health Organization. Geneva, Switzerland. In press.

EDWARDS, G., M. M. GROSS, M. KELLER, J. MOSER & R. ROOM, Eds. 1977. Alcohol-Related Disabilities. Offset Publication No. 32. World Health Organization. Geneva, Switzerland.

GROUPE, V. & G. C. SALMOIRAGHI, Eds. 1979. Alcohol and Cancer Workshop. Cancer Res. **39:** 2815–2908.

INSTITUTE OF MEDICINE. 1982. Legislative Approaches to Prevention of Alcohol-Related Problems: An Inter-American Workshop (proceedings). Publication No. IOM-82–003. National Academy Press. Washington, D.C.

ROOTMAN, I. & J. MOSER. 1984. Guidelines for Investigating Alcohol Problems and Developing Appropriate Responses. Offset Publication No. 81. World Health Organization. Geneva, Switzerland.

TUYNS, A. J., G. PEQUIGNOT & O. M. JENSON. 1977. Le cancer de l'oesophage en Ille et Vilaine en fonction de niveaux consommation d'alcool et de tabac: Des risques qui se multiplient. Bull. Cancer. **65**: 45–60.

WORLD HEALTH ORGANIZATION. 1981. Community Response to Alcohol-Related Problems, Phase I. Final Report. Geneva, Switzerland.

WORLD HEALTH ORGANIZATION. 1983. Community Response to Alcohol-Related Problems, Phase II. Final Report. Geneva, Switzerland.

# Current World Health Organization Activities on the Control and Prevention of Alcohol-Related Problems

MARCUS GRANT

*Division of Mental Health*
*World Health Organization*
*1211 Geneva 27, Switzerland*

## BACKGROUND

Ever since the First World Health Assembly in 1948, the World Health Organization (WHO) has recognized its role as a focal point for international concern about alcohol-related problems.

Within WHO's Seventh General Program of Work, a major objective for the Division of Mental Health is "to cooperate with Member States in preventing and controlling the problems related to alcohol and drug abuse" (WHO, 1982). This objective reflects a number of Assembly resolutions which have directed and guided WHO's efforts over the years. It also reflects increasing concern from countries throughout the world about the seriousness of trends in alcohol consumption and alcohol-related problems.

The range and severity of alcohol-related problems vary considerably, from country to country as well as within countries. Nevertheless, the accumulated research evidence of recent years demonstrates that there is generally a positive association between trends in alcohol consumption and trends in alcohol-related problems. This needs to be understood both from an individual and a social perspective. The relationship between consumption and problems is certainly complex, since, even within a single country, it cannot be assumed that drinking behavior is evenly spread throughout the population. It is also important to be aware that there may be groups who are particularly at risk. In many countries, increases in alcohol consumption by women and young people have already been noted.

Even without increases, problems might worsen at current levels of consumption because of the increased complexity of modern life. Protracted high levels of alertness are, for example, required in traffic, in factories, and on construction sites. At the same time, however, great care has to be taken in extrapolating from one group of countries to another. There is a great difference in approach needed if, for example, in one country the great majority of the population drinks a relatively small amount of alcohol on a regular daily basis compared with another country where only 15% of the population drinks alcohol at all. An increase in per capita consumption in such a country would therefore mean something very different from a comparable increase in a country where everybody drinks, since it would lead to quite different patterns of alcohol-related problems.

Recent decades have witnessed considerable increases in alcohol consumption and in alcohol-related problems in countries in all regions of the world. Within the WHO

European Region, the number of countries with an annual per capita intake of more than 10 liters of pure alcohol increased from 3 in 1950 to 18 by 1979. Countries in the WHO Western Pacific Region report sharp increases in alcohol-related health damage, in alcohol-related crimes, and in alcohol-related accidents during the 1970s. Similar reports have emerged from countries in other WHO regions, including those with long traditions of abstinence from alcohol. Although some countries in Western Europe and North America are now reporting a levelling off and even a modest decline in alcohol consumption, the global trend is still that of continuing growth, with particularly sharp increases in commercially produced alcoholic beverages in some developing countries in Africa, Latin America, and the Western Pacific.

Not only the alcohol-dependence syndrome itself, but also a wide range of disabling and sometimes fatal physical and psychological conditions, can be attributed either wholly or in part to excessive drinking. In addition, alcohol-related traffic accidents account for significant proportions of deaths in many countries, especially among young people. Other accidents, including accidents in the work setting, are more frequently related to alcohol consumption than is widely recognized. In more general terms, the disruption of family life caused by the excessive drinking of one or more family members causes distress and can also result in violence and neglect. Other areas of concern include drinking by young people and drinking by pregnant women, because of the possible harm to vulnerable populations. Drinking practices in some developing countries, which do not have long historical traditions of consuming commercially produced beverages of the range and strength available in most developed countries, may lead to a concentration of alcohol-related problems among technicians and professionals, who are the scarcest resource, or among young people, who represent the country's investment in its future. In such circumstances, the real cost to the community is greater than would be apparent from a simple statement of alcohol-related mortality.

## RECENT WHO DECISIONS AND ACTIVITIES

It was at the Twenty-eighth World Health Assembly in 1975 that the Director-General was requested " . . to direct special attention in the future programme of WHO to the extent and seriousness of the individual, public health and social problems associated with the current use of alcohol in many countries of the world . . ." (WHA28.81).

During the Sixth General Program of Work, WHO's activities in the area of alcohol abuse were concentrated on gathering information and initiating action. During this time, the concept of "alcoholism" was replaced with a much broader range of "alcohol-related problems" as well as a more narrowly defined "alcohol-dependence syndrome." Information from 80 countries on the prevention of alcohol-related problems was collated and published (Moser, 1980) and an Expert Committee on Problems Related to Alcohol Consumption formed (WHO, 1980). In addition, WHO carried out a large collaborative study in measuring and improving community responses to alcohol-related problems in Mexico, Scotland, and Zambia (Rootman and Moser, 1983; Rootman, 1983).

Throughout this time, the activities stimulated and coordinated by WHO's regional offices have remained an essential part of all the main directions of work.

Following the recognition, at the Thirty-second World Health Assembly in 1979, ". . . that problems related to alcohol, and particularly to its excessive consumption rank among the world's major public health problems . . . " (WHA32.40), the Technical Discussions three years later brought together participants from more than 100 countries. In the report of their discussions, four basic messages were emphasized: that alcohol-related problems are health problems; that action to reduce them is urgent; that there is sufficient consensus on priorities; and that explicit commitment must replace token action (A35/TD/6).

These themes were echoed in a further resolution at the Thirty-sixth World Health Assembly, which urged Member States "to formulate comprehensive national policies, with prevention as a priority, and with attention to populations at special risk, within the framework of the strategy of health for all" (WHA36.12). This resolution demonstrates the importance of the alcohol program to WHO's global strategy of health and expresses the collective decision of all member states of WHO to deal with major risks to health through a resolute program of action involving all sectors of government.

## CURRENT WHO ACTIVITIES

The WHO Executive Board, when reviewing the Organization's program budget proposals for 1984–1985, identified the prevention of alcohol-related health problems as one of the areas requiring more resources. Additional funding was therefore allocated from the Director-General's Development Program for strengthening the Organization's activities along the following lines:

i.   WHO's advocacy of public health measures for the prevention and control of alcohol problems;

ii.   the development of techniques for the identification, prevention and management of alcohol problems in individuals, families and the community; and

iii.   collaboration with countries in the development of national alcohol policies.

These activities are reinforced by WHO's active role in international coordination of action against health-related alcohol problems.

The WHO alcohol program therefore consists of a number of distinct but interrelated activities, which include:

*1. Increasing the awareness of governments, the general public and the scientific community about health consequences of alcohol consumption and about the possibilities for preventive intervention.*

An international meeting on alcohol and health held in Geneva in November 1983 identified effective advocacy approaches. This meeting involved media practitioners and communication scientists. The recommendations are now being implemented through the Division of Mental Health and the Division of Information and Education for Health. National and international meetings and workshops are being organized to develop, promote, and test specific approaches to the prevention of alcohol-related public health problems, with special emphasis upon the needs of developing countries.

A review was undertaken of the various documents on alcohol production, consumption, and related health problems issued or drafted by the Organization during the past few years. This review revealed that the information available had been insufficiently exploited for advocacy purposes. It also highlighted some discrepancies between various sets of data. Action has now been initiated for improving our data base and for producing a series of documents on alcohol production, consumption, and health-related problems. These include an analysis of alcohol production and trade, which documents major trends, discusses their public health implications, and suggests areas for future work (Walsh and Grant, 1985).

*2.  Collaboration in the development and evaluation of effectiveness of national policies and programs concerned with health aspects of alcohol abuse.*

Following a comprehensive review of the world literature, a basic publication is being prepared on policy options for decision-makers. It distinguishes between those policy measures for which there is now sufficient objective evidence of effectiveness, those for which the evidence is mixed, and those for which there is widespread popular support but little objective information. It is hoped that this publication will be of use in a wide range of countries, and that opportunities will arise for working with countries to help test the impact of different approaches to policy development and implementation.

In the meantime, intercountry and national workshops are being organized in a number of countries, particularly in the WHO African Region.

*3.  Promoting the development and use of sound national and international data bases on alcohol-related problems and their changes.*

The lack of adequate statistical information in this area has been repeatedly deplored in World Health Assembly resolutions and in requests from member states. A first consultation on this project was held in October 1982. Following detailed planning, it has now been established that collaborating centers are especially well placed to play a leading role in developing activities in this area. The Addiction Research Foundation (Canada) and the National Institute on Alcohol Abuse and Alcoholism (USA) would bring together groups of scientists from a range of countries to review the existing situation and to plan for specific international collaborative work. The first meeting concentrated on the improvement of the measurement of the alcohol component in casualty statistics.

*4.  Development of social and technological measures to reduce alcohol problems in the employment setting.*

In collaboration with the International Labor Organization (ILO) and the International Council on Alcohol and Addictions (ICAA), WHO has already produced six regional reviews of alcohol-related problems in the employment setting and the responses that are currently offered to them. A global summary has also been prepared. Discussions are now continuing with the ILO regarding further collaborative work, involving a number of different ILO technical units. The vocational and social aspects of drug and alcohol abuse in the work setting is the subject of a technical paper which the ILO presented for discussion at the Inter-Agency Meeting on Coordination in Matters of International Drug Abuse Control (ILO Geneva, September 1984). On the basis of discussions at that meeting and elsewhere, more specific proposals have been developed for possible joint action by ILO and WHO, focusing upon preventive measures appropriate for employment settings.

*5.  Development of social and technological measures to reduce alcohol problems in the family setting.*

Very little specific work has been undertaken by WHO in the area of alcohol-related problems in the family setting. A review of the world literature on the prevention and management of alcohol problems in the family setting has been commissioned in order to determine ways in which WHO might approach this complex field and become usefully involved. While this remains a topic of very great potential importance, no clear line of WHO work has emerged. It is, however, important within both the advocacy area and the treatment area.

*6.  Coordination of research on biological risk factors for alcohol dependence.*

This project aims to test the hypothesis that genetically determined differences in aldehyde dehydrogenase (ALDH) isoenzyme activity influence sensitivity to alcohol, drinking patterns, and the development of alcohol dependence. As a first step towards developing the studies, a draft for more comprehensive research protocols to standardize methods for determining biological measures has now been prepared. This line of work is seen as a long-term international collaborative effort, involving several centers, which would participate in research and exchange data on ethnic differences of alcohol-related enzymes.

7. *Development of technology for early detection of problems related to harmful consumption of alcohol and development and evaluation of measures to be used for the treatment and management of alcohol-related problems in primary health care settings.*

The project on early detection of alcohol problems aims to develop a simple procedure that will be useful in primary health care settings. Various existing methods for this purpose have been compared in order to determine which items should eventually be included in the screening instrument, which was then tested in a number of countries (Australia, Bulgaria, Kenya, Mexico, Norway, and the United States of America). A number of publications relating to the first phase of this work will be produced, and will appear in the near future.

The results of this project will feed directly into work on the development and evaluation of measures to be used for treatment and management of alcohol problems in the primary health care setting. The project on treatment emphasizes the development of effective and simple low-cost methods, designed to increase (a) the number of people that will be reached, (b) the likelihood that health systems can incorporate the relevant knowledge, and (c) the likelihood that countries can afford the cost. Centers in eleven countries (the six listed above, together with Costa Rica, France, the United Kingdom of Great Britain and Northern Ireland, the Union of Soviet Socialist Republics and Zimbabwe) have begun making preparations for the pilot phase. A simple advice session will be compared with a counselling session and self-help manual, in order to test their effectiveness in reducing consumption and/or alcohol-related problems in problem drinkers. The results will be used in drafting a set of guidelines for treatment and management of alcohol-related problems.

Efforts in this area are supplemented by a descriptive survey of the role of general medical practitioners in the management of alcohol-related problems in a range of developing and developed countries. Reports based upon studies from fourteen centers in twelve countries have been prepared in order to achieve a better understanding of the current practice and the future potential of general practitioners in identification, treatment, and prevention of alcohol-related problems.

## CONCLUSION

As is apparent from this brief description of the current WHO activities on the prevention and control of alcohol-related problems, the intention is to establish a program that makes the most cost-effective use of scare resources, that will attract the support of relevant national and international interests, and that will contribute significantly to the efforts of the Organization to work with countries to achieve the goal of health for all.

Since these activities fall within the work of the Division of Mental Health in relation to the prevention and control of alcohol and drug abuse, it is important to be aware of the strong links that exist between efforts to alleviate alcohol-related problems and efforts to alleviate drug-related problems. For many of the activities described above for the alcohol program, there exist parallel activities to counteract the abuse of other psychoactive drugs. Some issues are of particular relevance to one area or the other, but many benefit from the development of a common approach to alcohol and drug abuse.

Equally, the prevention and control of alcohol and drug abuse need to be seen within the context of the complete program of work of the Division of Mental Health. In order to achieve its goals, the program gives central attention to the development of ways that can help in the preservation and enhancement of mental health at all ages and in the specific sociocultural contexts of member states. Alcohol-related problems impinge upon many areas of physical and mental health as well as upon social functioning. National and international efforts to prevent and control alcohol abuse are best seen as part of the broader health concerns which are reflected in the strategies to achieve health for all by the year 2000.

## REFERENCES

INTERNATIONAL LABOUR OFFICE. 1984. Social and vocational aspects of drug/alcohol abuse in the work setting. Unpublished manuscript. Geneva, Switzerland.

MOSER, J., Ed. 1980. Prevention of Alcohol-Related Problems: An International Review of Prevention Measures, Policies and Programmes. Alcohol and Drug Addiction Research Foundation. Toronto, Ontario, Canada.

ROOTMAN, I. & J. MOSER. 1984. Community Response to Alcohol-Related Problems. A World Health Organization Project Monograph. U.S. Department of Health and Human Services. Washington, D.C.

WALSH, B. & M. GRANT. 1985. Public Health Implications of Alcohol Production and Trade. WHO Offset Publication No. 88. World Health Organization. Geneva, Switzerland.

WORLD HEALTH ORGANIZATION. 1983. Handbook of Resolutions and Decisions of the World Health Assembly and the Executive Board, Vol. II. Geneva, Switzerland.

WORLD HEALTH ORGANIZATION. 1982. Alcohol Consumption and Alcohol-Related Problems: Development of National Policies and Programmes. Report of the Technical Discussions. A35/Technical Discussions/6. May, 1982.

WORLD HEALTH ORGANIZATION. Seventh General Programme of Work Covering the Period 1984-1989. Health for All, Series No. 8. Geneva, Switzerland.

WORLD HEALTH ORGANIZATION. 1980. Problems Related to Alcohol Consumption. Report of a WHO Expert Committee. Technical Report Series No. 650. Geneva, Switzerland.

# Concluding Remarks

DWIGHT B. HEATH

*Department of Anthropology*
*Brown University*
*Providence, Rhode Island 02912*

It has been gratifying to watch, over the past decade or so, as the importance of social and cultural perspectives has come to be increasingly accepted by colleagues throughout the broad field of "alcohol studies." We have reached the point where almost everyone feels constrained to give at least lip service to the mutual relevance of various viewpoints if we are to understand the interplay of alcohol and human behavior. This is epitomized in the frequent allusion to alcoholism as "a biopsychosocial phenomenon," but is much more meaningfully illustrated in the fact that a conference such as this was conceived, organized, and carried through, with such broadly multidisciplinary and international participation, on the focal theme of alcohol and culture.

Although anthropologists have catalogued some 200 explicit definitions of "culture," the concept has generally been used in recent years to refer to a *system of patterns of beliefs and behavior that are familiar to, and in significant degree, shared by a given population.* It is that usage that is fundamental to "the sociocultural model" as developed by Bales, Heath, Pittman, Whitehead, and others, which holds that attitudes, values, norms, and other beliefs about alcohol and its effects shape not only the ways people drink but also the ways in which they behave while drunk, the kinds of problems, if any, that they may have with drinking, and the rate at which such problems are likely to occur. Such a view of culture emphasizes the fact that various populations not only have different beverages but also attach different meanings to them, to various acts of drinking, to various potential drinking companions, and so forth, as well as attaching different values to various outcomes of drinking.

Presumably most of the participants in this conference would accept such a general formulation of the interrelationship between alcohol and culture. Nevertheless, only a few of the papers that were presented had an emphasis that coincides with such a view. The reasons for this apparently anomalous disjuncture appear to have something to do with methodology and also to relate to some divergent ideas about how cultures relate to populations.

The methodologic issue to which we refer is connected only in part to the way in which data are collected. At a much more fundamental level, it relates to what kinds of data are sought. This problem was strongly hinted at during the first day, when Österberg, in summarizing the ISACE project, said that the abundant quantitative data on consumption and on problems were less helpful to him in understanding what had happened in those seven countries than were the relatively sparse and imprecise data on the meanings of drinking. Roizen,[a] despite his dogged and imaginative manipulations and transformations of the data collected by WHO's Community Responses to Alcohol-Related Problems study, apparently remains unconvinced that the

---

[a] In a paper ("Alcohol Dependence Symptoms in Cross-Cultural Perspective") read at this conference, but not published here.

"symptoms" elicited on the questionnaire (a standard instrument, translated for use in various countries) should seriously be regarded as "problems"; Campillo[b] obviously agreed, recommending that ethnographic, epidemiologic, and clinical perspectives should normally be used to complement such survey-research. The need for information about meanings and values — the underlying "patterns of belief" — is patent, even if it means that the apparent precision of pre-coded responses must be sacrificed, and respondents be given an open-ended opportunity to express their viewpoints. It is ironic that Room[c] implied that a survey, allowing choice only among a few alternatives phrased in alien terms, is more "democratic" than interviewing. For that matter, the cross-cultural validity and reliability of "standardized tests" is by no means assured. What "standardization" has been done usually relates to a literate population in the mainstream of Western Euroamerican culture, so that merely translating the questions and converting units of measure do not necessarily result in meaningful instruments.

Even where locally sensitive instruments have been devised, it is noteworthy that they have not often addressed the crucial issues of meaning and value. A striking illustration of this occurred in the discussion that followed Kandel's tightly organized and amply documented presentation[d]; when asked to "explain" or "account for" some of the differences that she had found between French, Israeli, and U.S. youth, she went beyond admitting that her data had not addressed that issue, and went on to speculate in terms that nicely fit "the sociocultural model," emphasizing integrative drinking in a supportive family context, and so forth. Perhaps the time is ripe for ethnographers and social psychologists to collaborate in attempting to develop instruments that might be more sensitive to such issues. Certainly much of the discussion at this conference, both formal and informal, was focused on questions of meaning and value that everyone seems to consider important, but that few of the speakers attempted to measure or to report on systematically.

Although his data were more synthetic, using studies made by others, Miller came close to laying bare some of the fundamental premises and feelings of a large population when he contrasted the peculiar disease concept of alcoholism that dominates in the United States with views about alcoholism elsewhere. Muller's comparison of ethnic subgroups among Swiss youth (not reprinted in this volume) also revealed norms, as well as discrepancies between the "real" and "ideal" in terms of peer and parent modeling. There is a major dichotomy between what people do and what they say ought to be done, that Vaillant appropriately stressed, and the data from his extraordinarily large-scale long-term prospective study of the natural history of a population lend striking support to the proposition that ethnic differences in alcohol use are reflected in very real differences in kinds and rates of problems. In dealing with a more widespread and diverse population, Babor and Mendelson appropriately reminded us that "basic demographic variables" may sometimes be important, as well as religious, ethnic, and racial categories such as are often uncritically designated "special populations," and inappropriately treated as if each were a homogeneous group.

The question of homogeneity is another thorny issue that seemed rarely to be addressed explicitly, but that implicitly colored much of what was said (and unsaid) throughout this conference. Although there is a long tradition of referring to "the

[b] In informal discussion.

[c] In a paper read at this conference, but published elsewhere: ROOM, R. 1984. Alcohol and ethnography: A case of problem deflation? Current Anthropology 25: 169–191.

[d] In a paper read at this conference, but published elsewhere: ADLER, I. & D. B. KANDEL. 1982. A cross-cultural comparison of sociopsychological factors in alcohol use among adolescents in Israel, France, and the United States. J. Youth Adolescence 11: 89–113.

Irish," "French drinking," and so forth, when introducing listeners first to the concept of culture as it relates to alcohol, few social scientists would be comfortable using such grossly diverse populations as meaningful units for analysis. Yet a number of the presentations did just that, with little indication of what kind of sample had been selected. A case could be made that referring to a comparison of Norwegians with Americans, or of French with French-Canadians and people of the U.S., and so forth, represents a convenient shorthand way of talking about *specific* populations sampled in specific ways for specific purposes. But a real problem seems to occur too often when the label takes on a sort of misplaced concreteness and we begin to talk about supposed national differences on the basis of such data.

When authors did focus on smaller populations which have less pluralistic cultural systems, and to address meanings and values, many participants seem to have felt that the data were more compelling, even if they were not presented in quantitatively sophisticated form. Westermeyer's identification of risk factors among Minnesota Indians is one example; Hall's introduction to a range of native modalities of treatment is another. The striking contrasts that can occur between an outsider's view and that of a member of the population under study were illustrated in Smart's impressionistic account of some Latin American patterns, and Campillo's reaction to it.

Mäkelä seems to have hit on an especially fruitful approach to cross-cultural study, that of controlled comparison among populations that are different in some key respects, but not different in so many respects that it is difficult even to be cognizant of all the variables. In a sense, Hall, Westermeyer, Vaillant, and Babor used the same relatively limited approach. This is not to imply that more contrastive cross-cultural studies are inappropriate — they hold enormous promise and more should be done, but such research should probably include more consistent attempt at specifying how and why samples were drawn, and at identifying the meanings and values that are crucial contextual factors for the other kinds of data that are collected.

The one paper read at the conference that did focus on traditional approaches to such questions has been published elsewhere so it is not included in this volume. It is just as well, inasmuch as it is flawed by major misunderstandings. Room has misrepresented ethnography no less than he has misrepresented epidemiology, and it is disturbing that his endorsement of a culturally relativistic point of view is not broad enough to allow for the possibility that a population may have few or no alcohol-related problems, even with widespread heavy drinking and frequent drunkenness.[e] The empirical evidence presented in the large-scale cross-cultural studies that we do have from ICASE, WHO, and the inter-American workshop lend quantitative support to the "sociocultural model," even if the editorial frontmatter and "consensus documents" ignore such data.

In a very real sense, the simple fact that a conference such as this was conceived, organized, and so effectively carried out signals a kind of "coming of age" of cultural concerns in alcohol studies. Although he had no professional training in the social sciences, Jellinek was an avid amateur culture historian and much of what he wrote

---

[e] Like William Miller's paper on the disease concept of alcoholism (reprinted in this volume), Robin Room's presentation, "Alcohol and Ethnography: A Case of Problem Deflation?" drew attention to a sensitive ideological issue pertaining to the philosophy of social science. To capture some of the flavor of the debate generated by that presentation, the reader is referred to the published text of Room's article, as well as the Comments to it provided by Michael Agar, Linda Bennett, Sally Casswell, Dwight Heath, Joy Leland, Jerrold Levy, William Madsen, Mac Marshall, Jacek Moskalewicz, Juan Carlos Negrete, Miriam Rodin, Lee Sackett, Margaret Sargent, David Strug and Jack Waddell, in *Current Anthropology* 25: 169–191.

—*Editor*

laid great emphasis on variations among populations. Selden Bacon's key role in the Yale Center (and later at the Rutgers Center) of Alcohol Studies supported this, and, ironically, the best known general theory about why people drink (i.e., to reduce anxiety) was given its most forceful exposition in Horton's large-scale cross-cultural study. During recent years, it has come to be increasingly recognized that qualitative data (dealing with attitudes, values, and meanings, as well as other aspects of data) are often collected in ways that meet traditional scientific criteria of reliability and validity, and that they can provide insights that are not otherwise available. The participants in this conference have collectively taken a giant step in attempting, for the first time on such a scale, to come to grips with the important but slippery issue of how alcohol relates to culture. Let us all hope that the next international conference on the subject of alcohol and culture, wherever it may be, will see many more presentations that combine qualitative with quantitative data, that identify the cultures in terms that more nearly reflect reference groups that are meaningful to the people themselves, and that combine a sensitivity to context with scientific rigor and systematic comparison.

# Index of Contributors